Behavior

Human Operant Behavior

Analysis and Application

Second Edition

Ellen P. Reese
Mount Holyoke College

with

Jane Howard
Western Michigan University

T. W. Reese
Mount Holyoke College

WM. C. BROWN COMPANY PUBLISHERS
Dubuque, Iowa

Printed in the United States of America
10   9   8   7   6

Figure and Table Credits

Several of the graphs and tables derive from other sources; we are grateful to the following authors and publishers for permission to reproduce or adapt their material.

Figure 1.1. Reproduced by permission of B. F. Skinner.

Figure 2.2. From: *Behavior Theory in Practice* by E. P. Reese. (film) Copyright 1965 by Appleton-Century-Crofts. (Distributed by Prentice-Hall.) Reproduced by permission of the author and Prentice-Hall, Inc.

Figure 2.4 and 4.7. From: *The Analysis of Human Operant Behavior* by E. P. Reese. Copyright 1966 by Wm. C. Brown Company. Reprinted by permission of the author and publisher.

Figure 2.5. From: "Operant conditioning methods in diagnosis" by O. R. Lindsley, in *The First Hahnemann Symposium on Psychosomatic Medicine.* Copyright 1962 by Lea & Febiger. Reprinted by permission of the author and publisher.

Figure 2.6. From: "Operant conditioning techniques in the measurement of psychopharmacologic response" by O. R. Lindsley, in *The First Hahnemann Symposium on Psychosomatic Medicine.* Copyright 1962 by Lea & Febiger. Adapted by permission of the author and publisher.

Figure 3.1. From: "An instructional aid for staff training in behavioral assessment" by P. N. Alevizos, P. L. Berck, M. D. Campbell, and E. J. Callahan, in *Journal of Applied Behavior Analysis*, 1974, 7, 472. Flow chart obtained from the authors and adapted with their permission.

Figure 3.2. From United Feature Syndicate, Inc., 1972.

Figure 3.3. From: "Effects of teacher attention on digit-reversal behavior in an elementary school child" by J. E. Hasazi and S. E. Hasazi, in *Journal of Applied Behavior Analysis*, 1972, 5, 157-162. Copyright 1972 by the Society for the Experimental Analysis of Behavior, Inc. Reprinted by permission of the authors and publisher.

Figure 3.4. From: "The 'Reinforcement Menu': Finding effective reinforcers" by M. F. Daley, in *Behavioral Counseling: Cases and techniques* edited by J. D. Krumboltz and C. E. Thoresen. Copyright 1969 by Holt, Rinehart and Winston, Inc. Reprinted by permission of the author and publisher.

Table 3.7. From: "Intrinsic reinforcers in a classroom token economy" by T. F. McLaughlin and J. Malaby, in *Journal of Applied Behavior Analysis*, 1972, 5, 263-270. Copyright 1972 by the Society for the Experimental Analysis of Behavior, Inc. Adapted by permission of the authors and publisher.

Table 3.8. From: *Self-directed Behavior: Self-modification for personal adjustment* by D. L. Watson and R. G. Tharp. Copyright 1972 by Wadsworth Publishing Company, Inc. Reprinted by permission of the authors and the publisher, Brooks/Cole Publishing Company, Monterey, California.

Figure 3.5. Reproduced by permission of Brian and Peggy Iwata.

Figure 3.6. From: "The control of eating behavior in an anorexic by operant conditioning techniques" by A. J. Bachrach, W. J. Erwin, and J. P. Mohr, in *Case Studies in Behavior Modification* edited by L. P. Ullmann and L. Krasner. Copyright 1965 by Holt, Rinehart and Winston. Photographs reprinted by permission of the authors and publisher.

Figure 3.7. From: "Interpretation of symptoms: Fact or fiction" by T. Ayllon, E. Haughton, and H. B. Hughes, in *Behaviour Research and Therapy*, 1965, 3, 1-7. Copyright 1965 by Pergamon Press Ltd. Reprinted by permission of the authors and publisher.

Table 3.10. From: "Behavioral contracting within the families of delinquents" by R. B. Stuart, in *Journal of Behavior Therapy and Experimental Psychiatry*, 1971, 2, 1-11. Copyright 1971 by Pergamon Press Ltd. Reprinted by permission of the author and publisher.

Table 3.11. From: "Behaviorally disordered peers as contingency managers" by C. M. Nelson, J. Worell, and L. Polsgrove, in *Behavior Therapy*, 1973, 4, 270-276. Copyright 1973 by the Association for Advancement of Behavior Therapy. Reprinted by permission of the authors and the publisher, Academic Press.

Table 3.12. From: "Accountability in psychotherapy: A test case" by T. Ayllon and W. Skuban, in *Journal of Behavior Therapy and Experimental Psychiatry*, 1973, 4, 19-29. Copyright 1973 by Pergamon Press Ltd. Reprinted by permission of the authors and publisher.

Figure 3.8. From: "The teaching-family model of group home treatment" by D. L. Fixsen, E. L. Phillips, E. A.

Baer, E. R. Brawley, and F. R. Harris, in *Journal of Applied Behavior Analysis*, 1968, *1*, 73-76. Copyright 1968 by the Society for the Experimental Analysis of Behavior. Reprinted by permission of the authors and publisher.

Figure 4.6. From: "Modification of behavior problems in the home with a parent as observer and experimenter" by R. V. Hall, S. Axelrod, L. Tyler, E. Grief, F. C. Jones, and R. Robertson, in *Journal of Applied Behavior Analysis*, 1972, *5*, 53-64. Copyright 1972 by the Society for the Experimental Analysis of Behavior, Inc. Reprinted by permission of the authors and publisher.

Figure 4.8. From: "Amount and distribution of study in a Personalized Instruction course and in a lecture course" by D. G. Born and M. L. Davis, in *Journal of Applied Behavior Analysis*, 1974, *7*, 365-375. Copyright 1974 by the Society for the Experimental Analysis of Behavior, Inc. Figures redrawn by permission of the authors and publisher.

Figure 4.9. From: "Instatement of stuttering in normally fluent individuals through operant procedures" by B. Flanagan, I. Goldiamond, and N. H. Azrin, in *Science*, 1959, *130*, 979-981. Reprinted by permission of the authors and publisher.

Figure 4.10. From: *Managing Behavior 3: Behavior Modification: Applications in school and home* by R. V. Hall. Copyright 1971 by H & H Enterprises, Lawrence, Kansas. Reprinted by permission of the author and publisher.

Figure 5.1. From: "The elimination of tantrum behavior by extinction procedures" by C. D. Williams, in *Journal of Abnormal and Social Psychology*, 1959, *59*, 269. Copyright 1959 by the American Psychological Association. Reprinted by permission of the author and publisher.

Figure 5.2. From: "Modification of symptomatic verbal behaviour of mental patients" by T. Ayllon and E. Haughton, in *Behaviour Research and Therapy*, 1964, *2*, 87-97. Copyright 1964 by Pergamon Press Ltd. Reprinted by permission of the authors and publisher.

Figure 5.3. Illustrations by David Thorne from *Elementary Principles of Behavior* by D. L. Whaley and R. W. Malott. Copyright 1971 by Appleton-Century-Crofts. Reprinted by permission of the authors and the publisher, Prentice-Hall, Inc.

Figures 5.4, 5.7, and 5.8. From: "Intensive treatment of psychotic behaviour by stimulus satiation and food reinforcement" by T. Ayllon, in *Behaviour Research and Therapy*, 1963, *1*, 53-61. Copyright 1963 by Pergamon Press Ltd. Reprinted by permission of the author and publisher.

Figure 5.5. From: "The timer-game: A variable interval contingency for the management of out-of-seat behavior" by M. M. Wolf, E. L. Hanley, L. A. King, J. Lachowicz, and D. K. Giles, in *Exceptional Children*, 1970, *37*, 113-117. Copyright 1970 by The Council for Exceptional Children. Reprinted by permission of the authors and publisher.

Figure 5.6. From: "Treating overweight children through parental training and contingency contracting" by J. Aragona, J. Cassady, and R. S. Drabman, in *Journal of Applied Behavior Analysis*, 1975, *8*, 269-278. Copyright 1975 by the Society for the Experimental Analysis of Behavior, Inc. Reprinted by permission of the authors and publisher.

Figure 5.9. From: "Modification of seizure disorders: The interruption of behavioral chains" by S. Zlutnick, W. J. Mayville, and S. Moffat, in *Journal of Applied Behavior Analysis*, 1975, *8*, 1-12. Copyright 1975 by the Society for the Experimental Analysis of Behavior, Inc. Reprinted by permission of the authors and publisher.

Figure 5.10 and 5.11. From: "A behavioral-educational alternative to drug control of hyperactive children" by T. Ayllon, D. Layman, and H. J. Kandel, in *Journal of Applied Behavior Analysis*, 1975, *8*, 137-146. Copyright 1975 by the Society for the Experimental Analysis of Behavior. Reprinted by permission of the authors and publisher.

Figure 5.12. From: "Use of aversive stimulation in behavior modification" by B. Bucher and O. I. Lovaas, in *Miami Symposium on the Prediction of Behavior, 1967: Aversive stimulation* edited by M. R. Jones. Copyright 1968 by the University of Miami Press. Reprinted by permission of the authors and publisher.

Figure 5.13. From: "Manipulation of self-destruction in three retarded children" by O. I. Lovaas and J. Q. Simmons, in *Journal of Applied Behavior Analysis*, 1969, *2*, 143-157. Copyright 1969 by the Society for the Experimental Analysis of Behavior, Inc. Adapted by permission of the authors and publisher.

Figures 5.14, 5.15, and 5.16. From: "Building social behavior in autistic children by use of electric shock" by O. I. Lovaas, B. Schaeffer, and J. Q. Simmons, in *Journal of Experimental Research in Personality*, 1965, *1*, 99-109. Copyright 1965 by Academic Press, Inc. Reprinted by permission of the authors and publisher.

Figure 6.2. From: *Learning Foundations of Behavior Therapy* by F. H. Kanfer and J. S. Phillips. Copyright 1970 by John S. Wiley & Sons. Reprinted by permission of the authors and publisher.

Figure 6.4. From: "Quantitative relationships in the systematic desensitization of phobias" by J. Wolpe, in *American Journal of Psychiatry*, 1963, *119*, 1062-1068. Copyright 1963 by the American Psychiatric Association. Reprinted by permission of the author and publisher.

Figure 6.5. From: "Transvestism and fetishism: Clinical and psychological changes during faradic aversion" by I. M. Marks and M. G. Gelder, in *British Journal of Psychiatry*, 1967, *113*, 711-729. Copyright 1967 by Headley Brothers Ltd. Reprinted by permission of the publisher.

Figure 6.6. From: "Case report: Avoidance conditioning therapy of an infant with chronic ruminative vomiting" by P. J. Lang and B. G. Melamed, in *Journal of Abnormal Psychology*, 1969, *74*, 1-8. Copyright 1969 by the American Psychological Association. Reprinted by permission of the authors and publisher.

Figure 6.7. From: "Treatment of overweight by aversion therapy" by J. P. Foreyt and W. A. Kennedy, in *Behaviour Research and Therapy*, 1971, 9, 29-34.

Copyright 1971 by Pergamon Press Ltd. Reprinted by permission of the authors and publisher.

Table 8.3. Client-Therapist Treatment Contract by Richard B. Stuart. Champaign, Illinois: Research Press, 1975. Reprinted by permission of the author and publisher.

To
FRED S. KELLER
in whom rigor, wit, clarity, and style so
joyously combine. Your contributions to our
libraries, laboratories, and classrooms proclaim
a model for all seasons.

Contents

Ethical and Other Concerns   242

8

Preface

Four years ago, I started to revise a little book called *The Analysis of Human Operant Behavior*.* It was clearly out of date, and the publishers had called for a new edition. I readily agreed; but where I had expected to revise and update, I found myself writing a new book. There are now a dozen journals founded expressly for the publication of research in basic and applied behavior analysis and for the discussion of issues raised by this research. There are hundreds of books, many thousands of articles. Behavior analysis and behavior modification are expanding at such a rate that the more I wrote, the farther behind I got. Like Alice, I had to run to stand in the same place. The basic data are, of course, the basic data. But the ingenuity and inventiveness of those engaged in basic and applied research have extended this science of behavior to problems, settings, and levels of analysis that few had envisioned in 1966.

Soon, the little book had grown to monstrous proportions. It was time to call for help. Tom Reese, my friend, husband, and mentor, and Jane Howard, my friend, colleague, and former student, came to the rescue. They cut the manuscript to something like its present length—and then patiently stood by while I proceeded to rewrite most of it for the third time. They also contributed many suggestions which I have gratefully incorporated.

We now have a book of modest length which describes the ways in which an experimental analysis of behavior is contributing to the analysis and amelioration of a broad range of problems: in education and therapy, in counseling and rehabilitation, in medicine, in business and industry, and in self-control or the management of one's own behavior. Beyond its contributions to the solution of existing problems, we have attempted to describe some of the ways in which a science of behavior can enhance the freedom of individuals and contribute to the survival and evolution of a culture.

In Chapter 1, and again in Chapter 8, we discuss the potential of a science of behavior, its contributions to date, and many of the issues that are raised when one examines the control of behavior. Chapter 2 is a brief exposition of basic terms and procedures. The core of the book is Chapter 3 which offers a general procedure for applied behavior analysis that can be adapted to a wide variety of situations and settings. This is not a "how to" manual. Rather, it includes a description of the rationale and the often complex issues involved in the assessment of problems and in the selection of goals and of procedures to achieve them. Since both education and therapy are defined in terms of their results, a good deal of space is devoted to measurement and evaluation, the underlying assumption being that the only measure of the teacher or therapist's success is the student or client's success. And since we cannot merely assume that therapeutic gains will be maintained in the natural environment, the chapter describes several procedures which can facilitate maintenance and transfer to natural settings.

*Wm. C. Brown, 1966; now in its nineteenth printing.

Operant procedures for changing behavior are described in Chapters 4 and 5, together with guidelines for maximizing their effectiveness. Chapter 6 is devoted to respondent procedures and therapies. While the major emphasis is the management of anxiety, we have discussed and attempted to analyze the effects of a number of respondent procedures in the treatment of a variety of problems.

Chapter 7 applies the general procedure described in Chapter 3 to the analysis and management of one's own behavior. For several years, our students have designed and conducted self-control projects, and their experience has shaped this revision of the chapter.

Ethical issues are stressed throughout. In Chapter 3, we are concerned with the selection of goals that will enhance the freedom of individuals by helping them attain their full potential without endangering the welfare of others or the environment that supports us all. We are also concerned with evaluation, so that counselors, educators, and therapists may be fully accountable to their clients and to their profession. Another way to facilitate accountability is by contracting. We have included several examples of contracts that specify the contingencies of behavioral programs—the arrangement of goals, procedures, and consequences—and the privileges and responsibilities of each party. Examples of self-management contracts are included in Chapter 7. The widespread application of behavioral procedures, documented in Chapter 8, has aroused the concern of behaviorists, as well as others, about the potential misuse of these procedures. So we return to the matter of accountability and offer guidelines for the protection of clients involved in behavior modification or *any other* form of therapy.

Just as behavior analysis draws from many fields, we believe that it has something to offer many fields. There is nothing about the model that cannot be incorporated into other disciplines or approaches. The book is thus addressed to a wide audience: to undergraduates taking courses in introductory, experimental, educational, and clinical psychology; to graduate students of other persuasions who want a review of the concerns and contributions of applied behavior analysis; to people already engaged in teaching, counseling, social work, or medicine; to parents and other paraprofessionals; and to anyone else who may be concerned about the ways in which behavior is controlled by its antecedents and consequences. To illustrate the current "domain" of applied behavior analysis, we have selected examples and case histories from a broad range of areas and settings. While the result is neither a source book nor a handbook of applications, Chapter 8—together with some 600 references—should enable the reader to pursue areas of particular interest.

I have already indicated my indebtedness to Tom Reese and Jane Howard, without whose help I should probably be starting Chapter 2, having arrived at page 2091. I would add my thanks to Jack Michael, whose marginal glosses (Bah! Too cognitive! Why??) enabled me to delete a number of inanities, and whose many constructive suggestions I have gratefully accepted. Judi LeBlanc, Edith Post, Wendy Leys, and Robert Shilkret also reviewed the entire manuscript and made many thoughtful and helpful suggestions; and Sue Uber contributed many examples to Chapter 6. I should have given up long ago were it not for Leanna Standish, Kent Johnson, and our students at Mount Holyoke and the University of Massachusetts, all of whom maintained my writing behavior by positive reinforcement in a situation otherwise dominated by avoidance contingencies. I would also thank Beth Sulzer-Azaroff who refused to read a word of the manuscript because she is writing a behavioral book of her own. I haven't the slightest doubt that many of "my" best ideas have derived from conversations with her.

To a considerable degree, the usefulness of a book depends upon its subject index. Marylou Reid has deciphered our hieroglyphics and put this one together, thereby earning our gratitude and admiration.

At Wm. C. Brown, my thanks go to Editors Don Rivers and Ed Bowers, to Copy Editor Joe Zullo, and to Ruth Richard and Jan Henkel in the Production Department.

My greatest debt, of course, is to those who have provided the data which called for the revision. Their names appear in the author index.

E. P. R.
South Hadley, Massachusetts

1

The Analysis of Behavior

One of our more notable characteristics as human beings is a curiosity about the causes of our behavior. For most of us, this curiosity is more than academic: Not only do we wonder about human behavior, we actively seek to change it. We try to change the behavior of others by persuasion, by setting an example, by reason, and by force; and we try to change our own behavior by self-control. Sometimes we want people to *stop* doing something: lying, cheating, procrastinating, dropping bombs on other people. And sometimes we want them to *start* doing something: getting good grades, being compassionate toward others, conserving natural resources. Either way, the more we know about the variables that affect our behavior, the more successful we will be in our efforts to understand and to change it.

Behavior is affected by several kinds of events, or *variables*, including genetic endowment, past experience, and current conditions. If you know someone who has been diagnosed as profoundly retarded, and if her mother and her eight brothers and sisters are also retarded, you might suspect that genetic endowment is a relevant variable.[1] Similarly, if you are working with a high-school student who grew up subsisting largely on carbohydrates and whose family shared a single room with rats and roaches rather than books or toys, then you might conclude that his social and academic difficulties in school are related to his past experience.

We can deplore the long-term effects of nutritional, social, and intellectual deprivation during early childhood, and we can elect public officials who will try to eliminate the conditions that produce these deprivations. We can also support basic research on behavioral genetics and the effects of early experience. But once childhood is over there's not much we can do about a person's genetic endowment or early experience. Fortunately, we need not abandon all hope. The immediate antecedents and consequences of behavior are very important in

determining what we will—or will not—do in a given situation; and these are conditions we very often *can* change.

A. Orientation

1. Behavioral Approach

Behavioral psychologists, as the name implies, study behavior; and behavior is anything that people do, including what they say and what they think and feel. The only restriction on behavior as subject matter is that it must be observable and measurable. In an applied situation, highest priority is given to those classes of behavior considered most important to the welfare of the particular individual and other members of society. It thus becomes necessary to find ways of observing and measuring such important classes of behavior as anger and fear, cooperation and self-control.

Behavioral research takes place in the community, the classroom, the home, and the laboratory. But many procedures now proving useful in education and therapy were first developed from studies of animal behavior. Despite the many important differences among species, research with animals frequently uncovers variables that may also affect human behavior and points to ways in which these variables might be studied. For example, at the turn of the twentieth century Pavlov's investigations of conditional reflexes showed how one stimulus can replace another in eliciting a response—how new reflexes can be added to those that are part of an organism's biological inheritance. Pavlov's work with dogs was extended to human behavior by Watson and Rayner (1920). Their famous experiment with Little Albert (discussed in Chapter 2 and 6) demonstrated that human fear can be *acquired*, a

1. This was actually the case in a study reported by Foxx and Azrin, 1972.

finding that has important ramifications. If inappropriate fears can be conditioned, perhaps accidental conditioning of this kind can be prevented; and if preventative measures fail, perhaps fears that have been conditioned can also be eliminated.

The important relations in Pavlovian, or classical, conditioning pertain to the stimulus conditions preceding the response. We now know that the manipulation of these *antecedent conditions* can result in the production or elimination of many kinds of behavior termed "neurotic."

The principle that behavior is affected by its *consequences* was formulated in Thorndike's Law of Effect (1898); but its importance was not generally appreciated until B. F. Skinner demonstrated the kinds and the degree of control exerted by events that follow a given activity (Skinner, 1935, 1938, 1953). Skinner rewarded lever pressing by a white rat confined in a small chamber, and discovered several basic principles of operant conditioning. It is a very long way from a "Skinner Box" to the natural environment and from a few Norway rats to a large number of people. Nonetheless, the way has been heavily traveled. Many of Skinner's early findings are applicable to people as well as to other animals and to such complex activities as aggression, cooperation, and teaching.

In their efforts to develop a science of behavior, Pavlov and Skinner and their students have developed a number of procedures that are now proving useful in education and therapy. These procedures—now known variously as behavior therapy, behavior modification, behavioral engineering, contingency management, and educational technology—are useful for two reasons: 1) They can be adapted to a wide variety of situations, and 2) since they have been derived from observable and measurable phenomena, they can be stated precisely.

The professional who can specify therapeutic procedures can teach them to others and thereby serve many more people. Teacher's aides, hospital attendants, parents, and other paraprofessionals can learn behavioral procedures, and they can learn them without years of expensive training. Since family, teachers, or institutional personnel are the very people who interact most closely with a client in his daily life, they are in the best possible position to help or to hinder the client's progress. The chances of helping improve when therapeutic procedures can be stated precisely.

2. Comparison with Traditional Approaches

The behavioral approach to education and therapy differs from many traditional approaches in that the procedures focus on specific, quantifiable behavior, rather than on theoretical constructs or internal mechanisms. Because they study behavior rather than internal mechanisms, and because they can specify their procedures precisely, behavioral psychologists are in a good position to measure the success of their efforts. And the ability to objectively evaluate their efforts allows behaviorists to be accountable to their clients with respect to the goals, the procedures, and the outcome of any programs they design. In addition, the procedures can be evaluated continuously throughout the program, which means they can be revised and adapted to the particular needs of the individual.

Emphasis on the individual is an important feature that the behavioral approach has in common with general clinical practice. In many other areas of experimental psychology, different groups of subjects are given different "treatments," and any obtained differences are evaluated statistically. Behavioral psychologists, however, are not very happy with statistical analyses or with group data, which necessarily obscure the performance of the individual. Even in research with animals, the basic method is the case study. A given procedure is introduced and continued until its effects can be determined. Additional subjects are run to replicate findings, *not* so that their data may be averaged. If the results are not clear, one doesn't add subjects—one looks for other variables affecting the results.[2]

3. Credo

Skinner and his colleagues share a guiding philosophy, a *credo*: "The subject knows best" or "The subject is always right." Ogden Lindsley, one of Skinner's most eminent students, tells us that Skinner used to say, "The rat knows best; that is why we have him in the

Figure 1.1.   The subject knows best. A rat teaches B. F. Skinner some basic principles of learning.

experiment. If we knew so much, we could put a mechanical rat in" (Lindsley, 1971, p. 56).

This credo means two things. First, in basic research, if we want to find out what the rat will do under a given set of conditions, we set up the conditions and watch. Sometimes, on the basis of prior information, we think that we can predict what he will do, but our predictions are not verified. When this happens, it is not the rat that is wrong, it is our predictions.[3] We must then take another look at the situation and try to find out what made the rat behave as he did. In other words, when our data are inconsistent, or when our predictions are inadequate, we conclude that there is another variable to be investigated.

Years ago, when our students first conditioned lever pressing in rats, we used feeders that delivered powdered rat food. During conditioning, when the students trained their rats to press a lever, a measured amount of food was delivered automatically every time the lever was depressed. Then, after the rat had pressed the lever and eaten the food 20 times, the feeder was disconnected so that lever pressing no longer delivered food. Under these conditions, we expect a burst of rapid responding before the behavior gradually drops out or extinguishes. Now, a problem with those early feeders was that they sometimes jammed and failed to deliver the powdered food. Occasionally, a rat would start to press rapidly during the conditioning period, and the student would call out "My feeder's clogged." She did *not* call out "I

2. Research designs to evaluate the effects of procedures with individual subjects are discussed in Chapter 3.

3. Probably the earliest published statement of this philosophy appears in *Walden Two* where Frazier (speaking for Skinner) says,

I remember the rage I used to feel when a prediction went awry. I could have shouted at the subjects of my experiments, "Behave, damn you! Behave as you ought!" Eventually I realized that the subjects were always right. They always behaved as they should have behaved. It was I who was wrong. I had made a bad prediction.

(Skinner, 1948, p. 240.)

have a crazy rat." She knew that the extinction process had begun, even though she had not planned it that way. The rat was right—and so was the student. We always treasured such incidents because they allowed us to say, "You have just done something important. You have correctly diagnosed the breakdown of a carefully engineered and relatively expensive piece of electromechanical apparatus because of the predictability of the behavior of a living organism."

This credo is equally important when we are working with people in applied settings. When progress is not as rapid as we might expect, we must look for relevant variables and then redesign the program. The credo does *not* mean that 7 is the sum of 2 + 3, or that Shakespeare was the author of *Paradise Lost* just because a student says so on an examination. It *does* mean that behavior is lawful, and that the exception that tests the rule merits further investigation. It is misleading to say that the subject is wrong or that the student has failed when, in fact, it is our predictions which are wrong or our teaching procedures which have failed.

Remember this *credo* when problems arise in a self-control program. When you are trying to control your own behavior, you are behaving in two roles at once: as teacher-therapist and as student-client. Since you (the client) are always right, a setback in the program means that you (the therapist) haven't yet succeeded in identifying or controlling the variables that determine your behavior. It is not *you* who have failed, it is the program; and recognizing that fact is the first step in designing a better one.

4. Applications

Behavioral procedures are now proving helpful in education at all levels, from preschool to graduate school, and with people diagnosed as normal, retarded, hyperactive, learning disabled, delinquent, or emotionally disturbed. The range of programs extends from academic subjects and social skills to physical education and vocational training. Behavioral procedures are also widely employed in therapy, counseling, rehabilitation, and social work; in medicine, nursing, and physical therapy; in business, industry, and the armed services; in the community and in the home. Recently, attention has been directed toward the solution of environmental problems such as the conservation of natural resources and population control, and there has been a concentrated effort to analyze the variables that allow us to manage our own behavior. Behavioral procedures for self-control are discussed in Chapter 7; the range and diversity of other major areas of concern are described in Chapter 8.

In the English language alone, there are now nine journals devoted exclusively to behavioral publications, five annuals, some 600 books, and thousands of articles.[4] In this brief summary, more space is devoted to operant (or Skinnerian) procedures than to respondent (or Pavlovian) procedures. This is mainly because the former are generally more applicable to our ordinary behavior at work, at home, and in the classroom; and because they can be applied with greater safety by the layman. There is another reason for the emphasis on operant procedures. Whether or not we realize it, and whether or not it is our intention, we all use operant procedures whenever we interact with another person. Everything we do, and even those things we refrain from doing, are likely to affect the behavior of others. Since we cannot avoid using operant procedures, they would seem to merit our close attention.

B. A Science of Behavior

Science is the search for lawful relations between natural events or variables. Scientists start with the observation of some phenomenon.

4. See Chapter 8 for a listing of journals, annuals, and bibliographies.

They then look for the variables that may affect this phenomenon and measure their effects in a systematic fashion. We may never know whether or not Galileo actually pushed two balls—one weighing one pound, the other, one hundred pounds—from the top of the tower of Pisa. But we do know that after a series of careful observations, he concluded that (discounting the effects of air resistance) all falling bodies, whatever their weights, fall at the same rate.

As information accumulates, scientific facts can be stated as laws, and these laws can be organized into a model that describes some aspect of the empirical world. Scientific data are cumulative; each empirically derived fact makes the next investigator's task that much easier. Galileo also determined that the rate of a free falling body increases as it approaches the surface of the earth. Galileo's formula was later subsumed under Newton's law of gravitation; and Newton's law, in turn, was subsumed under Einstein's model of space and time.

The determination of scientific verities or laws is possible only if nature is, in fact, lawful. If nature is capricious or chaotic, then lawful relations cannot obtain.

Is human behavior lawful and thus a proper subject of scientific investigation? A number of psychologists are proceeding under the assumption that it is. The application of scientific procedures to the study of behavior has established several lawful relations, and this encourages the search for others.

1. Scientific Method

A scientific description of behavior begins with the observation of some behavior. For example, while walking across campus with a friend on a bright day, you might note that the pupils of his eyes are very small. Later on, perhaps at dusk, you might note that his pupils are much larger. You might call his attention to the fact, and, in so doing, you would learn one of the first rules of

science: it must be *communicable*. To communicate with others who will wish to verify their findings, scientists must be able to define their terms. To define the observed change in pupillary size, one might simply hold up a ruler in front of someone's eye and measure the diameter of the pupil at different times of day.

After isolating and defining the behavior, one then locates the variables that affect, or control, it. You have already noticed a change in pupillary diameter at different times of day. You might also notice a change when your friend was frightened or excited about something or when he had taken medication. At this point, you might want to analyze the relation by measuring the behavior while you systematically change the value of a variable that you thinks affects that behavior. Even though most behavior is affected by a great many variables, you would probably examine the effects of one variable at a time. If you were measuring pupillary diameter at different times of day, you would try to make sure that the changes you observed were not attributable to another variable, such as drugs.

It is not always easy to isolate a relevant variable. After taking many measurements on bright and dreary days, you would eventually conclude that the amount of illumination, rather than the time of day, affects pupillary size. An analysis of this relation, based on observations taken at various levels of illumination, would reveal that the size of the pupil varies inversely with the intensity of the illumination cast upon the eye. After establishing this relation, you could *predict* the size of the pupil if you knew the intensity of the illumination; and you could *control* the size of the pupil if you could control the intensity of the illumination.

When we fail to look for relevant variables, we sometimes jump to erroneous conclusions. Here is one of Israel Goldiamond's stories:

Arthur and Stanley were two laboratory rats, brothers and litter mates. Shortly after birth they were parted and placed in separate cages because a scientist was interested in studying the effects of diet deficiencies. Stanley was given plenty of food, water, and vitamins. He thrived. Arthur, on the other hand, did not fare so well. First, he was deprived of vitamin D, and his teeth fell out, and he developed rickets. Next, vitamin C was taken away, and his gums became swollen and bloody, and he developed a fine case of scurvy. When the scientist took away vitamin A, poor Arthur's hair fell out and he could not see in the dark which, as we all know, is the best time for rats to play. In short, Arthur was a wreck.

One day, the laboratory assistant accidentally left open the door to Arthur's and Stanley's cages. Taking advantage of the situation, they went for a stroll along the laboratory corridors. Rounding a corner, the two brothers collided. Arthur recognized Stanley immediately. Stanley could only wonder whether the old and pathetic sight before him was truly a rat. Arthur cried out, "Stanley, it's me! Arthur! Your brother!" Stanley gulped, turned pale, and said, "But Arthur, what's happened to you? You look awful!" Arthur replied, "Terrible things have been happening in my life. First my teeth fell out and I got rickets. Then I got scurvy. Now I'm losing my hair —and I can hardly *see* you." The next few moments passed in strained silence. Finally, Arthur spoke up, "But Stanley; you look so well! Tell me, how did you do it?" Stanley, who was happy to change the subject, answered promptly: "It was easy. Just good, clean living; plenty of hard work; getting up early; and a little faith."

2. Prediction and Control of Behavior

We expect that reflexes such as pupil dilation, respiration, and heartbeat will occur predictably. When they don't, we look for a relevant variable or consult a physician who will look for a relevant variable—so certain are we that these classes of behavior obey natural laws. Nonetheless, many people are distressed to think that other classes of behavior are also subject to natural laws, despite the fact that most of us spend most of our waking hours predicting and—either deliberately or accidentally—controlling the behavior of other people. Drivers approaching a stop sign make very important predictions about the behavior of pedestrians

and other drivers; and their immediate behavior is controlled in large measure by the behavior of these other people.

We are particularly adept at predicting the behavior of our families and friends because we have observed their behavior under a variety of conditions. We are accustomed to making predictions about our parents with such certainty that there are whole classes of requests we don't even make because we are so certain they will be denied. And when a "reasonable" request is made and denied, we generally attribute the denial to another variable and make further predictions about father's day at the office or about traffic conditions on the way home. Television scriptwriters behave so predictably that the outcome of most situation comedies can be predicted after the first fifteen minutes. In fact, society functions to a great degree on the predictability of behavior; and a person whose behavior is sufficiently *un*predictable is likely to wind up in an institution.

When we think about the control of behavior, we are apt to think of frightening rather than benign examples. (However, the very words "misuse of control" imply that there are occasions when its use is proper.) We conjure up vivid images of mad scientists and political dictators rather than the softer images of gentle parents and parish priests. The word "control" has acquired ominous connotations, but as it is used in science, "to control" means only "to have an effect upon." The effect may indeed be frightening, but not necessarily. The mother who comforts her child and the priest who comforts a bereaved parishioner are trying to control the behavior of other people. *Control refers to any procedure that reliably produces a specifiable change in some event.* We try to manage variables that control human behavior whenever we attempt to teach people something or to entertain them or to win their allegiance to a cause.

In some cases, this control is assumed as a

natural right or obligation; in others it is implicit in the nature of the job. Specialists in the control of behavior include not only law-enforcement officers and military personnel, but also parents and politicians, teachers and therapists, doctors and lawyers, scout leaders and cheerleaders, con men and ad men, actors and writers, anti-war demonstrators and the clergy.

We also expend a good deal of effort so that our *own* behavior will be controlled. At this writing, I am housebreaking a puppy, and one of the most powerful controls over my behavior just now is a puppy at the door asking to go out. No matter what the hour, and no matter what I may be doing, her wish is my command.

"No man is an island, entire of itself"; we are inescapably "involved in mankind."[5] Our behavior is controlled by those around us and we, in turn, control the behavior of others, whether or not we admit it or call it by another name. To disguise our efforts beneath labels like "suggestion" or "persuasion" is not only to deceive ourselves, but to run a dangerous risk: when persuasion fails, there are those who resort to punitive and oppressive measures. Perhaps the surest way to protect ourselves from oppression, and to maximize our potential as human beings, is to examine the ways in which our behavior is controlled. A scientific analysis of behavior can increase our freedom by showing us ways to control our own behavior and to improve our relations with others. Catania (1968, p. 3) puts it this way: ". . . it is difficult to see how man's behavior can be called free if he fails to understand the conditions that control his behavior . . . there can be no loss of human dignity as man comes to understand his own behavior. In fact, the claim to dignity·must be questioned as long as such understanding is absent."

Questions are often raised about what classes of behavior should be controlled, and by whom. The answers to both of those important questions must be decided by all of us, as indi-

viduals and as socially-responsible citizens. The particular job of the behavioral psychologist is the analysis of the many variables that affect behavior so that the *facts* of behavioral control may be understood. A better understanding of these facts can enhance our best efforts in education, therapy, and government. Ignorance of these facts is a luxury we can no longer afford. There is some urgency about this, as B. F. Skinner noted more than 20 years ago.

We are all controlled by the world in which we live, and part of that world has been and will be constructed by men. The question is this: Are we to be controlled by accident, by tyrants, or by ourselves in effective cultural design?

The danger of the misuse of power is possibly greater than ever. It is not allayed by disguising the facts. We cannot make wise decisions if we continue to pretend that human behavior is not controlled, or if we refuse to engage in control when valuable results might be forthcoming. Such measures weaken only ourselves, leaving the strength of science to others. The first step in a defense against tyranny is the fullest possible exposure of controlling techniques. . . .

It is no time for self-deception, emotional indulgence, or the assumption of attitudes which are no longer useful. Man is facing a difficult test. He must keep his head now, or he must start again—a long way back. (Skinner, B. F. Freedom and the control of men. *American Scholar,* 1955, 25, 47-65 [pp. 56-57].)

C. Ethical Principles

It seems an inescapable conclusion that much of our behavior is controlled, or affected, by the behavior of others. In recognition of this fact we accept a great many civil and moral laws designed to limit this control. The first ten amendments to the Constitution of the United States (the Bill of Rights), for example, and legislation against child abuse are designed to control the ways in which we control one another's behavior. Members of certain professions who are in a position to exercise an unusual de-

5. John Donne *Devotions,* XII.

gree of control, either through special mandate or through special knowledge, have generally adopted codes of ethical behavior to further limit the ways they may control the behavior of others. As is the case with doctors, lawyers, judges and police officers, the professional activities of psychologists are governed by standards that extend beyond those they accept as ordinary citizens.

1. Professional Standards

The American Psychological Association has published several documents that detail the ethical standards governing the behavior of its members, e.g., *Ethical Standards of Psychologists* (1963) and *Ethical Principles in the Conduct of Research with Human Participants* (1973). (Standards for animal research and for educational and psychological tests have also been established.) These codes cover two sorts of ethical issues: those pertinent to all psychologists; and those that cover specific activities of certain individuals, activities such as teaching, therapy, or research. The codes were developed from thousands of descriptions of actual incidents involving ethical decisions—incidents submitted by practicing psychologists. The standards eventually adopted and published by the American Psychological Association cite many of these incidents, which puts the principles vividly in context.

Copies of *Ethical Standards* and *Ethical Principles* should be available in any psychology laboratory. We urge you to look at them. They are probably the most carefully derived and the most detailed examination of ethical behavior published by any professional organization.[6]

2. Accountability

Naturally, applied behavioral psychologists—like psychologists of any other orientation—are governed by the ethical standards of their profession. They are, however, more specific than most psychologists about the therapist's responsibility to the client and the educator's responsibility to the student.

One defining characteristic of behavior analysis is the objective evaluation of treatment. This means (1) that educational and therapeutic procedures *derive* from empirical research, and (2) that as these procedures are *applied* to individual cases, objective criteria are used to evaluate their effectiveness in each particular case. These two features of behavior modification allow the client to examine both the research concerning any procedure that may be proposed and the effectiveness of any procedure actually employed in his behalf. The protection this affords the client is part of what we mean by accountability.

After examining the alternatives, the client (or his representative) can help the therapist select the precise goals of therapy and the procedures that will be followed to attain these goals. Often these are incorporated into a written agreement, or contract, that spells out therapist-client responsibilities and includes the client's right to terminate treatment. Sometimes, the contract specifies that part of the therapist's fee will depend on the success of treatment. These and other dimensions of accountability are important (see Chapter 8); but we maintain that *there can be no accountability without data*. Data—those quantitative records which have long been the security blanket of the behaviorist (Figure 1.2)—are also essential to the security of the client. For clients, objective evaluation is an ethical matter: they are entitled to know how the treatment is going. For psychologists, it is also a practical matter: they,

6. The Department of Health, Education and Welfare (DHEW), which financially supports much of the behavioral research in this country, has also established regulations regarding research with human subjects to protect their rights and welfare (DHEW, 1974: Chapter 45, Code of Federal Regulations, Subtitle A, Part 46).

too, must know how the treatment is going so they can revise the procedures, if necessary.

D. A Brief Description of Behavior Therapy and of Behavior Analysis

1. Behavior Therapy and Behavior Modification

The following description of behavior therapy is taken from *AABT*, the newsletter of the Association for Advancement of Behavior Therapy:

Behavior therapy involves primarily applications of principles derived from research in experimental and social psychology to alleviate human suffering and enhance human functioning. Behavior therapy emphasizes a systematic monitoring and evaluation of the effectiveness of these applications.

Behavior therapy typically involves environmental change and social interaction, rather than direct intervention by medical procedures. The aim is primarily educational. The techniques are generally intended to facilitate improved self-control by expanding the skills, abilities, and independence of individuals. In the conduct of behavior therapy, a contractual agreement is usually negotiated, in which mutually agreeable goals and procedures are specified. Responsible persons using behavioral approaches are guided by generally accepted ethical principles.

(AABT, 1974, *1* (No. 3). p. 7.)

One purpose of this book is to expand and document this description of behavior therapy (or behavior modification) and *to present a general procedure that can be adapted to a variety of particular situations in education and therapy*. Another purpose is to describe the research from which the principles and applications were developed.

2. Behavior Analysis

Although the procedures often overlap, behavior therapy and behavior modification are primarily *applications* of research while behavior analysis is the research *itself*. The gener-

Figure 1.2. Data — The security blanket of the behaviorist. (Copyright, Ellen P. Reese, 1975.)

ally accepted definition of *applied behavior analysis* is an article by Baer, Wolf, and Risley (1968), which appeared in the first issue of the *Journal of Applied Behavior Analysis*. The authors distinguish basic and applied research mainly on the basis of the kinds of behavior and the kinds of variables studied: While basic (or nonapplied) research may examine any class of behavior and any variable that may control it, applied research is concerned with socially important behavior and the variables that may improve it.

Until the mid-sixties, most behavioral research, even with human subjects, was basic research. Often, the goal was to analyze how effectively a procedure could increase or decrease the rate of an arbitrarily selected class of behavior, such as pushing a button. Later, the procedures were evaluated in natural settings and applied to behavior of social importance: academic skills, and interpersonal relations, for example.

Even though we shall emphasize applied research, the occasional introduction of basic research provides more than historical perspective. In some cases, such as punishment, relatively little applied research has been con-

ducted, and much of the available evidence comes from basic research. In other areas, basic and applied research progress along parallel lines. Basic research often suggests variables that may prove important in applied settings; and problems that arise during application often prompt a return to the laboratory for study under more controlled conditions. For example, when Terrace (1963a) first showed that pigeons can learn to peck a red disk and not a green one *without ever making an error*, his "errorless" learning procedures were quickly adopted for use with human subjects (see Chapter 3). Even as applied research is demonstrating the usefulness of these procedures in teaching academic skills, basic research continues to examine the precise role of errors in learning.

2

Basic Terms and Procedures

A. Behavior
B. Respondent Procedures
    1. Reflexes
    2. Respondent conditioning
    3. Respondent extinction
    4. Generalization and discrimination
C. Operant Procedures
    1. Reinforcing consequences
    2. Punishing consequences
    3. Conditioned reinforcers and punishers
    4. Basic operant procedures
        a. Reinforcement
        b. Punishment
        c. Escape (negative reinforcement)
        d. Response cost
        e. Avoidance
        f. Omission training
        g. Extinction
        h. Recovery
    5. Stimulus control
        a. Generalization
        b. Discrimination
        c. Discriminative stimuli
    6. Contingencies
D. The Free Operant Method

Like all specialized fields, behavioral psychology has a technical vocabulary; and in many cases, familiar terms have a restricted meaning. The advantage of redefining familiar terms instead of coining new words is that a wide audience already knows the approximate meanings. A disadvantage, however, is that the technical term is often misused. For example, Skinner selected the word *reinforcement* as the name of a procedure that *strengthens behavior*. People seem to remember that to reinforce means to strengthen, but they often forget that the term applies to behavior. Technically speaking (common misusage notwithstanding), there is no way we can reinforce *people*. Fortunately, we can reinforce *behavior*.

Technical vocabulary enables us to define terms operationally. An *operational definition* states what must be done (including any necessary measurements) to observe the phenomenon being defined. The term "observe" refers to the detection of the event and includes seeing, hearing, feeling, smelling, tasting. When special apparatus such as a cardiograph or a breath analyzer monitors the event, then what is observed is the record produced by the apparatus.

A. Behavior

Behavior is defined here as any *activity of an organism that can be observed by another organism or by a measuring instrument*. Behavior thus includes external movements (gestures, vocalizations, writing, playing a violin), internal movements (heartbeat, bladder distension, vascular dilation), and glandular activity (salivation, hormone secretion). As the examples suggest, the unit of behavior may be as small as a muscle twitch, or it may comprise a number of movements as in playing a violin.

For research purposes, the *product* or result of behavior, rather than the activity itself, is sometimes measured. Pavlov recorded the number of drops of saliva, rather than secretion; and Skinner recorded the closing of an electrical circuit, rather than the behavior of the rat pressing the lever. In a study of disruptive noise in a classroom, Schmidt and Ulrich (1969) read the overall noise level from a decibel meter rather than attempting to record and classify the vocalizations of individual students.

B. Respondent Procedures

1. Reflexes

Some activities are reliably elicited by specific stimuli: salivation is elicited by food, perspiration by heat, and pupillary contraction by an increase in the amount of light reaching the eye. The relation between a particular stimulus and the response it elicits (usually involving the smooth muscles or glands innervated by the autonomic nervous system) is called a *reflex*. Another familiar reflex is the knee jerk, which is elicited by a tap on the patellar tendon. These stimulus-response relations are called *unconditional reflexes*[1] because they occur prior to any known conditioning history. We do not have to *learn* to jerk our knee in response to a tap on the patellar tendon, nor do we learn to perspire in hot weather. These reactions are part of our biological inheritance. The stimulus is thus called an *unconditional stimulus*, and the response is called an *unconditional response*. In the knee jerk reflex, the unconditional stimulus is the tap on the patellar tendon, and the unconditional response is the knee jerk.

2. Respondent Conditioning

Among the earliest laboratory studies of learning are Pavlov's (1927, 1928) famous condition-

1. According to Franks (1969), the terms *conditional* and *unconditional* appeared in the first of Pavlov's books to be translated into English, but later translations substituted the words *conditioned* and *unconditioned*. The mistranslations have now become well established in the literature.

ing experiments with dogs. These showed how new reflexes can be added to those that are part of our biological inheritance. While Pavlov was studying digestive secretion in dogs, he noticed that salivation occurred when the dog could see the food container, the person who brought the food, or even when it heard the sound of this person's footsteps—*before* food was placed in the dog's mouth (Pavlov, 1927). Salivation to these preliminary events appeared to represent learned reflexes, as opposed to innate or inherited reflexes. Pavlov and his colleagues then investigated the ways in which a new reflex can be established.

In respondent conditioning, a "neutral" stimulus is one that does not elicit a given response. For example, the sounding of a bell does not normally elicit salivation in dogs. But a neutral stimulus can *acquire* the ability to elicit a specific response when it is repeatedly paired with an unconditional stimulus that does elicit this response. Pavlov found that when the sound of a bell was paired with food a sufficient number of times, the sound of the bell could elicit salivation even without food.

The basic paradigm for respondent conditioning is shown in Figure 2.1. The unconditional reflex, in which food elicits salivation, is shown by the relation US → UR. In step 1, food is paired with the sound of a bell, a neutral stimulus (s) with respect to salivation, although the bell may elicit some other response (r) such as the dog's raising its ears. The neutral stimulus is presented slightly before the US. Step 2 shows that after repeated pairings, salivation will occur slightly before the presentation of food, which indicates that the bell is acquiring some control over the response. In step 3, the bell elicits salivation even in the absence of food, and the conditional reflex has been established. This repeated pairing procedure is called *respondent conditioning*, and is also known as *Pavlovian*, or *classical*, conditioning.

Pavlov called the acquired reflex a *conditional reflex* because of its temporary nature and

because it was conditional on the previous operation of pairing the neutral stimulus with one that already elicited the response. The previously neutral stimulus was termed the *conditional stimulus* (CS), and the response it elicited was the *conditional response* (CR).

Pavlov and other early theorists believed that the acquisition of a conditional reflex was primarily due to the short temporal interval between presentation of the CS and the US. Recently this "pairing" analysis has been shown to be an oversimplification. Pairing of the CS and US does not result in the acquisition of a conditional reflex if the US is also presented equally

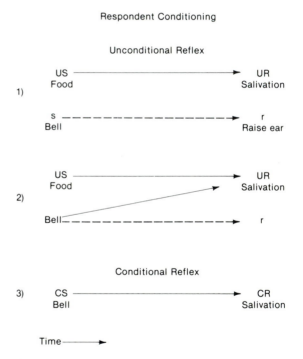

Figure 2.1.   Paradigms illustrating respondent conditioning. (1) Unconditional reflex. Food (US), which elicits salivation (UR), is paired with the sound of a bell. The bell is a neutral stimulus (s) with respect to salivation, but may elicit some other response (r) such as the dog's raising its ears. The neutral stimulus slightly precedes the US in time. (2) After repeated pairings, salivation will slightly precede the presentation of food, indicating that the bell is acquiring some control over the response. (3) Conditional reflex: The bell elicits salivation, even in the absence of the unconditional stimulus.

often in the absence of the CS (Rescorla, 1968). A tone-salivation reflex, for example, does not develop unless food is presented in the presence of the tone more often than in the absence of the tone. In other words, it appears that the conditional reflex develops only when presentation of the CS reliably "predicts" the occurrence of the US.

In respondent or reflex conditioning, the *strength of the reflex* is measured by (1) the *magnitude of the response*—e.g., the number of drops of saliva, (2) its *latency*—the time that elapses between the onsets of the stimulus and the response; and sometimes by (3) the *absolute threshold* of the stimulus—the intensity required to elicit the response. A "strong" reflex is one in which the magnitude of the response is relatively large, the latency is relatively short, and the threshold is relatively low.

A classic example of respondent conditioning in humans is the experiment performed by Watson and Rayner (1920) in which they conditioned an emotional response in an eleven-month-old child. The case is sometimes known as Little Albert and the White Rat. Prior to the experiment, Albert had been tested for fear reactions to a number of stimuli: loss of support, burning newspapers, masks with and without hair, and several animals including a rabbit, a dog, and a white rat. None of these objects elicited a fear reaction, and no one had ever seen Albert in a state of fear or rage. The first stimulus that elicited fear was a loud noise, produced by striking a hammer on a steel bar.

The fear response was conditioned by presenting a rat together with a loud noise. After the rat and the sound were paired seven times, the rat became a conditional stimulus eliciting startle and crying. This fear response also *generalized* to stimuli other than the rat: a rabbit, a fur coat, and Watson's hair. Watson and Rayner suggested several ways in which this fear might be eliminated, but unfortunately Albert left the hospital before they had a chance to try them out.

The ethical restrictions which govern experimentation today had not been formulated in 1920. The importance of the Watson and Rayner study is that by showing that fears can be acquired, they opened up the possibility that maladaptive fears can be eliminated. Many of the therapeutic procedures suggested by Watson were carried out by his student, Mary Cover Jones, working with other children whose fears and anxieties were in no way attributable to laboratory conditions. Jones (1924) explored several ways of eliminating children's irrational fears, and she can be considered the forerunner of behavior therapy.

3. Respondent Extinction

One procedure for eliminating conditional reflexes is called *respondent extinction*. If the conditional stimulus continues to be presented without occasional pairings with the unconditional stimulus, the conditional reflex will gradually weaken and eventually disappear. *Respondent extinction refers to the elimination of a conditional reflex when the conditional stimulus is no longer occasionally paired with the unconditional stimulus.* The conditional bell-salivation reflex described in Figure 2.1 would extinguish if the bell were presented often enough in the absence of food. Additional measures may be required to eliminate conditioned fears, partly because people usually avoid exposure to the conditional stimulus and thus the opportunity for extinction to occur. One of the most successful procedures —systematic desensitization—is described in Chapter 6.

4. Generalization and Discrimination

We might decide to train a dog to salivate to the sound of a one kHz tone. Then—if we were sufficiently curious—we might present other tones and see what happened. Pavlov was sufficiently curious. He discovered that salivation will also be elicited by tones of higher and lower frequencies, even if these tones have never been paired with food. This phenomenon is called *stimulus generalization*. Generalization can be defined as an increase in response strength in the presence of stimuli other than the one to which the response was originally conditioned. Pavlov also found that tones closer to the conditional stimulus elicited a greater amount of saliva than those more remote. This variation along the range of elicited responses is called a *generalization gradient*.

If we have frequently been hurt or frightened in a dentist's chair, the physiological components of anxiety may be elicited by sounds similar to those of the dentist's drill. This sort of generalization would not be adaptive for the dentist or for someone who works with other electric tools. But, as Pavlov discovered, experience with a variety of stimuli that are *not* paired with the unconditional stimulus restricts the occurrence of a conditional response. If, for example, salivation generalizes from a one kHz tone to neighboring tones, the range can be restricted by pairing the one kHz tone with food and presenting the other tones without food. Gradually, the response to the other tones will extinguish, so long as the dog is able to discriminate between them. *Discrimination* occurs when the conditional response is elicited by one stimulus (or a narrow range of stimuli) and not by other stimuli. A carpenter or machinist who has experienced pain in conjunction with the sound of a dentist's drill has also had many opportunities to discriminate the sounds made by various kinds of drills.

Discrimination training can produce emotional side effects. Pavlov established a discrimination between a circle and an ellipse, and then presented the dog with ellipses that more and more closely resembled circles. Eventually, the procedure produced an "experimental neurosis;" the discrimination broke down, and the dog had to be given a rest cure. In other Russian experiments, Krasnogorski (1925) used a metronome beat as the conditional stimulus in his work with children. One child, a six-year-old boy, quickly discriminated 144 metronome beats per minute from 92 beats, and then from 108 beats. The experimenter's notes during this period record such comments as "goes to the experiment quickly and laughing, gets into the apparatus by himself . . . a calm, well-balanced and quiet child." When required to discriminate 144 from 120 beats per minute, the child became irritable and refused to go to the laboratory; and when the final discrimination between 144 and 132 beats was attempted, he fell asleep. The accompanying notes read, "Is rude, fights with other children; insists on being discharged from hospital; doctor's (sic) report from the ward that his behavior is insupportable, he is extremely excited, fights and is disobedient" (Krasnogorski, 1925, p. 757). Like Pavlov's dog with the ellipses, the child was apparently incapable of the discrimination, and the experiment was discontinued.

Rudeness, disobedience, aggression, and various forms of "copping out" such as daydreaming, sleeping, or physically leaving the situation are not uncommon when excessive demands are made upon our abilities. This is true of operant discrimination training, described below, as well as respondent discrimination training. One solution is to reduce the demands; and, in the case of discriminating the frequency of metronome beats, this might be the only solution. There are, after all, built-in limits to our sensory capacities. But, in many cases, these kinds of recalcitrant behavior are an indication that discrimination training is proceeding too rapidly, or that conflicting demands are being made, or that consequences are being inconsistently applied. The fault may lie in the teaching, not the student. We need not necessarily lower our expectations. A comprehensive program, like that described in Chapter 3, enables many people to accomplish feats that are well beyond their presumed abilities.

Respondent conditioning, generalization,

and discrimination play an important role in our lives. After a bad automobile accident, for example, the physiological components of anxiety may be aroused by the sound of squealing brakes, the sight of a wrecked car, by stimuli associated with the scene of the accident, or by recalling the accident to others. Many fears are adaptive. For most people, under most conditions, it would be foolhardy to enter a burning building or to approach a snarling dog. On the other hand, *indiscriminate* fear of all fires or all dogs is not adaptive. At the least, such generalized fear can be an inconvenience. At the worst, it can be quite debilitating.

An intermediate example recently came to my attention during the course of student advising. It was the fourth time in three semesters that I was helping Linda, one of my sophomore advisees, rearrange her schedule. Each time we had blocked out a tentative four-year program. Each time there was some reason she had to postpone the intermediate-level lab course that was a prerequisite to all the advanced laboratory courses she wanted so badly to take. About the time that I realized she was actively avoiding this course, she told me the reason why. It wasn't that she minded the work: like 99% of our students she is highly motivated. And it wasn't that she objected to spending half of the semester working with animals: she had really enjoyed the two pigeon labs in the introductory course. But she simply could not face the idea, let alone the actuality, of working with rats. Why? Two years earlier, when she was a volunteer worker in an impoverished neighborhood, Linda had entered a dismal room to investigate the sound of a baby crying. The room appeared to be empty, except for a baby who was lying in a make-shift crib. As Linda approached, there was a sudden movement of the bed clothes; and a rat, which was gnawing at the baby's throat, scuttled from the crib, crossed the floor by her feet, and disappeared into the debris in the corner of the room.

As she described this horrifying scene, Linda paled, spoke haltingly, and exhibited other signs of emotional distress. Recalling the episode elicited an emotional reaction, and so—to a lesser degree—did our subsequent discussion of the animal section of the intermediate course.

After assuring Linda that she did not *have* to work with rats (we could devise similar studies with pigeons or doves), we went to the rodent quarters to see how severe her reaction would be. Even standing in the doorway was difficult. The emotional response had *generalized* from the predatory brown rat of the ghetto to the tame white rats in our vivarium. It had not, however, generalized to gerbils. She walked right up to our gerbil cages, and we considered the possibility of working with them instead of rats. But Linda did not want to live in dread of rats, and so we discussed the possibility of extinguishing her fear. (Actually, we would be establishing a *discrimination*: Both of us would retain a healthy respect for city rats).

First, we wondered if baby rats, like gerbils, were discriminated from adult rats. One baby rat, held a distance of several feet, provoked only a moderate reaction. (I was careful not to put it near my throat). We thus decided to try a combination of graduated extinction and modeling, with Linda retaining the option to work with gerbils or birds. We had approximately two months before the course would start.

We started with a young female rat, which Linda decided to call "Precious," and found a friend (Tim Mustaine) who was willing to make her a house pet during Christmas vacation. By the time Linda returned, Precious would be the friendliest rat ever; although of course she would be a good deal larger. Linda and Precious first got acquainted in Tim's room and office, far away from the other rats in the vivarium. Precious was kept a little hungry so that Linda could feed her. Gradually, Linda learned to take Precious in and out of her cage and how to handle and weigh her. By the time the course started, Linda wouldn't hear of working with any other animal. By then, Precious was back in the vivarium, and Linda marched right past all the other rats to take care of her daily feeding and weighing. Shortly thereafter some of her friends were away for the weekend, and Linda volunteered to take care of their rats as well as her own. Naturally, Precious proved to be the cleverest rat in the course, and we promised to keep her for breeding stock.

C. Operant Procedures

The respondent procedures described above involve the pairing, the presentation, or the withholding of stimulus events that *precede* behavior. A stimulus elicits a response, and the relation between these two events is called a reflex. Some psychologists, notably J. B. Watson (1924), have tried to describe all learning in terms of respondent conditioning procedures. But many examples of learning do not seem to fit this paradigm, and many activities are difficult to describe in terms of reflexes. It would be difficult, for example, to conceive of stimuli that could elicit the behavior of clearing a four-foot-high jump. A loud noise or a shock to the feet might elicit startle and a jump of a few inches. A louder noise or stronger shock might elicit a slightly higher jump. The word "jump" might be paired with a loud noise and eventually elicit elevation: but no increase in intensity of the word, or of any other conditional stimulus, would elicit a higher jump than the noise. Even if we could control all known reflexes, we would not get our subject sufficiently airborne; and yet thousands of people can easily clear a four-foot bar, and some athletes manage seven feet.

Something is missing from the respondent conditioning paradigm, and that "something" is an analysis of the consequences of behavior, of the events that follow it. An expert learns how to clear a seven-foot high jump through a past history of successes and failures in jumping lesser hurdles. Good physical condition is necessary, but the exquisite muscular control involved in the approach and take-off, as well as in clearing the jump, requires many hours of practice during which the jumper gets differential feedback from many sources. Clearing the bar without fouling is the ultimate consequence, but comments from the coach and the way the body feels at various stages of the performance are also important.

1. Reinforcing Consequences

Many of the things we do, including sports and games, reading, speaking, cooking, and playing a musical instrument, are learned and maintained by their consequences. Consequences that increase the likelihood or probability that a given activity will be repeated are called *reinforcers* or *reinforcing events*. Some activities such as playing tennis, working in a garden, and listening to music are inherently reinforcing. Reinforcing activities may be used to increase the strength of other, less preferred activities—the First Work Then Play principle. Sometimes behavior is maintained by consequences that follow naturally. For example, if organizing papers into a filing system permits you to find things quickly and easily, then it is likely that you will continue to file your papers in the future. And sometimes behavior is maintained by reinforcers that are somewhat arbitrary: many people work for wages, but money is not a naturally occurring consequence of labor.

Parents often say that they want their children to read for the pleasure it provides, for its inherent reinforcing value. The trouble is, a certain level of competence is necessary before one can enjoy reading "for its own sake," and other reinforcers may be helpful in strengthening the necessary skills to achieve this level of competence. Early efforts at reading are often reinforced with attention and special privileges. Artificial reinforcers are frequently used in therapy and education, but the long-term goal is to strengthen behavior to the point where normal sources of reinforcement can take over.

One of the ways in which the technical term *reinforcer* differs from the familiar term *reward* is that a *reinforcer is defined only in terms of its effect on behavior*. A reinforcer is any event or activity that increases the probability that the behavior it immediately follows will be repeated. If you thank your son whenever he picks up his clothes, and he picks them up more often than he did before you started thanking him, then your thanks are reinforcing. If he doesn't pick up his clothes more often, then try something else!

The only way to determine whether or not something is a reinforcer is to put it to an empirical test. This means that you must first select some behavior and measure how often it happens—perhaps the number of math homework problems that are correctly completed. Then make some event contingent on the behavior, perhaps five minutes of television for every problem that is answered correctly. If, and only if, the number of correct answers increases, can watching television be considered a reinforcer. If it is a particularly effective reinforcer, you may find that students ask the teacher for extra problems so they can answer them correctly and earn more television time.

To make sure that the improvement is due to the reinforcing effects of television and not to something else, you might then start a phase where television is no longer contingent on answering problems correctly. You might not allow the student to watch television no matter how many problems he has answered correctly, or you might let him watch even if he hasn't answered any problems correctly. In either case, if the number of correct answers decreases

to its original level then you should be reasonably confident that television is a reinforcer and that it was responsible for the improvement in homework.

A reinforcing event has two properties—*it increases the strength of behavior that produces it* (as we have just seen), and *it decreases the strength of behavior that removes it*. So there is another way to test whether or not an event such as watching television is a reinforcer. If you take away the privilege of watching television whenever a child comes home late for dinner, and if this behavior occurs less often, then watching television is a reinforcer.

The important thing to remember is that the reinforcing properties do not reside in the event, but rather, in its effect on behavior. It follows that some events will be reinforcers for some people but not for others, and that a given event may be a reinforcer at one time but not at another. The opportunity to watch a favorite television program may be reinforcing under most circumstances, but not when the individual has a headache, is tired, or has tickets to a football game.

2. Punishing Consequences

Behavior is also controlled by consequences called punishers. Like reinforcers, punishers have two properties—they decrease the strength of behavior that produces them, and they increase the strength of behavior that removes them. If the *presentation* of an event follows the occurrence of some behavior and that behavior subsequently occurs *less frequently*, then the event is a *punisher*. Alternatively, if behavior that *removes* an event subsequently occurs *more frequently*, then the event is also a punisher.

If stealing, or whining, or teasing one's sister is consistently followed by a spanking, and if these activities subsequently occur less often, then a spanking constitutes a punishing event. Needless to say, many classes of behavior that one would want to punish also have reinforcing consequences. Whether or not a given unpleasant event will actually decrease the frequency of any particular class of behavior depends on many variables, some of which are discussed in Chapter 5.

Events are also punishers if their removal increases the strength of behavior. Nagging, for example, is sometimes effective in getting children to do their homework or pick up their rooms. If the frequency of these activities increases when they terminate nagging, then nagging is a punishing event. This is usually a circular state of affairs, because the fact that the homework gets done or the room gets picked up reinforces the parent's behavior of nagging.

Reinforcing events increase the strength of behavior that produces them and decrease the strength of behavior that removes them. Punishers decrease the strength of behavior that produces them and increase the strength of behavior that removes them. These two definitions should make it easy to identify examples of reinforcing and punishing consequences. But for some reason, even professional psychologists find it difficult to accept the fact that reinforcers and punishers (as used in behavior analysis) are defined in terms of their effects on

behavior. Since the behavioral definition is what makes the terms so useful, we belabor the point in Figure 2.2, which shows lever pressing maintained by three different procedures. The rat at the left (A) is pressing a lever with his right paw. Lever pressing automatically turns on the light and delivers a pellet of food into the cup. Before lever pressing produced food, the rat pressed the lever less than once every ten minutes. (This rate, prior to any known conditioning, is called the *operant level*.) When food was made contingent upon lever pressing, the rate increased one hundredfold, to ten times a minute. This is why food can be called a reinforcer. If the rat had had continuous access to food for 24 hours, or if a particular part of the limbic system of his brain had been removed, then food would not have increased the rate of lever pressing, and could not be called a reinforcer.

The infant monkey (Figure 2.2B) is also pressing a lever, but in this case lever pressing terminates or avoids shock. A one kHz tone is sounded for 10 seconds before the shock is turned on. The monkey can terminate the shock by pressing the lever or can avoid it altogether by pressing while the tone is on. In an hour's time, the monkey avoided all the shocks that would have been delivered had lever pressing not been occurring at a high rate. The rate of lever pressing under these conditions far ex-

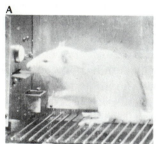 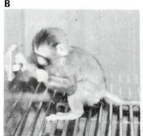 

Figure 2.2.   Lever pressing conditioned and maintained by three different procedures. A: Lever pressing produces pellets of food; B: lever pressing in the presence of a tone postpones or terminates electric shock; C: lever pressing produces electrical stimulation of the brain (the onset of electrical stimulation is shown on the oscilloscope at left of figure, and lever pressing is recorded by the cumulative recorder in the foreground). (From the film, *Behavior theory in practice.* Reese, 1965.)

ceeds the rate before these consequences were imposed. Since the increased rate of lever pressing can be attributed to the *removal* or termination of shock, shock onset can be called a *punisher*.

The rat in Figure 2.2C is also pressing a lever at a high, sustained rate. Each press delivers a brief, electrical stimulus to the region of the posterior hypothalamus of the brain. (The pulse is delivered through wires that are permanently implanted in the rat's brain. The experimenter monitors the electrical stimulus on the oscilloscope shown at the left of the picture, and lever pressing is recorded by a cumulative recorder in the foreground.)

Under this procedure, which is called intracranial self-stimulation, lever pressing may persist for many thousands of responses. Since electrical stimulation is contingent on lever pressing, and since lever pressing is maintained way above operant level, stimulation is by definition a reinforcer.

If the electrodes are implanted in a different area of the brain, the effects may be very different. Stimulation of certain regions of the brain is by definition punishing; an animal will respond at a high rate when lever pressing *terminates* stimulation. When electrodes are implanted in still other regions, the consequence of lever pressing (either stimulation or the termination of stimulation) does not affect the rate of the behavior. To repeat: the reinforcing or punishing properties do not lie in the event, but rather in its effects on behavior.

3. Conditioned Reinforcers and Punishers

Some events are reinforcing or punishing before any special training has taken place. Food, warmth, the odor of certain flowers, and the sound of certain rhythms are generally unlearned or unconditioned reinforcers. A sudden, loud noise and a painful blow are unlearned or unconditioned punishers.

Other events have acquired reinforcing or punishing properties by being paired with events that already had these properties. Money, trading stamps, and the word "excellent" written by a teacher across a student's paper are examples of conditioned reinforcers. The word "no," a poor grade on a report card, or being told to go to the end of the line for recess are conditioned punishers. It is easy to see that the events that function as conditioned reinforcers or conditioned punishers could vary not only among cultures but among individuals within the same cultures.

In terms of the effect on behavior, it usually makes very little difference whether the reinforcing or punishing event is unconditioned or conditioned. But it is often easier for a parent to say "good" than to deliver an unconditioned reinforcer when a child is engaging in praiseworthy behavior, or to say "no" when a child is endangering life or property. Probably a great proportion of the consequences that control our own behavior have acquired their reinforcing or punishing properties.

4. Basic Operant Procedures

There are several ways in which behavior can be modified by its consequences. Behavior can produce, remove, or postpone a reinforcing or punishing event; and once established, any of these dependencies can be terminated. Eight basic procedures are shown in Table 2.1, where the shaded areas indicate procedures that weaken behavior ("bad" happenings) and the unshaded areas indicate procedures that strengthen behavior ("good" happenings). Please note that our definitions have not changed. "Good" and "bad happenings" are not technical terms. Furthermore, they refer to procedures, not to reinforcing or punishing events.

REINFORCEMENT and PUNISHMENT involve the presentation of reinforcing and punishing events, respectively; ESCAPE and RE-SPONSE COST involve their removal; AVOID-ANCE and OMISSION TRAINING involve their postponement (see left of table). Whether the procedure involves reinforcing or punishing events is stated beneath the name of each procedure.

When the contingencies are terminated, there is no procedural consequence of behavior. Discontinuing any of the strengthening or conditioning procedures results in EXTINC-TION; discontinuing any of the weakening or suppression procedures results in RECOVERY. The arrows and shading indicate the direction of the behavior change. Note that some conditioning procedures involve punishers and that some weakening procedures involve reinforcers.

a. Reinforcement
A procedure to *increase* the strength of behavior by *presenting a reinforcer* contingent upon that

behavior. If the behavior is not strengthened, then the consequence is not a reinforcer, and the procedure cannot be called reinforcement. The most common measures of "strength" of behavior are its frequency and duration. A professor who is interested in helping students contribute more to class discussions might follow each contribution with comments about the importance of the issue raised by the student. If the number or the extent of the students' contributions then increases, the professor's comments are reinforcers. And, since the students' behavior produces the comments, the procedure is reinforcement.

b. Punishment
A procedure to *decrease* the strength of behavior by *presenting* a punisher contingent upon behavior. A procedure cannot be called punishment unless the behavior weakens over time. There must be reduction in the frequency,

Table 2.1   Basic operant procedures. Above: Technical names of six procedures when behavior produces, removes, or postpones a reinforcing or punishing event. Below: Names of procedures when contingencies are terminated. Arrows indicate direction of behavior change (increase or decrease). Shaded areas indicate reductive procedures ("bad" happenings); unshaded areas indicate strengthening procedures ("good" happenings).

Consequence *Behavior:*	CONTINGENCIES IN EFFECT	
	CONDITIONING ←	SUPPRESSION ←
Produces event	**Reinforcement** Behavior produces *reinforcer*	**Punishment** Behavior produces *punisher*
Removes event	**Escape (Negative Reinforcement)** Behavior removes *punisher*	**Response Cost** Behavior removes *reinforcer*
Postpones event	**Avoidance** Behavior postpones *punisher*	**Omission Training** Behavior postpones *reinforcer*
	CONTINGENCIES TERMINATED	
	EXTINCTION ←	RECOVERY ←
No consequence	Discontinue: Reinforcement, Escape, or Avoidance	Discontinue: Punishment, Response Cost, or Omission Training

duration, or severity of the behavior. Teachers sometimes scold children when they annoy other students; but if the annoying behavior does not decrease, then the procedure is not punishment. The teacher may feel better, but not much is being done to remedy the situation. In fact, a child may annoy other students *more* frequently, either because teacher attention is a reinforcer or because the child is receiving reinforcers from peers for being "a tough guy to handle."

c. Escape (negative reinforcement)[2]

A procedure to *increase* the strength of behavior by *removing a punisher*, contingent upon that behavior. The monkey in Figure 2.2 was trained to press the lever by an escape procedure. Every so often, shock was delivered through the floor of the cage; and when the lever was pressed, the shock was terminated for a period of time. Lever pressing removed shock and was rapidly conditioned. There are many examples of escape conditioning in the natural environment. We can escape pain by taking medication, cover our ears to shut out painful noise, or hang up the phone to terminate a distressing conversation.

d. Response cost

A procedure to *decrease* the strength of behavior by *removing a reinforcer*, contingent upon that behavior. A fine for a traffic violation is a common example of response cost. In many applied situations, the reinforcer that is removed is money or points that could have been exchanged for other reinforcers. Parents use this procedure when they dock a child's allowance contingent upon some misbehavior, as do teachers when they subtract points from the grade if a paper is turned in late.

e. Avoidance

A procedure by which behavior is *strengthened* when it *postpones or prevents a punishing event*. Much of our behavior seems to be learned and maintained by avoidance procedures. Students often study to avoid getting a bad grade; children may clean their rooms to avoid being scolded, or learn to look both ways before crossing the street to avoid being hit by a car. People pay income taxes to avoid fines or imprisonment.

The monkey in Figure 2.2, in addition to being trained to lever press under an escape procedure, could also avoid shock by pressing the lever when a tone sounded. Changing from escape to avoidance contingencies is probably the most common method of establishing avoidance behavior. But most of us do not have to be hit by a car or punished for tax evasion before we learn ways of avoiding these events. We learn to recognize generalized warning signals or threats, which are much like the preshock tone to the monkey. We learn to avoid certain dangers because of the verbal instructions we receive from others. Learning to react to verbal

---

2. The term "negative reinforcer" is sometimes used instead of the word "punisher." And the procedure we are calling *escape* is sometimes called *negative reinforcement*, the rationale being that behavior is strengthened—or reinforced—by the removal of a negative reinforcer. We find, however, that no matter how carefully we describe the operations, and no matter how often we point out that negative reinforcement is a "good" happening, our students persist in using the word negative reinforcement as a synonym for punishment. To escape these punishing signs of ineffective teaching, we have finally restricted the words "negative reinforcer" and "negative reinforcement" to footnotes and parentheses. Michael (1975) reviews the historical development and the changes in definitions of these technical terms. He suggests that we abandon the distinction between presentation and removal and refer to "good things" having a strengthening effect on behavior as reinforcement, and to "bad things" having a weakening effect as punishment. Thus reinforcement would include both the presentation of a reinforcer and the removal of a punisher, and punishment would include both the removal of a reinforcer and the presentation of a punisher. This seems the simplest solution to our current terminological confusion, but I favor retaining the distinction between presentation and removal as useful in describing the actual procedures. However, Jack Michael is usually light years ahead of his colleagues, and quite likely the rest of us will come around in time.

instructions or other generalized warning signals means that we can avoid many punishing events without ever personally encountering them.

f. Omission training (DRO)[3]
A procedure by which behavior is *weakened* when it *postpones a reinforcing event*. In this procedure, which is normally used to reduce behavior occurring at a high rate, each occurrence of the behavior postpones the delivery of a reinforcer. Because reinforcement is delivered only when the behavior is omitted for a specified time period, the procedure is called omission training. Its essential feature is that a specified period of time must elapse when the behavior does not occur. If the behavior does occur, then the time period starts again. One of our students got his roommate to stop smoking by giving him a dollar for every 24-hour period he went without a cigarette; (24-hour periods that occurred over a weekend were worth two dollars). If the roommate smoked a cigarette at any time during the 24-hour period, even after 23 hours of abstinence, the opportunity to earn a dollar was postponed for a new 24-hour period. The program was so successful that the student's financial resources were depleted at the end of a month. Nonetheless, both roommates were happy at the outcome. In the six weeks following the program, the student reported that his roommate had lighted one cigarette, taken one "drag," and then snuffed the cigarette out.

g. Extinction
The two procedures at the bottom of Table 2.1 refer to the termination of the procedures listed above them. At the present time there are no separate names for the termination of reinforcement, escape, and avoidance contingencies. Termination of all these conditioning procedures is called *extinction*.

Not surprisingly, behavior occurs less frequently when the procedure that maintained it is no longer in effect. Extinction occurs when reinforcement is discontinued (complaining no longer results in sympathetic attention) or when escape and avoidance are no longer possible (when excuses no longer get one out of mowing the lawn). Extinction refers to both the *effect* (the decrease in the strength of behavior) and to the *procedure* (the termination of reinforcement, escape, or avoidance contingencies). Since extinction is a weakening procedure, it can be used to reduce the frequency or duration of problem behavior—*if* one can identify and withhold the consequences maintaining the behavior, a feat which may be easier said than done.

h.   Recovery
Not surprisingly, behavior is likely to occur more often when the procedure that weakened it is no longer in effect. Unless special measures are taken, behavior generally *recovers* when punishment, response cost, or omission training is discontinued. As in the case of extinction, there are no separate names for terminating these procedures, so we shall use the one term, *recovery*.

Procedures to prevent the extinction of desirable behavior and the recovery of problem behavior are described in Chapter 3. No educational or therapeutic program can be considered complete until it provides for the gains to be maintained in the natural environment.

On the other hand, it is possible to take advantage of recovery to strengthen desirable behavior. This means identifying the consequences which are weakening the behavior and then removing them. A male supervisor might find that he is getting little feedback from his employees regarding the effectiveness of his management skills, even though he has asked for suggestions. An analysis of the situation might show the supervisor that he was actually punishing the very feedback that he wanted. By

3. Omission Training, abbreviated OT, is sometimes called DRO (Differential Reinforcement of Other behavior). See Chapter 5.

withholding his negative reactions to the employees' criticisms, the frequency of suggestions might recover and he might well get the feedback that would help him to do a better job.

These basic procedures are summarized in the paradigms of Figure 2.3, where R stands for behavior,[4] S^R for reinforcer, and S^P for punisher. The arrow ($\rightarrow$) shows the temporal relation between the events and indicates that the contingencies are in effect. Thus the reinforcement procedure, in which behavior ("response") produces a reinforcer, is symbolized by R→S^R; punishment by R→S^P. A slash through the symbol ($\cancel{S}^R$; $\cancel{S}^P$) indicates the removal or termination of a reinforcer or punisher. Escape, where the behavior removes or terminates a punishing event, becomes R→$\cancel{S}^P$; and response cost: R→$\cancel{S}^R$.

Alternative paradigms are given for avoidance and omission training because these procedures can be viewed in two ways. The behavior postpones the event, so we use an extended arrow ($\rightsquigarrow$) to indicate this temporal relation. On the other hand, we could say that the omission of behavior ($\cancel{R}$) produces reinforcement or punishment. In our example of avoidance, R$\rightsquigarrow$$S^P$ seems more descriptive of the monkey whose lever pressing postpones electric shock (Figure 2.3). But in our example of omission training, $\cancel{R}$→S^R may be more descriptive of the college student who earned a dollar by not smoking for 24 hours.

4. Even though we believe the term *behavior* is more appropriate than *response* when one is describing operant procedures, we have retained the symbol "R" in these paradigms.

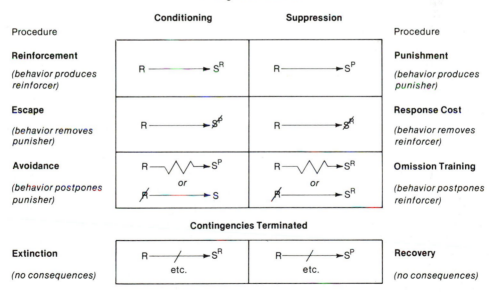

BASIC OPERANT PROCEDURES

Figure 2.3 Paradigms for basic operant procedures. R: behavior, S^R: reinforcer, S^P: punisher, $\cancel{S}^R$: removal of a reinforcer, $\cancel{S}^P$: removal of a punisher. The arrow shows the temporal relations between the events and indicates that the contingencies are in effect. The extended arrow ($\rightsquigarrow$) means that the behavior postpones the consequence. The slashed arrow ($\nrightarrow$) means that the former contingencies have been terminated and that the behavior is no longer followed by the particular consequence. An alternative paradigm is offered for avoidance and omission training (see text).

The slashed arrow ($\not\rightarrow$) in the paradigms for extinction and recovery indicates that the contingencies have been terminated: the behavior occurs but is no longer followed by the particular consequence.

5. Stimulus Control

a. Generalization

Whatever its consequences, behavior does not occur in a vacuum. And behavior that has been reinforced in one situation is likely to occur in other situations. Just as in respondent conditioning, the effects of operant procedures may *generalize* to different settings. A child who is learning to talk may speak his first words in the presence of his mother, who usually has more opportunities than other people to reinforce this behavior. He soon "speaks" to other members of the family and to strangers. When he is taken to a strange place, speaking usually generalizes to the new surroundings. All of which is fortunate. Without generalization, we would probably spend most of our time relearning the same few skills in each new situation, and be able to develop only the most limited behavioral repertoires.

The more situations in which a given activity is reinforced, the more likely it is to generalize to new situations. A frequent problem in education and therapy is the transfer of skills to situations outside the classroom or clinic. To facilitate the generalization of newly acquired behavior, special measures may be necessary to insure that the behavior is reinforced in a variety of settings.

b. Discrimination

Of course there would be utter confusion if there were complete generalization, with any behavior likely to occur in any situation; but we learn that "There is a time and place for everything." We *discriminate*—that is, we behave differently in different situations. A driver stops at red traffic lights and not at green ones. Rather than asking for a larger allowance when the teacher has called home to report some misbehavior, a child awaits the arrival of a good report card. In these examples, a red traffic light has been discriminated from a green one, and a situation in which a request for additional money is likely to be refused has been discriminated from one in which the request is likely to be granted. *Discrimination is a consistent difference in behavior in the presence of different stimulus situations.* A *differential response* is essential to any behavioral definition of discrimination. We can say that the driver discriminates differences in traffic lights, or the child discriminates among occasions to ask for money, *only* if they behave differently in the different situations.

If a differential response is lacking, it may be because the person is not capable of making the discrimination—some people are color blind—or it may be because the behavior has not been brought under stimulus control. If a driver does not stop at a red light unless there is other traffic or a police car on the horizon, then it is these other stimulus events, not the color of the lights alone, which control the driver's behavior. Teachers face a different problem. When asked to read a list of words, a child may say the word "saw" for the letters "w-a-s" as well as for the letters "s-a-w." Yet if asked to circle the letter "s" and not the letter "w", this same child might do so with no trouble. In this case, the letters "w" and "s" are discriminated when presented singly, but not when presented in the context of a word. In the context of words, there is no differential response; stimulus control remains to be developed.

Stimulus control is developed by discrimination training. Although several different procedures exist, all of them require that when the behavior occurs in *different situations*, it is followed by *different consequences*. The behavior could be reinforced in one situation and extinguished in another; it could be reinforced in one situation and punished in another; different classes of behavior could be reinforced in different situations, and so forth. A child learning to speak is likely to meet up with all of these variations of *differential reinforcement*. Initially, many parents react with joy whether the word "doggy" is bestowed upon a dog, a cat, or a doorstop in the shape of a horse. Generalization is accepted, if not encouraged, in their enthusiasm over baby's first words. Later on, they will probably reserve their admiration for those occasions when the word "doggy" is addressed to a dog or to a picture or statue of a dog. They may also ignore (extinguish) the usage of this word in the presence of other animals; they may punish the generalized response; or they may try to establish a differential response by reinforcing different verbalizations in different stimulus contexts. If the child were pointing to a cat, for example, they would not only extinguish the word "doggy", but also shape and reinforce an expression such as "ki'y kat."

c. Discriminative stimuli

Events that precede or accompany reinforcement or punishment are called discriminative stimuli *if* a differential response occurs in their presence. If a child says "doggy" when shown a picture of a dog, but not when shown a picture of a cat or a hippopotamus, then the picture of a dog is a discriminative stimulus for the vocalization "doggy." Verbal instructions, the ringing of a telephone, an ambulance siren, and signs such as QUIET, ENTER, or SPEED LIMIT 45 M.P.H. are familiar examples of discriminative stimuli designed to control our behavior. Certain classes of behavior are more likely to occur in the presence of these stimuli than in their absence. Discriminative stimuli are signals or cues or instructions; but, like reinforcing or punishing events, they are defined by their effects upon behavior. Even a young child or a foreigner who cannot read English can probably discriminate

a difference between the signs LADIES and GENTLEMEN, if only because one word is longer. But unless they enter the appropriate door, we cannot say that the signs are discriminative stimuli for this class of behavior.

Discriminative stimuli do not elicit behavior in the sense that a bell can become a conditional stimulus for salivation. Rather, they control behavior in the sense that a given class of behavior is more likely to occur in their presence than in their absence—because the behavior has been reinforced more often in their presence than in their absence.

Understanding the stimulus control of behavior is sometimes easier when we start with a simple, laboratory example, such as the pigeon in Figure 2.4. The pigeon "reads": at least he responds differentially and appropriately to written commands, pecking when the sign says PECK and turning a full circle when the sign says TURN. Food reinforcement is delivered when the feeder is raised (Figure 2.4H). Between reinforcements, it is lowered out of the bird's reach. The bird was first taught to peck at a circular pattern placed in the stimulus window. Later the letters PECK appeared in the window, and the response generalized: the bird pecked the letters. When pecking the letters was well established, the sign was changed so that the letters TURN were centered in the window. At this point, discrimination training—or differential reinforcement—was started: pecking was not reinforced when TURN was in the window. The two words were presented in random order, but pecking was reinforced only in the presence of the word PECK. A differential response was established as pecking was maintained in strength to the word PECK and extinguished to the word TURN.

Meanwhile, turning was conditioned to the word TURN. Rather than waiting for the bird to execute a full turn, the experimenters *shaped* turning by reinforcing behavior that more and more closely resembled turning. First, reinforcement was presented when the bird turned his head toward the Plexiglas front of the box. Then reinforcement was withheld until he turned his body. Gradually, closer approximations to turning a full circle were demanded: lifting his foot, moving both feet a quarter turn, moving a half turn, and so forth.

This example illustrates: *generalization* of pecking from the circular pattern to the letters; *differential reinforcement* of pecking in the presence of PECK, and nonreinforcement of pecking in the presence of TURN; a *differential response* (hence discrimination) of frequent pecking to PECK and infrequent pecking to TURN; *shaping* of turning by differential reinforcement of closer and closer approximations of turning; and finally, *differential reinforcement* of pecking to PECK and turning to TURN, with concomitant differential responding to these two stimuli. The word PECK was thus established as a *discriminative stimulus* for pecking, and the word TURN for turning.

The bird in Figure 2.4 was trained by two undergraduates taking their first laboratory course in psychology. After the initial conditioning of pecking, it took them less than an hour to establish a reliably literate performance. It could have been *any* pigeon—and it could have been *any* undergraduate. (The discrimination was facilitated by printing the words in different colors and then gradually making the letters the same color after the bird was responding appropriately. This procedure, called *fading*, is described in Chapter 3.)

6. Contingencies

An adequate description of operant procedures must specify not only the *behavior* and its *consequences*, but also the *conditions* under which the consequences will or will not be forthcoming. Taken together, these three classes of events constitute the *contingencies* of operant procedures. Restrictions may be placed on the form, frequency, rate, or duration of the behavior itself; further restrictions may be placed on the conditions in which the behavior will occur. For example, the completion of a

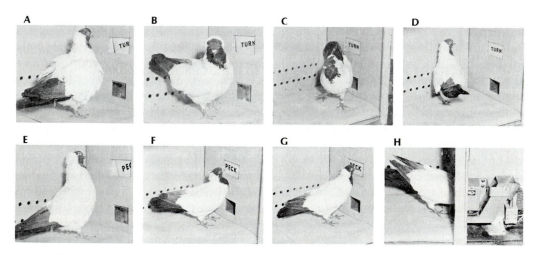

Figure 2.4.   Pigeon "reading," i.e., pecking or turning appropriately to written commands. Commands appeared in window in random order. A: looking at letters as sign changes; B: starting to turn; C: halfway through the turn by the time letters are centered; D: completing the turn; E: observing the sign; F: starting to peck; G: pecking the panel; H: reinforcement—feeder is raised and bird can reach the grain in the hopper. (Photographs by Max Kotfila. From Reese, 1966, p. 10.)

homework assignment might be reinforced only when the paper was handed in on time, 90% correct, and sufficiently neat to be legible. Shouting might be punished in the library, but not in the gym, and only when the noise level exceeded a certain intensity.

The major contingencies in effect for the pigeon in Figure 2.4 specified that when the word PECK was in view, pecking would produce food reinforcement; and when the word TURN was in view, turning a circle would be reinforced. Actually, the bird had to peck an average of 10 times before food was delivered, and the (single) turn had to be in a clockwise direction. On the other hand, the contingencies did not include any restrictions on the rate or force of pecking, nor were there any consequences (such as punishment) for failure to respond appropriately.

Changing behavior is largely a matter of locating effective reinforcers, establishing discriminative stimuli, and arranging appropriate contingencies. Contingency management is the essence of successful teaching and of self-control.

D. The Free Operant Method

One of Skinner's early contributions was the design of a laboratory apparatus in which a rat was "free" to move about a small enclosure and engage in a number of activities, such as grooming, exploring, or pressing a lever. Everything is relative: the rat was free compared to Pavlov's dogs which were restrained in harnesses. Skinner was *not* trying to simulate the rat's natural environment, nor was he trying to study any particular class of behavior such as reproduction or aggression. He was interested in the effects of the *consequences* of behavior, and the frequency and pattern of lever pressing provided a convenient measure of these effects.[5]

Lever pressing is easily conditioned, and

the rate of lever pressing can serve as a baseline for measuring the effects of various programs of reinforcement or punishment. Other activities can be added, and complex sequences of behavior can be developed. Since lever pressing is something many animals can do easily and repeatedly, the rate can vary between zero and thousands of times an hour, and a wide range of effects can be detected. This can provide a sensitive measure of discrimination or motivation or the effects of many other variables of interest. A particular rate or pattern of responding may be maintained for hours, and this allows the experimenter to measure such things as the onset, duration, and long-term effects of a given drug.

The free operant method is now used in many areas of biology and psychology. In most basic research, the subject is still confined in a small enclosure. But there is now a good deal of evidence from applied research that the principles discovered in "Skinner boxes" appear to hold in larger "boxes" such as hospital wards, businesses, the home, and the classroom.

Lindsley (1956, 1960, 1962) was the first to adapt the free operant method to systematic studies with institutionalized psychotic patients. In the study described below, which illustrates some of the advantages of the free operant method, he investigated the effects of the drug, benactyzine, on both normal and psychotic behavior (Lindsley, 1962a, b).

The subject was a chronic psychotic adult who exhibited the hallucinatory behavior of talking and shouting to nonexistent people. Lindsley developed a technique to record this vocal behavior automatically and, simultaneously, to record the simple, manual activity of pulling a plunger. The experimental enclosure

5. One advantage over other apparatus of the 1930s, such as the maze and the puzzle box, was that the subject could emit the specified behavior (e.g., lever pressing) at any time. The experimenter did not have to intervene and disrupt the animal's behavior in order to begin a new trial.

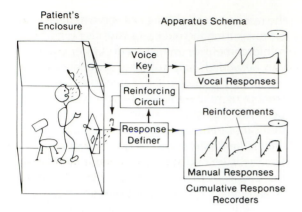

Patient's Enclosure

Apparatus Schema

Voice Key

Reinforcing Circuit

Response Definer

Vocal Responses

Reinforcements

Manual Responses

Cumulative Response Recorders

Figure 2.5. Diagram of apparatus for simultaneous recording of two classes of behavior: vocal output and pulling the plunger. (From Lindsley, 1962a, p. 51.)

was a six-foot square, indestructible room (Figure 2.5, left). *Pulling the plunger was occasionally reinforced* with candy, delivered through a chute. *Hallucinatory vocal responding, which was never reinforced*, was picked up by a microphone hidden at the ceiling, transduced by a voice key, and transmitted to another cumulative recorder. Continuous recordings of both classes of behavior were obtained throughout sessions lasting five hours or more. The severity of vocal hallucinations could be measured by their frequency and duration and also by the extent to which responding on the plunger decreased.

Lindsley's technique permits the screening of hallucinogenic and antihallucinatory drugs. In one such study the patient was given 20 mg. benactyzine, a drug reputed to have psychotherapeutic value. The results are shown in Figure 2.6: vocal behavior (upper graph, Voc) and manual responding on the plunger (lower graph, Man) were recorded for five hours. The pens of the cumulative recorders reset to zero after 500 responses.[6] Initially, the manual response occurred at a high rate (five columns or 2,500 responses in 18 minutes), and there were no vocalizations. But 18 minutes

after the drug was administered, hallucinatory vocal behavior began and continued for more than three and a half hours. Coinciding with an increase in vocalizations was a decrease in the rate of the manual response, with maximum reduction occurring one to one and a half hours after ingestion of the drug. By the fourth hour, responding on the plunger was back to the high and stable rate, and vocalizing had greatly diminished. From this session, and from long control sessions during which lactose tablets were given as a placebo instead of benactyzine, Lindsley could draw two major conclusions. First, benactyzine was a hallucinogenic drug rather than a therapeutic one; and, second, a 20 mg. dosage produced hallucinatory behavior

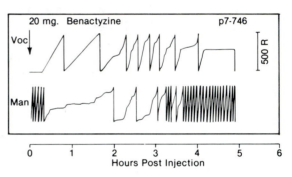

20 mg. Benactyzine   p7-746

Voc

500 R

Man

0   1   2   3   4   5   6
Hours Post Injection

Figure 2.6. Effects of a single dosage of 20 mg. benactyzine upon simultaneously recorded hallucinatory vocal behavior (Voc) and reinforced plunger pulling (Man) of an hallucinatory chronic psychotic adult. (Adapted from Lindsley, 1962b, p. 377.)

6. Skinner devised the cumulative recorder to provide a continuous, graphical record of behavior as it occurs. A cumulative recorder consists of a paper tape that moves at a constant speed and a marking pen that moves upward a constant distance as each response is recorded. Note that a period in which no responses occur will be shown as a horizontal line. Cumulative records are used when the experimenter wants to examine the rate or pattern of thousands of responses occurring continuously over time. They are extraordinarily useful in basic research. In many applied studies, however, data from a single subject are averaged over sessions or days, and in these cases conventional (noncumulative) records are usually presented.

with a latency of 18 minutes and a duration of three and a half to four hours. These findings were subsequently supported by clinical field trials.

A general procedure for applied behavior analysis is described in Chapter 3, but two of the essential features are illustrated by Lindsley's basic research with psychotic patients.

1) Emphasis is placed on the performance of the individual rather than a group. In many other research designs, different groups of subjects are given different "treatments", and any obtained differences are evaluated statistically. However, behaviorists are not particularly interested in using statistical analyses to predict what will happen, on the average, to an "average" subject. They believe that averaging subjects' data obscures important individual differences.[7] With the free operant method, individual subjects serve as their own controls. To evaluate the effects of benactyzine upon hallucinatory vocal behavior (Figure 2.6), Lindsley conducted many long control sessions without the drug. He could thus compare this particular patient's behavior with and without the drug, and he could replicate the study with other patients to assess the generality of his findings. The free operant method usually requires the psychologist to work with a few individuals over long periods of time rather than with groups of individuals over short periods of time. A given procedure is introduced and continued until its effects are reliably determined. Additional subjects are run to replicate findings, *not* so that their data may be averaged. If the results are not clear, one doesn't add subjects; one looks for the variables that account for the individual differences.

2) The other essential feature of behavior analysis is the precise definition and measurement of behavior. Reliable measures are especially important when one wants to monitor behavior continuously (or repeatedly) over long periods of time. Lindsley's setting allowed him to monitor both classes of behavior with automatic recording equipment. But since automatic recording is seldom feasible in an applied setting, the reliability of observational recording has been a major concern of behavior analysts. Many recording procedures have been developed for different settings or different classes of behavior. Some demand the full-time attention of one or more trained observers; others can be employed by parents or teachers without interrupting their other work (see Chapter 3).

7. See Murray Sidman's *Tactics of Scientific Research* (1960) for an elegant statement of this position and Jack Michael's discussion (1974) of the potentially harmful effects of relying on statistical analyses. Alan Kazdin (1976b) also addresses the issue of statistical analyses in within-subject experimental designs.

3

A General Procedure for Applied Behavior Analysis

A. Preliminary and Continuing
  1. Observe
  2. Consult
  3. Evaluate
B. Designing the Program
  1. Analyze the current situation
  2. Ethical issues in the selection of goals
    a. Attaining freedom
    b. Exercising freedom
  3. Establish priorities
  4. Specify goals
    a. General goals or objectives
    b. Specific goals: behavioral definitions
      i. Identify the behavior
      ii. Context
      iii. Criterion levels
      iv. Measurement
    c. Recording behavior
      i. Why bother?
      ii. Automatic recording
      iii. Permanent products
      iv. Observational recording
      v. Subjective reports
    d. Interobserver agreement
      i. Percentage agreement, totals only
      ii. Interobserver agreement, by intervals
    e. Naming the class of behavior
    f. Teaching objectives
  5. Motivation
    a. Reinforcers
      i. Varieties of reinforcers
      ii. Token economies
      iii. Locating reinforcers
      iv. Increasing reinforcer effectiveness
    b. Punishers
  6. Select procedures
    a. Consider the options
    b. Examine the evidence
    c. Attend to the personal equation
    d. Balance the costs
    e. Select combinations of procedures
    f. "Symptom substitution"
  7. Specify contingencies
    a. Stating contingencies
    b. Contingency contracts
  8. Design a favorable situation
  9. Adaptation
  10. Select evaluation procedures
    a. Group designs
    b. Replication
    c. Reversal designs
    d. Multiple-baseline designs
    e. Combined designs
    f. Changing-criterion designs
C. Carrying out the Program
  1. Review of program design
    a. Preliminary and continuing review
    b. Analyze current situation
    c. Ethical issues and priorities
    d. Specific goals
    e. Procedures and contingencies
    f. Favorable situation and adaptation
    g. Evaluation
  2. Baseline
  3. Build from repertoire
  4. Program the task and the material
    a. Shaping
    b. Backwards chaining

  c. Fading
  d. Gradually raise the requirements
5. Evaluate
6. Maintenance and Generalization
   (Transfer)
   a. Incorporate natural settings
   b. Select goals that will be supported
      by the community
   c. Incorporate naturally occurring
      reinforcers
   d. Decrease density of reinforcement

and increase the delay
   e. Extend contingencies to new settings
      and individuals
   f. Train parents, teachers, peers
   g. Program reentry into the community
   h. Self-management
7. Follow-up
   a. Duration of follow-up
   b. Follow-up measures
   c. Long-term evaluation of a program
      for alcoholics

As all behavior modifiers quickly learn, the principles are easier to state than to apply. When you are serious about helping yourself or someone else accomplish a goal, you are likely to wind up with a program that resembles the flow chart suggested in Table 3.1. Table 3.1 is a revision of an earlier attempt (Reese, 1966) to provide a general procedure that can be adapted to a wide variety of situations. It also incorporates suggestions from Sulzer and Mayer (1972) who have provided a similar model for school personnel. In the past few years several helpful books have appeared that describe the use of behavioral procedures in specific applied settings.[1] Table 3.1 is a more general description, and it includes certain steps that we believe to be implicit, if not explicit, in other programs. It might serve as a guideline for setting up a behavioral program, or it might provide a useful checklist in conjunction with an ongoing program.[2]

Obviously the first step in behavior modification is for someone to decide that someone's behavior should be changed. It could be the individual client who decides that his own behavior must be changed; it could be a concerned relative or friend or teacher, another professional, or institutional personnel. The professional behavior modifier then assumes the role of consultant, helping the concerned individuals decide what behavior to change, toward

what ends, and how. In helping to formulate these decisions, behavioral consultants assume responsibility to their clients and to society for any program that is designed with their approval.

The consulting role of the professional is important because behavior modification endeavors to help people learn to manage their own behavior. Even in cases where self-management is an unrealistic short-term goal, someone other than the professional will be carrying out the program, usually parents, teachers, or hospital staff. These people can often suggest effective reinforcers and identify aspects of the situation that may influence the selection of procedures. An effective program is therefore likely to be one that is designed with the help of the person who will carry it out.

Many of the procedures effective in changing the behavior of someone else are also effective in managing one's own behavior. The application of Table 3.1 to self-management, or self-control, is discussed in Chapter 7, but you might want to keep a particular self-control project in mind as you read this chapter.

---

1. See Chapter 8.

2. The film, *Born to Succeed* (Reese, 1971a) shows how this general procedure was used in a program to teach number concepts to retarded children.

Table 3.1   A general procedure for applied behavior analysis.

A GENERAL PROCEDURE FOR APPLIED BEHAVIOR ANALYSIS

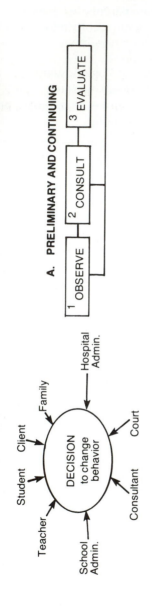

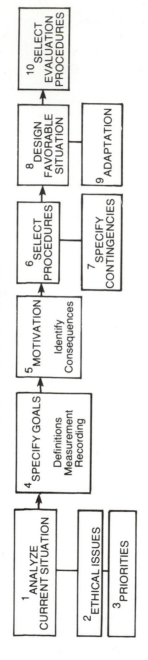

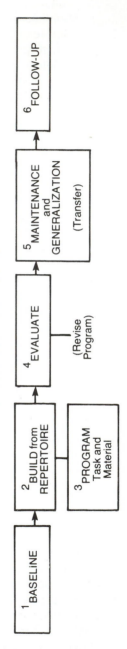

A. Preliminary and Continuing

The first three steps continue to be important all during the program, right through to the follow-up assessment.

1. Observe: Know thy . . .
(child) (student) (patient)
(parent) (spouse) (self)

Behavioral procedures must always be adapted to the individual and to the situation.[3] We are all unique, with our own special problems to solve, and our own special potential to nourish. "Knowing thyself" or another involves identifying the individual's strengths and weaknesses, as well as identifying those people and situations that are major determinants of the individual's behavior.

There are two reasons for discovering the individual's particular skills and capabilities. For one thing, these are the classes of behavior to build on. For another, even though problem behavior may be conspicuous simply because it is aversive, it often takes considerable effort to identify another's abilities (or one's own, for that matter). Yet when we take the trouble to look, we can always find *something* to work with, something to appreciate; and this will enhance the social context in which behavior change must take place. As part of a program to improve the self-esteem of a group of inner-city children, Bill Conway[4] gave their parents the following assignment: each parent was to discover the child doing something right, and then *immediately* praise or thank the child. Bill made a videotape at a subsequent meeting with the parents, and I recall a deeply moving sequence in which one mother said, "You know, I never liked that kid before. I couldn't stand him. But now we get along fine. For the first time in his life, he kissed me when he left for school this morning." *Catch them being good* is an important maxim in behavior modification. The

strengths that one can build on include general intelligence and good will as well as particular social, academic, or athletic abilities.

It is also important to know the person's deficits, the problems that must be overcome or worked around. For example, it is often difficult to determine whether a person is retarded or has a hearing deficit; but the extent of both of these possible limitations is an important consideration in selecting both remedial aids and effective teaching programs.[5]

This background information on general strengths and weaknesses, together with information concerning peer and family relations and medical, educational, and work histories, helps to define the context in which the problems occur and usually must be treated. It is also important in defining the goals of treatment. Guidelines for clinical assessment in behavioral counseling with adults are described by Hersen and Bellack, 1976; Goldiamond (1974); Kanfer and Saslow (1969); and Lazarus (1972). For counseling with parents, see Holland (1970, 1976). Bijou (1968) and Kazdin and Straw (1976) are excellent sources for those working with retarded children.

2. Consult With Those Who Will Implement or Maintain the Program

Since most human behavior occurs in a social context, it is important to identify the people who influence the individual's behavior—for better or for worse. The people who are ad-

3. Successful programs for *groups* of individuals allow for, and are responsive to, individual differences.

4. Dr. William Conway, University of Massachusetts School of Education. The mother's statement is as I remember it.

5. Behavioral procedures are providing sensitive measures of auditory and visual capacities in handicapped people. (See Bricker & Bricker, 1970; Macht, 1971; Meyerson & Michael, 1964; Reese, Howard, & Rosenberger, 1977; Rosenberger, 1974; Sidman & Stoddard, 1967.)

mired, those who are resented; the people who may help with the program, those who may hamper it. Relatives, friends, and employers are all people who can make or break a program and whose own conflicting needs may have to be considered.

A behavioral program will be carried out by parents, teachers, institutional staff members, and, wherever possible, by the client. Usually these people will be more interested in maintaining a program that they have helped to design than one to which they have contributed nothing; and they will be better able to modify the procedures as the need arises.

3. Evaluate: Incorporate Procedures to Evaluate the Success of the Program

Perhaps the most important characteristic of behavior modification is that the procedures *can* be and *must* be evaluated. Behavior modification is, of course, more than a collection of procedures. It is an attempt to apply a science of behavior to the solution of particular human problems. But when a given procedure, or combination of procedures, has been selected, its effectiveness must be subjected to empirical test. This emphasis on evaluation distinguishes behavior modification from many schools of therapy. Even with practical projects of limited application, continuous evaluation is necessary to assess the effectiveness of the program, to provide feedback on the success or failure of the various procedures. If something isn't working very well, you would try something else—but first, you would have to know exactly how well it *is* working.

When a program is going well, the data can be powerful reinforcers for those who are carrying out the procedures. When a program is not going well, data constitute an "early warning system," and changes can be made before things get out of hand. Data are more reliable and more sensitive to small changes than

are subjective impressions. A child's problem behavior may actually decrease by half; but a single rude and cutting remark to the teacher may mean that the improvement goes unnoticed.

B. Designing the Program

1. Analyze the current situation

The first step in designing a program is an analysis of the current situation. It may be obvious that *something's* got to change, but this does not necessarily mean that the problems have been clearly identified. If a teacher complains that a student is uncooperative, does this mean that the student behaves aggressively toward classmates or is it a matter of failure to complete assignments? If aggression, does the student usually precipitate the action, or does the aggressive behavior occur in self-defense? If the problem is failure to complete assignments, does the student have the materials and the prerequisite skills? Is this a problem in all classes, or only one? Have hearing and vision been checked recently?

A preliminary analysis of the situation is important for two reasons. First of all, you need a reasonably objective measure of the frequency or duration of any problem behavior, whether it is something that occurs too often or too seldom. Subjective estimates are often unreliable. It may *seem* as though fighting or tantrums occur "all of the time" or that a child "never" complies with a request; but such estimates usually turn out to be exaggerations. Reliable estimates of frequency and duration are necessary because the procedures selected may well depend on the severity of the problem.

Second, even when behavior modification consists only of the reinforcement of desired behavior and the extinction of problem behavior, you need to know *which potential rein-*

forcers to present or withhold and in *what context*. The behavior of concern has had a past history of reinforcement and nonreinforcement in various contexts that may or may not be discoverable; but the variables *currently* controlling the behavior can often be identified if one takes the trouble to look. General questions to ask include:

1) When does the behavior occur? With whom? Where? What time of day?
2) What kinds of events precipitate it? (e.g., criticism, fatigue, failure, being rushed.)
3) What reinforcers may be maintaining it?

And if the problem is a behavioral deficit:

4) Does the individual have the prerequisite skills?
5) What approximations of the behavior occur?
6) What behavior may compete with the desired behavior?

There are many kinds of recording instruments and data sheets, some of which will be described below. What is essential at this stage is to get a reasonably objective measure of the frequency or duration of the behavior, the context in which it occurs, and the consequences that may maintain or suppress it.

It sometimes turns out that behavior that seems to be a problem doesn't really occur all that often, or it occurs only in rather specific situations. Many children are said to have very short attention spans or to be unable to concentrate. We filmed the classroom behavior of a six-year-old boy, David, who was labeled hyperactive and unable to concentrate.[6] We discovered that he was attending to work approximately two thirds of the time. Considering that less than half of a college class is paying good attention at any given time (Cameron & Giuntoli, 1972), we decided that inability to concentrate was not a problem. But David also spent a lot of time running around the room and

going to the blackboard to embellish his own work and that of the other children. He drew boxes around his work, filled in the tops and bottoms of letters, added embellishments in colored chalk, and so forth. Not surprisingly, these activities attracted the attention and admiration of the teacher and other students, and reduced the amount of time available for academic work. When the teacher ignored this behavior during work periods and encouraged it during free periods, the problem disappeared.

Thus on the basis of a sequence analysis of the current situation, it is possible to separate the real problems from the apparent ones, and then to establish priorities, state specific goals, and select procedures to achieve them.

2. Ethical Issues in the Selection of Goals

As individuals, behavior modifiers, like everyone else, have personal values. Professional ethics prevent them from trying to impose their beliefs on their clients, but this is easier said than not done. When two people interact, they differentially reinforce, extinguish, and punish each other's behavior, if only by selective attention. Therapists and counselors influence the behavior—and by implication, the decisions—of their clients, whether they want to or not. This is an important consideration in the selection of goals, so it is a good idea to find out what your counselor or therapist "believes in" before you embark on a joint program.

There seem to be two fundamental values or beliefs that characterize the philosophy of most behaviorists. Taken together, they constitute what might be called *pragmatic humanism*.

a. Attaining freedom: maximizing potential
Goals are selected that will help individuals realize their potential and function to the upper

6. The film is part of a training program on observing, defining, and recording behavior (Reese, 1977).

limit of their capacities. These are goals that maximize the development of social, physical, and intellectual skills, because it is the *depth and diversity of his behavioral repertoire that enable the individual to exercise options*. This is the behavioral view of *freedom*.

b. Exercising freedom: future consequences of behavior

How one uses one's freedom—the options one selects when one has a behavioral repertoire that allows freedom of choice—is a matter that vitally concerns the freedom of others and the future of society. One can select options that either enhance or suppress the freedom of others; and one can select options that will preserve or destroy the environment in which we live. The inhabitants of this earth and the environment that supports them are mutually dependent, and the options we now select will have long-term, often irreversible effects. Related to this point is the survival of the culture, the major issue Skinner addresses in *Beyond Freedom and Dignity*. Maximizing the physical, intellectual, and social skills of the individual is not enough, because the options we exercise as individuals may endanger not only the happiness of others but the survival of the culture. In our counseling and teaching, including the goals that we are willing to help a client attain, and in the examples that we set, *we must recognize the future consequences of our behavior* if the culture and the environment that sustains it are to survive. Like the evolution and survival of the culture, the effects of our behavior on others and on our environment are the concern of humanitarians of every persuasion and every academic discipline. What the behavioral psychologist may be able to contribute is a better understanding of the ways we can control our own behavior in order to attain long-term goals, even when their attainment means forfeiting immediate gratification.

The future consequences of changing behavior are important considerations for the individual as well as for society. If a particular class of problem behavior, such as excessive drinking or self-mutilation, has important consequences for the individual and for others in the environment, then elimination of this behavior would seem to be a high-priority goal. However, not all problems are debilitating and, as Kanfer and Saslow point out, we should ask, "What new problems in living would successful therapy pose for the patient?" (Kanfer & Saslow, 1969, p. 432.)

It is also difficult to decide how best to allocate one's time and resources. In an important and thought-provoking paper, Hawkins (1975) points out the pressing need for research in several areas related to the selection of goals. We lack, for example, the empirical data that would tell us *which* physical, social, and intellectual skills will prove most useful—to the student and to society—when a student leaves the classroom. We assume that reading, writing, and arithmetic are essential skills for children to acquire in school, and most schools require algebra as well. But do we have any idea how often most adults use algebra in their daily lives?

LeBlanc and her colleagues are making progress in this important area with respect to preschool programs and special education classrooms. From a survey of public school teachers and from extensive recording in the normal classroom, they have identified specific academic and social skills that are expected of entering kindergarten and first-grade children. They have also identified the types of instructions the children will be expected to follow and the sorts of reinforcers and punishers the teachers will be most likely to dispense (LeBlanc & Etzel, 1976). Normative data of this sort should be useful to preschool teachers and those in special classrooms when they try to select goals that will help their pupils make a successful entry into regular classroom programs. (The authors were not, of course, attempting to *evaluate* the goals of the regular classroom or of educational curricula in general.)

3. Establish Priorities

When several classes of problem behavior must be eliminated, or several deficits need remedial work, priorities must be established. As a start, the general goals can be ranked in order of importance. If one class of problem behavior is more pervasive or more damaging than others, it is usually handled first. This is partly because such behavior as temper tantrums, withdrawal, or violence will interfere with attempts to modify other behavior.

It is also a good idea to start with a goal that is important but not too difficult to accomplish. If problem behavior includes both "teasing sister" and "fighting with other children," and if fighting usually occurs away from home, the parents might be advised to start with "teasing sister," which occurs in a situation where they will be better able to identify and control the relevant variables.

Sometimes the major problems are behavioral deficits: the individual is "unable to concentrate" or lacks expected physical, social, or academic skills. Here, the *initial* goals must be set according to current capabilities, and as these are reached, more demanding goals can be set and achieved.

Since most behavioral programs are carried out by parents, teachers, and institutional staff, it is wise to get their help in setting priorities. Behavior modification is not easy, but it can *seem* easier if you see progress towards a goal you really care about. Progress reinforces the trainer's use of behavioral procedures and also helps develop confidence in the procedures. Where self-maintenance skills such as dressing, feeding, and going to the toilet are missing, institutional attendants often want to start with them. However, the last time I asked a group of attendants to arrange their own lists of goals in order of importance, one attendant gave "bad language" the highest priority!

Often (but, alas, not always) the remediation of one or two classes of behavior has salutory effects on collateral behavior. Other problems may "evaporate," especially if the behavior tackled first is something like "noncompliance" or "aggression," which is important in many social situations.

4. Specify Goals

a. General goals or objectives

Since it is difficult to define specific behavioral goals and ways to measure them, it is a good idea to start with general goals. Sometimes a parent will say, "I just want Tommy to 'be good' like his sister." That's a little too general to be useful, but it's a start on thinking in terms of behavior: on describing what Tommy *does*, or doesn't do, that's causing trouble (or what his sister does or doesn't do that's so great). "Good" behavior can turn out to be anything from being polite to his grandmother to washing his hands and buttoning his fly. "Bad" behavior can be anything from procrastinating to terrorizing every kid in the neighborhood. Sometimes a single, severe problem is mentioned, such as frequent temper tantrums or a debilitating fear of going to school. Some parents and teachers will be particularly concerned about good manners, others about the child's work habits, cleanliness, self-esteem, or relations with peers. It is often useful to identify (1) general classes of problem behavior to be reduced or eliminated and (2) general classes of desired behavior to be learned or strengthened. Unfortunately, many parents who seek help emphasize the child's problem behavior rather than the skills that need developing (e.g., Berkowitz & Graziano, 1972). For this reason, it is important to look for positive goals right from the start. The reinforcement of positive behavior can also be a way to reduce problem behavior, if only because they can not occur at the same time. The elimination of problems by the reinforcement of alternative behavior provides an opportunity to develop skills that will be useful to the individual and to society. When problem behavior is replaced by desirable behavior, there is a net gain over methods that simply remove the problem.

A mother might start off by saying of her ten-year-old son, "He's lazy and inconsiderate, and he resents me—just like his father." Maybe the parents should be talking with a marriage counselor; but if they are seeking help with their son, they might be persuaded to talk about the boy's behavior, and a list of general goals might read:

Desired behavior

being polite
being on time
paying attention
doing his homework
helping with chores
calming down
getting all A's

Problem behavior

procrastinating
guessing all the time
teasing his sister
using bad language
sloppiness
never doing what he's asked
no ambition

Some of these goals might turn out to be related.[7] Perhaps the boy's "sloppiness" refers to the fact that he doesn't clean up his room, and that is the main household chore that the mother cares about. And perhaps all the specific examples she gives of "procrastinating" and "never doing what he's asked" also relate to his messy room. Maybe she nags him about it, and he

becomes rude and resentful and just doesn't pay attention when she tells him for the fiftieth time, "clean up your room." And his father just says, "Lay off the kid, will you; I'm trying to work." In this situation, one might design a program to help the boy keep his room neat. Solving that problem would meet most of the mother's other complaints.

Now, assume that general goals have been selected and that priorities have been arranged. And also assume that an analysis of the current situation has established which activities actually constitute problems by virtue of their frequency, duration, or severity. And further assume that the analysis has revealed the antecedents of the problem behavior and the consequences which might be maintaining it. Now we can begin to define specific goals.

b. Specific goals: Behavioral definitions

Specific behavioral goals are defined in terms of the behavior itself, the context in which it is to occur, and any relevant performance criteria (such as accuracy or neatness). A behavioral goal also states how the behavior is to be measured. The four components of a behavioral definition—behavior, context, criteria, and measurement—will be discussed separately. But first it may be worth distinguishing behavior-in-progress from the products of behavior, and noting the advantages and disadvantages of each.

Behavior-in-progress would include such activities as working, playing, fighting, paying attention, smiling, writing, speaking, singing, and playing a guitar. Products, or results, of behavior include math problems completed, pages written, units assembled in a factory, goals scored, weight gained, blood alcohol

---

7. Mager's book *Goal Analysis* (which, like everything else he writes, is brief, witty, and eminently useful) suggests that the more general goals we list, the more clearly we see the situation.

level, and electrical recordings of heart rate or brain waves. It is often easier, and sometimes sufficient, to measure the product rather than the behavior itself. But the distinction should be clearly drawn: weight and blood alcohol level are *not* classes of behavior; eating and drinking *are*. In designing a program to control the product, we may ignore the behavior to our peril.

In a learning situation, the product of behavior may be the measure of success, but the behavior *leading up to* the product is important to both student and teacher. What does the golfer do that *results* in his sinking a 20-foot putt? How does a child *arrive* at a correct or incorrect answer to a problem? A student asked to tutor a fourth-grade child in math was told "she can't subtract" and shown numerous work sheets to prove the point. There were columns of problems, like those below, and the number of incorrect answers certainly indicated that this child had difficulty subtracting.

$$
\begin{array}{ccccc}
73 & 97 & 48 & 26 & 61 \\
-56 & -45 & -21 & -17 & -35 \\
\hline
X\ 23 & C\ 52 & C\ 27 & X\ 11 & X\ 34
\end{array}
$$

Since this had been going on for months, it didn't seem that looking at the answers (the products of behavior) and marking them "right" or "wrong" was helping this child learn how to subtract. The child was not present, so we could not watch what she was doing while she was subtracting. But there were enough correct answers to tell us that she understood at least part of the process—she couldn't have answered as many as she did just by guessing. After looking at all the problems, including those answered correctly, we decided that it wasn't any particular number, and it wasn't the size of the numerals in the problem or the answer, so we examined what we would have to do to arrive at the answers the child had written down. In every case we got the same answer by looking at the right-hand numerals (as if we

were subtracting one-digit rather than two-digit problems) and subtracting the smaller from the larger, disregarding which numeral was on top. It looked as though the child could subtract all combinations of numerals from 1 through 9, but that she hadn't learned to carry the "10" and subtract from numbers up to 19. The next tutoring session was spent subtracting single numerals from "teens," and after this "drill," the child was able to handle the two-digit problems. It seems likely that this child could have been helped a lot sooner if someone had watched her behavior as she was doing the problems. For example, she might have covered the left-hand column with one hand, or indicated with her pencil that she was subtracting the smaller numeral from the larger, regardless of which was on top.

i. Identify the behavior. General goals such as "reduce disruptive behavior" or "improve academic performance" are first broken down into classes of behavior that constitute disruption and academic performance. In a particular case, disruptive behavior might include shouting, being out of seat, interrupting, touching other people or their property, and breaking things. Academic performance might include attention to work during class, answering questions asked by the teacher, submitting homework, and grades on tests. Identifying these examples helps to clarify what one means by disruptive behavior and academic performance, but we haven't really defined any of the examples.

To develop a behavioral definition of any class of behavior, one has to specify exactly what must be seen, heard, felt, or otherwise *observed*, so that someone can decide whether or not the behavior is occurring. The difficulty lies in specifying what must be observed with sufficient precision so that *two or more observers will AGREE on the occurrence or nonoccurrence of the behavior*. For example, "talking" in class would usually be defined in terms of both auditory and visual components, unless the observers recognized the sound of all of the students' voices. The observers would have to hear the sound of talking and simultaneously see the student's lips moving. If this definition were not sufficiently precise to produce high agreement, then one would go on to specify what sorts of verbalizations constituted talking, perhaps eliminating whispering, singing, and vocalizations that the observer could not identify as words. When we are concerned with social interactions, the behavior of more than one person may have to be specified. "Noncompliance with requests," for example, would require that we observe one person making a request and another person failing to comply with that request. Most definitions are tested and revised several times until interobserver agreement reaches a criterion of 90 percent or better. As Hawkins and Dobes (1976) point out, a behavioral definition should be objective, clear, and complete. It should be unambiguous and clearly delineate the "boundaries" by specifying which classes of behavior are to be included and which excluded. As little as possible should be left to the observer's judgment.

Refining a definition to the point where different observers will agree on the occurrence of the behavior is a good deal more difficult than it seems before one actually tries to *use* the definition. Suppose that you are a teacher with a class of high-spirited second-graders. One child in particular, Billy, seems "always" to be out of his seat, interrupting your attempts to teach arithmetic. Now, you don't want to turn Billy into a zombie; on the other hand, he hasn't much of a future if he doesn't learn how to add and subtract. Just how much of the time *is* he out of his seat? Is it really anything to worry about? The only way to find out is to get an objective record. Take a moment and write a definition of out of seat, specifying what you would have to observe to decide that Billy is, indeed, out of his seat.

Now, *according to your definition,* is Billy out of seat in the situations described in Table 3.2? Put a check by the situation if he is out of seat, and compare your answers with those of someone else. (Actually, it would be better to agree on the definition with someone else, check the items independently, and then compare the results.) If you agree on all the items, your definition has probably taken into account the other components of a behavioral definition.

ii. Context. A behavioral definition specifies the context in which the behavior will occur: the conditions, restrictions, or exceptions placed on the definition. Essentially, the context deals with the four questions of journalism: Who? What? When? Where? To a definition of out of seat, you might want to add that the child is to be in his *own* seat. As an exception, you might want to exempt those occasions, such as erasing the board, when you have asked him to do something that requires him to leave his chair. You would also be likely to exempt out-of-seat behavior during recess and free play. While precision is essential, it's nice to have a definition that is useful. At this point, you might decide that you don't really want to know all the times Billy is out of his seat; you want to know how much of the time he's out of his seat when he "ought" to be in it. So you decide to define "*inappropriate* out of seat," and you add to your original definition of the behavior itself those conditions that would make the behavior inappropriate.

iii. Criterion levels. What constitutes noise in a noisy classroom? How soon after a request is made does a child become disobedient? If Catherine Dwight Gregory is asked to write her name, must she spell it correctly? Include her middle name? Distinguish capital and small letters? Or will we settle for CAthy? Many definitions fail the test of interobserver agreement because the observers impose different

Table 3.2   Exercise in defining behavior.

Defining Behavior

Write a definition of out-of-seat behavior, specifying what you would have to observe to decide that a child, Billy, is out of seat. *According to this definition,* is Billy out of seat in the following situations? Place a check beside the situation if he is out of seat.

_____ 1. He is rocking back and forth on his hands, but his thighs are in contact with the seat of the chair.

_____ 2. He is kneeling in the chair.

_____ 3. He is sitting quietly in someone else's chair.

_____ 4. He is standing up in his own chair.

_____ 5. You have asked a question of the class, and Billy jumps up and says "I know, ask me!"

_____ 6. He is standing on the floor beside his chair, leaning on the back of the chair.

_____ 7. He's squirming around a lot, and you can't really see.

_____ 8. He has placed his chair on top of a table and is sitting in it regally, surveying his domain.

_____ 9. You are working at the blackboard with another child who is adding numerals. Billy goes quietly to the other end of the board, copies the problem, and gets the right answer.

_____ 10. You have finished working at the board and ask Billy, who is seated, to erase the board. He does.

Check your answers with someone else, preferably someone with whom you previously agreed on a definition.

qualifications or criteria on the occurrence or nonoccurrence of the behavior. Eventually the criteria are agreed on and incorporated into the definition.

The chief criteria are accuracy, latency, duration, frequency, amount, and intensity. These are the most easily measured. But other criteria may be imposed. For classroom work, they might include neatness, legibility, and the kind and amount of help that is allowed.

iv. Measurement. The final component of a behavioral definition is a statement of how the behavior will be measured. If you still want to know whether Billy is inappropriately out of seat too much of the time, the answer will depend on how you decide to measure the behavior. On Monday you might decide to measure *frequency,* so you count the number of times he is out of his seat. No problem: he's out of seat only once. He leaves his seat two minutes after the class starts, and he's still out of seat when the bell rings for recess. On Tuesday, you decide to measure *duration,* so you start a timer when he leaves his chair and stop it when he returns. As it happens, Tuesday is one of those days he's up and down like a jack-in-the-box, and you completely lose track of the time. Wednesday, you decide to measure *latency* and see how long it takes him to sit down once you've asked him to; and on Thursday you decide to count the number of times you have to ask him to sit down before he complies with your request. On Friday, you measure the loudness or *intensity* of your voice as you shout these requests, and you are grateful for the weekend to recuperate. The point is, of course, that you haven't really defined a class of behavior until you decide how it is to be measured. And that decision will depend upon the recording procedure you choose.

Different measures and recording techniques are appropriate for different situations and for different classes of behavior. But beyond that, some require very little time or effort, while others require the observer's undivided attention. The most common recording procedures and the measures they provide are summarized below.

c. Recording behavior

i. Why bother? Most of us have occasional speech disfluencies, but our hesitations and repetitions do not mark us as stutterers. Most of us withdraw into daydreams, but we're not considered schizophrenic. Most of us make errors, but we are not considered retarded. Generally, it is not *what* we do that is a problem for ourselves or others; it is how often or how much of the time we do it. Subjective estimates are often unreliable, and we need valid measures for two reasons. First, to decide whether or not some presumed behavioral excess or deficit is, in fact, a problem. Preliminary recording helps to establish priorities and saves considerable misdirected effort. Second, we need to measure behavior so that we will be in a position to evaluate our efforts to help. We need reliable feedback on the success or failure of our procedures.

There are three general methods of recording behavior: automatic recording, direct measurement of products of behavior, and observational recording of ongoing behavior (Hall, 1971a). Observational recording includes several methods that allow a human observer to record behavior while it is in progress. The various methods and their major applications are summarized in Table 3.3 and Figure 3.1.

ii. Automatic recording. Lindsley obtained continuous records (Figures 2.5, 2.6) of hallucinatory vocal behavior by means of a microphone and voice key. With the help of automated recording equipment, he was able to record and analyze as many as 780 sessions from some of his patients over a period of six years. Automatic recording equipment is also used to monitor physiological activities. The "lie detector" polygraph, for example, measures changes in heart rate, respiration, and skin conductance. Physiological measures are particularly useful when we are interested in emotional behavior, and several examples are given in Chapter 6.

Automatic recording equipment can monitor behavior at incredible distances (e.g., outer space) and for long periods of time. But it can be expensive to design and maintain, and there are many classes of behavior, such as "play," for which recording equipment does not exist. Behavior can, of course, be recorded on film or videotape, but these media do not yield direct quantitative outputs. Films and tapes are immensely useful because they can be played back repeatedly and at different speeds; but a human observer is needed to interpret, analyze, and quantify the data.

iii. Permanent products. Permanent products of behavior are not restricted to the outputs of automatic recording equipment. Written solutions to math problems are products of behavior, and so is a thank-you note or a model airplane. Some products of behavior, for example, a clean room, are relatively impermanent; but once defined, such products are readily observed and counted. They are therefore useful and generally reliable measures of the success of a program, and wherever possible should be included among any other measures that are taken.

iv. Observational recording. Observational recording includes several methods by which a human observer can record behavior while it is in progress. The observer's judgments may be transmitted to recording equipment, as when we press buttons which activate counters or recording pens; but it is the observer, not the equipment, who decides whether or not the behavior has occurred. Since observational recording does not require elaborate equipment, it is useful in a variety of situations where apparatus might be impractical or obtrusive. It is also possible to observe a great many activities that cannot be recorded automatically. Observational recording procedures include:

Narrative recording, also called continuous or anecdotal recording, is particularly appropriate in the early stages of a study, before one has decided which classes of behavior are important and how they will be defined and measured. The observer attempts a narrative description of behavior in progress, including its relation to objects and other individuals in the situation. This may be written on paper or spoken into a tape recorder. Narrative recording may be considered a substitute for film or videotape in that it "captures" behavior in progress. Further analysis is necessary for quantitative data, but relations between behavior and its antecedents and consequences are often revealed. Although it involves exacting and exhausting work, it provides excellent training in observational skills, and is often used in a preliminary analysis of the current situation.

Time sampling is a convenient technique when the observer is involved in other activities and cannot engage in continuous recording. Time sampling consists of noting whether or not a given class of behavior is occurring at specified times. It has thus been called *momentary* time sampling (Powell, Martindale, & Kulp, 1975). A teacher might glance at a particular student once every 10 minutes and note whether or not the student was attending to work. Alternatively, the teacher might survey the class and note how many students were engaged in a particular activity. The interval one selects for time sampling depends on the situation. One might check only three times a day to see if a child is wearing an orthodontic device (Figure 4.6). Time sampling is the easiest and least obtrusive of all the observational recording techniques, and it can provide parents, teachers, and institutional staff with considerable data without restricting their other activities.

Frequency, or event, recording is appropriate when it is important to know how often an activity occurs. If it occurs rather seldom (turning in a homework assignment, arriving late to class, giving a good lecture) or if the exact total is important (the number of goals scored in a sporting event) then we would probably want to count every occurrence of the behavior. But if the behavior occurs frequently and intermit-

tently, we can take sample counts during selected periods of time. A teacher might count the number of times in a 10-minute period that a child asks for help or leaves the room. Frequency counts by themselves have little meaning unless they are turned into rates: it makes a difference whether something is happening twice a minute or twice in a lifetime. Frequency recording is not appropriate when the behavior is occurring at very high rates or when it is difficult to determine when the behavior starts and stops. However, it requires only a pencil and paper (or a golf or knitting counter) to tally the occurrences of behavior. Other ways of keeping track of the number of times an activity occurs include strings of beads attached to a bracelet or watch band and used as an abacus, or simply moving a paper clip from one pocket to another.

Duration recording is used when the duration, rather than the frequency, of behavior is important. The length of time one spends studying or sleeping or going without a cigarette is usually more important than the frequency with which these activities occur. A student might be out of seat only once during a class period—but might get up at the beginning of a class and still be cruising about the room at the end of the period. Duration is usually recorded with a clock or stop watch. If the behavior occurs relatively infrequently, bedtime temper tantrums, for example, then one would probably record the duration of every occurrence. With something like attention to work, repeated samples at random intervals would be more appropriate. Like frequency, duration should be stated for a given period of time. Does daydreaming occur 25 minutes an hour or 25 minutes a day?

Latency is a special case of duration. In experimental psychology, the term refers to the time between the onset of a stimulus and the beginning of a response. The term originally applied to reflexes, but has been extended to the time that elapses between a signal—such as a

Table 3.3   Methods of recording behavior.

Method	Application	Measure
AUTOMATIC RECORDING: Behavior is monitored by electronic or electromechanical relay equipment.	Physiological activities (including biofeedback training). Lever press and other manipulanda. Intensity or frequency of vocalizations. Location of individuals (sensors).	Depends on apparatus. Can include frequency, duration, intensity, inter-response time, wave length amplitude, and various transformations of these and other measures.
OBSERVATIONAL RECORDING *Narrative (Continuous) Recording.* A running account of behavior in progress. Information may then be ordered in a sequence analysis, enumerating the antecedents of the behavior, the behavior itself, and its consequences.	Used in early stages of analysis to identify potentially important variables including events that may precipitate the behavior and those that may be maintaining it. A precise behavioral definition is not required.	Does not provide quantitative data.
(Permanent) Product of Behavior. The observer measures the effect or outcome of behavior. Products include data provided by automatic recording equipment.	Number of tasks (items) completed; number of problems correct; grades; time punched on a time clock. Weight or blood alcohol level. Does not require continuous observation or interfere with the behavior.	Depends on product. Number or percentage of items completed; percentage correct; time of arrival, departure; records obtained with automatic recording equipment, e.g., heart rate or intensity of noise level.
Frequency (Event) Recording. The observer counts the number of times the behavior occurs during a specified period of time (minute, hour, day, week).	Number of social contacts initiated, number of questions asked, number of aggressive acts. Behavior must be discrete (observer can identify beginning and end of each instance). Rate must be low enough to count. Separate occurrences should have relatively constant durations.	Rate. (Frequency per unit time)
Duration. The observer measures the total length of time that the behavior occurs, either (a) for single occurrences or (b) during a given time period.	(a) Duration of temper tantrum, crying episode; sustained conversation. (b) Time (per hour, day) spent attending to work, out of seat, engaging in cooperative behavior. Behavior should be continuous rather than intermittent, and beginning and end of each occurrence must be determinable.	(a) (Average) duration of a single occurrence (e.g., tantrum). (b) (Average) amount of time (per hour or day) spent engaging in the behavior.
Latency. The observer measures the time between the onset of a signal and the response to the signal.	Time to "settle down" to work after bell or other signal given; time to start complying with a request; time to get up after alarm rings. Must be able to identify the signal and the beginning (or end) of the criterion behavior.	Time.

Table 3.3   Continued

Method	Application	Measure
Interval Recording. A period of time is divided into brief intervals (e.g., 10 sec., 1 min.), and the observer notes whether or not the behavior occurs *at any time during the interval.* (Neither frequency nor duration is measured; only the occurrence or nonoccurrence of the behavior.)	Often used in classrooms or institutional settings to monitor various classes of "appropriate" or "inappropriate" behavior. Provides an estimate of the proportion of time various activities are in progress. Requires continuous observation throughout interval; but several classes of behavior can be monitored, and it is not necessary to specify beginning and end of each occurrence.	Percentage of intervals in which behavior occurs.
Time Sampling. At specified periods of time (e.g., once every 10 min.) the observer notes whether or not the behavior is occurring *at that moment.* Alternatively, the observer might note how many individuals are engaged in a particular activity at that moment.	An alternative to interval recording, useful when observer is involved in other activities and cannot engage in continuous recording. Easy and unobtrusive.	Percentage of samples in which behavior was occurring or, Average number or percentage of people engaged in particular activity(ies).
SUBJECTIVE REPORTS The individual may count the occurrences of some class of covert behavior or time its duration or estimate its intensity, preferably in relation to environmental events.	Anxiety, attitudes, urges, feelings. Cannot be independently verified, but often used in conjunction with objective measures, especially in self-management projects.	Usually frequency, duration, or intensity (in subjective units).

bell or gesture or request—and the behavior that constitutes a "response" to that signal. It is the time before an activity starts rather than the duration of the activity. By extension, then, latency is a measure of promptness or reaction time. Latency would be an appropriate measure when it is important to know how quickly a child gets dressed in the morning or complies with a request, or how soon after the bell rings a class settles down to work.

Interval recording provides a compromise between frequency and duration recording. An observation period is divided into equal intervals, and the observer notes whether or not the behavior occurs *at any time* during the interval. This differs from time sampling in that interval recording requires the observer's attention throughout the interval, whereas time sampling requires attention only at the end of the interval or at specified instances of time.[8] You don't record how often or how long, only whether or not the behavior occurs at all during the interval. Interval recording was introduced to the field of applied behavior analysis by Bijou, Peterson, and Ault in 1968, and it now appears to be

8. Powell et al. (1975) consider interval recording to be a variation of time sampling. According to their usage, there are three variations of time sampling: (1) *whole interval time sampling,* when the behavior must occur throughout the interval if it is to be scored; (2) *partial interval time sampling,* when the behavior may occur during any part of the interval; and (3) *momentary time sampling,* when the behavior must occur at the end of the interval. We are retaining the customary terminology, using interval recording whenever the observer must attend to the behavior throughout the interval, and time sampling (or momentary time sampling) when the observer need attend only at specified moments. Before using interval recording, the observer must decide whether or not the behavior has to occur throughout the entire interval if it is to be scored. If so, this becomes one of the criteria of the definition itself. One might decide, for example, that attention to work would have to occur throughout the interval, but that verbal behavior or physical contact could occur at any time during the interval. This criterion would likely differ for different classes of behavior.

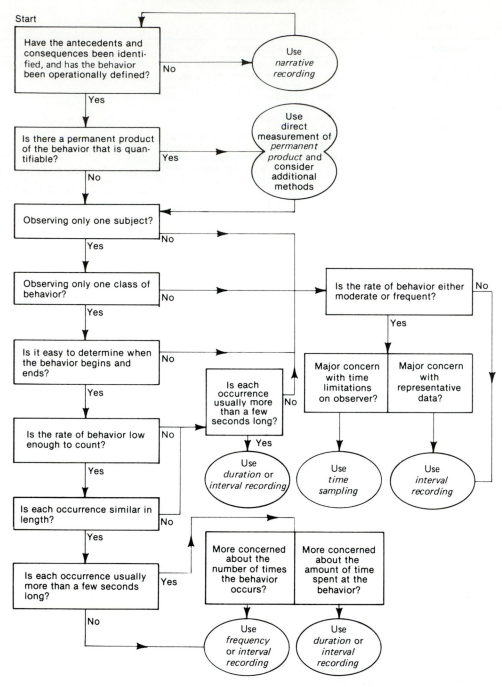

Figure 3.1. Flow Chart for selecting an appropriate recording technique. (Derived from chart designed by P. N. Alevizos, M. D. Campbell, E. J. Callahan, Neuropsychiatric Research Program, UCLA, Camarillo, CA 93010 and P. L. Berck, University of Illinois, Urbana.)

the most widely used method of observational recording.

In Table 3.4, a three-minute observation period has been divided into 10-second intervals, and an observer has checked the appropriate code letter if the behavior (as previously defined) occurred at any time during the interval. This is a sample recorded from film (Reese, 1977) of the behavior of a six-year-old boy labeled "retarded," "hyperactive," and "learning disabled." The code letters stand for A: attention to work for at least five seconds of the interval; O: inappropriately out of seat; NC: noncompliance with teacher's request; TO: talk out, interrupting the teacher or another student. In some intervals, none of these activities was observed, while in other intervals more than one activity was scored. In this sample, the child who was thought to be inattentive actually attended to classroom work during 12 of the 18 intervals, including the last half of the third minute when he was out of seat watching another child work at the blackboard. The scores at the right of the table show that he paid attention to work during 67 percent of the intervals, but was out of seat, noncompliant, or talking out during 50 percent, 39 percent, and 28 percent of the intervals, respectively.

v. Subjective reports. Thus far, we have described methods for recording overt behavior, usually by one or more independent observers. We can use any of these recording techniques to record our own behavior; and when self-recording is involved, we can monitor covert as well as overt behavior. In self-control projects, for example, people sometimes record the number of times they want food or a drink or a cigarette, or the amount of time they spend daydreaming or feeling anxious or angry or depressed. Sometimes they develop a rating scale to measure their self-esteem or the intensity of pain or anger. When we report the frequency, duration, or intensity of covert behavior, the data are usually referred to as subjective reports because they cannot be confirmed by an independent observer.

Table 3.4   Interval scoring. Three-minute sample of four previously defined classes of behavior scored during 10-second intervals. Scored intervals are summed at the right, and the percentage of intervals during which each class of behavior occurred is indicated.

INTERVAL RECORDING

Time (sec)

min	0-9		10-19		20-29		30-39		40-49		50-59		SUM A	O	NC	TO
1	A	NC	A	NC	A	NC	A	NC	A	NC	A	NC	6	1	2	3
	O	TO	O	TO	O	TO	O	TO	O	TO	O	TO				
2	A	NC	A	NC	A	NC	A	NC	A	NC	A	NC	—	5	5	1
	O	TO	O	TO	O	TO	O	TO	O	TO	O	TO				
3	A	NC	A	NC	A	NC	A	NC	A	NC	A	NC	6	3	—	1
	O	TO	O	TO	O	TO	O	TO	O	TO	O	TO				
											Sum		12	9	7	5
											%		67	50	39	28

A: Attention to work   NC: Noncompliance

O: Inappropriately Out of Seat   TO: Talk out

d. Interobserver agreement

When the success of a program is evaluated by a product of behavior—test scores, completed homework assignments, the number of items produced by a worker—it is relatively easy to determine whether or not the goals have been achieved. But when the success of a program is measured by observational records, we need to know just how accurate these records are. The accuracy, or validity, of observational records is usually inferred from the degree of agreement between independent observers. There are several formulas for measuring interobserver agreement, only two of which will be described here. (See Hawkins, Axelrod, & Hall, 1976; Hawkins & Dotson, 1975; and Kazdin, 1976a.)

i. Percentage agreement, totals only. If two people have counted the frequency of some behavior, they can compare their totals and compute a percentage agreement score by dividing the smaller total by the larger. If one observer recorded 10 instances of the behavior and the other recorded 11, the percentage agreement would be a very respectable 91 percent. However, it is conceivable that one observer noted the behavior 10 times at the start of the recording session while the other observer noted it 11 times at the end of the session. In this case, the actual agreement would be zero, and the calculated agreement quite misleading.

ii. Interobserver agreement, by intervals. Measures of interobserver agreement are more convincing when the observation period is divided into intervals, and agreement is calculated over the intervals. In Table 3.5, one observer (x) has recorded 10 occurrences of an activity over a period of six minutes. Another observer (o), recording the same behavior in the same individual during the same time period, has reported that the behavior occurred 11 times. If we compare the *totals* (Table 3.5A) the percentage agreement is 91 percent. If we look at the agreement within each interval, however, we find that they agreed nine times (twice in the first interval, twice in the third, once in the fourth, and four times in the fifth), and they disagreed three times (once in each of the first, fifth, and sixth intervals).[9] If we now calculate percentage agreement by dividing the number of agreements by the number of agreements *plus* disagreements, we arrive at a score of 75 percent. This is a much lower index of agreement, and one which suggests that the observers should redefine the behavior and start again.

This same formula can be used for interval recording where the observer notes only the occurrence of behavior, not its frequency, as in Table 3.4. If two observers record the same class of behavior in the same interval, this counts as an agreement. If one observer, but not the other, records the behavior, this counts as a disagreement. Intervals in which neither observer records the behavior are not counted. This is because if both scored and unscored intervals are included in the calculation, the agreement will often be spuriously high. If, for example, the behavior was scored once in 100 intervals by one observer and never scored by the other observer, a percentage agreement based on all 100 intervals would be 99 percent, even though the agreement on the occurrence of the behavior was actually zero percent.

In writing up research that employs observational recording, authors should describe both the particular method of recording used and the way in which interobserver agreement was calculated. They should also report the number of times agreement was assessed and the values obtained. Vance Hall and his colleagues go one step further: they indicate on their graphs those points for which interobserver

---

9. In the first interval, for example, we assume that two of the instances reported by (o) coincide with the two reported by (x). This assumption may not be valid, but the shorter the interval, the less likely are errors of this sort.

agreement was calculated. (See Figures 3.12, 3.14.) It would be even more informative if authors plotted the actual data obtained by the different observers.

Learning to observe and record behavior is time-consuming and often exasperating, but it brings many rewards. Trained observers are better able than most people to appreciate what goes on around them, whether it be the movements of a dancer or the expression of sheer joy on the face of a retarded child who has just learned to count. And observational skills are useful even when one isn't recording data. A Christmas card from a former student,[10] now working with "problem" children in California, brought the following message. "Thanks to my time spent with gerbils, I'm a pretty good observer. I can spot a hearing problem, a two-month pregnancy, a domineering mother, or a fight brewing—at a glance."

e. Naming the class of behavior

A final word on the topic of definitions. A problem arises when different observers qualify the definition by some interpretation of the *name* given the class of behavior. Suppose a child frequently fails to follow the teacher's directions and requests, and you label this behavior "noncompliance." Observers may begin to score the behavior on the basis of whether or not they thought the child *meant* to comply, or on the basis of whether or not the child had *understood* the teacher. This is very different from scoring on the basis of whether or not the behavior actually occurred; and it raises two important points.

First, it is best to avoid emotionally-toned words as well as those that require a judgment of intent. It is notoriously difficult to judge another person's intent, and notoriously easy to project your own motivation into a situation. Thus, while "noncompliance" is undoubtedly a better name than "disobedience," "stubbornness," or "defiance," it apparently carries a negative connotation that affects the judgments of many observers. (Actually, noncompliance is often to be desired. Just as guide dogs for the blind must learn to disobey commands that would endanger their owners, so must children learn to disregard many beguiling requests.) The use of neutral words increases the observers' agreement by reducing the chances that a given activity will be included or excluded on the basis of unspecified criteria.

The second point is that we may do the

10. Lucy Herman Kirshner, December, 1973

Table 3.5 **Interobserver agreement.** Different agreement scores can be calculated from the same data using two different formulas: (A) Totals only, and (B) interval-by-interval agreement.

INTEROBSERVER AGREEMENT

	1	2	3	4	5	6	Sum	Agree	Disagree
	xx		xx	x	xxxxx		x=10	9	3
	000		00	0	0000	0	0=11		

A. Percent Agreement (Totals only) $\frac{10}{11} = 91\%$

B. Interobserver agreement $\frac{\text{No. Agree}}{\text{No. Agree + Disagree}} = \frac{9}{12} = 75\%$

individual a great disservice by failing to report occurrences of behavior that are not specifically excluded in the definition. To pursue the example of noncompliance, suppose that a teacher asks your help with a child whose frequent noncompliance with requests is creating a problem in the classroom. You agree on a definition and then you record the behavior to find out how much of a problem really exists. Now, further suppose that you arbitrarily exclude all those occasions when you think the child doesn't hear or understand the teacher's request. Then you show the teacher your data. The teacher "knows" the child is frequently noncompliant; your records "prove" that he is not. Thus ends what might have been a promising collaboration. How much more helpful to all concerned had your records shown that yes, the child was frequently noncompliant, but mostly on those occasions when he might not have heard or understood the teacher's request. A number of possibilities now open up. In addition to checking the child's hearing, one could look at the situations in which the child fails to comply. If it generally happens in math or reading, perhaps he lacks some prerequisite skills in these areas. If it generally happens first thing in the morning, perhaps there is a problem at home.

f. Teaching objectives

Perhaps the widest and most controversial application of behavioral definitions has been in the field of education. Teaching objectives state what the student will *do* to demonstrate that learning has taken place: they specify the performance and how it will be evaluated. If the general goal is that a child "learn to add," specific subgoals would state the kinds of addition problems that would be solved: numerals up to 9, or 99, or 999; pairs or columns of numerals; whole numbers or fractions; and so forth. Specific goals would also state any restrictions: time limits; whether or not the child might count on his fingers or use a calculating machine. Finally, specific goals would state what constituted an acceptable performance.

It is frequently argued that behavioral objectives must, of necessity, be trivial. While it may be easier to write "knowledge" items such as "state the formula for the area of a rectangle," the student can instead be asked to *apply* the formula by calculating the area of a football field. I used to ask my students to write a formula for measuring interobserver agreement and calculate the agreement for exercises like the data in Table 3.5. Now I send them into the field or to a television set where they select some class of behavior, define it, and then record until they reach an interobserver agreement level of 90 percent or better. Actually obtaining interobserver agreement is a better evaluation of my general goal than is writing about it, because (in this part of the course) I am trying to teach recording skills. In addition to application, behavioral objectives can require:

analysis:

"Diagram the structure of a classical string quartet identifying, if present, the major and minor themes, major key changes, bridge passages, development, and coda."

(Vargas, 1972b, p. 127.)

synthesis:

"Make your own Halloween mask out of a paper bag. The mask must be designed so that you can see out and it must have at least one moving part controlled by a string you can pull while wearing the mask."

(Vargas, p. 127–128.)

evaluation:

"Criticize a research study on the appropriateness of statistical methods for the problem selected, using the text as a reference."

(Vargas, p. 130.)

Some activities are relatively easy to specify, and acceptable standards are generally agreed upon. These activities would include reading, spelling, and arithmetic; laboratory work in the sciences; and motor skills such as athletics and shop work. Most teachers can specify at least some of the things they expect of their students in these areas, and what is an acceptable performance.[11]

Vargas (1972b) lists three criteria of behavioral objectives and three functions. The *criteria* of a behavioral objective are (1) that it refer to the student's behavior, not the teacher's; (2) that it describe observable behavior; and (3) that it specify a level or criterion of acceptable performance. The *functions* are (1) to help the teacher select appropriate learning experiences; (2) to communicate what is expected of the student (to the student, and also to parents, school personnel, and the public); and (3) to provide standards for evaluating progress.

Charles Schulz makes this last point very neatly in Figure 3.2.

Many teachers deplore the whole idea of teaching objectives. They appear to be more

11. Among the many books now available to help teachers generate objectives are Mager's (1961) paperback that started the whole movement, Popham and Baker (1970), and Vargas (1972b). In addition, Kapfer's (1971) collection of papers covers a wide range of topics including art, music, and English *style*; values, and creative behavior. Julie Skinner Vargas, who is a musician as well as an educator, also tackles the problem of teaching creative behavior and offers many useful suggestions (Vargas, 1972b). Further ideas can be obtained from the Instructional Objectives Exchange (IOX), Box 24095, Los Angeles, CA, 90024. The IOX was founded on the assumption that it is easier to *select* objectives from many alternatives than it is to write one's own. Collections of objectives available from IOX cover many topics including most academic subjects, business, home economics, and auto mechanics, to name a few.

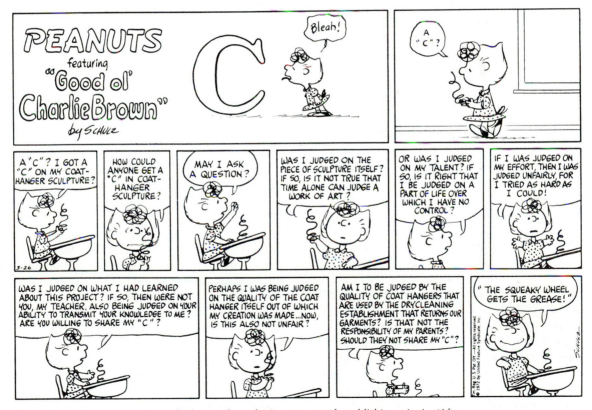

Figure 3.2. The art of getting a higher grade or the importance of establishing criteria. (After Schultz; Copyright United Feature Syndicate.)

comfortable teaching their students to "understand" and to "appreciate" music or art or poetry or scientific method, without ever specifying what it is the students will do to demonstrate their "understanding" and "appreciation." Mager (1961, p. 47) challenges this position by saying ". . . if you are teaching skills which cannot be evaluated, you are in the awkward position of being unable to demonstrate that you are teaching anything at all."

Proponents of teaching objectives argue for accountability in education. This means first specifying what students will learn and then devising methods that assure learning will take place. Ideally, every student will earn an "A"; it's just that it will take a little more time and ingenuity to help some students reach that goal than others. It is curious that teaching is virtually the only profession in which performance is not assessed by results. Surgeons who lose an appreciable number of their patients on the operating table, or trial lawyers who lose an appreciable number of their cases, will lose their clientele if not their license to practice. Educators, on the other hand, who lose an appreciable number of their students are likely to be commended for their "high standards." Few educators seem willing to adopt the philosophy that the only measure of the teacher's success is the student's progress.

5. Motivation

At one point or another, nearly all operant programs include changing the consequences of behavior. In a particular situation, we might first select a procedure and then look for the reinforcers or punishers that would be effective. But since we shall urge that *all* programs include reinforcement of *some* class(es) of behavior, it seems appropriate to discuss motivation first. Besides, when we can locate really effective reinforcers, we may not have to consider aversive procedures.

When we say that someone is not "motivated" to do something—to study, for example, or to get enough exercise—we usually mean that even though the capability and the opportunity are present, the behavior seldom occurs. When referring to someone else, we might speak of motivation as some inner force that "incites" or "impels" the individual to action. That may be all very well when motivation is present and on the job, but inner forces are hard to locate when they step out for a walk. It might prove more useful to look at motivation from the vantage of the person who lacks "it."

If we ask a child why he doesn't study, three sorts of answers are likely: "Why bother?", "I've got better things to do", or "Quit nagging me, will you?" These answers are suggestive. "Why bother?" suggests that, for this particular child, there are no discernable rewards inherent in studying or as a consequence of studying. "I've got better things to do" suggests that some sort of competing behavior has greater reinforcing consequences. And "Quit nagging" suggests that while nagging may be aversive, it is not sufficiently aversive to ensure that studying will be maintained just to avoid the nagging.

When we look to outside sources of motivation, we find that much of our behavior is maintained (or motivated) by reinforcing consequences or by the avoidance of punishing consequences. To a great extent, managing behavior amounts to managing the consequences of that behavior. It is important to identify both reinforcing and punishing consequences. If we want to increase the time or efficiency of studying, we can make sure that it is followed by reinforcing consequences; but we may also have to identify and temporarily withhold the reinforcers maintaining competing behavior. In other cases, we may need to locate punishers, not only because we might want to punish some behavior such as running in front of cars, but also because behavior is often maintained by avoidance of punishment. A child may be running in front of cars to avoid being called "chicken." One of the reasons for analyzing the current situation before deciding on specific goals is to locate the reinforcers that may be maintaining problem behavior and the punishers that may be suppressing desired behavior. Another reason for developing a sensitivity to the consequences of behavior is that many of the things we say and do are reinforcing or punishing without our even realizing the fact.

In this section, we shall discuss the many kinds of reinforcers and punishers that are available. Suggestions for using them effectively are offered in Chapter 4.

a. Reinforcers

Human felicity is produced not so much by great pieces of good fortune that seldom happen, as by little advantages that occur every day.

Franklin

A Rolls Royce Silver Ghost or a first folio of Shakespeare, the Nobel Prize or an invitation to climb Mount Everest could be powerful reinforcers, but as Franklin suggests, "little advantages" are likely to prove more useful in a practical situation.

An effective reinforcer is one that can be presented immediately following the desired behavior, one that can be presented repeatedly with minimum satiation, and one that is in reasonable supply. Social reinforcers such as praise usually meet these criteria. M & M candy used to be popular as a reinforcer: M & Ms being the ones that "melt in the child's mouth not in the psychologist's hand." (Whaley & Malott, 1971, p. 28.) In many cases, generalized reinforcers, such as stars or tokens, are even more useful. They can be delivered immediately and exchanged later for a variety of back-up reinforcers.

i. Varieties of reinforcers. Some activities, such as reading, swimming, and solving puzzles can be *intrinsically reinforcing*. But they may achieve this status only after a certain level of proficiency is reached. Other activities are not especially reinforcing in themselves, but they have *natural reinforcing consequences*. Weeding a garden is usually considered a chore; but removing the weeds increases the chances of getting healthy flowers and vegetables which can be enjoyed, given away, sold, or maybe even win a blue ribbon at the fair. Learning how to do arithmetic increases job and educational opportunities and allows one to play games such as poker and bridge. Praise and applause are natural reinforcing consequences of doing something that pleases or amuses another person.

Obviously, behavior that is intrinsically reinforcing poses no problems in motivation. Behavior for which reinforcing consequences follow naturally poses no problems either, except when the consequences are delayed. Exercising and dieting are good ways to lose weight, but it takes a long time to lose ten pounds, and we may need a little help along the way. The natural reinforcing consequences of "being good" and "working hard" are also likely to be remote. This being the case, our motivation to be good or work hard often derives from *un*natural consequences: money or prestige; entrance into heaven or the threatened loss of same. Four classes of reinforcers are described below, and recommendations for using them effectively are discussed in Chapter 4. The four classes are social reinforcers, reinforcing activities, edible and tangible reinforcers, and generalized reinforcers.

Social reinforcers, such as expressions of warmth, affection, interest, and approval are among the most powerful reinforcers controlling our behavior. Sometimes they are natural consequences of behavior: parents' delight at their baby's first words, the laughter that follows a good joke. Some social reinforcers are conferred: honorary degrees, citations for valor in battle or for selling the most cars. Some, like a nod of agreement, may be nearly imperceptible. This is an area where all of us use and misuse behavioral procedures, often capriciously, unknowingly, insensitive to their effects.

We tend to misuse social reinforcers in two ways: (1) we do not always use them when we "should," and (2) we do not realize that some of the things we do *are* reinforcing, so we use them when we should not. We often act as though people and animals should be good "for goodness sake"; "virtue is its own reward." Children should be helpful around the house because it is their responsibility as members of the family, a dog should come when called to please its master. We can simply expect these activities to occur as socially responsible behavior, but we are far more likely to see them occur if we make an appropriate social response such as "thank you" or a pat on the head.

Unfortunately, it is ever so easy to ignore appropriate behavior, especially when we are busy or harrassed. When children are playing quietly or students are doing their work, we can attend to our own problems. It is not so easy to ignore inappropriate behavior; and, as a result, it receives a good deal of attention. Problems arise when the attention is reinforcing. Institutionalized patients are more apt to get attention from the staff when they undress in the day hall or bang their heads against a wall or attack another resident than when they are behaving "normally." Social reinforcers being a rare commodity in institutions, it is not surprising that these activities are maintained.

Sometimes our very best efforts turn out to be misguided. The Zimmermans (1962) described a child who made repeated spelling errors, despite the teacher's special help and attention. When the teacher subsequently ignored the errors and reserved her attention for correct spelling, spelling markedly improved. A similar study by Hasazi and Hasazi (1972) contains an important message for those who work so diligently with children labeled "retarded" or "learning disabled" or "minimally brain damaged." Bob was an 8-year-old boy who did well in class except when it came to adding numbers. If the sum contained two digits, he nearly always reversed the order: for example, the sum of 5 + 7 would be written 21. The teacher was particularly conscientious in helping Bob with this problem. When she corrected his papers, she pointed out the answers where he had reversed the digits and then gave him extra help. She prompted the correct answer and used special teaching aids such as counters and number lines.

The Hasazis suspected that the teacher's help might be reinforcing, rather than eliminating, these errors, partly because Bob frequently pointed out reversals to the teacher when she failed to notice them. They decided to take a closer look, and to analyze the effects of the teacher's help. The class did 20 addition problems a day. During baseline, Bob reversed the digits in his answers in 18 to 20 of the problems (Figure 3.3). He thus received extra help on nearly all of them. During the next phase of the study, the teacher ignored his digit reversals and gave special praise for the sums that were written correctly. The first two days (day 8 and 9 in Figure 3.3) he wrote no correct sums, so he received no special attention. On the next day, he answered two correctly, and when the teacher corrected his paper—after all 20 problems were completed—these answers were praised. On the very next day, the errors dropped dramatically. The data suggest that he knew how to write digits correctly all along, but, of course, he could have learned during this part of the study. So, to increase their confidence that the digit reversals had really been maintained by teacher attention, the procedure was reversed. On the 15th day, the teacher went back to giving extra help for digit reversals. Since there were no errors, Bob did not receive extra help that day. On day 16, he reversed two answers, got extra help, and thereafter missed every problem every day. During the final phase of the study, attention was again made contingent upon correct answers. After none of the 20 reversals made on day 22 produced extra help, the number of errors dropped immediately.

No one is suggesting that all "learning disabilities" are maintained by misguided teacher attention. The point is that clinical labels may serve to discourage the investigation of relevant variables, especially in those cases where "treatment" consists of repeated doses of amphetamines. Fortunately, a good deal is being done to develop special teaching materials for children diagnosed as learning disabled. This

study indicates that we should also concern ourselves with reinforcement contingencies. Labels and drugs are unlikely to help a child acquire important skills; but an analysis of the contingencies of reinforcement very well may.

Sometimes we need special reminders, even special training, to notice and reinforce the behavior we want to encourage. Patterson and Reid (1970) train parents to use social reinforcers with their children, *and vice versa*. They have sometimes found it necessary to reward parents by subtracting part of the clinic fee when they appropriately reinforce their children's behavior (Patterson, McNeal, Hawkins, & Phelps, 1967).

Sometimes parents and teachers can join

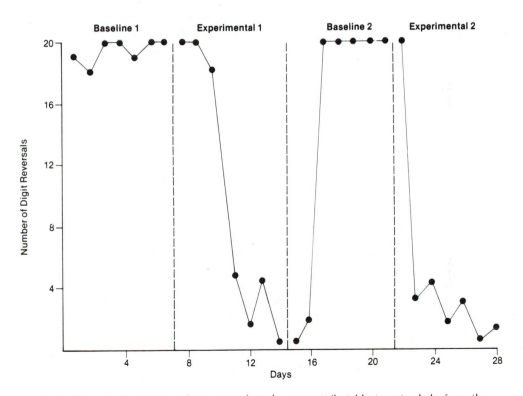

Figure 3.3.   Inadvertent reinforcement of math errors attributable to extra help from the teacher. Baseline: extra help from teacher maintains errors; experimental treatment: withholding attention for errors and reinforcing correct answers decreases errors. (From Hasazi & Hasazi, 1972, p. 160.)

forces to reinforce appropriate academic behavior. A six-year-old girl who was completing only about 60 percent of her daily classroom assignments completed every single one of them for the rest of the year when the result was her mother's attention. The teacher sent home a card noting the number of papers completed each day. Each paper earned three minutes of the mother's undivided attention which could be claimed that day or saved up for a special occasion (Robert Hawkins, personal communication, July, 1976. Similar studies are reported in Hawkins, Sluyter, & Smith, 1972).

When using praise, it is best to be specific: "I like your enthusiasm"; "I admire your persistence"; "That work shows you were very patient and careful." Social reinforcers also include nods and other gestures of approval, physical contact such as a pat on the head, and smiling. Nonverbal attention can be even more effective than verbal approval in increasing appropriate classroom behavior (Kazdin & Klock, 1973). It is almost always a good idea to combine social reinforcers with any other reinforcer one may be using: it helps the transition from special help to the normal situation.

Activities that are inherently reinforcing can be made contingent on other classes of behavior. Along with social reinforcers, the opportunity to engage in an activity is probably the reinforcer used most frequently in behavior modification projects today. The procedure has been around as long as parents have been allowing their children to play once their chores are completed. It's called *Grandma's Law*: "First work, then play" or the *Premack Principle*, after its author, David Premack (1959, 1965). The Premack Principle states that if one activity occurs more often than another, the higher probability behavior will be an effective reinforcer for the lower probability behavior. Rats, for example, learn to press a lever if the opportunity to run a running wheel is contingent upon lever pressing. Thus, if children spend more time running around the classroom or doing puzzles than they spend working, then the opportunity to run around the room could be used to reinforce the lower probability classroom behavior. This is exactly what happened when Lloyd Homme and his colleagues applied the Premack Principle with nursery school children. One way they predicted high probability activities was to think of things the children might do that would ordinarily be punished. They came up with throwing a plastic cup across the room and kicking the waste basket, both of which turned out to be dandy reinforcers. Another effective reinforcer which they had not predicted was the opportunity to push the experimenter around the room in a chair equipped with casters (Homme, deBaca, Devine, Steinhorst, & Rickert, 1963). In this first study, the experimenter occasionally blew a whistle while the children were working and announced, "Everybody run and scream" or whatever high probability behavior was to be used as the reinforcer for studying. Now it's gotten more sophisticated. Before settling down to work, a child is shown a Reinforcement Menu: a brochure with line drawings of possible reinforcing events such as those shown in Figure 3.4. The child selects a reinforcer and then proceeds to earn it by doing classroom work (Daley, 1969; Addison & Homme, 1966).

Free time has been used as a reinforcer in many programs, including one with deaf children (Osborne, 1969). This occasionally causes raised eyebrows. When one teacher announced to members of a teachers' workshop that she was using five minutes of free play to reinforce correct spelling, most of the other teachers disapproved. The teacher pointed out that the child played freely all of the time anyway—she was only allowing him to *earn* the opportunity! (Zimmerman, Zimmerman, Rider, Smith, & Dinn, 1971.)

One reason for the widespread use of activities as reinforcers is that many of them are

Reinforcement Menu

a. Talking

b. Writing

c. Coloring

d. Drawing

e. Reading

f. Swinging feet

g. Record

h. Hugging

i. Dancing

j. Walking

k. Drawing on Board

l. Telephoning

m. Puzzle

n. Blocks

o. Jumping

p. Drinking

q. Using Colored Pencils

r. Singing

s. Swinging on Door

t. Moving Chair

u. Erasing Blackboard

v. Looking out Window

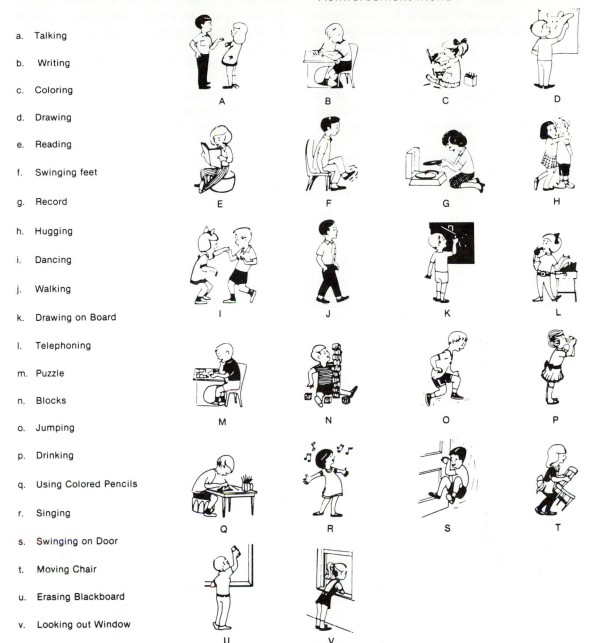

Figure 3.4.   Activities offered in reinforcement menu for school children. Students earn the opportunity to select and participate in these activities by performing classroom work. (From Daley, 1969, p. 44.)

free. This is important in school programs and for families on limited budgets. It is also important for most people who want to manage their own behavior. Some of the reinforcers used by our students in self-control projects are listed in Table 3.6. They include: reading for pleasure, writing or telephoning a friend, buying or giving someone else a present, watering the plants, playing bridge or watching the evening news,

sunbathing, sewing, going to the greenhouse or the gym, going on a bird walk, going to any of the free concerts, lectures, plays, or art exhibits on campus.

Activities can also be educational. Students have raised their grades in math to earn access to the school library, and even to take more advanced courses in math. Whaley and Malott (1971) found that high-school drop-outs would

Table 3.6   **Potential reinforcers** for young children (above), and for older students and those involved in self-control projects (below).

Potential Reinforcers

YOUNG CHILDREN

Things	Activities	
Candy, pretzels	Cut out paper forms	Draw, paint, color
Carrot sticks, fruit	Play with toys, puzzles	Play with water
Milk, fruit juice	Use playground equipment	Model clay
Toys and trinkets	Write on blackboard	Make collage
Stickers, stars	Read; be read to	Make noise
Ribbons, barrettes	Sing song; listen to song	Extra recess
"Pop" beads	Look at pictures, slides, films	Watch television
Marbles, jacks	Listen to music, stories, piano	String beads
Football cards	Listen to own voice on tape	Dress up
Books	Blow up balloon, let it go	Make popcorn
Paper dolls	Be pushed on swing, pulled on wagon	Plant seeds
Doll's clothes, furniture	Push adult in swivel chair	Feed pets
	Lead in "follow the leader"	Help an adult
	Choose activity for class	Help a child

(See also *838 Ways to Amuse a Child,* Johnson, 1960)

HIGH-SCHOOL AND COLLEGE STUDENTS; SELF-CONTROL PROJECTS

Sports equipment	Read for pleasure	Drive family car
Hobby equipment	Listen to radio, records	Stay out late
Kitchen utensils	Play bridge, chess, poker, frizbie; do a	Have mother (friend) clean room or
Furniture, rugs	puzzle	type paper
Clothes	Paint, draw, model	Telephone friend
Jewelry	Knit, sew, cook	Write letter to friend
Add to collections: coins, stamps,	Write poetry, prose	Visit friend
models, charms	Try out for a part in play	Go to library, gym, music room
Records, posters	Attend movie, concert, sports	Visit greenhouse, zoo, museum
Books, magazines	Participate in music, dance, political	Sunbathe
Tickets to concerts, sports events	rally	Take a walk
Gift certificate	Buy or wear new clothes	Work in garden, shop
Green stamps	Buy or eat snacks (low calorie for	Watch television
FOOD	weight control)	Go out for dinner
MONEY	Comb hair, brush teeth, take shower	Go away for weekend
GAS FOR CAR	Buy someone else a present	Play with pet
	Give someone else the present	Feed or train pet
	Earn points for someone else	Water plants; garden
	Take someone out	SLEEP LATE
	Tutor someone	FREE TIME

work through 20 math problems for the opportunity to spend only two minutes on a Russian program. They suggest "the frequency of working on Russian might have been high because it would allow the boys to write messages in Russian which the fuzz could not read" (p. 316). Group educational activities are also effective reinforcers: special films or field trips to museums and zoos, for example. One can well argue that children should be taken on field trips *anyway*, but there is an advantage in making at least some of them contingent on productive work: when high quality work is produced in less time, there is room on the tight school calendar for *extra* trips and educational programs.

Finally, students often select as reinforcers activities that help others as well as themselves. A first-grade student who had trouble with arithmetic chose as a reinforcer the opportunity to tutor classmates in the "low reading group" (Zimmerman et al., 1971); and a sixth-grade student improved his spelling when he earned the privilege of tutoring first-graders (Hall, 1971b). In several studies, children have worked for reinforcers that would be divided among their peers (Allen, Turner, & Everett, 1970; Patterson & Brodsky, 1966; Wolf, Hanley, King, Lachowicz, & Giles, 1970).

It is important to remember that it takes high probability behavior to strengthen an activity that occurs less often. Even something mundane and routine will do. One of our students allows herself to wash her face in the morning only if she has kept to her diet the previous day. At this writing, she has lost 25 pounds. In counseling a couple who had been married for nearly ten years, and whose sexual relations were limited to approximately two contacts a year, Goldiamond (1965) urged them to seek effective reinforcers. They had tried scheduling the wife in the husband's appointment book, but there were no special consequences for keeping these appointments. They had also tried having the husband read *Playboy* magazine as a stimulus to sexual activity, but he fell asleep reading it. Now, both subjects were extremely well dressed and well groomed; the wife went to the hairdresser every week, and the husband to the barber every other week. They decided to make their trips to the hairdresser contingent upon sexual relations. Goldiamond reports that they looked somewhat bedraggled the first week, but not thereafter.

Edibles, tangibles, and other reinforcing events. Yes, people do still use M & Ms, frosted cereal, trinkets, and stickers. These items are particularly useful with people for whom social reinforcers are not effective and who have not yet learned the "value" of generalized reinforcers such as tokens or points. They can also be delivered automatically, in various dispensing machines, which makes them useful in research.

Many therapy programs start with edibles and tangibles and then gradually transfer control to other, less contrived reinforcers. Two films illustrate the process. Lovaas (1971) describes the acquisition of speech and other social behavior in autistic children. Initially, sounds are imitated and reinforced with frosted cereal; later, as more complex verbal behavior is shaped, reinforcement is primarily social.

In a program to teach number concepts to retarded children (Reese, 1971a), the subjects select reinforcers from a "cafeteria" of M & Ms, pretzels, stickers, or trinkets. Later, praise, including applause from the other children, maintains their behavior. In one case, doing arithmetic apparently became a reinforcing activity. This child went home, wrote problems for herself, solved them, and proudly showed them to her mother.

Large items, such as bicycle or stereo equipment, can be earned over a period of time, but it is usually a good idea to indicate progress along the way. Getting a bicycle for a whole year of straight A's is usually too distant a goal to maintain study behavior. Smaller reinforcers can be given at more frequent intervals, and progress toward the larger goal can be marked by accumulating points or by putting money in a special savings account. As with any potential reinforcer, the goal must be contingent upon the desired behavior. A fourth-grade boy we know was putting in extra time on his math to earn a dog. He worked very hard—until his parents gave him the dog for Christmas.

Generalized reinforcers. The special advantage of generalized reinforcers, such as points, tokens, or money, is that they can be delivered immediately and later exchanged for a *variety* of back-up reinforcers. The earliest study to take advantage of this broad motivational base was published by Staats, Minke, Finley, Wolf, and Brooks in 1964. Preschool children earned marbles for working on a reading program. The marbles could be exchanged immediately for trinkets, pennies, or candy; or they could be saved up for an "expensive" toy. In this case, the child dropped the marbles into a plastic container under the toys and collected the toy when the container was full.

ii. Token economies. By 1965, Ayllon and Azrin were using tokens as reinforcers on a psychiatric ward,[12] and Birnbrauer and his colleagues had introduced tokens into a classroom for retarded children (Birnbrauer, Wolf, Kidder, & Tague, 1965). Token reinforcement programs have since been established with every conceivable population. They have been used to strengthen academic, social, and self-managed behavior as well as to decrease problem behavior. (See Kazdin & Bootzin, 1972; O'Leary & Drabman, 1971; and Patterson, in press, for reviews, and Kazdin, 1972b for an annotated bibliography.) Don Bushell's Follow Through programs in public schools have now helped more than 10,000 children.[13]

A token economy for fifth- and sixth-grade students combined token reinforcement in the form of points for appropriate classroom behavior with response cost for inappropriate behavior (McLaughlin & Malaby, 1972). The back-up reinforcers for the points earned were intrinsically reinforcing activities available in the classroom. These activities and their price in points are shown in Table 3.7. The activities that earned or lost points are shown in Table 3.7B. A sixth-grade child could work on a special project (price, 25 points) and listen to a record (five points) by completing all assignments and earning 30 points for accuracy, so long as no points were lost for inappropriate social behavior. The system, in effect for most of an academic year, effectively increased the number of assignments the students completed. The program required *less than 25 minutes a week* for the teacher to administer and relied on reinforcers normally available in the elementary classroom.

Burchard (1967) established a token economy for "anti-social" retarded boys whose offenses included arson, theft, and property damage. His goals included academic skills, shop skills, and skills that would be necessary for the boys to get along in the world if they were released from the institution. These included such skills as using the telephone and public transportation, budgeting money and purchasing items, caring for clothes, and patience in performing a dull task. The boys earned tokens for shop and academic work and used the tokens to purchase meals, clothing, commissary items, recreational activities, and trips. All of this was in preparation for an outside world that

12. According to O'Leary and Drabman's (1971) review of classroom token economies, Staats and Ayllon and Azrin started their respective programs in 1961.

13. For a brief description of effective classroom teaching see Bushell's *Classroom Behavior: A Little Book for Teachers*, 1973. For information about Follow Through programs in various parts of the country, write him at the Department of Human Development, University of Kansas, Lawrence, Kansas, 66045.

would be more than a welfare program. All purchases required a purchase order as well as the requisite number of tokens. This gave the

Table 3.7   Contingencies in a fifth- and sixth-grade token economy using reinforcers already available in most classrooms. Students could select any of the privileges listed in (A) by accumulating the specified number of points for each activity. Points were earned or lost by the students for engaging in the activities shown in (B). (Adapted from McLaughlin & Malaby, 1972, p. 264, 265.)

A. Weekly Privileges

Privilege	Price in Points Sixth	Fifth[a]
1) Sharpening pencils	20	13
2) Seeing animals	30	25
3) Taking out balls	5	3
4) Sports	60	40
5) Special writing on board	20	16
6) Being on a committee	30	25
7) Special jobs	25	15
8) Playing games	5	3
9) Listening to records	5	2
10) Coming in early	10	6
11) Seeing the gradebook	5	2
12) Special projects	25	20

[a]Privilege costs were determined separately for the two grades. Also, fifth-grade children were in the room less time per day than were the sixth-grade children.

B. Activities that Earned or Lost Points

Activities That Earned Points	Points
1) Items correct	6 to 12
2) Study behavior 8:50-9:15	5 per day
3) Bring food for animals	1 to 10
4) Bring sawdust for animals	1 to 10
5) Art	1 to 4
6) Listening points	1 to 2 per lesson
7) Extra credit	Assigned value
8) Neatness	1 to 2
9) Taking home assignments	5
10) Taking notes	1 to 3
11) Quiet in lunch line	2
12) Quiet in cafeteria	2
13) Appropriate noon hour behavior	3

Activities That Lost Points	Points
1) Assignments incomplete	Amount squared
2) Gum and candy	100
3) Inappropriate verbal behavior	15
4) Inappropriate motor behavior	15
5) Fighting	100
6) Cheating	100

boys practice in using their newly acquired skills in writing, spelling, and addition, and also gave them experience with order forms. To encourage the saving and budgeting of money, Dr. Burchard set up a bank and paid interest.

iii. Locating reinforcers.   One way to discover potential reinforcers is to watch what people do in their spare time. *Then apply the Premack Principle.* Ayllon and Azrin (1965) have noted that one of the characteristics of psychotic patients is the apparent absence of effective reinforcers; but by carefully watching what their patients did, or tried to do, Ayllon and Azrin came up with a long list of potential reinforcers, ranging from recreational activities to private audiences with the psychologist or social worker. (The study is described in Chapter 4 where the reinforcers are listed in Table 4.2.)

The most obvious approach is to *ask* people what they want to work for, but it is surprisingly difficult for most people to come up with concrete suggestions. Sometimes a *list of suggested reinforcers* is helpful. Children can select from a reinforcement menu such as the one shown in Figure 3.4. Our students often get ideas from Table 3.6. Juvenile delinquents in a federal prison selected reinforcers from a Sears, Roebuck catalogue—after the gun and knife pages had been removed (Cohen & Filipczak, 1971). Cautela and Kastenbaum (1967) have published a long list of potentially reinforcing activities which can be used in two ways. Clients can select activities that they will actually engage in (overt reinforcement) or that they will imagine (covert reinforcement). A client who has turned down a second helping of dessert or completed 20 pages of assigned reading might spend the next few seconds imagining skiing down the advanced slope on a bright day, with perfect snow conditions.

Another helpful probe is the *list of questions* in Table 3.8. The questions were prepared by Watson and Tharp (1972) for students work-

Table 3.8   Questions to ask when trying to locate reinforcers. (From Watson & Tharp, 1972, p. 108.)

Questions to Ask When Trying to Locate Reinforcers

1. What kinds of things do you like to have? _____
2. What are your major interests? _____
3. What are your hobbies? _____
4. What people do you like to be with? _____
5. What do you like to do with these people? _____
6. What do you do for fun, enjoyment? _____
7. What do you do to relax? _____
8. What do you do to get away from it all? _____
9. What makes you feel good? _____
10. What would be a nice present to receive? _____
11. What kinds of things are important to you? _____
12. What would you do if you had an extra five dollars? Ten dollars? Fifty dollars? _____
13. What behaviors do you perform every day? _____ (Do not overlook the obvious, the commonplace.)
14. Are there any behaviors that you usually perform instead of the target behavior? _____
15. What would you hate to lose? _____
16. Of the things you do every day, what would you hate to give up? _____

ing on self-management projects, but they are helpful in other situations as well. Even when someone else is designing the rest of the program, the client is often the most appropriate person to select the reinforcers. These questions are a useful adjunct to a general list of reinforcers because they are personal: What do you do for fun? What people do you like to be with? What would you hate to lose? What would be a nice present to receive?

If you're as perceptive as three-year-old Chrissy Iwata, you don't need a list of questions to select a present or a reinforcer. Chrissy was looking for a birthday present for her father, Brian, and it had to be something special. Now, she might have asked her father what he

wanted, or she might have heeded the advice of advertisers who claim to know what fathers like. Chrissy needed help from no one to discover the one present her father would prize above all others, and she seems to have discovered the Premack Principle all by herself. What does Daddy spend his time at? What does Daddy do for fun? Daddy is a behavioral psychologist, and Chrissy *knows* what turns him on. She has kindly allowed us to reproduce her present in Figure 3.5.

iv. Increasing reinforcer effectiveness. There are at least three ways to increase the effectiveness of potential reinforcers: modeling, reinforcer sampling, and deprivation. *Modeling*

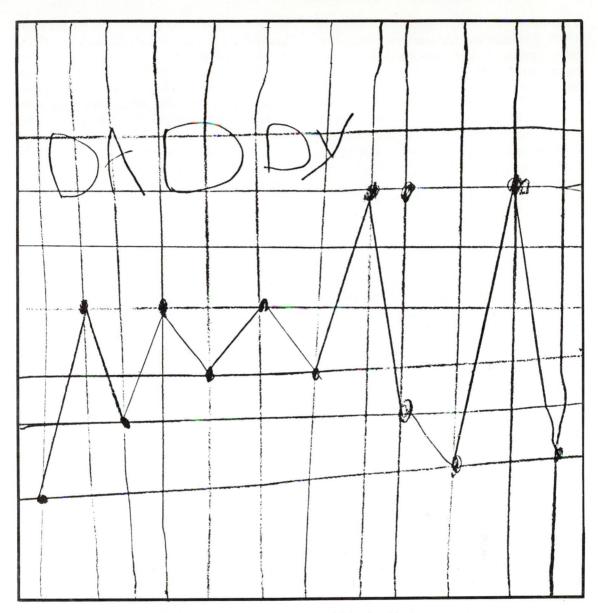

Figure 3.5. Dr. Brian Iwata's birthday present from his three-year-old daughter Chrissy.

is illustrated in a study reported by Engelmann (1975). A student teacher, working with a rather difficult group of eight-year-olds, was reinforcing correct answers with M & Ms. If an answer was incorrect, the teacher gave the correct answer and then ate the candy with obvious enjoyment. The procedure was highly successful in reducing disruptive behavior and increasing academic work, except for the fact that the student teacher gained 15 pounds in three weeks. Engelmann thereupon cut up pieces of yellow paper and told the students that each time they answered correctly, they could choose between an M & M or a piece of yellow paper. He added that he realized the students were young and would probably choose an M & M, but that *he* was going to choose the yellow paper whenever he had the chance. Only once did anyone choose another M & M. For the remainder of the class, every child opted for yellow paper, voicing comments such as "Look how smart I am; I got seven yellow papers" and "That's nothin'. I got eight."

Reinforcer sampling is a technique developed by Ayllon and Azrin (1968) who instituted a token economy in a state hospital and used a wide variety of back-up reinforcers. They found that some of these potential reinforcers were rarely chosen, even though other evidence indicated that the patients enjoyed the activities. To increase the frequency of exchanging their tokens for different reinforcers, the patients were required to participate in a potentially reinforcing activity whenever it was available. However, the participation was so brief that the reinforcing event was only sampled. The technique was evaluated for three events: going for a walk, watching a movie, and attending a music session. In all three cases, these reinforcers were subsequently selected more frequently and by more patients than before the sampling procedure was introduced. The authors have since supplied a rule for token economies: "Before using an event or stimulus as a reinforcer, re-

quire sampling of the reinforcer in the situation in which it is to be used" (Ayllon & Azrin, 1968, p. 91). Support for this rule also comes from Sulzer and Mayer (1972) who note that (like movie audiences) children are more apt to spend points on a film when they have seen a short preview of the film than when they have not.

Deprivation. When a generalized reinforcer or a variety of reinforcers is used, specific deprivation procedures are usually unnecessary. However, in serious cases that demand immediate attention, it may be necessary to withhold whatever reinforcers can be identified so that they can be made contingent upon desired behavior. This was the case with a patient treated by Bachrach, Erwin and Mohr (1965). The patient suffered from *anorexia nervosa*, a chronic failure to eat, and was in danger of death. She is shown in Figure 3.6A as she looked at the start of behavior therapy. At this time, she was 5 feet, 4 inches tall, weighed 47 pounds, and could stand only with assistance. In the words of the authors, she gave "the appearance of a poorly preserved mummy suddenly struck with the breath of life" (Bachrach et al., 1965, p. 154). Before therapy, she lived in an attractive hospital room with pictures, flowers, and a pleasant view; and she had free access to visitors, radio, television, and a record player. Because she appeared to enjoy these things, she was moved to a barren hospital room and allowed no visitors. She was deprived of visitors, television, music, flowers, so that these events could be used to reinforce eating behavior. The only reinforcer she was allowed was her knitting, and this was available at all times. (The hospital personnel were apprised of the reasons for this "inhuman treatment" and convinced that it was more humane than allowing the patient—who had not been cured by eight previous hospitalizations—to die.)

The attention and sympathy with which the nurses had formerly coaxed the patient to eat

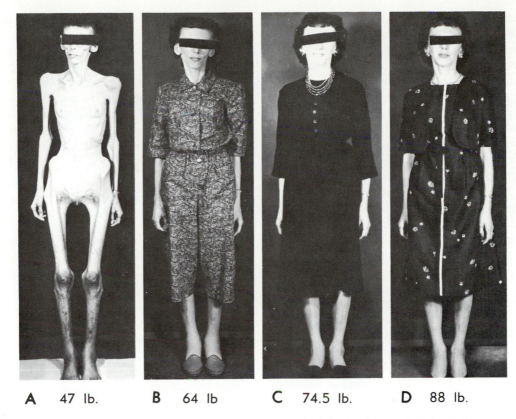

A   47 lb.   **B**   64 lb   **C**   74.5 lb.   **D**   88 lb.

Figure 3.6.   Successful treatment of an anorexic patient by behavior therapy. A: Patient before therapy, weighing 47 pounds. B: After eight weeks of therapy just before discharge as an outpatient. C: After ten months as an outpatient, prior to readmission to hospital for a month of further therapy during which she gained an additional seven pounds. D: Three months after final discharge, shortly before patient completed home-study course in practical nursing and received her cap and uniform. (Adapted from Bachrach, Erwin, & Mohr, 1965, p. 154, 155.)

were also withdrawn. Each of the authors ate one meal a day with the patient; the nurses were allowed to say only "good morning" when they entered the room to attend her other needs. Thus the social reinforcers which had helped to maintain *non*-eating behavior were withdrawn so that they could be used to strengthen eating.

The authors shaped eating behavior by talking with her when she picked up her fork, lifted food toward her mouth, chewed food, and so forth. They also shaped the amount of food eaten by allowing her the radio or television after meals at which she ate increasing amounts of the food on her plate. Later on, as she began to gain weight, other reinforcers were introduced; she was allowed to choose her own menu, invite another patient to dine with her, or dine with the other patients. Note that these reinforcers were directly related to, as well as contingent upon, eating behavior. Still later, the reinforcers included walks, visits, and mail. The effectiveness of this treatment can be judged from the remaining photographs of Figure 3.6.

When she was discharged as an outpatient, new methods had to be devised to replace those that were possible in the hospital. The help of the patient's family was enlisted, and they were cautioned against making an issue out of eating or reinforcing invalid behavior (incompatible with normal eating). They were never to let her eat alone, and were to discuss only pleasant topics at meals (social reinforcement during eating). They were to follow a rigid schedule for meals, with an alarm clock and a purple tablecloth as discriminative stimuli; and they were to encourage her to dine out with other people under enjoyable conditions.

Three years after behavior therapy was started (and nearly a year after she was finally discharged) the patient had completed one training program and was enrolled in business school. In addition to classes and extra activities, she was a dormitory advisor for 25 girls. Although she had lost some weight, she was eating regularly and enjoying an active life. Five years after the start of therapy, we learned from Dr. Bachrach that the patient was maintaining her weight between 78 and 80 pounds (self-report) and that she was working "happily and successfully in a university hospital newborn nursery."

b. Punishers

Like reinforcers, punishers come in assorted colors and sizes, both natural and contrived, and they include social events, activities, and physical pain.

Natural punishing events occur when we let a match burn down too close to our fingers, when we bump into something solid or slam the car door on our hand, and when we walk into a patch of nettles. There are also natural punishing consequences of eating, drinking, and smoking too much; but they are often too delayed or too "mild" to compete with the reinforcing consequences of the behavior. Only to the extent that they actually suppress behavior can they be considered punishing.

Social punishers include criticism and ridicule—but again, only to the extent that behavior is suppressed. Parents' eternal squabbling may be sufficiently punishing to keep children away from home; children's eternal squabbling in the car may be sufficiently punishing to keep parents from taking them on trips.

Activities that may be punishing include "hard labor" and labor that seems pointless. The favorite punishment of my seventh-grade teacher was to have us stay after school and copy the dictionary, including every blasted punctuation mark:

A, a (ā), n.; pl. A's, A'S, As, AS, AES (āz). 1. The first letter of the English alphabet. A comes from Latin A, which came from Greek A (*alpha*), which in turn was derived from the first letter of the Phoenician alphabet. 2. The sound of this letter A . . . .

Being a model child, I never got beyond "abomination (-na'shun), n." In other words, this was an effective punisher. In weight-control projects, people sometimes make themselves do 15 minutes of calisthenics for every 100 calories they consume beyond the limit they have set. Other aversive events selected by students for self-management projects are listed in Table 3.9.

Table 3.9   Aversive events used in self-management projects by Mount Holyoke College students.

Punishers

Do 15 push ups
Do all the homework problems (even the optional ones)
Clean the room
Wash the dishes
Spend time being nice to someone I dislike
Wear a sign on back saying "I blew it"
Confess to boyfriend
Wear a ski mask indoors
Buy and eat cottage cheese
Get up at 6 A.M. and STUDY
Take bus, instead of drive, to Amherst
Call friend on pay phone in hall instead of phone in room

Response Costs

Can't open mail
Can't receive a phone call from _____
No tea at breakfast
Can't brush teeth (shower, wash hair) in morning
Give _____ (friend) a dollar
Give _____ my blue sweater

Physical pain that is not a natural consequence of behavior would include spanking a child; whipping (20 lashes), keelhauling, and, of course, the rack and the Iron Maiden. (See any James Bond novel for elegant variations.) Punishers used in research have included electric shock, loud noise, unpleasant odors, temperature extremes, pinching, and delayed auditory feedback where one speaks into a microphone and hears one's own voice played back with a fraction of a second delay. In one form of aversion therapy for smoking, a blast of stale cigarette smoke is blown into the clients' face every time they take a drag. Parents, too, can think of ways to let the punishment fit the crime. My younger sister used to indulge in the unattractive and painful practice of kicking people in the shins. One day, with brilliance born from desperation, our mother returned the compliment. One swift kick was all it took.

A punisher is a punisher only if it suppresses behavior. In many cases, what is assumed to be punishing may actually be reinforcing. Madsen and Madsen (1971, p. 51) describe what might be the actual consequences when a teacher sends three disruptive boys to the principal's office: "Jim is delighted; his payoff is that he caused the teacher to lose his cool. Alex's payoff is that he maintained his reputation among the rest of the class for being a tough guy. Pete does not care anything about the teacher or the class; the people he wants to impress are Jim and Alex, and he is happy because their friendship and approval are his payoff."

6. Select Procedures

When goals have been established, there will almost certainly be alternative ways to reach them. Sometimes the choice is fairly obvious. If a sequence analysis suggests that parents have been inadvertently, but fairly consistently, rein-forcing procrastination, they would probably decide to extinguish procrastination and, instead, reinforce doing things on time. In other cases, the decisions will be more difficult. If the goals involve developing, increasing, or maintaining the strength of behavior in one or more settings, then the program will probably include some form of conditioning, often in conjunction with other procedures. If the goals involve reducing or eliminating behavior, or restricting it to specific settings, then one or more of the many "reductive" procedures may be used, preferably in conjunction with procedures to strengthen alternative, more adaptive behavior.

The basic operant and respondent procedures were introduced in Chapter 2. The major variations of the operant procedures are discussed in Chapters 4 and 5. Chapter 5 ends with guidelines for their use. The major variations of respondent procedures— most of which require close professional supervision—are described in Chapter 6. (Discussion of these procedures was moved to later chapters because we think they can be examined more realistically following a description of the entire program shown in the flow chart of Table 3.1. The selection of a particular combination of procedures may well depend on the particular problems to be encountered during maintenance and transfer, when the gains must be consolidated in the natural environment.)

The selection of procedures is likely to require many decisions; and if a client-therapist relationship is involved, this is a major area of therapist accountability. A great many matters must be considered before a client is in a position to give informed consent to a particular program of treatment:

a. Consider the options

This is pretty obvious. Why spend all that time analyzing the situation and defining precise goals only to plunge into the first procedure that comes to mind. If the first choice remains the best, well and good. But remember that a client can't give *informed* consent unless other options have been considered. Also, the consideration of other procedures may help the client carry out the one(s) that are selected.

b. Examine the evidence

Behavioral procedures are based on experimental data, so the evidence is there for anyone to see. Look for the long-term as well as the short-term effects. Reductive procedures vary considerably in the speed, extent, and durability of suppression. Extinction and punishment may be accompanied by aggressive behavior or anxiety. The respondent procedure, implosion, involves considerable stress and has a mixed history of success. (Unlike surgical procedures, behavioral procedures are reversible, but one still should anticipate and prepare to handle any possible "side effects.") Some operant procedures to increase behavior require a minimal behavioral repertoire; others, like modeling, are most effective when used in combination with reinforcement.

c. Attend to the personal equation

A behavioral program starts with "knowing" the individual, and this continues to be of major importance when it comes to selecting procedures. The severity of the behavioral deficit or excess is obviously relevant, but so is the rest of the behavioral repertoire. Which skills need building, and where must one start? What problems, medical or otherwise, must be circumvented? Which personal attributes—conscientiousness, meticulousness, social aptitudes, motivation to change—will make certain procedures easier to carry out than others? What environmental variables, social and economic, must be considered? To what extent is the individual now able to manage the details of the program? How much responsibility will be assumed? Who else must be involved?

d. Balance the costs

In weighing the pros and cons of various procedures, many "costs" must be considered. There's money—possibly for therapist fees and transportation; possibly for apparatus or back-up reinforcers. But the least expensive procedure isn't necessarily the most appropriate one, or the one with the best long-term prognosis. There's time—both overall time in days, weeks, or months, and uninterrupted time. A program developed by Azrin and Foxx (1974) and field tested by Butler (1976) enables most parents to toilet train their children in less than a day[14]; but they have to find a day when they can devote at least four hours to training and nothing else. (The Foxx and Azrin (1973) program for toilet training retarded individuals may require an attendant's attention for 24 hours or more.) In some cases, the more painful or stressful procedures such as punishment or aversion therapy will probably produce the most rapid and enduring effects, so several costs must be balanced. Where the problem is extreme self-injury or aggression towards others, one may not be able to afford an alternative procedure like extinction, simply because the time required would involve too much danger for the individual or others. Finally, there are costs in terms of inconvenience. It is often easier to punish or to impose Response Cost than to notice and reinforce incompatible behavior. And all procedures have to be evaluated by objective data. Some records are much easier to keep than others. It's usually no great hassle to weigh yourself once a day, but you might not care to keep records of all calories consumed in food and all those expended in exercise. You'd probably lose weight much faster, and maintain the loss

14. The parents in Butler's study attended three training classes as well as read the Azrin and Foxx book. Seventy-seven percent succeeded in toilet training their children, with the gains maintained during a two-month follow-up.

much longer, in a program that required you to keep count of calories—but only if you stuck to the program.

e. Select combinations of procedures

If the goal is to reduce problem behavior, probably any procedure will be more effective when combined with extinction and the reinforcement of alternative, incompatible behavior. Common sense dictates that we try to locate and withhold the reinforcers maintaining the behavior we want to reduce; common decency dictates that we also strengthen behavior that will benefit the individual and society. Combinations of procedures are also appropriate when the goal is to develop or extend an area of competence: procedures such as modeling and self-recording are generally more effective when combined with reinforcement.

f. "Symptom substitution"

Throughout this section we have, of course, been talking about procedures to change *behavior*. Psychologists of other orientations sometimes claim that in dealing with behavior, we are dealing only with "symptoms" rather than with the real "causes" of the client's problem. These psychologists and psychiatrists tend to view maladaptive behavior as the symptom of some underlying pathology; and they predict that treating the symptom, rather than the underlying cause, will lead to *symptom substitution*: eliminate one symptom and it will inevitably be replaced with another.

The use of the word "symptom" derives from medical practice where a skin rash, for example, might be a symptom of dietary or endocrine imbalance; or swollen glands might be a symptom of practically anything. In medicine, the phenomena called symptoms are related to observable, measurable variables. In some models of psychiatry and psychology, however, maladaptive behavior is viewed as a symptom

of a hypothetical inner process rather than as a function of the measurable variables of biochemistry, physiology, anatomy, or external stimulus conditions. There is a world of difference between these two views. Scientists have frequently postulated the existence of matter before the means were available to observe and measure it: the atom, the planet Pluto, and the rods and cones of the retina, are examples. But these were *potentially* measurable phenomena belonging to the empirical world, whereas some of the constructs used to explain behavior are held to be not of the empirical world.

It is, of course, behavior which brings the client to a psychiatrist or a psychologist. As Ayllon, Haughton, and Hughes (1965, p. 5) point out,

Relatives, neighbours, or friends do not initiate commitment procedures to a psychiatric institution because a person fails to resolve his Oedipus Complex. Institutionalization becomes necessary only when the patient engages in a socially deviant behaviour and spends a sufficiently large amount of time at it to disrupt normal functioning.

Ayllon and his associates have successfully modified a number of kinds of deviant behavior without recourse to hypothetical constructs. It has not been necessary to determine how the deviant behavior was first acquired, although that information would undoubtedly be helpful as well as important theoretically. There is available, however, at least one case history where the origin, development, and treatment of deviant behavior are a matter of record. Ethical considerations would prevent the following study, conducted by Ayllon et al. in 1965, from being undertaken today. Ayllon, himself, is foremost among those who insist that patients be taught only useful skills. In fact, his relevance-of-behavior rule is a guideline for setting goals: "teach behavior that will be functional for the individual after he leaves the institution, clinic, or other formal training situation'' (Ayllon & Azrin, 1968). Nonetheless, the study *was* conducted in 1965, and it has important implications for the disease model of maladaptive behavior and its corollary, symptom substitution.

The patient exhibited the compulsive behavior of standing and holding a broom or carrying it about while she paced the floor. The patient (Figure 3.7) was observed through a one-way window by a board-certified psychiatrist who described her in the following words:

Her constant and compulsive pacing, holding a broom in the manner she does, could be seen as a ritualistic procedure, a magical action .... Her broom would be then: (1) a child that gives her love and she gives him in return her devotion, (2) a phallic

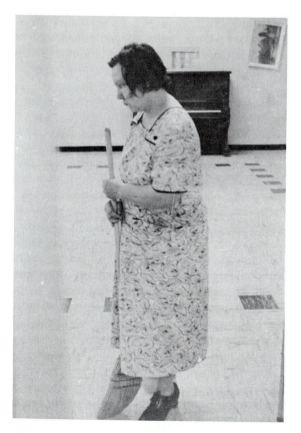

Figure 3.7. Psychiatric patient displaying a symptom: remaining in an upright position and holding a broom. (From Ayllon, Haughton, & Hughes, 1965, p. 3.)

symbol, (3) the sceptre of an omnipotent queen .... this is a magical procedure in which the patient carries out her wishes, expressed in a way that is far beyond our solid, rational and conventional way of thinking and acting. (Ayllon, Haughton, & Hughes, 1965, p. 3.)

In actual fact, this ''symptom'' was conditioned, maintained, and eventually extinguished by Ayllon et al. to demonstrate that psychotic behavior can be experimentally produced and eliminated by the simple (and measurable) manipulation of reinforcement contingencies.

The patient was a chronic schizophrenic who had been hospitalized for 23 years and who spent most of her time in bed or lying on a couch. Since she was a heavy smoker, cigarettes were selected as a reinforcer. During the 25-day baseline period, she spent 60 percent of her waking time in bed and approximately 20 percent sitting and walking, but never carrying a broom. During this period she was limited to one cigarette per meal.

The behavior that was to be conditioned was defined as the patient being in an upright position and carrying a broom. During shaping, one nurse gave the patient a broom and another then gave her a cigarette. On the second day of shaping, the patient picked up the broom by herself. Thereafter, the behavior was maintained on a variable interval schedule that was gradually increased from 15 minutes to eight hours. The patient continued to carry the broom for nine months until reinforcement was completely withdrawn during extinction. As the behavior of carrying the broom decreased, the former behavior of lying in bed increased.

This study, of course, does not prove that all psychotic behavior is learned or that the elimination of one form of psychotic behavior will never result in the appearance of another. But there are many well-documented cases where the withholding of social reinforcement has resulted in the elimination of maladaptive behavior, and this looks very much like extinction. Also, the incidence of ''symptom substitution'' following treatment with behavioral procedures is extremely low (Baker, 1969; Cahoon, 1968; Hampe, Noble, Miller & Barrett, 1973; O'Leary & Wilson, 1975; Yates, 1958). The most likely reason is that steps are taken to strengthen adaptive behavior at the same time the maladaptive behavior is eliminated. If "symptomatic" behavior has brought a person social reinforcers in the form of attention or sympathy, and this behavior is then eliminated, we would expect an increase in any other behavior that produces these social reinforcers. The alternative behavior, if left to chance, might well be another "symptom"; in a well-designed program, it would be something useful to the individual and to society.

7. Specify Contingencies

Goals, procedures, and reinforcing events are the essential components of a program, but the arrangement is all-important. We must specify exactly what progress toward exactly what goal will be followed by exactly what reinforcers; and we must make sure that the reinforcer *depends on* the progress. Many children get a clearly specified weekly allowance, and many are expected to perform clearly specified chores around the house. From the parents' view, the allowance is bestowed as a present and the chores are demanded as a responsibility. From the child's view, the allowance is an inalienable right, and the chores constitute taxation without representation. Often the chores are accomplished grudgingly—if at all—to avoid nagging or unpredictable reprisals such as the withdrawal of a privilege. Of course, there is no *a priori* reason that chores and allowance be related. But the chores are more likely to be accomplished when the allowance or some other privilege or expression of appreciation follow as a consequence. And, when given the option, many children prefer earning their allowance to a "welfare" status. Perhaps they see their parents being paid for *their* work,

and earning an allowance makes them feel more grown up. Or perhaps it's that a formal agreement about work and allowance can minimize nagging and threats and the inconsistent withdrawal of other privileges if the chores are not accomplished. At any rate, a precise statement of contingencies favors both harmony and the achievement of goals.

a. Stating contingencies

A statement of contingencies specifies the behavior, including the context and all criteria, and the consequences that will follow when the behavior occurs or fails to occur. The contingencies for grades on math homework assignments are usually stated fairly explicitly: e.g., if the homework is turned in on time and is at least 90 percent correct, it receives a grade of A. If it is between 80–90 percent correct, it receives a B, and so forth. Additional contingencies might specify progressive penalties for degrees of lateness or bonus points for neatness or for doing extra problems.

A mother and son we know were in a continual hassle because Mike "never" took out the trash, which he was supposed to do as soon as he got home from school. On learning that the first thing he did after school was make a beeline for the refrigerator, it took only a few minutes for us to arrange the following contingencies. A large sign saying TRASH would be taped to the refrigerator door. Mike would earn a dime of his allowance if he took out the trash as soon as he got home, before opening the refrigerator. If he didn't take out the trash until dinner time, he'd forfeit a nickel of his allowance, and if he didn't take it out at all, he'd lose all 10 cents. *However*, if his mother nagged him about the trash, or even mentioned it, he could take it out any time during the day and still earn the full dime.

b. Contingency contracts

Probably the clearest way to specify contingencies is to state the provisions in a contingency *contract*. Behavioral psychologists are now writing therapeutic contracts with their clients and, in the case of marriage or family counseling, helping their clients write contracts with each other.

Lloyd Homme has been a leader in the use of contingency contracting in the classroom (e.g., Homme, Csanyi, Gonzales & Rechs, 1970) as has Richard Stuart in family and marriage counseling (e.g., Stuart, 1971). Stuart sees a behavioral contract as a means of scheduling the exchange of reinforcers among people, and he names five elements of a good contract: (1) The contract will specify the privileges all parties expect to gain *after* fulfilling their responsibilities. (2) The contract will specify the responsibilities essential to securing each privilege. (3) There will be sanctions for failure to meet responsibilities. (4) There will be a bonus clause to assure reinforcement for compliance with the terms of the contract. (5) The contract will provide some means of keeping track of the reinforcers given and received (Stuart, 1971). Among Homme's rules for contracting are those that the contract should call for *accomplishment* rather than sheer obedience and that the contract should be positive rather than negative or threatening. He also warns that a contract should be *fair*, *clear*, and *honest* (Homme et al., 1970).

One of Dr. Stuart's clients, referred by the local juvenile court, was a 16-year-old girl, Candy Bremer (pseudonym) who was confined to a psychiatric hospital for alleged "promiscuity, exhibitionism, drug abuse and home truancy." It took some negotiating, but finally Stuart was able to help Candy and her parents draw up the contract shown in Table 3.10. Candy was primarily concerned with her freedom; her parents with Candy's truancy, academic work, and household chores. The contract proved to be effective, and court wardship was terminated. As Stuart notes, many family arguments were eliminated because the con-

tract removed from the realm of contention the issues of privileges and responsibilities.

A number of family contracts have been arranged between husbands and wives. An alcoholic and his wife drew up a contract whereby he could have one to three drinks a day in her presence. Drinking on occasions other than those specified in the contract was forbidden and resulted in a fine of $20.00 to be spent by the wife on a frivolous, nonessential item. On the other hand, the wife was to refrain from criticizing her husband's drinking else she paid him a $20.00 fine. Drinking was brought under control in about a week and was maintained at an acceptable level of 0–3 drinks a day six months later (Miller, 1972).

Another husband and his 26-year-old wife negotiated a two-fold contract designed to help the wife to lose weight and to insure that 90 percent of the household chores were completed. Daily and weekly household chores were defined and divided between them. The contract specified that 10 percent of the chores could be neglected; but beyond that, the delinquent partner would have to take over an equivalent number of chores from the other's list. The weight-control contract provided for three alternative consequences, based upon weekly weigh-in sessions. If the wife lost half a pound or more, she received a predetermined reinforcer, and her husband continued his share of the work. If she weighed the same as the previous week, she forfeited the reinforcer, but there was no further penalty. If she gained weight, however, she forfeited the reinforcer and her husband resigned from his work contract for the following week. The wife lost 14 pounds and has maintained that loss for more than a year; and the completion of household chores has consistently met the 90 percent criterion (Lutzker & Lutzker, 1974).

Given a little advice and encouragement, youth is no barrier to contingency management.

Table 3.10   Behavioral contract between Candy Bremer and her parents. (From Stuart, 1971, p. 9.)

CONTRACT

Privileges	Responsibilities
General	
In exchange for the privilege of remaining together and preserving some semblance of family integrity, Mr. and Mrs. Bremer and Candy all agree to	concentrate on positively reinforcing each other's behavior while diminishing the present overemphasis on the faults of the others.
Specific	
In exchange for the privilege of riding the bus directly from school into town after school on school days	Candy agrees to phone her father by 4:00 P.M. to tell him that she is all right and to return home by 5:15 P.M.
In exchange for the privilege of going out at 7:00 P.M. on one weekend evening without having to account for her whereabouts	Candy must maintain a weekly average of "B" in the academic ratings of all of her classes and must return home by 11:30 P.M.
In exchange for the privilege of going out a second weekend night	Candy must tell her parents by *6:00 P.M.* of her destination and her companion, and must return home by 11:30 P.M.
In exchange for the privilege of going out between 11:00 A.M. and 5:15 P.M. Saturdays, Sundays and holidays	Candy agrees to have completed all household chores *before* leaving and to telephone her parents once during the time she is out to tell them that she is all right.
In exchange for the privilege of having Candy complete household chores and maintain her curfew	Mr. and Mrs. Bremer agree to pay Candy $1.50 on the morning following days on which the money is earned.
Bonuses and Sanctions	
If Candy is 1-10 minutes late	she must come in the same amount of time earlier the following day, but she does not forfeit her money for the day.
If Candy is 11-30 minutes late	she must come in 22-60 minutes earlier the following day and does forfeit her money for the day.
If Candy is 31-60 minutes late	she loses the privilege of going out the following day and does forfeit her money for the day.
For each half hour of tardiness over one hour, Candy	loses her privilege of going out and her money for one additional day.
Candy may go out on Sunday evenings from 7:00 to 9:30 P.M. and either Monday or Thursday evening	if she abides by all the terms of this contract from Sunday through Saturday with a total tardiness not exceeding 30 minutes which must have been made up as above.
Candy may add a total of two hours divided among one to three curfews	if she abides by all the terms of this contract for two weeks with a total tardiness not exceeding 30 minutes which must have been made up as above and if she requests permission to use this additional time by 9:00 P.M.

Monitoring

Mr. and Mrs. Bremer agree to keep written records of the hours of Candy's leaving and coming home and of the completion of her chores.

Candy agrees to furnish her parents with a school monitoring card each Friday at dinner.

_____
_____
_____

Youngsters in a summer camp for "behaviorally disordered and neurologically impaired" children managed contingency contracts with their peers (Nelson, Worell, & Polsgrove, 1973). The nine managers, who ranged in age from 8 to 11 years, were selected on the basis of interest and the counselors' impressions that the cooperative effort would be mutually beneficial. Their nine protégés, age 7–11, were selected primarily because of their disruptive behavior. The various goals for the different protégés included decreasing threats, name calling, "homesick" statements, and leaving the group, as well as increasing appropriate verbal behavior and completion of tasks. The exact goals and the responsibilities of protégé, manager, and counselor were written by the counselor and one of the authors. Contracts were then arranged with the protégés and managers, each of whose reinforcers depended on the protégé's progress toward his specified goal. One of these contracts is shown in Table 3.11. The protégé, 11-year-old Andrew, had been classified as neurologically impaired, and he engaged in a fair amount of self-stimulatory behavior which interfered with his ability to attend to work. The goal was to reduce his off-task behavior, as defined in Table 3.11. The manager, eight-year-old Frank, was diagnosed as having "a perceptual impairment with strong emotional overlay" and reported to be hyperactive, distractible, and lacking an attention span. The reinforcers for both Andy and Frank, and the responsibilities of Frank and the counselor, are shown in the table. With Frank's help, Andy's off-task behavior dropped from a baseline level of twenty-nine per half hour to only four. Comparable changes are reported for the other children. Unfortunately, the authors do not seem to have monitored changes in the *managers'* problem behavior: we would not be surprised if they also made therapeutic gains. Perhaps in another study, protégés and managers can assume both roles, and mutual contracts can be arranged.

Contingency contracts have proved useful in a great many settings. In schools, for example, we usually think of Homme et al., 1970 and the elementary classroom. But contracts have found a place in high-school physical-education programs (Fast, 1971; see also Rushall & Siedentop, 1972), and at the college level. The students in our advanced course in behavior analysis, for example, write contracts that specify what they will do in the way of readings, lab work, workshops, papers, and projects to earn a particular grade. The most difficult task is deciding how their performance on various projects will be evaluated, so students who don't want to write a contract from "scratch" can select among a list of options provided by the instructor. These students also carry out a self-management project and write contracts with themselves that specify the behavior they wish to change and the consequences for meeting or failing to meet their daily goals. These self-management contracts are usually set for short periods of time and revised every week or two. At the end of the course, they write a maintenance contract which usually includes a clause specifying that they must go back on the program if certain gains are not maintained (see Chapter 7). In a school for delinquent boys, Schlomo Cohen and his colleagues help the students and their parents negotiate contingency contracts that are signed by all parties. The contracts specify certain academic and social responsibilities that the student will meet, and the consequences that will attend success or failure. (See Cohen, Keyworth, Kleiner, & Libert, 1971; and the film, *ABCs of education*.)

The Mansfield Training School[15] is among those institutions that arrange individual contracts between the resident (or an advocate) and the institutional staff. Boudin (1972) has incorporated contingency contracting into a successful program to combat drug abuse and is now

15. Mansfield Training School, Mansfield Depot, Connecticut. Write Jack Thaw for further information.

Table 3.11   Contingency contract managed by a "behaviorally disordered" child to reduce the off-task behavior of another "behaviorally disordered" child. (From Nelson, Worell, & Polsgrove, 1973, p. 272.)

PROTÉGÉ: Andrew
MANAGER: Frank
TARGET BEHAVIOR: Off-Task
OBJECTIVE: Reduce off-task behavior to zero for
                     observation periods.

Definition of Behavior:

Given tasks requested or assigned by the counselor, off-task behavior is counted when Andrew:
1. Turns entire body 180 degrees from the task site
2. Places two feet outside the task area as designated below:
    a. Dining area—beneath dining canopy
    b. Kitchen area—beneath kitchen canopy
    c. Fire area—circle of rocks and trees at fireplace
    d. Wash area—circle of rocks and trees at wash place
3. Does not take hold of a task object within 30 seconds of being asked or does not move a task object from one position of function to another in accordance with task demands within a period of 30 seconds.

Observation Period: 30 minutes (during camp capers, when on-task behavior is expected).

Reinforcing Events:
1. Subject: For each observation period, if Andrew's off-task behavior falls below that of his baseline average, (28), he may have his choice of one event from the following menu:
    a. Five minutes of extra time in the shower alone
    b. Five swings on the grapevine
    c. Extra rest time
    d. Choice of songs and opportunity to lead them after mealtime
    e. Choice of songs and opportunity to lead them at group meeting
2. Manager:
    a. Five swings on the grapevine for each observation period in which frequency falls below 28.

Responsibilities of the Manager:
1. Remind Andrew he is off-task when he makes a 180 degree turn from the task site.
2. Tell Andrew he has done a good job when he finishes one phase of a task.
3. Check the count from the counselor and determine whether reinforcing events have been earned.

Responsibilities of the Counselor:
1. Remind manager of his responsibilities when he does not follow them.
2. Take count and help manager determine whether reinforcing events have been earned.

using contracting in a large-scale behavioral program that is an alternative to methadone maintenance (Boudin & Valentine, 1974). The initial contract leaves little room for client negotiation; but as treatment progresses, successive contracts turn over increasingly more control to the client.

There are two sorts of contracts negotiated between therapists and their clients that involve a portion of the therapist's fee. One is specifi-cally designed to motivate the client to stick to the program, particularly the record keeping. Knox (1973) reinforces this behavior in marriage counseling by reducing his fee. He also charges an extra fee if the client "forgets" to bring the data to a session. In family counseling, Eyberg and Johnson (1974) have required the parents to make an advance deposit which was gradually returned, contingent on attendance at treatment sessions and collection of data.

The other sort of therapist-client contract represents a major step in therapist accountability. The contract clearly states the responsibilities that the therapist will assume, and part of the therapist's fee depends on the success of therapy. The agreement made between Ayllon and Skuban (1973) and the parents of a child who had been refused admission to school is an excellent example. Their contract, shown in Table 3.12, merits careful reading. It starts with a review of the problem and the general goals of therapy, then states the precise goals and how success will be evaluated, specifies the setting and duration of treatment, and, finally, provides that one-third of the cost of treatment will depend upon the sucess of treatment.

On various occasions, Mike had been diagnosed as brain-damaged, emotionally disturbed, and autistic; and he was "untestable" (or retarded) by standard psychological measures. The overall goal was to reduce his extreme temper tantrums and disruptive behavior while developing social skills and self-control, so that he might be considered for admission to a special school. The program avoids the problem of transfer from a clinical setting to the natural environment by providing that therapy be conducted in a variety of natural settings, including the zoo, department stores, shopping centers, and restaurants. The "final examination" evaluates transfer of cooperative behavior from therapist to parents and to another adult whom Mike had never seen (see II, 3 of the contract).

When the final test was administered, Mike complied with 28 of the 30 requests, thus easily meeting the 80 percent criterion specified in the contract. The other condition of the contract —no more than one tantrum, and it could not last for more than one minute—was also met: he had one five-second tantrum. The conditions of the contract thus having been met, the parents were delighted, the therapist received the rest of his fee, and Mike was admitted into school.

Another child who would not have been admitted to school made the grade when Robertshaw and Johnson (1974) negotiated a remedial contract with his mother. The contract specified the responsibilities of the advisor, the instructor, and the mother, and was signed by all three. There was a modest charge of $2.00 per session. Most of the therapist's fee was contingent upon the child's achieving the several goals of the program: e.g., repeat the numbers from one to ten from memory ($10.00), trace and then print name ($20.00), play ball cooperatively with another child ($10.00), listen attentively to a five-minute story ($10.00).

8. Design a Favorable Situation

Some conditions favor productive behavior while others do not. Teaching seventh-grade math is not made easier when the high-school band is practicing outside the window. First-grade children are likely to find it difficult to pay attention and work independently in a classroom arranged so that all of the desks are touching. And, as many teachers, parents, and publishers well know, some of us don't really do our best writing at 3 A.M.

A favorable situation increases the likelihood that the desired behavior will occur and decreases the likelihood of competing behavior. It provides discriminative stimuli for the desired behavior, and removes the discriminative stimuli and the opportunity for competing behavior. Libraries are designed as favorable situations for studying: good lighting, quiet, moderately comfortable chairs (but not so comfortable as to encourage sleeping), books and other reference materials, and the presence of other students also studying. Studying at home or in the dormitory, though feasible, may have many discriminative stimuli for competing behavior: friends, magazines, letters to be answered, phone calls. It is possible to remove some of these discriminative stimuli for competing be-

Table 3.12   A contingency contract for therapy. (From Ayllon & Skuban, 1973, p. 22, 23.)

I. Overview of problem and therapeutic program

The overall objective of this therapeutic program is to develop and stabilize Mike's behavior patterns so that he may be considered for admission to school this fall. In general, this will involve strengthening some requisite behaviors such as following commands from an adult, and eliminating others, such as the screaming and tantrumming that accompany most of his refusals to follow instructions.

Mike has a discouraging behavior history for most teachers to consider working with. Because his characteristic reaction to requests is to throw tantrums, he is considered "untestable" by standard psychological means. This does not necessarily mean that he cannot do the items on a test, but rather that he has little or no control over his own behavior. His uncooperativeness quickly discourages most people from making much of an effort to work with him. What is clearly needed is an intensive rehabilitation program designed to enable Mike to build patterns of self-control which would lead to the elimination or drastic reduction of his disruptive behavior. This, in turn, would open other possibilities for developing Mike's potential, that is, the avenues which are blocked by his unmanageable behavior.

The overall goal of this 8-week program will be the development of self-control with its reciprocal outcome of decreasing or eliminating tantrums and disruptive behaviors. Implementation of this program will require that the child and his trainer engage in such activities as trips to the zoo, museums, parks, movies, swimming pools, shopping centers, supermarkets, and so on as well as having lunch and snacks together. These settings are included to expose Mike to a maximal number of normal situations where expectations of a standard of conduct are imposed by the setting itself.

As much as possible, the techniques used in the day program will be designed with the ultimate objective of utilization in the home. An attempt will be made to see that procedures used in the program are transferred to home management at the termination of treatment. The therapist will give instructions weekly to the parents by phone to insure that efforts both at home and in rehabilitation do not conflict.

II. Behavioral objectives of therapy

1. The objective of the therapeutic program is to teach Mike to comply with between 80-100 percent of the verbal commands given to him by an adult(s). Compliance will be defined as Mike's beginning to perform the behavior specified by the command within 15 sec after it has been stated and then completing the specified task.

2. In addition, we intend to eliminate or drastically reduce Mike's excessive screaming and tantrumming. The goal is not to tantrum more frequently than once out of 30 commands and for no longer than 1 min at a time.

3. Evaluation of treatment outcome: The decision as to the attainment of these specific objectives will rest upon Mike's performance during a 30 min test session to be conducted in a classroom situation. At this session the therapist, the parents, and an additional person will make 10 verbal requests each of Mike, for a total of 30 verbal requests. Mike must comply with 80-100 percent of these requests for the program to be considered a success. In addition, he must have tantrummed not more than once, and for not more than 1 min, during this final evaluation.

III. Time and place of therapeutic intervention

1. The therapeutic program will start on _____ and terminate on _____. Evaluation of the effectiveness of treatment will be held on or about the termination date of the therapeutic program.

2. Location: The meeting place will be at the _____. Session activities, however, will involve time spent elsewhere, for example, having lunch, trips to shopping centers, amusements, and other special events. If the facility is not available, some other place agreeable can be designated as meeting and base center.

3. Days of training: Therapy sessions will be scheduled 5 days per week. The specific days may vary from week to week to comply with the objectives of the program. The family will be advised of the therapy schedule 1 week in advance.

4. Hours per day: Therapeutic sessions will be scheduled for 7 hr a day. Session time may be extended when therapeutically necessary as decided by the therapist.

5. Absences: There will be 4 notified absences allowed. The mother is expected to notify the therapist at least 1 hr before the scheduled therapy session. Any additional absences will require an additional fee of $10 per absence.

IV. Fees

Achievement of the behavioral objectives is expected to take 7 weeks of training from _____. This training will cost a total of _____. The monies will be disbursed in the following manner.

1. A check for 2/3 of the total amount will be given to the therapist at the beginning of therapy.

2. The balance of 1/3 will be paid to the therapist upon the achievement of the program objectives as specified above on about the date of termination of the program. In the event that the above objectives are not reached by this date, therapy will be discontinued and the balance will be forfeited by the therapist.

3. All expense incurred during training will be defrayed by the therapist. This will include admission to baseball games, the city zoo, swimming pools, and so on, as well as the cost of field trips, lunch, and snacks.

* * * * *

By my signature I do hereby attest that I have read the above proposal and agree to the conditions stated therein.

_____   _____
Parent   Supervising Therapist

_____   _____
Date   Co-Therapist

havior by posting a note on the door: STUDY-ING—GO AWAY. But then, of course, one has to be careful not to reinforce interrupting behavior by answering a knock on the door. A favorable situation does not preclude the opportunity for "extraneous" behavior unless it is incompatible with the desired behavior. For many people, drinking coffee or listening to "background" music is not incompatible with studying.

In a study of the effects of play materials on the play of seven-year-old children, Quilitch and Risley (1973) alternately provided "social toys" such as checkers and playing cards, and "isolate toys" such as Play Doh and a jigsaw puzzle. They found that social play occurred 78 percent of the time with social toys and only 16 percent of the time with isolate toys. Providing toys that encourage social play could be more efficient than an elaborate program to encourage and reinforce social interaction. And if the toys alone were not enough, they would nonetheless provide a favorable situation for the shaping of social behavior in excessively shy or isolated children.

9. Adaptation

The importance of adaptation as a requisite for behavior therapy can be seen in the report by Salzinger, Feldman, Cowan, and Salzinger (1965) on the conditioning of verbal behavior in speech-deficient children. One child showed a marked fear of strangers and of leaving the hospital ward; and adaptation to the experimenter and the experimental room took four weeks. The experimenter first visited the ward once or twice a day and was very gradually established as a source of praise and candy in the environment to which the child was already adapted. The boy was then picked up for brief periods and then carried about, but not toward the exit from the ward. Next, a member of the ward staff accompanied the child and the experimenter to

the experimental room where pieces of candy were conspicuously in evidence. Soon after, the experimenter reinforced the child's walking to the experimental room, presenting candy after every few steps. Presently, he was taken to the room but allowed to leave when he wished; and finally he remained in the room for periods up to an hour. Without this period of adaptation, it is doubtful that the conditioning of verbal behavior would have taken place. The child's reaction of panic to the presence of a stranger and to unfamiliar surroundings was clearly incompatible with the development of normal speech. The authors note that when the child was discharged from the hospital, approximately 20 months after they began to work with him, he was speaking almost entirely in sentences, was using a variety of grammatical structures, and showed marked improvement in many other aspects of his social behavior.

A more familiar example is the problem of adaptation on the first day of school or summer camp. This problem can be acute if the discriminative stimuli for the child's behavior have been restricted to the home and family. Children whose behavior is controlled by a wide variety of discriminative stimuli have a much easier time: many classes of behavior will be available under many stimulus conditions. They will already have encountered strange children at their own houses and at other people's houses; and other children will have become discriminative stimuli for behavior such as talking and playing and eating. They will already have encountered groups of children, perhaps at birthday parties. They will have developed a repertoire of behavior in the presence of adults other than their parents, and the verbal behavior of other adults will have acquired stimulus control. In short, they will have behaved appropriately under a wide variety of stimulus conditions. Adaptation to school is further facilitated when children are taken for a preliminary visit to see the school and meet the teacher, and if, when they must stay at school, they are accompanied by a parent or a friend.

10. Select Evaluation Procedures

An essential step in designing a program is deciding how to evaluate its success. When we find a way to measure behavior, we can determine the extent of its change in the desired direction. If it does change in the desired direction, there is every reason to rejoice; but it is always possible that the change can be attributed to something other than the program we designed and carried out. Suppose, for example, that we decide to teach a nonverbal, "emotionally disturbed" child to talk by first reinforcing any imitative behavior and then reinforcing only vocalizations that increasingly resemble human speech. Two months later, the child has developed a working vocabulary of 30 words, which we attribute to our program. But perhaps the child was put on—or taken off—drugs during those two months. Or perhaps someone at home was teaching him to talk by another method. Or perhaps his constantly quarreling parents separated, and life was more peaceful at home. How can we decide whether or not the improvement that accompanies our program is related to our program? Several experimental designs, appropriate to different situations, can help us answer this question.

The experimental designs used by most psychologists are group designs. These are appropriate for statistical analyses of the differences obtained from groups of subjects who have experienced different procedures. Applied behavior analysts, however, tend to favor "within-subject" designs. They generally rely on replication, rather than statistical analysis, to increase their confidence that the experimental procedure, rather than some unidentified variable, is responsible for the observed change in behavior. Both sorts of designs are useful, and both may be employed within a single study. A few designs are described below, with the emphasis placed on within-subject designs since they are not yet included in most standard texts on design and measurement. For a more detailed discussion of this important topic, see Baer (1975), Barlow and Hersen (1973), Kazdin (1976a,b), Hersen and Barlow (1976), Paul (1969a), and Sidman (1960).

a. Group designs

When group designs are employed in education or therapy, we would expect them to meet the minimum requirements enumerated by Meehl (1955): (1) there should be experimental and control groups, (2) evaluation should be taken before and after therapy, and (3) follow-up data should be collected.

One evaluation that meets these requirements is the evaluation of Achievement Place, a behavioral program for delinquent youths established in 1967 by Elery and Elaine Phillips (Fixsen, Phillips, Phillips & Wolf, 1976; Phillips, 1968; Phillips, Phillips, Fixsen, & Wolf, 1973). The Phillips were the "teaching parents" in the original Achievement Place at Lawrence, Kansas, and the data to be reported are based on that program. There are now several dozen family-style homes patterned after Achievement Place; and, some 400 delinquent boys and girls have benefited from this alternative to prison.

Sixteen youths from Achievement Place were compared to fifteen youths committed to the Kansas Boys' School and thirteen placed on formal probation with respect to recidivism, police and court contacts, grades and school attendance, and school drop-out rate. Although the boys were not assigned randomly to these locations, the juvenile court did not specify any particular conditions for placement; and the Achievement Place boys scored no higher on any of these measures before treatment than did the boys from the other groups. Figure 3.8 compares the percentage of boys who were in school before, during, and after

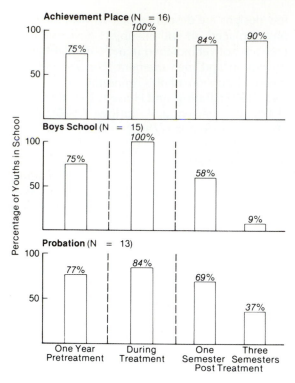

Figure 3.8.   *Group design.* Percentage of youths in school before, during, and after treatment, for boys at Achievement Place and for comparison groups. (From Fixsen, Phillips, Phillips, & Wolf, 1976, p. 318.)

their assignment to one of the three programs. Three semesters after their release, 90 percent of the Achievement Place youths attended public school, while only 9 percent of the Boys' School youths and 37 percent of the Probation youths were still in school. Similar comparisons held for the other measures: two years after release recidivism was less than 20 percent for the Achievement Place group and more than 50 percent for the other populations; police and court contacts were much lower for the Achievement Place boys, and their school grades were higher. Not only is the program successful in accomplishing its major goals, but the operating costs of Achievement Place are *less than one-half* the operating costs for the Kansas Boys' School.

The selection of subjects for control groups is a complicated matter, and many studies include two or three experimental groups and two or three control groups to evaluate different aspects of the program. Paul (1969a) offers excellent suggestions as well as warnings. Serious questions have been raised about the ethics of using control groups because this denies those individuals the possible benefits of therapy. One solution is the "delayed-treatment" control in which the control subjects receive the most successful treatment after they have served as no-treatment controls for purposes of evaluation. Brown, Wienckowski, and Stolz (1975) suggest that when a new (experimental) procedure is to be evaluated, the control subjects be given the best available alternative treatment. The control subjects in the Sobells's program for alcoholics (e.g., Figures 3.23 and 3.25) were given counseling and therapy and encouraged to join Alcoholics Anonymous.

b. Replication

The problem with group data is that they obscure important individual differences. When we want to evaluate the effects of a particular procedure on the behavior of one or several particular individuals we should look at individual data. If instituting a procedure (e.g., reinforcement) is accompanied by a change in behavior (e.g., an increase in cooperative play), the change could be due either to the procedure or to something else. One way to determine which, is to discontinue the reinforcement procedure. If cooperative behavior returns to its baseline level, we will be a little more confident that the change was related to the procedure. We would be even more confident if we could repeat, or replicate, this apparent relation. Most experimental designs that evaluate the effects of procedures on individual behavior are based on replication. (Of course, it is also appropriate to try to replicate the findings of group studies —one wishes it happened more often.)

"Within-subject" designs replicate data in another way. In the example of reinforcing cooperative play, we would obtain repeated measures of cooperative play both before and after introducing reinforcement. This replication of data *within* a condition provides a measure of day-to-day variability that is lost if we have only one "before" and one "after" measure. It also allows us to examine the course of behavior when a procedural change is introduced. Sometimes the accompanying change in behavior is gradual; sometimes abrupt.

c. Reversal designs (ABAB)

Reversal designs replicate a finding by introducing a procedure and then removing it as often as necessary to observe whether or not a change in behavior reliably accompanies a change in the procedure. This design has been used to evaluate a procedure for getting impoverished rural children in a Head Start program to eat the nutritional, but unfamiliar, breakfasts provided in school by the county school system (Madsen, Madsen, & Thompson, 1974). The food con-

sisted of middle class items such as scrambled eggs, sausages, bacon, toast, pancakes and waffles, milk, and fruit juice. With the exception of bread, these were unfamiliar foods, and the children were reluctant to eat them. After observing one school employee try to pour milk down the throat of a child for "his own good," the authors decided to try reinforcement procedures. The teachers were told to circulate among the children during breakfast and to deliver praise and sugar-coated cereal contingent upon eating the nourishing food: "William, it makes me proud and I'll bet you feel proud, too, when you drink your milk like that."

Figure 3.9 shows that before this reinforcement procedure was introduced, the children were eating approximately 75 percent of their food. With contingent praise and sugar-coated cereal, the children ate more than 90 percent of the food. The reinforcement procedure was continued for five days, and the average percentage of meals consumed was consistently high. Even so, the improvement might have been due to some unknown variable, so

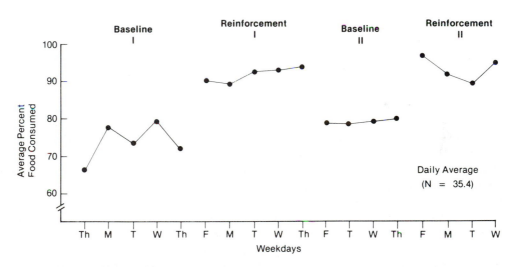

Figure 3.9.   *Reversal design.* Average percent of breakfast meal consumed by children in Head Start program under baseline and reinforcement conditions. (From Madsen, Madsen, & Thompson, 1974, p. 262.)

the conditions were "reversed" in a return-to-baseline design. Now, this is a case where reversing the procedure might *not* have been accompanied by a reversal in behavior: the children might have gotten to like the nourishing middle-class food during the five days that they were encouraged to try it, and the behavior might not have returned to baseline. In that case, the authors would not have known for certain whether or not the reinforcement procedure was responsible for getting the children to eat more of the different foods, but at least the children would be getting a better diet. However, the percentage of food eaten did decrease when reinforcement was discontinued (Figure 3.9, baseline II), and it did recover when reinforcement was reintroduced. So this return-to-baseline version of a reversal design evaluated the effectiveness of a reinforcement procedure in getting economically impoverished children to eat the only nutritional food available. This is an ABAB design, where A stands for baseline conditions and B for treatment. In this particular example, the data for subjects have been averaged, *but the comparison is between conditions, rather than between groups of subjects.* (Within-subject designs with individual subjects will be illustrated in a moment.)

There are several ways of carrying out a reversal design. The Madsen study was a return to baseline. Instead of returning to baseline conditions, one could make reinforcers (or punishers, if punishment was the procedure being evaluated) noncontingent during the reversal phase or contingent upon some other behavior. Alternatively, one could alternate reinforcement and extinction or alternate the reinforcement of two different classes of behavior. The Hasazi data shown in Figure 3.3 is another example of a return-to-baseline reversal design. In this case, the experimental treatment consisted of extinction (withholding extra help when Bob made errors), and the reversal was a return to reinforcement. The ABAB design:

reinforcement–extinction–reinforcement–extinction. The baseline condition is whatever conditions are in effect before an experimental procedure is introduced; and sometimes, as in Figure 3.21, these conditions are not known. In this Kazdin study, the subjects exhibited very little social interaction during the baseline period (which is not shown), but it would be difficult to say "why." Maybe the behavior was being punished by some unknown event; maybe competing behavior was being reinforced; or maybe the behavior was not within their repertoire. At any rate, the phases in this reversal design start with reinforcement and include: reinforcement–extinction–reinforcement–extinction. Figure 4.10 is another return-to-baseline design, but the treatment is an avoidance procedure. A husband picks up his clothes when he thereby avoids doing the dishes: baseline (unknown conditions)–avoidance–baseline–avoidance–follow-up.

A good example of a reversal design with noncontingent reinforcement as the reversal phase is the Hart et al. study shown in Figure 4.5. In this case, the design is ABCBC: baseline–noncontingent reinforcement–reinforcement of cooperative play–noncontingent reinforcement–reinforcement of cooperative play. Figure 5.2 is a reversal design in which two different classes of behavior are alternatively reinforced and extinguished.

d. Multiple-baseline designs
It is sometimes difficult, impossible, or unethical to "reverse" behavior in an attempt to evaluate the effectiveness of a procedure. If classroom disruptive behavior has been reduced, few teachers will be eager to return to baseline conditions or to employ any other procedure that would allow disruptive behavior to recover. Some behavior is essentially irreversible. Once acquired, skills cannot usually be unacquired, though they may decline from lack of practice. It may be unethical to allow behavior to revert to

its former level. If a procedure has been used to reduce self-injurious behavior, we would want to find some way of evaluating the procedure that did not require the recovery of self-injury. Finally, a reversal of procedures may not result in a reversal of behavior simply because other consequences have come to control the behavior. As we noted in conjunction with Figure 3.9, the Head Start children might have come to *like* middle class food and kept on eating it even when the other reinforcers were withdrawn. In most cases, there would not be a return to baseline if therapy were successful. The program would include provisions to maintain the behavior in the natural environment.

Multiple-baseline designs provide a solution to these problems; they do not require a reversal of conditions or behavior. Instead of replicating effects by repeatedly introducing and removing the treatment procedure, multiple-baseline designs replicate across different subjects or settings or classes of behavior by introducing the procedural variable at different times.

A *multiple-baseline design across subjects* has been used to assess the effects of praise by the school principal on the attendance of three kindergarten and first-grade children. The data, from Copeland, Brown, and Hall (1974), are shown in Figure 3.10. A baseline condition, with no special contingencies for attending school, was in effect for all subjects for several weeks. Then, *while baseline continued for the other subjects*, the procedure (praise) was introduced for Elbert. His attendance increased from approximately 50 percent to better than 80 percent, while that of the other children who were still on baseline varied considerably but showed no systematic change. The procedure was introduced for Yolanda during the eleventh week, while Lynnette continued on baseline and Elbert continued to receive praise from the principal. Two weeks later, the procedure was introduced for Lynnette. The procedure was introduced at

different times for different subjects in an effort to control for other (unknown) variables that might have accounted for a change in behavior if the procedure had been introduced for all subjects at the same time. Since the change in procedure was made at different times and was accompanied by a change in behavior in all three cases, one can be reasonably confident that the change in behavior is directly related to the procedure. During the final phase of the study, daily praise from the principal was replaced by intermittent praise. (This phase was introduced simultaneously for all children and

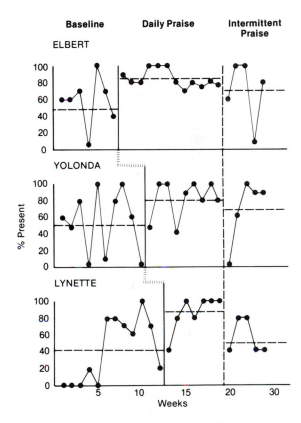

Figure 3.10. *Multiple baseline across subjects.* Percentage of time three students attended school. Baseline: before experimental procedures. Daily Praise: principal entered classrooms daily and delivered praise for school attendance. Intermittent praise: principal delivered praise two or three times a week. (From Copeland, Brown, & Hall, 1974, p. 79.)

is not part of the multiple-baseline design.) Elbert's attendance was much less consistent under this condition; Yolanda was absent all of the first week, but thereafter she attended as often as when the principal had delivered daily praise; but Lynette's attendance was little better than during baseline.

A *multiple-baseline across different classes of behavior* is shown in Figure 3.11. Fawcett and Miller (1975) developed a public-speaking training program designed to teach the students to look at the audience, make appropriate gestures, and perform a number of other classes of behavior such as acknowledging the introduction, greeting the audience and smiling, repeating questions, and so forth. The three main "packages"—eye contact, gestures, and speaking behavior—were introduced at different times as shown in Figure 3.11. The rapid improvement which coincides with the introduction of each program strongly argues for the success of the program; and these results were replicated with other subjects.

The third variation is the *multiple-baseline design across different settings*. Here, the subject and the class of behavior are the same, but the procedure is introduced at different times in different settings. One example is shown in Figure 5.10. This study demonstrated that reinforcement of academic behavior reduced hyperactivity to the same degree as did medication, producing at least two benefits for the children: their academic skills improved greatly, and they were spared the potential ill effects of continuing medication. The data in Figure 5.10, which were replicated with other children, show that during both math and reading the increase in academic behavior and the decrease in hyperactive behavior coincide with the introduction of the procedure.

e. Combined designs

In some cases, it is possible to double your confidence by doubling the design. Figure 3.12

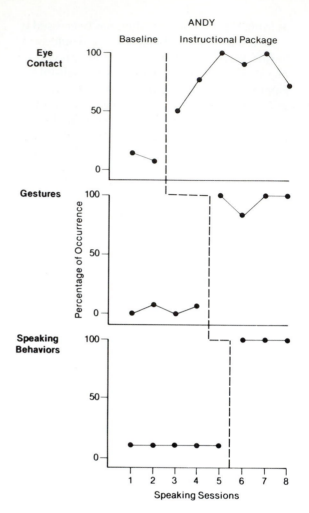

Figure 3.11.   *Multiple baseline across behavior.* The percentage occurrence of target activities for each category of public-speaking behavior. Vertical dotted lines indicate point at which the instructional package was introduced for each category. (From Fawcett & Miller, 1975, p. 129.)

shows a combination of a return-to-baseline reversal design with a multiple baseline across two subjects (Fox, Copeland, Harris, Rieth, & Hall, 1975). The behavior differs—David has poor vision and doesn't wear his glasses, while Greg has poor hearing and doesn't wear his hearing aid—but in both cases the procedure was token reinforcement contingent on wearing

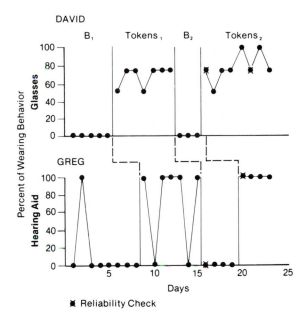

DAVID

Figure 3.12. *Combined reversal and multiple-baseline design.* Percentage of time samples that each of two second-grade students wore his hearing aid or glasses during baseline and during periods when tokens (backed by special activities) were contingent upon the behavior. Interobserver agreement calculated for points marked with (X). (From Fox, Copeland, Harris, Rieth, & Hall, 1975, p. 140.)

these objects. The procedure was introduced later for Greg, who remained on baseline three days longer than David in a multiple-baseline design. The ABAB reversal design was also staggered for the two boys. The abrupt change in behavior that accompanies the change in procedure argues that the tokens were responsible for the change.

A within-subjects reversal design was combined with a between-subjects group design to evaluate the effectiveness of paying Mexican industrial workers for coming to work on time (Hermann, de Montes, Domínquez, Montes, & Hopkins, 1973). Six of 12 workers who were frequently late for work served as a control group, while the other six received a bonus for punctuality during the treatment phases of a reversal design. The maximum

bonus possible was $0.80 per week. The results of this study, which continued for more than a year and a half, are shown in Figure 3.13. Each point is the percentage of tardiness for the six subjects in the group during a two-week block of time. Each time the bonus for punctuality was introduced (treatment phase, lower graph), there was a marked reduction in tardiness; and each time the bonus was discontinued (during a return to the baseline conditions), the percentage of tardiness increased. The first reversal phase was relatively short, but during the second reversal phase (blocks 18–23) the percentage of tardiness gradually approached and might have exceeded the original baseline level. This trend would not be seen had the data been averaged instead of plotted for each block of time. During the final phase of the study, when the punctuality bonus was in effect for approximately eight months, tardiness remained at a low level.

These within-subject replications strongly suggest that the small bonus for punctuality was an effective way to reduce tardiness in these workers. However, there is a problem with reversal designs in that it is difficult to assess the possible sequential effects of the procedures. Performance during a return to baseline, for example, may be affected by the fact that some other procedure has been in effect and has now been discontinued. To take a practical example: if the second return to baseline had continued longer, and if the percentage of tardiness then exceeded the original baseline, one might conclude that once a punctuality bonus is introduced it must be maintained, or management will have to contend with more tardiness than before the program started. If the level of tardiness did not fully recover when the bonus was discontinued, we might also infer sequential effects deriving from the nature of the design. Adding a control group to a within-subjects design is a way of estimating what would have happened had a procedure never been intro-

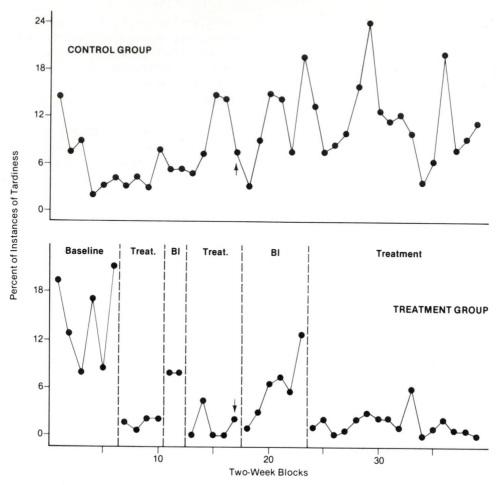

Figure 3.13.   *Combined group and reversal design.* Effects of bonus for punctuality upon the tardiness of industrial workers (lower graph). Data from control group shown in upper graph. Arrows indicate points based on one (not two) weeks data. (Adapted from Hermann, deMontes, Domínguez, Montes, & Hopkins, 1973, p. 567.)

duced. In this study, the data from the control subjects (upper graph in Figure 3.13) indicate what would have happened if the punctuality bonus had never been introduced. These data show a slight increase in tardiness over the 80 weeks of the study.

f. Changing-criterion design

Another design, recently introduced by Axelrod, Hall, Weis, and Rohrer (1974), demon-

strates the control of behavior in a very different way. The changing-criterion design shows the extent to which behavior matches a progressively changing criterion. If the behavior is to be decreased, as in Figure 3.14, control is demonstrated to the extent that the behavior stays within the limits set by the criterion. The subject in Figure 3.14 is a graduate student who decided to gradually eliminate smoking. The procedure was an avoidance one: if the number of ciga-

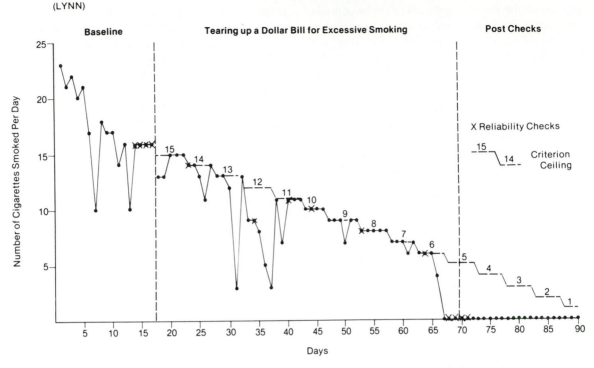

Figure 3.14. *Changing–criterion design.* The number of cigarettes smoked per day by a graduate student. Interobserver agreement calculated for points marked with (X). (From Axelrod, Hall, Weis, & Rohrer, 1974, p. 81.)

rettes smoked exceeded the criterion set for the day, the student, Lynn, had to tear up a dollar bill. When I show these data to students, they are horrified at the very idea of tearing up money; why not give it to charity? That procedure might or might not have been effective. This one was. How many times did Lynn tear up a dollar bill?

This design can also be used to assess the effects of a program designed to gradually increase a class of behavior. For example, a student might program a gradual increase in time spent studying and use the changing-criterion design to evaluate the success of the self-control procedures selected.

There are other useful within-subject designs, notably the *simultaneous-treatment de-*

sign (McCulloch, Cornell, McDaniel & Mueller, 1974) and the *multielement-baseline design* (Ulman & Sulzer-Azaroff, 1975). However, the reversal and multiple-baseline designs are presently those most frequently used in applied behavior analysis.

C. Carrying out the Program

Even though applied behavior analysis now includes all of the steps outlined in Table 3.1C, the emphasis will vary considerably. In some cases, the major time and effort is devoted to assessing and then strengthening specific capabilities, thus broadening the individual's repertoire of behavior. In others, the major emphasis may be placed on the maintenance and transfer of goals that were relatively easy to attain in a highly structured situation. To provide continuity, we shall illustrate this section with a single study, adding material from other authors where our own program provides insufficient detail.

The program[16] was designed and conducted by an honors student, Debbie Werden —with a little help from her friends, particularly the classroom teacher, Barbara Blank. (Reese, 1971b; Reese & Werden, 1970). Debbie wanted to teach number concepts to retarded children, and she went through all of the steps summarized in this chapter:

1. Review of Program Design

Teaching Number Concepts to Retarded Children

a. Preliminary and continuing

First, Debbie got to know the children: five girls from a public-school class for trainable retarded children, age 6-13, whose I.Q.s ranged between 38–49. Debbie spent several weeks in the classroom, helping the teacher and identifying the children's skills she could build on and the deficits she would have to overcome or work around. She found that some of the children had speech handicaps, so she designed a number program that would not depend on verbal ability. Had she relied on *verbal* skills she might have underestimated the children's *number* skills. She might also have used inappropriate teaching procedures. For similar reasons, Debbie decided not to require the children to write numerals. One can recognize and count four objects without being able to draw the numeral "4," and vice versa.

The teacher was consulted almost daily —before, during, and after the program. Not only did she make many invaluable suggestions, she agreed to stop trying to teach number skills by traditional methods for the duration of the program. She recognized that we could not evaluate the program if the children were receiving additional instruction; and she had enough faith in the program to let us take over that aspect of the curriculum.

b. Analyze current situation

An analysis of the situation revealed that the children recognized some numerals but not their relation to actual numbers of objects. And many could reel off the numbers 1 to 5, but could not bring five spoons to the table. The children could state that the human face had two eyes and one nose; they could match objects by color; and their abundant goodwill to the teacher seemed to generalize to us.

c. Ethical issues and priorities

Ethical considerations included the advisability of attempting a number program, its possible value to the children, and Debbie's qualifications to conduct such a program. We all decided that the acquisition of basic number skills was a high-priority goal; that the future options of the children would be improved if they could count objects and recognize numerals; that even if the program failed, the experience would produce no ill effects; and that Debbie's general background, conscientious attitude, and previous experience with retarded children qualified her to conduct the program under the guidance of the classroom teacher and the thesis advisor.

d. Specific goals

Concept of number was defined by nine tasks. There were two counting tasks: counting a given number of objects (the only task that required the children to speak) and counting out a requested number of objects from a set of 30. The

16. This program, and another designed to teach arithmetic, are the subjects of the film, *Born to Succeed: Behavioral procedures for education*, (Reese, 1971a). For a much more elaborate behavioral analysis of mathematical skills and concepts, see Resnick, Wang, and Kaplan (1973).

children were also asked to identify the numerals from 1 to 10 by pointing to the numeral Debbie named. Finally, there were six matching tasks in which the child selected from several sets of objects the one that matched a sample numeral or set of objects. Figure 3.15 shows one subject matching sets of two-dimensional objects to numerals. These tasks included: matching numerals to numerals, matching sets of two-dimensional objects to a two-dimensional sample, matching sets of three-dimensional objects to a three-dimensional sample, and the three combinations of these matching tasks. Performance was measured in terms of time and accuracy.

When it came to counting and matching actual numbers of objects (as opposed to numerals) we wanted to make sure that the children would attend to the number, rather than to some other dimension of the objects. If we had used rows of black circles, for example, the children might have matched correctly by judging the length of the row of circles or the total amount of blackness. They might not have judged number at all. Our three-dimensional objects were "junk objects"—glass and wooden beads and buttons, and various metal objects—which differed in size, shape, color, brightness, and texture, so that only judgments based on number would be consistently correct. The two-dimensional objects were different colored geometric shapes—circles, triangles, squares, and hexagons—painted on cards.

e. Procedures and contingencies

The major procedure was reinforcement in the context of certain programming techniques described below. The reinforcers were praise and tokens which could be exchanged for trinkets, pretzels, animal crackers, M&Ms, or colored stickers of plants and animals. Each correct match or count produced praise and a token; and when five tokens were accumulated, they were exchanged for a back-up reinforcer.

f. Favorable situation and adaptation

Several steps were taken to ensure a favorable situation. Since the training would involve matching, we used a display board[17] to hold the cards containing the various sets of objects (Figure 3.15A). The sample was presented near the

17. The display board was designed and built by Nancy Bachman and Edward A. Chittenden III.

A
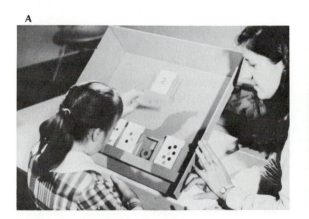

B
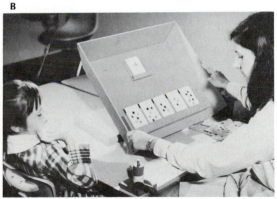

Figure 3.15.   Display board for teaching the concept of number to retarded children. A: Token is recessed behind card that is correct choice. B: Child places token on spindle and teacher rearranges stimuli for another trial. (From the film, *Born to Succeed*, Reese, 1971a.)

top of the display, centered above five alternative choices. A token was recessed behind the correct choice. The board was mounted on a swivel base so that the teacher could quickly turn it away to change the cards and put another token in the recessed compartment. This is shown in Figure 3.15B: the subject has just placed a fourth token on the spindle in the center foreground. When the spindle is full, the five tokens will be exchanged for a back-up reinforcer. The children in this study always seemed to look at the sample before making a choice, but normal children in a later study were a bit casual about checking the sample. We therefore covered the sample with a door that the child had to open before making a choice, hoping this would favor attention to the sample.

Originally we had hoped to conduct the training sessions in a private room, but since this was impossible, they were conducted in a corner of the regular classroom. Somewhat to our surprise, this turned out to be a favorable situation: the children saw each other working, learning, and earning praise and tokens; and all were eager to take their turns. Staying in the regular classroom also eased the problem of adaptation. The children had to become accustomed to working with Debbie, but she had been in and out of the classroom for weeks before the program had started. The various stimulus materials were gradually introduced.

g. Evaluation

The study was designed to test the effectiveness of a fading procedure in teaching number concepts to retarded children and to see if training on two of our nine tasks would transfer to the other seven. We decided to assess baseline performance on all tasks, train on two of them, and then reassess the children's performance on all nine tasks. The experimental design was thus an ABA procedure in which we hoped there would be no return to baseline. The next step was to carry out the program.

2. Baseline

There are two reasons for measuring baseline. First, we need to know where to start. In building skills, we must identify the individual's current repertoire; and in reducing problem behavior, we need to assess its extent and severity before we can select appropriate procedures. Second, baseline provides the basis of comparison so that we can evaluate the success of a program.

Debbie tested the children on all nine tasks, reinforcing all correct answers with praise and tokens. She started with one object (or the numeral 1) and went as far as the child could go. The criterion for passing a given task was two correct responses out of three tries. Figure 3.16 shows the baseline performance of Betsy; it was the highest in the group. Betsy could count three objects if only three were given her, but she could count only two objects from a collection of thirty. She could match all the numerals from 1 to 10; but without a sample, she did not recognize 3, 4, 5, or 6 when they were asked for by name. Matching numerals is essentially the same as matching pictures, and the ability to recognize a numeral does not necessarily mean that the numeral stands for a given number of objects. On all of the matching tasks involving actual numbers of objects, Betsy's baseline was two.

3. Build from Repertoire

The attainment of most goals requires a repertoire of prerequisite skills. Students of Greek or Russian must first learn the Greek or Cyrillic alphabet. There is misery for all concerned when a student of algebra has not mastered arithmetic. *Modeling* and *prompting* are often helpful. If you are trying to develop conversational speech and a child is able to imitate, start with that ability. Model the sounds or phrases, and reinforce the child's attempts to imitate.[18]

18. Modeling is discussed in Chapters 4, 5, and 6.

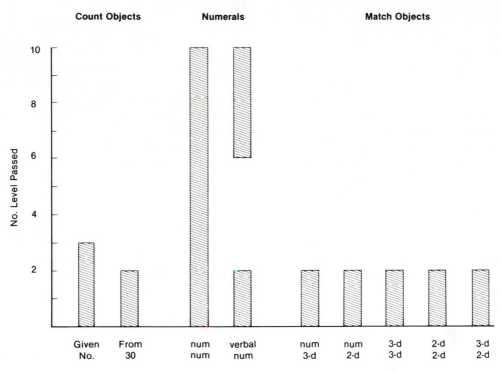

Figure 3.16. Baseline performance of one subject (Betsy) on nine tasks defining concept of number: counting a given number of objects; counting out a requested number from a set of 30 objects; matching numerals; identifying a numeral on verbal request; and combinations of matching numerals, sets of two dimensional objects, and sets of three dimensional objects. (From Reese, 1971b, p. 4a.)

Then you can progress to naming objects, answering questions, telling stories about pictures, and on to conversation. Lovaas illustrates such a program in his film, *Behavior Modification*. Along with modeling, you can prompt the appropriate behavior. In the case of imitative speech, the teacher can say the first syllable of a word, or the first letter, and let the student fill in the rest. Suggestions or hints are other prompts useful in the early stages of learning.

The display board and the matching-to-sample task were new to the children in the number program. Since they had previously matched colored blocks and papers, we intro-

duced the board with cards of different colors. There were a few errors, but the children quickly mastered the task. We then had them match pictures of familiar objects. Only when they could handle familiar material in this new situation did we proceed to measure baseline with numerals and numbers of objects.

4. Program the Task and the Material

Generally, programming refers to a gradual progression from an easy or possible task to a more difficult one. Nearly all teaching is based on this principle, but three programming procedures are worth mentioning because they have often proved successful when ordinary teaching procedures have not. The three procedures are shaping, backwards chaining, and fading. Since we did not emphasize the first two in our number program, we will illustrate these procedures with material from other sources.

a. Shaping

When it comes to increasing a student's repertoire, shaping is one of the most useful procedures in the teacher's repertoire. Shaping has already been described in connection with Figure 2.4, the student being a pigeon who follows written instructions to peck a certain pattern or to turn a circle.[19] Given the physical and biological limitations on what an individual *can* do—and these limitations are sometimes exaggerated, simply because shaping has not been tried—we can develop behavior that seldom or never occurs by reinforcing increasingly closer approximations of that behavior. Strengthening even a distant approximation of the desired behavior increases the likelihood that a closer approximation will occur. If a pigeon's head is near a display bearing the letters PECK, he is more likely to make a pecking motion toward the display than if he is preening or pacing along the far wall of the apparatus. If we then reinforce a slight movement of the head toward the display, the bird will make more head movements, some of which will be closer to the display. The idea is to increase the frequency of behavior that makes it likely for the subject to emit other behavior that is even closer to the goal.

As new approximations are reached and reinforced, earlier ones are allowed to extinguish. Shaping "works" because behavior is variable. But if a given approximation is reinforced too often, we lose that variability. The behavior may become so firmly established that there is little chance for other, closer approximations to occur. On the other hand, if we progress too rapidly, demanding an approximation that is

not yet likely to occur, then the behavior we have already shaped is likely to extinguish. In that case, we have to backtrack to an earlier approximation and gradually work up again.

Skillful shaping consists of selecting the "right" behavior to reinforce and in knowing how often to reinforce each approximation. When a good approximation occurs, the reinforcer must be delivered immediately or other behavior will intervene—and then it will be the intervening behavior that is strengthened. When working with an animal that moves quickly, you can't wait for some activity to occur and then *decide* whether or not to reinforce it. There is no time for decisions. You have to *anticipate* the behavior if you are to reinforce it immediately. You must know your subjects very well to predict what they will do under various conditions. Timing the delivery of reinforcement may be even more important when one is dealing with pathological behavior. A good way to eliminate problem behavior is to shape alternative, incompatible behavior, but this requires careful timing. In serious cases of persistent self-injury or self-stimulation, the desired behavior may rarely occur. If we are slow in delivering the reinforcer, the problem behavior may well intervene, and we will find ourselves reinforcing the very behavior that we are trying to eliminate.

---

19. Although pigeons normally eat off the ground with a pecking motion, and although they sometimes turn circles while courting another pigeon, neither of these activities is quite like the behavior one sees in the laboratory. In the case of pecking a pattern on the wall of the apparatus, the difference is largely a matter of position: unlike woodpeckers, pigeons don't usually peck at a vertical surface, but they can easily be trained to do so. The turning behavior that is conditioned by reinforcing successive approximations of a turn appears to be quite different from anything one observes in a feral pigeon. Turning during courtship is usually accompanied by vocalizations and is interrupted by bowing movements, side steps, hesitations, tail drop, or running steps (depending on the variety of pigeon) none of which characterizes the rapid, smooth, uninterrupted turn of a pigeon in the usual laboratory demonstration.

Along with modeling, shaping plays an important part in the way normal children learn to talk. Although the student of a foreign language may have convictions to the contrary, Osgood (1953) has concluded that the human infant makes all of the vocal sounds that an adult produces, including those of foreign languages. But even in the babbling stage, the infant's vocal behavior is changing and becoming more like the language spoken by those around him, as certain sounds are reinforced while others extinguish. At first, parents are likely to reinforce rather distant approximations. For example, the sound "kuh," emitted in the kitchen at the right time of day, may produce a cookie as well as praise. Later, closer approximations will be required. The level of performance may be raised deliberately, as when the parent delays reinforcement by asking the child to repeat the request or tells the child to say "cookie" and then accepts "kuhkuh." Or, once the child begins to talk, the parents may not work so hard to find a semantic connection between the vocalizing and the environment, and so they simply may not understand the more distant approximations. As children speak to people other than their parents, still closer approximations to adult verbal behavior will be required before their requests and commands can be understood and reinforced. Later on, even though the meaning may be quite clear, "baby talk" will be extinguished if not punished.

b. Backwards chaining

Much of our behavior occurs in sequences that are chained in the sense that each activity functions as a discriminative stimulus for the next activity in the sequence. Closing the car door is usually a discriminative stimulus for fastening the seat belt, which is in turn a stimulus for putting the key in the ignition, checking the gear before turning the key, and so forth. To establish a chain of behavior, we often insert stimuli between the activities. These stimuli function as reinforcers for the behavior that precedes them and as discriminative stimuli for the behavior that follows. After a student driver had put the key in the ignition, for example, the instructor might say "Good! Now check the gear." Later, the student might say this subvocally, and still later the behavior itself might become the discriminative stimulus for the next link in the chain.

An example of chaining that has received nationwide publicity is the performance of a rat named Barnabus. Barnabus was trained by Rosemary Pierrel Sorrentino and Gil Sherman while they were at Barnard College and Columbia University (Pierrel & Sherman, 1963). Barnabus performs in a four-story "house." When he is placed on the first floor, a light goes on, the discriminative stimulus which initiates the following chain of events: he climbs a spiral staircase to a platform, pushes down a raised drawbridge and crosses to another platform, climbs a ladder, hauls in a car by pulling a chain hand over hand, pedals the car through a tunnel, climbs another flight of stairs, and runs through a tunnel to an elevator. At this point, he raises the Columbia banner over the elevator, which starts the elevator on its downward journey to the ground floor. A buzzer sounds, Barnabus departs the elevator and moves to a lever which he presses and receives a pellet of food. When the buzzer stops, he runs to the spiral staircase and makes another tour of his house, repeating the same sequence of events. Pierrel and Sherman and their students have trained several generations of Barnabi, and their feat has been widely applauded and replicated. Robert Karen (1974) has trained Rodent E. Lee in a similar chain, illustrated in Figure 3.17.

Barnabus and Rodent E. Lee started their careers by learning to press the lever that delivered food. The chain of behavior was trained by starting at the last step and then working backwards. For Barnabus, the buzzer was made a discriminative stimulus for lever pressing. The

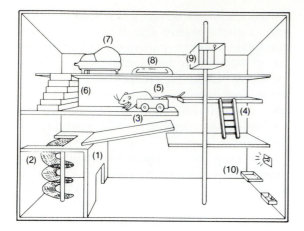

Figure 3.17.   The ten-link chain of behavior performed by Rodent E. Lee who (1) goes through a door, (2) runs up a spiral staircase, (3) continues across a drawbridge, (4) climbs a ladder, (5) drives a cable car, (6) climbs another staircase, (7) plays a toy piano, (8) crawls through a tunnel, (9) pulls a chain and rides an elevator down to the first floor, and (10) presses a lever and receives a pellet of food. (From Karen, 1974, p. 130.)

buzzer was also used as a conditioned reinforcer to shape the behavior of entering the elevator while it was on the ground floor. Entering the elevator produced the buzzer, which was also the discriminative stimulus for lever pressing, which was maintained by food. Next, Barnabus was placed in front of the elevator while it was on the top floor and trained to raise the Columbia banner. This action lowered the elevator to the ground floor—and the opportunity to press the lever and get food. The whole sequence was established by gradually adding new links to the front of the chain.

This procedure of backwards chaining has been very helpful in training self-maintenance skills in retarded individuals. For most of us, the sequence of activities involved in dressing or feeding ourselves has become so automatic that we are hard put just to name the steps. Take putting on a T-shirt for an example. What if we had to think about each step in turn; and what if we weren't very skillful and got stuck part way. It

could be very frightening to have your arms stuck part way into the sleeves, especially if your head were covered by the shirt and you couldn't see or breathe very well. By breaking down these complex tasks into small steps, and by starting at the end of the sequence, people like Luke Watson have been remarkably successful in teaching even profoundly retarded people to feed and dress themselves, to make their beds, and to play games (Watson, 1974). Some of the steps in putting on a pullover shirt are shown in Figure 3.18. Initially, the trainer puts the shirt over the retarded person's head and his arms through the sleeves. She then pulls the shirt part way down his chest so that the trainee has only to pull down the hem of the shirt to his waist (A). He completes this last step and is liberally rewarded. Soon he can pull the shirt down from the top of his chest when both arms are free. Later, he can pull down the hem while one elbow is still partly confined in the sleeve (B). At this stage, he pushes up with his right arm while he pulls down the shirt with his left. After he can put his right arm into the sleeve and complete the rest of the sequence, he is helped to put his left arm into the sleeve (C). By this time, he knows how to find the other sleeve and get his arm through it. Further back in the chain, he pulls the shirt down over his head after the trainer has put it in the right position (D). Then he learns to lift the shirt to his head (E), and finally to grasp it correctly so that he will be able to get it over his head in one easy motion. As he learns each step, he completes the rest of the sequence and is reinforced for doing so.

c. Fading

Fading is a means of helping individuals acquire discriminations that are otherwise difficult or impossible. As in shaping, you start with behavior easily available to the individual and then gradually change the contingencies of reinforcement. In shaping, the *behavioral requirement* is gradually changed. In fading, it is the

BACKWARDS CHAINING

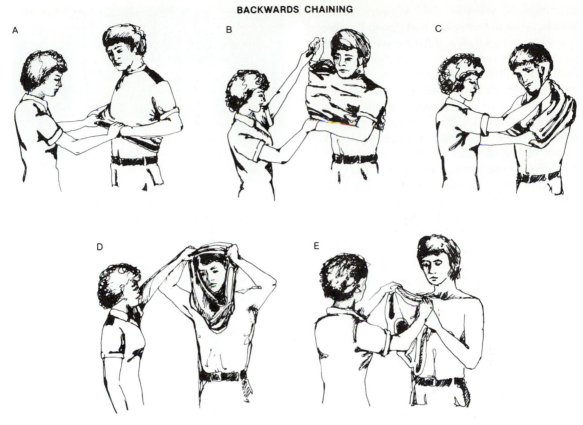

Figure 3.18. Backwards chaining to teach putting on a pullover shirt. A: Trainer puts shirt over client's head and puts his arms through sleeves; client has only to pull down hem of shirt. B: Trainer puts shirt over client's head, puts left arm completely through sleeve and starts the right arm; client will push right arm through sleeve and pull down hem of shirt. C: Trainer puts shirt over client's head and helps start left arm through sleeve; client will put other arm through sleeve and pull down hem. D: Trainer puts shirt in right position; client will pull shirt over head, put arms through sleeves, and pull down hem. E: Client grasps shirt before completing entire sequence. (From Watson, 1968, p. 19–20.)

stimulus context in which the behavior occurs that is changed. First, behavior is brought under the control of stimuli that are easy for the subject to discriminate. The pigeon in Figure 2.4 was first trained to peck the letters PECK printed in red, and to turn a circle when the letters TURN appeared in black. Such a color discrimination is easy for pigeons. Then control is gradually transferred to stimuli that are more difficult to discriminate. The pattern discrimination of letters is difficult for pigeons; but by gradually

darkening the letters PECK we were able to transfer the control of pecking and turning from the easy color discrimination to the far more difficult pattern discrimination.

When Terrace, in the early 1960s, first used fading to teach pigeons to peck a vertical line and not a horizontal one, and when they learned this discrimination *without making errors*, he precipitated something of a revolution in educational theory and practice. Theorists had held that errors are *necessary* for learning;

practitioners, whether they viewed errors as beneficial or detrimental, had generally agreed that they are inevitable. But there were Terrace's pigeons. And not only had they learned a discrimination that is normally very difficult for pigeons, they did not exhibit the emotional behavior that often accompanies errors and presumably interferes with learning. Furthermore, their performance remained impeccable, even under heavy dosages of drugs which greatly disrupted the performance of other birds trained by traditional procedures (Terrace, 1963a,b,c). Several studies with normal and retarded human subjects support Terrace's suggestions that high error rates are detrimental (Hively, 1962; Reese, Howard, & Rosenberger, 1977; Sidman & Stoddard, 1967; Stoddard & Sidman, 1967; Touchette, 1968). Generally, these studies have found that repeated errors impair retention and delay the acquisition of subsequent discriminations. A moderate number of errors, however, appears to favor retention and transfer to related tasks (Mosher & Reese, 1976).[20]

Our earlier success in teaching pigeons to "read" encouraged us to use fading procedures in the number program. Size fading was selected for the children, instead of color, largely because it was easier to make the stimulus materials. We also used a matching-to-sample task in which the learner selects from a number of alternatives the one that corresponds to, or matches, a particular sample. In the first fading program, the children selected from five sets of objects, the set that had the same number of objects as the sample. The objects in the correct choice were very large, the same size as those in the sample. The incorrect choices were very small for the first step of fading, but the objects were gradually increased in size as the program progressed. At the sixth and final step, all of the objects were the same size, and the correct choice had to be based on number. In the second task selected for fading, the children matched sets of two-dimensional

Figure 3.19.   Early step in fading program to teach number concepts. Correct choice in matching-to-sample task is large; incorrect choices are small and are gradually increased in size as program progresses.

objects to numerals, as shown in Figure 3.19. The figure shows the second fading step, where the objects on the incorrect cards were the next to smallest size.

d. Gradually raise the requirements

Programming includes a gradual raising of the requirements, as rapidly as progress permits. If a task that is too difficult promotes emotional behavior and inattention, a task that is too easy promotes boredom and inattention. If we are trying to develop competence in some area,

20. Fading procedures have proved useful in many areas of human performance. Fading has facilitated the acquisition of a variety of skills including handwriting (Skinner & Krakower, 1968), basic reading skills (Corey & Shamow, 1972; Hewett, 1964; McDowell, 1968; Mosher & Reese, 1976), number concepts (Reese & Werden, 1970; Suppes & Ginsberg, 1962), right-left position concepts (Jeffrey, 1958; Touchette, 1968), and form discrimination (Macht, 1971; Moore & Goldiamond, 1964; Sidman & Stoddard, 1967). Fading has also provided a means of assessing sensory capacities and psychophysical thresholds in profoundly retarded subjects (Macht, 1971; Reese et al., 1977; Stoddard & Sidman, 1967) and in subjects with known brain damage (Rosenberger, 1974) or suspected hearing loss (Bricker & Bricker, 1970; Meyerson & Michael, 1964).

failure to raise the requirements judiciously results in a loss of the individual's valuable time. A major advantage of personalized or self-paced instruction is that students may progress at their own pace. A common criterion for moving on to new material in a self-paced program is 90 percent mastery of the material. Mastery is usually measured by a test taken at the end of each unit. In programs where performance is monitored continuously, there is often a back-up procedure for errors. Such a provision prevents the student from getting ahead of competence; it is a sort of built-in mastery requirement.

Debbie's program included a back-up procedure for errors. Each fading step was presented for three trials before she moved to the next step—where the objects on the incorrect choice card would be slightly larger and more like the correct one. But if the child made more than one error, Debbie immediately backed up two fading steps to an easier discrimination. The rate of progress seems to have been about right because the children made few errors and they attended to the task 97 percent of the time.[21] In an academic program, there should also be periodic reviews of the material learned previously. In Debbie's program, the same back-up procedure used in training was used in review sessions.

A gradual change in the requirements, based on the level of success attained, also applies to programs designed to reduce problem behavior. If we want to reduce disruptive classroom behavior by reinforcing low rates of this behavior, and if the baseline rate is 10 instances per class period, we might allow the class a few minutes free time if no more than eight instances occur. When that criterion is sustained for several days, we might reduce it to six and gradually work down to whatever we consider an acceptable level. (See Dietz & Repp, 1973.) The changing-criterion design shown in Figure 3.14 is another example of programming a gradual reduction of problem behavior.

5. Evaluate

When continuous records are taken, it is possible to evaluate and revise a program while it is in progress. Debbie's program provided this sort of monitoring, and the back-up procedure for errors was a built-in evaluation and correction procedure. The matching-to-sample task had another convenient feature: if persistent errors occurred in the five-choice discrimination, we could reduce the number of alternatives presented on the display board.[22]

In approximately three and a half hours, spread over several weeks, all of the children learned to match two-dimensional sets containing as many as four objects. The second training program, in which they matched sets of objects to numerals, required only two hours.

The real effectiveness of the program was evaluated when Debbie repeated the baseline tasks with no fading. Working with the same number over and over again, while a size difference is gradually faded out, is very different from choosing among objects that are all the same size the first time you see a particular number. We could not be sure that we had succeeded in teaching number skills until the children could pass the baseline tasks without the fading program. And, of course, we wanted to see if training would transfer to the other tasks.

Betsy was available during the summer and received more training than the other children:

21. This figure is based on duration recording by a single independent observer; interobserver agreement was not computed.

22. This happened with one child who early in the program began to select any card with a yellow object on it. The simplest solution seemed to be to remove all the cards with yellow objects and to put only the correct choice on the display board. Under these conditions, she had to find a token beneath a card that did *not* contain a yellow object, and fortunately she did not shift to another color. Debbie gradually added cards to the display board, working back to five alternatives at fading step 1. The child continued to select the correct choice, so the program was resumed.

a total of eight hours. Whereas the others reached only four objects, Betsy continued the first program (where the sample was a set of two-dimensional objects) through eight objects and the second program (where the sample was a numeral) through six objects. Her data are compared to her baseline performance in Figure 3.20. Initially, she could count three objects if only three were given her. After the program she could count eight. Initially, she could count only two objects from a collection of 30; with no training on this most difficult of the tasks, her performance improved to five. Both before and after the program she could match the numerals from 1 to 10. Initially, she could identify the numerals 1 and 2 and 7 to 10 if she were asked

to point to them. After the program the gaps were filled in. On all matching tasks involving actual numbers of objects, Betsy's baseline limit was two. After the program, she reached seven on all but one task: when both the sample and the comparison objects were 3-dimensional junk objects, she could match as many as six.

6. Maintenance and Generalization (Transfer)

A full year later, all of the children were performing well beyond the level they had achieved at the end of the program, and their abilities with numbers extended beyond those skills we had helped them acquire. Some were using regular

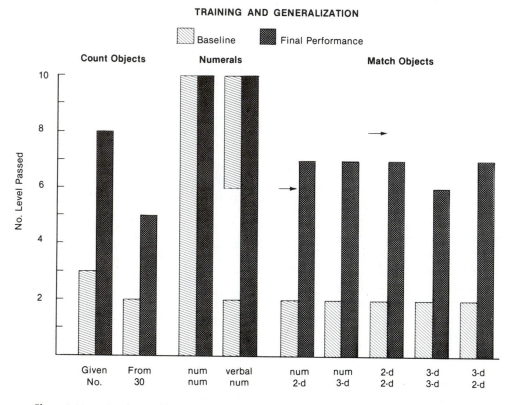

Figure 3.20.   Baseline and final performance of one subject (Betsy) following approximately eight hours of training on both programs. Arrows indicate that training continued through eight objects in first program and through six objects in second program. (From Reese, 1971b, p. 10b.)

school workbooks, and four of the five knew all of the numerals through 29. Most could tell time on the hour, and some could exchange five pennies for a nickel. The main reason that the gains were maintained in the regular classroom is that the teacher was interested in the training program and was part of it from the start. Not all programs—and students—fare so well.

Children who have developed academic skills and appropriate classroom behavior in a highly structured program do not *necessarily* maintain these gains when they enter a different classroom the next year; and retarded children who have learned self-maintenance skills in an institutional setting do not *necessarily* continue to care for themselves when they return home. The maintenance of gains after a program has been terminated, and the generalization or transfer of these gains to other settings are two of the most important responsibilities a program designer must assume. No matter how carefully a program is conceived and conducted, we have done little more than demonstrate the potential of the procedures until we can insure that the progress will be maintained when the program is terminated. Unless the program designer plans for maintenance and generalization to natural settings, the change in behavior may constitute but a brief reprieve for the individual and other concerned parties.

Until the 1970s, if we can judge by published reports, most people conducting applied behavior analysis concentrated on developing effective procedures to handle a variety of problems in a variety of settings. They also devoted considerable time and energy to developing and implementing experimental designs to evaluate the effectiveness of the procedures. Then, more often than not, the program or experiment was concluded, and follow-up data were seldom collected or reported. (See Keeley, Shemberg, & Carbonnell, 1976 for the data on the lack of follow-up data.) There are, of course, exceptions: several of the studies described in this book have reported long-term gains; and most of the work being done in private practice, where follow-up assessment is presumably routine, seldom sees the light of print. Nonetheless, we cannot simply assume that therapeutic gains achieved by dint of careful programming will be maintained in the natural environment when a program is terminated. On the contrary, the evidence from token-economy programs indicates that unless special measures are taken, these gains are likely to be lost (Kazdin & Bootzin, 1972; O'Leary & Drabman, 1971). As Baer et al. (1968, p. 97) have noted "generalization should be programmed, rather than expected or lamented."

There are several reasons why maintenance and generalization require special attention. For one, we generally pay more attention to behavior that is annoying, disruptive, or dangerous than we do to appropriate behavior. When a program succeeds, we are "left with" appropriate behavior—the sort we are long accustomed to ignore. If the important people in the client's environment do, in fact, ignore the gains, then it stands to reason the behavior will extinguish.

Another reason is that even people who are labeled retarded or psychotic seem to be awfully good at discriminating the conditions of reinforcement and punishment. They discriminate both the individuals who administer these consequences and the settings in which they are administered. Accordingly, they behave appropriately in these situations but not in others.

A third reason is that many programs employ reinforcers or punishers that differ from the naturally occurring consequences of appropriate behavior. In a token economy, for example, tokens may be earned for cooperative social interactions, performance on academic tasks, and a part-time job. When the individual leaves the program, and perhaps the institution, the consequences of appropriate social interactions will probably be nil (but inappropriate behavior may be punished); the consequences of academic achievement will be grades and perhaps praise; and the consequences of work will be money. To plan for maintenance and generalization, we must examine the current setting, discriminative stimuli, and consequences, and compare them with the setting, discriminative stimuli, and consequences that will be in effect when the program is terminated. Given this information, several steps can facilitate the maintenance of progress in the natural environment. Some have been mentioned already. But this is such a critical area, and such an important part of therapist accountability as defined in Chapter 8, that they bear repeating.

a. Incorporate natural settings

Obviously the best way to eliminate the problem of generalization *to* the natural environment is to conduct the program *in* the natural environment. This, of course, is one of the main advantages of training parents and teachers in the use of behavioral procedures, and it is the defining characteristic of *in vivo* desensitization (Chapter 6). But even when professional therapists are needed to carry out operant procedures, therapy can sometimes begin in the natural environment. This was the course taken by Ayllon and Skuban (1973) who managed to prepare the intractable Mike for admission to school (see Table 3.12 and accompanying text). Therapy was conducted in restaurants, shopping centers, the zoo, and in the homes of friends—the very settings where Mike's temper tantrums had created such a problem.

If remedial education and therapy do not start in the natural environment, they should at least end there. A program to teach retarded students to read restaurant menus ended in a restaurant where the students successfully read and ordered such items as hamburgers, barbecue, french fries, and chocolate milkshakes (Brown, Van Deventer, Johnson, & Sontag, 1974). Even when a program is conducted in a clinic or institutional setting, aspects of the natural environment should be incorporated whenever possible. This prescription extends from the selection of goals and reinforcers to the settings where treatment takes place; and it includes the training of staff members, parents, teachers, and peers so that they can carry out the program.

b. Select goals that will be supported by the community

The selection of goals should be based on Ayllon and Azrin's (1968) relevance rule—that we teach only those classes of behavior that will continue to be reinforced when the program is terminated. Burchard's program to teach vocational and community survival skills, such as the use of telephone and public transportation and the handling of money, is an excellent example. (See above, under token ecomonies.) Unfortunately, the selection of useful and appropriate goals is no guarantee that the behavior *will* be reinforced when a program is terminated. As noted above, we generally tend to ignore appropriate behavior, as though we expected it to be self-sustaining. Nonetheless, certain social, vocational, and academic skills are prerequisites for employment and many forms of recreation.

c. Incorporate naturally occurring reinforcers

Nearly all programs pair praise with tokens, candy, or the opportunity to engage in reinforcing activities. In addition to social reinforcers, many programs can incorporate reinforcers or punishers common in the setting to which the individual will return. In the home setting, common reinforcers include privileges, allowance, the opportunity to stay up late or watch television. Procedures to reduce problem behavior may include the withholding of these reinforcing events and social disapproval. Classroom reinforcers also include privileges and the opportunity to engage in reinforcing activities as well as grades and other commendations for academic progress. The most obvious reinforcer in a job setting is money, but an examination of union contract negotiations would reveal that many other conditions and benefits are important. A token economy has a good deal in common with other economic marketplaces, but tokens are more likely to be contingent upon actual performance than is salary. In some institutions, tokens may be exchanged for money when the resident goes home for a weekend; and the transfer from tokens to money continues when the resident assumes a part-time job, often in a sheltered workshop.

d. Decrease the density of reinforcement and increase the delay

The light usually comes on as soon as we flip the switch, and the car usually starts when we turn the key in the ignition. But reinforcement is seldom continuous or immediate when the behavior has required a program such as those described in this chapter. A gradual transition from continuous to intermittent reinforcement is one good way to prepare individuals for reentry into the natural environment. This was the procedure recommended by Skinner in *Walden Two* so that the children might "build tolerance for discouraging events."

Kazdin and Polster (1973) used token reinforcement to increase verbal interactions between two "social isolates" and their peers in a sheltered workshop for the mentally retarded. The subjects could earn tokens by conversing with other peers during three daily "breaks." Simple questions and answers wouldn't do. The speakers had to exchange informative statements about the weather, sports, news, or whatever; and only statements that produced a verbal response qualified for reinforcement. Initially, each conversation earned praise and a token, and the frequency of verbal interactions rapidly increased (Figure 3.21). During the subsequent reversal phase, these social interactions were essentially eliminated. Even though praise was continued, the frequency was lower than during baseline, which shows the dangers inherent in the abrupt termination of a program. During the next five weeks, token reinforcement was reintroduced. One subject (S₁) again received continuous reinforcement. For the other (S₂), the density of reinforcement was gradually "thinned" until he received tokens following only one of the three daily work breaks. He was not told which work break had been selected for reinforcement. This subject probably earned one-third the number of tokens earned by S₁, but the frequency of his verbal interactions was nearly as high. More important, when reinforcement was again discontinued during the last five weeks of the study, this subject's social interactions were maintained in strength, while those of S₁ rapidly extinguished.

The transition from continuous to intermittent reinforcement should be made slowly and carefully, and the behavior should be closely monitored. (Steeves, Martin, and Pear (1970) report an increase in tantrums with an increase in ratio size.) But the transition is worth making:

A dedicated person is one who remains active for long periods of time without reinforcement. He does so because, either in the hands of a skillful teacher or by accident, he has been exposed to a gradually lengthening variable-ratio schedule.

(Skinner, 1968, p. 165.)

The other procedure for attenuating reinforcement so that it more closely approximates the occurrence in the natural environment is to increase the delay between the delivery of a reinforcer and the behavior it maintains. The exchange of tokens, for example, can be gradually delayed for some minutes, then hours, then days. This procedure has successfully maintained a high rate of studying in the classroom of a state institution (Cotler, Applegate, King, & Kristal, 1972) and a low rate of inappropriate motor behavior among retarded children (Jones & Kazdin, 1975). Stumphauzer (1972) in-

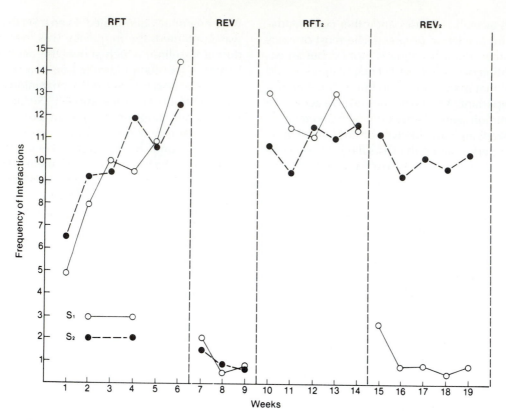

Figure 3.21. The effects of intermittent reinforcement upon the maintenance of behavior. The social behavior of one subject (S₂, solid circles) was intermittently reinforced during the second reinforcement phase (RFT₂) and was maintained after tokens were discontinued during the second reversal phase (REV₂). The social behavior of the other subject (S₁, open circles) was maintained by continuous reinforcement during both reinforcement phases and extinguished when tokens were withdrawn during the second reversal phase. (From Kazdin & Polster, 1973, p. 389.)

creased "delay of gratification" in young prisoners through imitation of peer models who chose a delayed reward over a smaller, immediate reward.

e. Extend contingencies to new settings and individuals

As noted above, clients sometimes discriminate the conditions of reinforcement or punishment. When they do, the effects of a program may be restricted to a limited number of settings and to the presence of a limited number of people. In a well-designed study with severely retarded boys

(Redd & Birnbrauer, 1969) one adult consistently reinforced cooperative play with food and praise while another adult consistently delivered these same events independent of the children's behavior. The adult who delivered reinforcers contingent on play soon became a discriminative stimulus for play, which commenced as soon as she entered the room and ceased when she left. The presence of the other adult had no effect on this behavior. The findings were replicated when the role of the adults was reversed.

Examples of the lack of generalization following punishment are described in Chapter 5. Lovaas and Simmons (1969) suppressed self-injurious behavior by extinction (Figure 5.12) and by punishment (Figure 5.13), but the effects were restricted to the setting and to the presence of the adult who administered punishment. The evidence from this and other studies suggests that generalization is greatly facilitated when at least two different people deliver the reinforcing or punishing consequences in at least three different settings (Birnbrauer, 1968; Bucher & King, 1971; Corte, Wolf, & Locke, 1971; Koegel & Rincover, 1974; Lovaas & Simmons, 1969; Redd & Birnbrauer, 1969; Stokes, Baer, & Jackson, 1974).

f. Train parents, teachers, peers in the use of behavioral procedures

This is far easier said than done. Skills in implementing behavioral procedures are not acquired overnight—or at a weekend workshop. (Yen and McIntire (1976) describe training programs for several populations.) A program can be designed with the help of the important people in the individual's environment, and in several cases the program has actually been carried out by nonprofessionals with the psychologist serving as a consultant. But when the program has been conducted in a different setting or by different personnel, the gains will generally be lost unless relatives or other relevant people are trained in the use of behavioral procedures. This is apparent from the follow-up data of Lovaas and his colleagues who have made dramatic gains with autistic children (Lovaas, Koegel, Simmons, & Long, 1973). One to four years after treatment was concluded, those children who had been returned to parents trained in the use of behavioral procedures had maintained their gains or improved still further. Those children who had been moved to institutions had lost most of the ground they had gained.

In comparing three procedures to facilitate generalization from a token economy to a regular classroom, Walker and Buckley (1972) had better results from training the children's peers than from training their teachers! When the children entered the regular classroom, they could earn points for appropriate academic and social behavior and exchange these points for a reinforcing activity for the entire class. One teacher made the earning of these points so aversive that the child asked her to stop giving them out.

g. Program reentry into the community

When individuals have been confined to an institution, halfway houses and sheltered workshops provide a setting in which they can gradually be reintroduced to the contingencies that control behavior in the natural environment. Leaving the institution for a few hours a day to work at a part-time job serves a similar purpose. Before these moves are made, the contingencies that apply to a highly structured program may be gradually reduced as the individuals are able to assume more control over their behavior (Kazdin, 1975a). And this brings us to the final suggestion for programming generalization: self-management.

h. Self-management

It seems likely that maintenance and generalization are probably positively related to the degree of self-management an individual exercises. Even though there is presently little research to support this supposition (Jeffrey, 1974; Kazdin, 1975a), most clinicians would urge that control be transferred to the client as rapidly and as fully as possible. Procedures for managing our own behavior are described in some detail in Chapter 7. While not all of these procedures can be undertaken by all clients, most people—given guidance and support—can assume some degree of control.

Self-instruction is one place to start. Meichenbaum reports good results from training normal and "impulsive" children and schizophrenic patients to verbalize the instructions for various tasks or for coping with difficult situations. Initially, the clients state the instructions out loud; later they verbalize them to themselves (Meichenbaum & Cameron, 1973, 1974; Meichenbaum & Goodman, 1971). Clients, including children, can also set the conditions for reinforcement, examine their own behavior, and determine the amount of reinforcement they have earned (e.g., Felixbrod & O'Leary, 1973; Kaufman & O'Leary, 1972; Lovitt & Curtiss, 1969). In the continuing saga of Achievement Place, delinquent and predelinquent boys assume increasingly more control over their behavior with respect to both school work and home life. (For a brief summary of this highly successful program by its designers, see Fixsen et al., 1976. Figure 3.8 is taken from this article.)

7. Follow-Up

Some behavioral programs are designed to help people acquire rather specific skills, e.g., competence in some social, academic, athletic, artistic, or occupational area. Once acquired, the skill—public speaking, playing a violin, reading a foreign language, or operating a milling machine—is part of the learner's repertoire, and is likely to be maintained by economic, social, or intrinsic reinforcing consequences. Little effort is made to determine how often people subsequently engage in these activities[23]— probably because it is assumed that, should the need arise, the performance will be forthcoming. If the skills are indeed useful, the learner will most likely keep "in practice." If they are not useful, or productive of reinforcers, presumably no great harm will come to the individual or to society if the behavior occurs infrequently or if the initial level of competence is not maintained.

On the other hand, a great many programs—particularly, but not exclusively, those designed to resolve problem behavior—*must* be evaluated in terms of the client's behavior after the program is over. One can "dry out" an alcoholic, and it's not all that difficult to lose ten pounds or to stop smoking. ("It's easy to quit smoking; I've done it a hundred times.") It is the *maintenance* of behavior change that is the true test of a program. This, of course, is why we have emphasized the importance of programming transfer from the clinical setting to the natural environment. And this is why we must continue to monitor the client's progress after a program has terminated. It is not solely a matter of scientific procedure, it is an ethical matter as well. In keeping with our definition of accountability (Chapter 8), we look forward to the day when therapeutic contracts will contain a provision for follow-up measures. Perhaps part of the therapist's fee will depend upon successful outcome at stated follow-up intervals.

a. Duration of follow-up

Sometimes follow-up data should be taken at a particular time or occasion. If students have participated in a program for test anxiety at the beginning of a semester, one would certainly want to assess their performance during final exams. If a child has been taken from the regular classroom to participate in a special program, one would assess the degree to which improvement transfers to the regular classroom; it would also be sound practice to monitor the child's progress in a new classroom at the start of the following year.

---

23. As noted above, it would be extremely useful to have this information, particularly when it comes to designing school curricula. Before deciding whether or not schools should *require* physics, algebra, or Latin, for example, we need to know how often adults actually engage in these activities and for which professions or vocations they are prerequisite skills. (See Selection of Goals, and Hawkins, 1975) Eventually, perhaps, all educational programs will be evaluated in terms of the learner's *postgraduate* performance, and the data will be used to determine both the usefulness of particular goals and the adequacy of instruction.

In other cases, there is no specific occasion on which to assess the outcome of treatment: the gains could be lost at any time. In such cases the duration of the follow-up period depends on the nature of the problem and the procedures employed. Probably the longer the duration the better, particularly when evaluating a new program of treatment. Beyond determining the extent to which therapeutic gains are maintained, we must look for possible adverse side effects of treatment. In some areas, such as the major psychoses and criminal and drug rehabilitation, government statistics on recidivism rates can serve as guidelines. If the usual treatment is successful for six months, but a high proportion of the clients have relapsed by the end of a year, then obviously the follow-up evaluation of a new program should continue for at least one year and preferably eighteen months.

Hunt collected data from 87 studies on the relapse rate following various treatments for cigarette smoking (Hunt, Barnett, & Branch, 1971). As shown in Figure 3.22, only 35 percent of the subjects abstained for three months; and within six months, this figure dropped to 24 percent. There was little further change between six months and a year. The data from three studies of heroin addiction are practically identical, and the data from one alcohol study follow the same trend. The rapid drop in these curves shows that, following these particular programs, most relapses have occurred within three to six months. If a new treatment showed a high percentage of abstainers at three months, this would be very encouraging. Even so, the outcome of treatment should be monitored for six months to a year.

The outcome of programs to lose weight seems to follow a different course. Hall and Hall (1974) reviewed 19 experimental studies, as well as 14 case studies, which employed various behavioral procedures in the treatment of obesity. Most of the programs were successful in that the subjects had lost significantly more

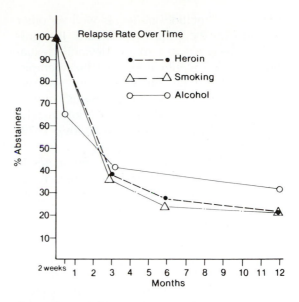

Figure 3.22.   Relapse rate over time for heroin, smoking, and alcohol. (From Hunt, Barnett, & Branch, 1971, p. 456.)

weight at the end of treatment than had the control subjects. Conclusions about long-term success, however, depended on the length of the follow-up period. For most studies in which the follow-up period was three months or less, the experimental subjects continued to weigh less than their controls; but for most studies with longer follow-up periods, the differences were no longer significant. Weight-control programs, like smoking programs, probably require long follow-up periods even in the face of encouraging short-term results.

b. Follow-up measures
Generally, one collects data on the same classes of behavior monitored during treatment. Additional measures of collateral behavior can also be informative. If a program centers on the reduction of disruptive classroom behavior, it will probably include differential reinforcement of academic work. Even if not, we would want to assess the effects of the program on general classroom performance, so follow-up data

could easily include grades as well as other measures on the child's report card. If a program is designed to reduce "deviant" sexual behavior, one would hope that the therapist would incorporate procedures to increase "normal" sexual behavior and would collect follow-up data in both areas. (Unfortunately, this is not always the case. See Barlow, 1973, for a review.)

Especially when a program terminates in release from a hospital or prison, therapeutic outcome may be evaluated by a broad range of measures that, taken together, indicate how well the individual is functioning. The data are usually gathered from collateral sources and relate to general health, family relations, and employment status as well as to parole violations or rehospitalization. These are the sorts of measures psychotherapists have been using for years. Their use in a behavioral program is exemplified in the work of Mark and Linda Sobell who have developed an unusually comprehensive program for the treatment of alcoholism.

c. Long-term evaluation of a program for alcoholics

In treating alcoholism—one of society's most pervasive problems—the Sobells have designed a group program incorporating individualized therapy and training in self-management skills (Sobell & Sobell, 1972a, 1973a,b,c). Each client's drinking behavior is analyzed, and a repertoire of alternative behavior is developed for situations that foster excessive drinking. Extensive data have been collected throughout a two-year period following treatment.

i. Rationale. There is a prevalent belief that alcoholism is a progressive disease for which total abstinence is the only cure. While abstinence may well be the best solution for many people, uncritical acceptance of the disease model can create problems. The belief that excessive drinking (as opposed to its physiolog-

ical effects) is a disease may allow some people to disavow responsibility for their behavior: one drink, and they are inevitably doomed to relapse. Perhaps more important, the Sobells (1973a) suggest that some alcoholics may refuse help because they fear being "condemned to abstinence for life." They cite a good deal of evidence that at least some alcoholics can learn how to control their drinking, and suggest that in some cases controlled drinking may be a more practical goal than abstinence (Mills, Sobell, & Schaefer, 1971; Sobell & Sobell, 1973a). Their program includes both treatment goals, the choice depending on the particular individual and the environment to which he will return.

ii. Patient characteristics and selection of goals. Seventy male alcoholics at the Patton (California) State Hospital[24] volunteered to serve as subjects in a program of research on alcoholism. Although baseline data are not presented, all of the patients had experienced such withdrawal symptoms as tremors, convulsions, blackouts, and hallucinations, and all had damaged their health, finances, and social standing as a result of drinking. They were approximately 40 years old, with a long history of problem drinking and several prior arrests and hospitalizations for alcoholism.

After medical and psychiatric examination, each patient was assigned to one of two treatment groups: nondrinking or controlled drinking. Patients who requested abstinence or who lacked outside social support for controlled drinking were assigned to the nondrinking group. Those who requested the controlled drinking program were placed in that group if they had outside support for controlled drinking and had practiced controlled drinking in the past. Forty patients were assigned to the controlled-drinking program and 30 to the ab-

24. The Sobells are now at Vanderbilt University, Nashville, Tennessee.

stinence program. Each group was then sub-divided: the patients were randomly assigned either to a control group that received conventional hospital therapy or to an experimental group that received 17 behavioral treatment sessions in addition to the conventional treatment. Note that patients in the control group were not simply left to shift for themselves. They were given the best available treatment, which included group therapy, drug, physiotherapy, industrial therapy, and Alcoholics Anonymous meetings.

iii. Treatment setting. At every stage of treatment, the Sobells incorporated procedures to facilitate transfer from the hospital setting to the patient's natural environment. Treatment was conducted in a situation closely resembling the setting in which the patient normally drank excessively. For those who customarily drank at home, there was a simulated home environment, completely and comfortably furnished. For those who customarily drank away from home, there was a simulated cocktail lounge with a mahogany-finished bar and a full-length mirrored display of bottles. A great variety of confiscated alcoholic drinks was available, and the bartender was a professional who, as a patient, had volunteered his services (Schaefer, Sobell, & Mills, 1971). Alcoholic beverages included straight and mixed drinks, beer, and wine. Soft drinks were also available.

iv. Individualized therapy and training in self-management. Even though the experimental design called for groups of subjects, the program included individualized training in self-management—another way to facilitate transfer from the therapeutic setting. Throughout treatment, the patients and staff were trained to identify and analyze the situations in which excessive drinking was likely to occur. When these antecedent conditions—such as losing an argument, working overtime, paying bills, see-

ing a particular friend—were identified, the patient worked out for each situation a large number of possible alternatives to drinking. The alternatives were then discussed with respect to probable long- and short-term consequences; and those that seemed most effective and constructive were practiced under simulated conditions.

A cumulative file of antecedent conditions and alternatives to heavy drinking was kept for each patient, and situations were devised so that the patient could experiment with and practice the various alternatives. In addition, all patients were trained to resist social pressures, and they acquired a repertoire for refusing alcoholic beverages. Another feature of the educational program was the playing of videotapes taken during the first two sessions, when the patient was allowed to get drunk, and later when he was sober. The early tapes demonstrated the patient's deficient responses to situations while the latter tape demonstrated his progress.

v. Punishment of inappropriate drinking and shaping of alternative behavior. There were seventeen sessions in the simulated bar or home environment, whichever more closely resembled the patient's usual drinking environment. During most of these sessions, inappropriate drinking was punished by electric shock delivered to the nondominant hand on a low variable ratio schedule. (All patients were fully informed about the purpose and rationale of the program and told when the various shock contingencies would apply.)

Patients in the nondrinking group might receive a one-second shock when they ordered an alcoholic drink. The drink was then served and could be consumed, but continuous shock was given from the time a patient touched the glass until he released it. He could thus escape continuous shock by putting down the glass, or he could avoid shock altogether by refraining from ordering alcohol. When a patient in the nondrinking group ordered no drinks for two consecutive sessions, he was offered a free drink (no shock) at the beginning of the next session. If he consumed this drink, shock contingencies were reinstated. If he refused the drink, he had to pour it down the sink. This procedure continued at 15-minute intervals throughout the 90-minute session.

Punishment contingencies for subjects in the controlled drinking group were more elaborate. The following activities produced a one-second shock on a VR 2 schedule: (1) ordering a straight drink; (2) taking a sip that was larger than one-sixth of a mixed drink or one-twelfth of a beer (the glasses were demarcated); (3) ordering a drink within twenty minutes of ordering a previous drink; (4) ordering more than a total of three drinks. After three drinks at any one session, these patients were placed on the same shock contingencies as patients in the nondrinking group. The controlled drinkers could thus avoid shock by sipping (as opposed to gulping) a mixed (as opposed to straight) drink, so long as they did not exceed the limit of three drinks and so long as the drinks were spaced at least twenty minutes apart. This program accomplished two things: inappropriate drinking was suppressed by punishment, while appropriate drinking —and self control—were established and maintained by the avoidance contingencies. The bartender and other people in the lounge gradually increased the social pressure with phrases such as "Oh come on, one more won't hurt you"—another example of programming transfer from the hospital. Three probe sessions without shock were scheduled during treatment. Even though the patients knew that they would not be shocked, the average number of drinks consumed during these probe sessions was *less than* three. Fewer than half of the subjects emitted any inappropriate drinking behavior during any probe session. (For further details on the program, see Sobell and Sobell, 1973a, or write for their 1972 monograph.)

vi. Outcome of treatment. The follow-up data do not assess the effectiveness of the separate components of the different treatment programs. That will have to come later. The data do, however, provide extensive information on the success of the total program during a two-year period following treatment.

Following discharge from the hospital, information was gathered every *three to four weeks* from the patients and from their collateral sources, which included friends, relatives, employers, and public and private agencies (e.g., telephone companies, credit bureaus, welfare departments, municipal courts, the California Department of Human Resources Development). One control subject died and another could not be located; but all experimental subjects were followed for at least a year, to places as distant as Hawaii, the Canary Islands, Italy, and Spain. Even at the end of two years, only five of the original seventy subjects could not be located. Missing were one subject from each of the experimental groups and three control subjects from the controlled-drinking group. An average of four to five collaterals was interviewed for each subject. Criminal records and driver's records were obtained every two months; and incarcerations in a jail or hospital were checked to determine whether or not the incarceration involved drinking.

Repeated measures were thus obtained for drinking behavior and for vocational and residential status, interpersonal relations, driving records, confinement in jail or hospitals, and the use of outpatient therapeutic support (Alcoholics Anonymous, outpatient counseling, etc.). Because of the frequent contacts with patients and their collaterals, an estimate of *daily* drinking behavior was possible. The drinking data are presented in five categories: drunk days, controlled drinking days, abstinent days, and days incarcerated in jail or hospital in relation to drinking.

A good measure of the program's success is

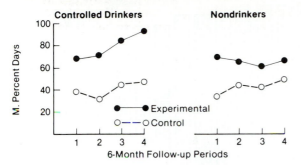

Figure 3.23. Percentage of days subjects "functioned well" (abstinent or controlled drinking; not incarcerated) throughout successive six-month follow-up periods. Left: Subjects from controlled drinking program and their controls; Right: Subjects from nondrinking program and their controls. (Data plotted from tables in Sobell & Sobell, 1973a, 1973b.)

the number of days the former patients were abstinent or controlled drinkers. Taken together, these categories indicate the percentage of days the subjects were "functioning well."

From the tables in Sobell and Sobell (1973 a,b) we have plotted the percentage of days the subjects were "functioning well" throughout each of the four six-month periods for which follow-up data are now available. These data are shown in Figure 3.23 for experimental and control subjects in the controlled drinking program and the nondrinking program. Throughout the two-year period, the patients in both experimental programs fared better than their controls who had received conventional treatment. Patients in the controlled drinking program fared best of all and improved over time. As a group, they practiced abstinence or controlled drinking (and were not incarcerated) during 92 percent of the days of the last six-month period. The differences between the controlled drinking subjects and their controls are significant (p < .005) for each six-month period and for each of the two years. The differences between the nondrinking subjects and their controls are significant for the first year (p < .005); the

second year these differences are less reliable (p > .05, < .10).

The pattern of drinking of the controlled drinking subjects changed over time. Figure 3.24 (also plotted from the Sobells's data) shows that the improvement is due to an increase in the number of abstinent days and a decrease in the number of drunk days. The number of days they practiced controlled drinking remains fairly constant at approximately 25 percent. Individual data for subjects in the controlled drinking program and their controls during the last six months are shown in Figure 3.25. Of the 20 subjects in the controlled drinking program, seventeen functioned well most of the time. The same can be said for only four of the 20 comparison subjects.

The other follow-up measures generally support the data on drinking disposition. For example, "total functioning" (an evaluation made by the collateral source who had the most extensive contact with the former patient) was rated significantly more improved for subjects in both experimental programs than for their respective controls during the first year.

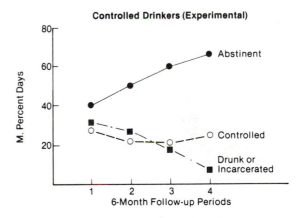

Figure 3.24. Percentage of days subjects from controlled drinking program were abstinent (closed circles), engaged in controlled drinking (open circles), or were drunk or incarcerated (squares) throughout successive six-month follow-up periods. (Data plotted from tables in Sobell & Sobell, 1973a, 1973b.)

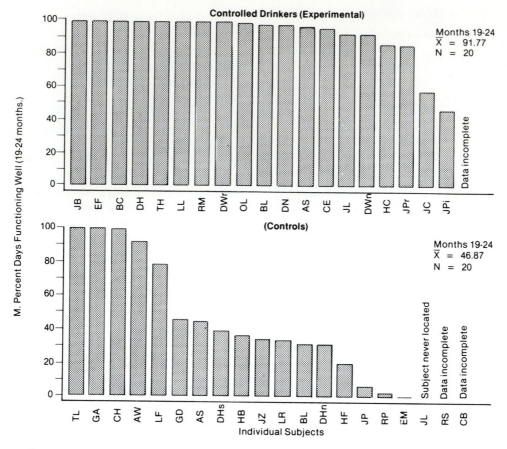

Figure 3.25.   Percentage of days subjects "functioned well" (i.e., abstinent or controlled drinking; not incarcerated) during last six months of two-year followup. (From Sobell & Sobell, 1973b, p. HO 4.)

This difference remained significant during the second year only for those who had been in the controlled drinking program. Likewise, at the end of the second year, vocational and occupational status were significantly higher for controlled drinking subjects than their controls; but not for nondrinking subjects compared to their controls.

The results are indeed promising and "economical" when one considers that therapy required only seventeen sessions. The extent to which the results are effected by frequent contacts during the follow-up period is not known, but such contacts are undoubtedly helpful. Even though they may confound the data (for controls as well as experimental subjects), they could —as the Sobells suggest—be incorporated into a therapeutic maintenance program.

4

Operant Procedures for Changing Behavior — I

A. Procedures that either Increase or Decrease the Strength of Behavior
   1. Self-recording
   2. Modeling
   3. Modifying the environment
   4. Biofeedback
B. Procedures that Increase, Maintain, or Extend Behavior
   1. Reinforcement
     a. Contingency
     b. Immediacy
     c. Amount
     d. Consistency
     e. Schedules of reinforcement

      i. Continuous reinforcement
     ii. Ratio schedules
    iii. Interval schedules
    iv. Differential reinforcement of rate
     v. Extinction following various schedules of reinforcement
    vi. Summary
   2. Escape conditioning (Negative reinforcement)
   3. Avoidance
   4. Recovery

Table 4.1 lists the major operant procedures used in applied behavior analysis. This list does not include respondent procedures, which are described in Chapter 6, nor does it include drug therapy or surgical interventions, which are not behavioral procedures.

The procedures at the top of the table are often used in conjunction with other procedures. Depending on the circumstances, they can either increase or decrease the frequency or duration of behavior. Self-recording and biofeedback provide information that can itself be reinforcing or punishing and can enhance the effectiveness of other procedures. Modeling and modifying the environment relate to the stimulus control of behavior.

The procedures at the left of the table may be used to increase the frequency or duration of behavior, to maintain behavior at a desired level, or to extend its occurrence to different situations. The procedures at the center may be used to restrict the occurrence of behavior to specified situations or to reduce its frequency or duration. These *reductive* procedures are described in Chapter 5. The covert procedures at the right of the table are described in Chapter 7 where we discuss self-management. (Covert respondent procedures are described in Chapter 6.)

In most practical situations, particularly those involving self-management, one would employ a combination of procedures. One might also combine operant and respondent procedures in what Lazarus (1967) calls "technical eclecticism" and Franks (1969) calls the "total behavioral approach." The fact that the

Table 4.1   **Operant procedures and their effects upon behavior.**

OPERANT PROCEDURES

Procedures that INCREASE or DECREASE Behavior
- Self-recording
- Modeling
- Modifying Environment
- Biofeedback

Procedures that INCREASE, MAINTAIN, or EXTEND behavior
- Reinforcement
- Escape
- Avoidance
- Recovery

Procedures that RESTRICT, REDUCE, or ELIMINATE behavior (Ch. 5)
- Extinction
- Satiation
- Response Cost
- Time Out
- Restraint
- Reinforced Omission (OT, DRO)
- Reinforced Alternative (Alt R)
- Reinforced Low Rate (DRL)
- Punishment

COVERT operant Procedures (Ch. 7) (increase or decrease)
- Covert Reinforcement
- Covert Punishment
- Covert Extinction
- Covert Satiation
- Covert Escape
- Thought Stopping

procedures are described separately is in no way a suggestion that they must be applied separately.

A. Procedures that either Increase or Decrease the Strength of Behavior

1. Self-recording

A distinguishing feature of behavior analysis is the emphasis on data collection. In most published research, the data are collected by someone other than the individual whose behavior is being measured: usually a parent, teacher, or friend. But it is becoming increasingly common for clients and students to record their own behavior. Sometimes it is inconvenient for someone else to do the recording; but sometimes— as in the case of thoughts or cravings—the behavior cannot be observed by others.

Recording one's own behavior can be accompanied by a beneficial change in that behavior, even before a treatment program is designed and put into effect. This being so, self-recording can be considered a procedure to change behavior. Zimmerman (1973), for example, has reported the case of a 17-year-old patient who was distressed by the number of times she had to go back and check things before she could leave her house. Had she turned off the stove? The faucet? When she started using a golf counter to record both her impulses to check and the number of times she acted on these impulses, she was horrified to discover that she had 103 impulses the first day of counting. Both the number of impulses and the number of times she acted on them decreased markedly over the seven days of baseline recording.

A similar, happy state of affairs can occur when parents record the number of times they attend to their children's appropriate behavior.

The frequency of attention to appropriate behavior increases, and—not surprisingly—so does the appropriate behavior (Herbert & Baer, 1972). In the classroom, Broden, Hall, and Mitts (1971) found that self-recording was effective in changing the behavior of two eighth-grade students, Liza and Stu. Stu recorded the number of times he talked out in class without his teacher's permission, and found that his frequency of "talk outs" decreased. Liza, who had requested help in improving her D— history grade, marked a data sheet whenever she happened to remember to record her studying behavior. She marked a (+) if she had been studying during the preceding few minutes and a (−) if she had not been studying. The result was an impressive increase in the percentage of time she spent studying—a result confirmed by an independent observer. In another academic setting, students who recorded their studying behavior earned significantly higher grades than those who did not (Johnson & White, 1971). Even first-grade children have benefited from self-recording. In one study, there was a marked decrease in the number of arithmetic errors when the children recorded and graphed their errors on a daily basis (Fink & Carnine, 1975).

A variety of devices has been used for self-recording purposes: index cards, tally sheets and wrist counters originally used by golfers to count golf strokes (Lindsley, 1968). One of the more innovative devices is the "countoon" described by Kunzelmann (1970) and shown in Figure 4.1. The "countoon" was developed by classroom teachers as part of a learning program called Precision Teaching and has been used by children to record their own behavior. The "countoon" as shown in Figure 4.1 has two components: (1) a *What I Do* sequence of pictures; and (2) a *My Count* column. The *What I Do* pictures illustrate the problem behavior, which is kicking a peer in Figure 4.1 (above). (Other "countoons" illustrate a variety of activities: saying "please", tying one's shoes, interrupting someone, and so forth.) In the *My Count* column, the child keeps track of the behavior by drawing a circle around the appropriate number each time the behavior occurs. If counting alone does not eliminate the problem, the "countoon" has a third component: a *What Happens* column. The "countoon" shown in Figure 4.1 (below) says that if the child hits his friend again, he will have to wear a mitten on his hand for three minutes.

Self-recording is an integral part of many classroom programs associated with the Schoolcraft Project, initiated in 1973 under the direction of Howard Farris and Rob Hawkins[1] of Western Michigan University. In some classrooms, which range from grades 2–10, every student records completion and accuracy of academic work on a daily basis. In this case, self-recording is not being used as a therapeutic technique but rather as part of a strategy to establish a positive motivational basis for learning. Figure 4.2 (left) shows Joyce, a second-grade student recording her progress in spelling. Spelling in Joyce's class is individualized so that students can progress at their own pace. Spelling tests are self-administered in that students

use a tape recorder to play a tape on which the teacher has prerecorded the spelling words in a particular unit. As each word is announced, the student spells it on paper. They can check their own work, and if they have achieved at least 90 percent accuracy they graph their success on the chart just as Joyce is doing. If 90 percent accuracy is not achieved, students are directed to a set of remedial exercises. They retake the test when they are ready, and color in the chart when they reach 90 percent accuracy. Bruce, a fourth-grader, is shown coloring in a square on the handwriting chart that indicates the letters of the alphabet he has mastered in his cursive writing class. Students in this class also work at their own pace and record their progress.

Self-recording has also been effective in increasing attendance at swimming practice (McKenzie & Rushall, 1974), in decreasing smoking (McFall, 1970; McFall & Hammen, 1971), and in other self-management programs (Watson & Tharp, 1972). However, many studies lack appropriate controls, and many report that self-recording alone is ineffective in producing durable behavior change. (See Kazdin, 1974c, for an analysis and a review.) Unlike Johnson and White (1971), Bristol and Sloane (1974) found no increase in test scores or time spent studying when college freshmen recorded the number of hours they spent studying. Self-recording failed to increase attention to their children's appropriate behavior in one of the three sets of parents in the Herbert and Baer study. And self-recording of their own disruptive behavior by boys in a remedial classroom failed to decrease disruptive behavior, even though the records showed high agreement with data collected by independent observers (Santogrossi, O'Leary, Romanczyk, & Kaufman, 1973). These and other studies suggest that motivation to change is probably a major variable in the effectiveness of self-recording as a procedure to change behavior.

A

B

Figure 4.1.   "Countoons" used by children to record their own behavior. (From Kunzelmann, 1970, p. 122, 123.)

1. Now at the University of West Virginia, Morgantown.

Figure 4.2.   Elementary school students from "Schoolcraft Project" recording their own academic progress. (Photographs courtesy of John Peterson.)

If self-recording makes us more aware of our behavior and the conditions under which it occurs, it is not surprising that self-recording is often accompanied by a change in the desired direction. We learn something about our behavior and the variables that control it. When the records show even a modest change in the desired direction, this can reinforce both record-keeping itself and the attention to behavior it requires. Self-recording may not be the most effective way to change behavior, and it may not produce the most durable changes; but it should not be overlooked as a viable means of control, particularly of self-control. At the very least, it can provide information that will be helpful when additional procedures are selected.

2. Modeling

Modeling is a familiar procedure to most parents and teachers, especially in teaching verbal and motor skills. A parent may pronounce the name of an object (modeling) and then reinforce the child's attempt to imitate the sound. When we learn to write, sing, or play golf, we are explicitly instructed to imitate the behavior the teacher models. Modeling is also used in programs for teaching public speaking and assertive behavior.

Imitation seems to occur naturally in most children, but in some populations imitative behavior must be carefully shaped and reinforced. Working with severely retarded children, Baer, Peterson, and Sherman (1967) started by shaping relatively simple imitative behavior—movements such as raising an arm, tapping a table, standing up—and progressed to such activities as building a tower with blocks and placing a box inside of a ring of beads. Eventually, they were able to establish a limited repertoire of verbal imitations with two of the three children. In their extensive work with autistic children, Lovaas and his colleagues also shaped imitative behavior, particularly to facilitate the acquisition of speech (Lovaas, Berberich, Perloff, & Schaeffer, 1966). (The Lovaas language program for autistic children, can be seen in his film, *Behavior Modification*.)

In other cases, teachers and therapists can take advantage of naturally occurring imitative behavior. Modeling has been used to reduce the number and letter reversals made by students in special-education classes (Stromer, 1975); to increase the use of descriptive adjectives by retarded children (Martin, 1975); to facilitate the learning of arithmetic computations by learning-disabled children (Smith & Lovitt, 1975); and to teach mildly retarded children to ask questions (Bondy & Erickson, 1976). In another context, Csapo (1972) used peer models to reduce inappropriate classroom behavior, and a number of people have used modeling to reduce anxieties and phobias (Chapter 6).

Modeling, or demonstrating the desired behavior, is an important teaching procedure, and in language and other areas it may be essential. However, imitation may occur without explicit instructions or encouragement. Cigarette advertising is now prohibited on television, but many parents model smoking and such other undesirable activities as lying and failing to observe traffic laws, including driving under the influence of alcohol. The extent to which children imitate parental and peer models is unknown, but the possibilities are frightening. Correlations do not prove causality, but apparently many parents who physically abuse their children were themselves victims of child abuse.

Many people would like to restrict the violence shown on television because of the vast audience exposed to this sort of modeling. Although the data are difficult to gather, newspaper reports of crimes sometimes quote the accused as saying that the crime was inspired by a particular movie or television program. Similarly, the rapid rise of skyjackings in the 1960s, and the recurrent cycles of bombings and other acts of terrorism, may be at least partly attributable to modeling and its attendant publicity. Fortunately, there is now a growing body of research on modeling and the variables that affect the degree to which a model's behavior is imitated.

One important variable is the consequence of the model's behavior. Bandura (1965) reported a series of studies in which children were shown films of adults modeling verbal and physical aggression. In one film, the model's aggressive behavior was reinforced, in another it was punished, and in a third there was no particular consequence. After viewing the films, the children were tested for imitation. Those who had seen the model's behavior punished exhibited significantly less aggressive behavior than did children from the other conditions. Later, the children were offered incentives for reproducing the model's behavior. Under these conditions, all groups showed an equivalent amount of learning from the film. All emitted more imitative behavior than they had when no incentive was offered; and those who had seen the model's behavior punished reproduced just as much of the model's behavior as did those who had seen this behavior reinforced. Similar findings have been reported by Rosenkrans and Hartup (1967).

There seems little doubt that aggressive behavior is imitated, especially when the model's behavior and the observer's behavior are reinforced. We question the encouragement of uncontrolled aggressive behavior by some therapists, even when the behavior itself is harmless (hitting a sofa with a bat board) or the attack is "merely" verbal (screaming at other members of the group). These rituals in the name of therapy are particularly worrisome when one recognizes that the encouragement of verbal aggression can lead to physical aggression. (See Berkowitz: The Case for Bottling up Rage, 1973, and Ulrich's film: Understanding Aggression, 1971.) Venting steam is fine for tea kettles, but it is not at all clear that "venting" anger is beneficial for people. In some cases, self-defense skills would prove more useful. And for the shy, passive, or harassed, more lasting benefits are likely to derive from social skills training, including assertiveness training.

Along with modeling, training in social

skills often includes *behavior rehearsals*. The teacher or counselor models behavior that would be appropriate in various situations, such as settling a family argument, asking for a date, or being interviewed for a job. The learner then imitates the manner, tone of voice, and general strategy of the model, but adapts them to a particular, personal situation. The teacher may then play the role of the learner's parent, date, or potential employer so that the learner has an opportunity to practice the newly acquired skills in a situation that is less provoking or intimidating than the one where they will be needed.

In addition to differential reinforcement of the model's behavior and of the observer's imitative behavior, two characteristics of the model appear to be important: the model's prestige and the perceived similarity of the model to the observer. Modeling did not prove to be an effective procedure in getting residents of one army psychiatric ward to increase their exercise by joining in a daily half-mile run. Perhaps the failure can be attributed to the fact that the resident selected as a model happened to be an army *officer* with whom the other residents did not identify (Boren & Colman, 1970). For a further discussion of the variables affecting modeling, see Bandura, 1965, 1971a, 1971b.

When employing modeling as a procedure to change behavior, we should use some care in selecting the model and make sure that appropriate imitative behavior is reinforced. We might also heed Bandura's rather chilling warning: "In the case of behavior that is ordinarily disapproved . . . seeing transgressions go unpunished seems to heighten analogous actions in observers to the same degree as witnessing models rewarded." (Bandura, 1971a, p. 25.)

3. Modifying the Environment

A careful look at the current situation may reveal conditions that are suppressing desired behavior or facilitating unwanted behavior. Some-

times the simplest solution is to modify the environment. This can be done by presenting discriminative stimuli for desired behavior, by removing discriminative stimuli for unwanted behavior, or simply by making it more difficult for unwanted behavior to occur.

Someone who is dieting may place fresh fruit and vetetables in a conspicuous and accessible place, while cookies and crackers are removed to a cabinet that can be reached only by standing on a chair. Someone trying to study more efficiently may clear the desk of photographs, magazines, letters, and other distracting material, and place the examination schedule in a prominent position. Modifying the environment by changing the stimuli that control behavior is an important feature of self-management and is discussed in some detail in Chapter 7.

Teachers may modify the environment by separating two children who usually make trouble when they are seated next to each other. A professor who is interested in facilitating discussions may arrange the chairs in a semicircle rather than in traditional rows. The director of an institution, wishing the staff to keep consistent records of their clients' progress, may display the graphs on a wall rather than keep them hidden away in a file cabinet. The parents of a child who is just learning to walk may remove valued objects from tables in order to prevent their breakage. Asphalt ridges in driveways are designed to make people drive slowly. "Childproof" caps on medicines and certain household cleaners are designed to prevent accidental poisonings.

My favorite example of preventing unwanted behavior is taken from a description of a Thanksgiving visit with Skinner, written by his daughter Julie. It reveals both the ingenuity and the gentleness of the man. Skinner, Julie, and her daughters are in Skinner's basement study. Five-year-old Lisa is writing letters of the alphabet for her grandfather to find and identify; and 18-month-old Justine is playing on the floor.

"Let's see if I can interest Justine in the organ," my father said. He turned on a timer patched into the cord. Years ago when the organ was new, my sister and I kept leaving the organ on after we had finished playing, and *rather than restrict our playing or punish us for forgetting to turn the organ off*, he had wired a timer into the cord which gave 60 minutes of uninterrupted playing and turned the power off automatically if we forgot.

(Vargas, 1972a, p. 20. Italics ours.)

4. Biofeedback

Under certain conditions, people can learn to control such physiological activities as heart rate, blood pressure, muscle tension, and the pattern of their brain waves. One procedure that allows the control of such "involuntary reflexes" is biofeedback. If we are given immediate (and preferably continuous) information about an autonomic function such as heart rate, for example, we may be able to increase or decrease the rate on request. In some cases, feedback is provided when the subject sees the record made by the apparatus recording his internal behavior. In other cases, feedback is provided by a visual or an auditory signal: a light or a tone would be presented while heart rate remained below a certain level or while the brain maintained an alpha wave pattern.

Snyder and Noble (1968) investigated the ability of human subjects to control the constriction of peripheral blood vessels. (When the blood vessels in our face constrict, we turn pale; when they dilate, we flush. These responses are relatively easy to observe.) Snyder and Noble presented two groups of subjects with a light flash (feedback) whenever their blood vessels constricted to a predetermined criterion. These experimental subjects thus received feedback contingent upon vasoconstriction. There were also two groups of control subjects. One group (B) received no feedback. The subjects in the other control group (C) were yoked controls: they received a light flash whenever the experimental subjects did, but the light flash was independent of (noncontingent on) their own level of

vasoconstriction. The results are shown in Figure 4.3. The four groups showed approximately the same number of constrictions during baseline. During biofeedback conditioning, with the light as reinforcer, the experimental subjects greatly increased the number of vasoconstrictions, while subjects in both control groups showed very little change. During extinction, when the light flash was no longer forthcoming, the number of criterion vasoconstrictions decreased for one of the experimental groups (EC) and stayed at approximately the same level for the other.

Other autonomic activities that people can control to some degree include heart rate and blood pressure, body temperature, muscle relaxation, and brain-wave patterns. Much of the basic research on biofeedback stems from the work of Neal Miller and his colleagues on the conditioning of autonomic responses in animals (e.g., Miller, 1969). His work has received a great deal of attention because of the potential importance of biofeedback research to therapy. If physiological activities can be controlled to a significant degree outside the

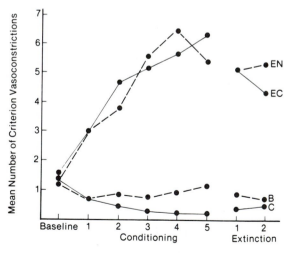

Figure 4.3.   Mean number of vasoconstrictions for successive five-min. periods for experimental (EC and EN), matched control (C), and baseline control (B) subjects. (From Snyder & Noble, 1968, p. 265.)

laboratory, heart patients may be able to control hypertension and irregular or too rapid heartbeats (arrhythmia and tachycardia); and people with tension headaches may be able to relax the muscles in their foreheads.

Though biofeedback appears promising, there is a relative lack of controlled research with long-term follow-up assessment. In addition, changes reported in laboratory studies are sometimes small compared to the changes needed in clinical practice. Statistical significance does not necessarily imply clinical significance. In a critical review of the literature to that date, Blanchard and Young (1974) concluded that the best evidence supporting the clinical effectiveness of biofeedback training is in the area of EMG (electromyogram) feedback for: (1) retraining muscular control in paralytic patients: (2) eliminating subvocal speech during reading; and (3) eliminating or reducing tension headaches. Areas in which the evidence is promising, but not conclusive, include the elimination of cardiac arrhythmias, the lowering of blood pressure, and reduction of various kinds of seizures. Meanwhile, workshops (and apparatus companies) proliferate as the research continues in these and other areas, including the treatment of insomnia, asthma, ulcers, and anxiety. Major articles are reprinted each year in the annual, *Biofeedback and Self-Control.*

B. Procedures that Increase, Maintain, or Extend Behavior

Sometimes the desired behavior is within the person's repertoire, but it may occur infrequently or for short periods of time, or it may occur only in limited situations. Our students often design self-management programs to increase their studying activities, not so much because they don't know how to study efficiently (although this is sometimes the case), but because they want to increase, maintain, or extend this class of behavior. They may want to study more often or for longer periods of time; or they may want to maintain their behavior in the face of competing activities over weekends as exam period approaches; or they may study efficiently in one course or in a particular setting such as the library and wish to extend the behavior to other contexts. The procedures described in this section are designed to accomplish these ends.

1. Reinforcement

The statement, "I tried reinforcement, but it didn't work" is not a possible statement within this model. If the Jones's 12-year-old son gets an allowance of five dollars a week, and they offer him 10 cents a day for completing his homework assignments, the frequency and accuracy of completing homework assignments may not increase. This result would be neither surprising nor proof that reinforcement "didn't work." It would, however, suggest that the Joneses had not found an effective reinforcer for increasing their son's homework performance. Like most procedures, reinforcement is easier to define than to apply. A great many factors determine whether or not a given event will be a reinforcer in a given situation. First, potential reinforcers must be identified; second, they must be used effectively.

We have described a great many kinds of potential reinforcers in Chapter 3: naturally reinforcing consequences, social reinforcers, reinforcing activities, edibles, and tangibles, and generalized reinforcers. Assuming that potential reinforcers have been identified, it remains to use them effectively so that they will, in fact, function as reinforcers.

a. Contingency
Although a reinforcer need not follow every occurrence of the desired behavior, one should be delivered only when the behavior occurs. The importance of making reinforcement *contingent* on behavior is shown clearly in Figure

4.4. The data are from one of Ayllon and Azrin's experiments in which a ward of 44 female psychotic patients worked for tokens that could be exchanged for the reinforcers listed in Table 4.2. During the first 20 days of this study, the patients worked at a job of their choice and were paid in tokens after the job was performed. The job assignments usually took less than an hour and usually paid fewer than ten tokens. Figure 4.4 shows that the 44 patients worked a total of approximately 45 hours when the tokens were contingent on job performance.

For the second 20-day period, the patients were paid the same number of tokens they had earned during the first part of the study, but they received the tokens *before* performing their jobs. They were told that they would get the tokens each day whether or not they worked, but that the staff was pleased with the work and hoped they would continue. When the tokens were no longer contingent on job performance, the number of hours worked gradually dropped to one hour a day. In the final phase of the study,

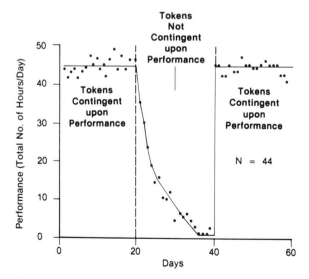

Figure 4.4. The importance of making reinforcement contingent upon performance. The total number of hours worked by 44 psychotic patients when tokens were contingent upon performance and when they were not. (Adapted from Ayllon & Azrin, 1965, p. 373.)

Table 4.2   Reinforcers available in token economy for female psychotic patients. (From Ayllon & Azrin, 1965, p. 360.)

Reinforcers	No. of Tokens Daily
I. Privacy	
Selection of Room 1	0
Selection of Room 2	4
Selection of Room 3	8
Selection of Room 4	15
Selection of Room 5	30
Personal Chair	1
Choice of Eating Group	1
Screen (Room Divider)	1
Choice of Bedspreads	1
Coat Rack	1
Personal Cabinet	2
Placebo	1-2
II. Leave from the Ward	
20-min walk on hospital grounds (with escort)	2
30-min grounds pass (3 tokens for each additional 30 min)	10
Trip to town (with escort)	100
III. Social Interaction with Staff	
Private audience with chaplain, nurse	5 min free
Private audience with ward staff, ward physician (for additional time—1 token per min)	5 min free
Private audience with ward psychologist	20
Private audience with social worker	100
IV. Devotional Opportunities	
Extra religious services on ward	1
Extra religious services off ward	10
V. Recreational Opportunities	
Movie on ward	1
Opportunity to listen to a live band	1
Exclusive use of radio	1
Television (choice of program)	3
VI. Commissary Items	
Consumable items such as candy, milk, cigarettes, coffee, and sandwich	1-5
Toilet articles such as Kleenex, toothpaste, comb, lipstick, and talcum powder	1-10
Clothing and accessories such as gloves, headscarf, house slippers, handbag, and skirt	12-400
Reading and writing materials such as stationery, pen, greeting card, newspaper, and magazine	2-5
Miscellaneous items such as ashtray, throw rug, potted plant, picture holder, and stuffed animal	1-50

when tokens were again made contingent on job performance, the number of hours worked by the patients immediately increased to its former level of 45 hours per day.

A study of cooperative play in a preschool child shows that the contingency relation between behavior and consequence is just as important with social reinforcement as it is with token reinforcement. It may be even more important because we are usually less aware of dispensing social reinforcers than we are of dispensing tangible reinforcers. The following study from the University of Washington preschool examined the effects of contingent and noncontingent adult attention on the cooperative play of five-year-old Martha (Hart, Reynolds, Baer, Brawley, & Harris, 1968).

It is sometimes assumed that inappropriate behavior results from a lack of attention and affection, that hostility or isolation reflect an insecurity that can be corrected by massive doses of noncontingent love. Although noncontingent love and attention can create a favorable and relaxed atmosphere, a favorable atmosphere may not be enough. Martha's story is a case in point. Despite the teachers' good intentions, noncontingent affection and attention apparently maintained Martha's uncooperative and antisocial behavior with other children. However, when the *same amount* of attention was given more selectively, Martha's cooperative play with other children increased dramatically.

At the start of this study, Martha's contacts with other children were described as brief and noncooperative. "Her refusals to play when invited, her taunts and competitive statements ('I can do that better than you'), and her foul language and rambling accounts of violent accidents perhaps made her aversive to other children." (Hart et al., p. 73.) Figure 4.5 shows the percentage of time in school she spent in

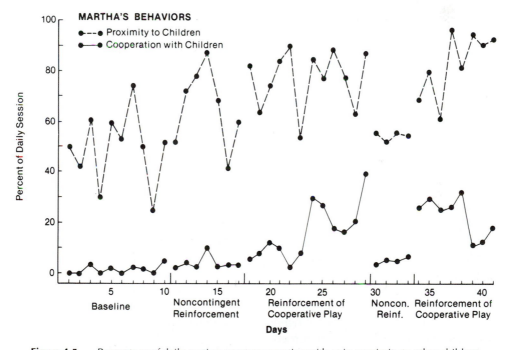

Figure 4.5.   Percentage of daily session spent cooperating with or in proximity to other children when teacher attention was made contingent on appropriate social behavior and when it was not. (From Hart, Reynolds, Baer, Brawley, & Harris, 1968, p. 75.)

proximity to another child and cooperating with another child. (Proximity was defined as being within three feet of another child when indoors, and within six feet outdoors.) During baseline, she was physically near another child approximately 50 percent of the session, but she rarely engaged in play. Teacher attention during this baseline period averaged 20 percent of the school day. (Teacher attention consisted of staying near Martha, attending to her behavior, and occasionally smiling, conversing, and supplying her with materials.)

During the next period (days 11–17 in Figure 4.5) this noncontingent attention was increased to 80 percent of the school day. Martha spent slightly more time in proximity to other children (65 percent), but the authors note that this may have been due to the other children being drawn to a situation where Martha was receiving nearly continual attention from a teacher. Despite this massive increase in teacher attention, cooperative play remained at less than 5 percent. Starting on the 18th day, the other children were primed to speak to Martha and to initiate play; and any approximation of social behavior on Martha's part was immediately followed by teacher praise and attention. By the 7th day of this procedure (day 24), shaping was no longer necessary, and reinforcement was contingent on real cooperative play. Proximity to other children increased to approximately 80 percent and cooperative play to 40 percent. At the end of this period, teacher attention had decreased to 20 percent of the day and was frequently given to the whole group rather than to Martha as an individual.

When *attention* was again *made noncontingent, both proximity and cooperative play dropped sharply* (days 30–33) *even though the total amount of attention was increased from 20 percent to 80 percent.* Note that cooperative play was not ignored during noncontingent phases; it simply was not selectively reinforced. In the final phase, teacher attention was reduced to 20 percent and again made contingent on

cooperative play, which promptly recovered. During the last few days, teacher attention was based on broader categories of play, and the authors note that the decrease in cooperative play indicates that this change was made too abruptly. Nonetheless, Martha was spending approximately 90 percent of the day in proximity to other children, and cooperative play was increasing to 20 percent. (The last point was taken on the last day of school.) This study clearly demonstrates that relatively infrequent but contingent teacher attention produced changes that abundant, but noncontingent, attention had not. The important thing to remember is that the change in behavior accompanied the contingency, not the attention *per se*.

Superstition. If we are ''on the outside looking in'' and decide that some reinforcer is contingent upon some class of behavior, we would probably call the resulting change in behavior *learning*. If, however, we decide that the temporal relation between the behavior and a reinforcing event is accidental, rather than contingent, we would probably call the change in behavior *superstition*.

Skinner (1948a) demonstrated the acquisition of superstitious behavior in the laboratory, using pigeons as subjects.[2] A food-deprived bird is placed in an experimental apparatus that makes food available for five seconds at intervals of fifteen seconds—no matter what the bird is doing. The delivery of food is not contingent on any specific behavior, but the bird is likely to be emitting some behavior when the food arrives. This behavior is therefore a little more likely to occur at the end of the next interval. Skinner found that different activities were thus accidentally conditioned in different birds, e.g., turning a circle, tossing the head, a pendulum motion of the head and body.

A short interval of fifteen seconds between food deliveries facilitates the accidental condi-

2. The acquisition of superstitious behavior is shown in the film, *A demonstration of behavioral processes* by B. F. Skinner (Reese, 1971c).

tioning because there is little time for the behavior to extinguish. Once the behavior is well established, however, the interval can be lengthened. The superstitious behavior acquired by one of Skinner's pigeons consisted of a hopping step from the right to the left foot. The interval between the noncontingent feedings was increased to one minute; and after some hours, a temporal discrimination developed: the behavior was delayed for ten to twenty seconds after each food delivery. When the feeder was disconnected, more than 10,000 responses were recorded in "extinction"—even though the food had never been contingent upon this or any other behavior.

It is essentially the matter of contingency that separates magic from science. We can consider the behavior of two men, both of whom wish rain to fall. One man engages in a rain dance, simulating rain by sprinkling water and imitating the motions of the clouds. The other man takes silver iodide crystals up in an airplane and discharges them into a cloud of a certain formation. Both sequences of behavior are followed by heavy rainfall. Both sequences of behavior are therefore likely to recur. We say "coincidence" to the Indian medicine man, "science" to the fellow with the silver iodide crystals—on the basis of our judgment of contingency.

The next time you watch a baseball game, examine the behavior of the batters. One will carry two bats to the plate and then toss one away. Another will touch his bat to the plate and make stereotyped swinging motions between pitches. One will remove and replace his cap, and perhaps another will hike up his trousers. The next time you start your car on a cold day or try to remove the distortion from your old television set, examine your own behavior.

b. Immediacy

In addition to contingency, the timing of reinforcement is important. If the potential reinforcer is delayed, some other behavior will intervene, and that will be the behavior that is strengthened because it immediately precedes the reinforcing event.

A study comparing the effects of delayed and immediate reinforcement was conducted by a mother with her 16-year-old boy to try and get him to wear his orthodontic device (Hall, Axelrod, Tyler, Grief, Jones & Robertson, 1972). Jerry started wearing dental devices when he was eight. Unfortunately, he did not wear them very often. "After eight years, four dentists, and approximately $3,300 in dental fees, Jerry's orthodontic condition was essentially unchanged" (p. 54). During baseline conditions, Jerry's mother just checked to see whether or not he was wearing the device. She did this five times during the day, at random intervals. Figure 4.6 shows that during these eight days, Jerry was wearing the device at only one or two of these checks. While she was collecting baseline data, Jerry's mother noticed that she gave Jerry attention in the form of a reprimand when he was *not* wearing the device. So, she decided that during the next phase she would ignore the occasions when he was not wearing the device and praise him when he was. This contingent social attention produced some improvement in that the number of times he was wearing the device increased to an average of 36 percent, but this was not enough to justify all the dentist bills. Next, Jerry's mother tried delayed monetary payoff: if Jerry was wearing the device when she checked he would earn 25 cents; if not Jerry would lose 25 cents. The "score" was kept on a calendar in the kitchen, and the money was paid at the end of the month. As Figure 4.6 shows, this contingency produced an immediate, but temporary effect. In the next phase, money was paid (or forfeited) immediately after each of the five daily checks. During 15 of the 18 days of this procedure, Jerry was wearing the device during all daily checks. To determine whether or not this contingency was responsible for the improvement, Jerry's mother returned to baseline conditions for five days. The amount of

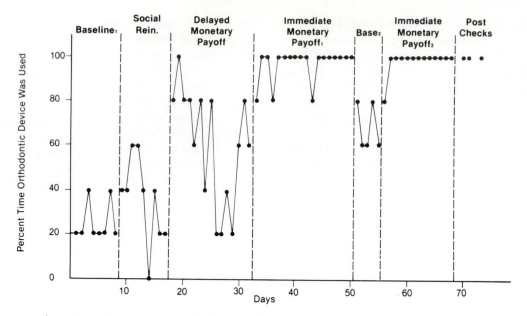

Figure 4.6. Percentage of mother's checks that son was wearing orthodontic device during various conditions of study: When there was no scheduled consequence for wearing the device (baseline), and when social or monetary reinforcement was immediate or delayed. (From Hall, Axelrod, Tyler, Grief, Jones, & Robertson, 1972, p. 57.)

time Jerry was found wearing the device decreased to 64 percent. When immediate payoff was reintroduced, the percentage quickly recovered to 98 percent.

The study ended at this point, but follow-up checks showed that Jerry was always wearing the device; and eight months later the dentist pronounced the good news that it was no longer necessary.

The previous study with Martha demonstrated the importance of the contingent relation between behavior and the reinforcing consequence. Jerry's mother discovered that the reinforcing event must also be delivered immediately. Sometimes, however, it is impossible to deliver the reinforcer immediately after the behavior. One way to bridge the delay is to immediately follow the behavior with praise and a token that can later be exchanged for a back-up reinforcer. With young children, an effective bridge is a picture of the reinforcer. Even better, cut up a picture of the back-up reinforcer,

which might be a model plane or a bike, and deliver a piece of the picture contingent on each occurrence of the behavior. Each time the criterion is met, the picture "rounds out" a little more. When the picture is complete, the child has earned the reinforcer. It is a good way to let children know just how close they are to receiving the back-up reinforcer, and putting together the picture is itself reinforcing.

c. Amount

Parents and teachers who contemplate reinforcement programs often ask how *much* of a reward they should give. The answer, of course, is "enough"; but there are certain guidelines. Too little of a potential reinforcer may not be reinforcing at all; and too much may be socially inappropriate, lead to rapid satiation, or compete with the activities one wants to strengthen. One hour's play for five minutes work would not be productive over the long run. Teachers have decreased disruptive classroom behavior by reinforcing academic work with free time for the students to engage in other activities of their choice. In these cases, the amount of the free-time reinforcer is a portion of the time the class has been wasting anyway, so there is a net gain in the time for educational activities.

Sometimes the amount of the reinforcer is determined by the quality of the performance. This is generally the case with academic grades, and the salaries paid to athletes generally depend on performance during the previous year. Pigeons apparently like to gamble and, when given a choice, prefer a variable amount of food to a fixed amount of food when the task requirements and the *average* amount of food are the same (Essock & Reese, 1974). People, of course, like to gamble, too; but they probably prefer their salaries in fixed installments.

In deciding the amount of reinforcement for a self-management program or for a program designed for someone else, we usually know what is a fair return for a given amount of work. But a couple of things are worth remembering. First of all, the more often behavior occurs and is reinforced, the more opportunities we have to learn. So, particularly when we are acquiring new skills, it is generally better when our efforts meet with frequent, small amounts of a reinforcer than infrequent, large amounts. Second, if we decide to work toward a major reinforcer contingent on a major effort, it is a good idea to program smaller reinforcers along the way. No matter how attractive it seems, the major reinforcer may be too distant in time to be maximally effective. (Exactly a year prior to this writing, I made a contract with myself and my publisher: If I hadn't turned in this manuscript by June 1, I would cancel the trip to England I'd been planning for more than a year. The trip was cancelled.)

d. Consistency

Consistency is yet another important consideration in the effective use of reinforcement procedures. Here, we must distinguish between the acquisition or learning of behavior and the maintenance of behavior that has already been learned. Learning takes place most rapidly when each occurrence of the behavior is reinforced. So, until the desired behavior is well-established, it is advisable to look for and reinforce its every occurrence. When children are learning the letters of the alphabet or how to write their names, they benefit from encouragement of each correct attempt. Continuous reinforcement is especially important when we have shaped behavior and—by definition—reinforced a variety of approximations before the goal behavior emerged. The learner will have a difficult time differentiating the goal from the approximations unless we are both liberal and consistent with the reinforcers. Time and again we have watched the students in our introductory course carefully shape the behavior of a pigeon, training it to peck a small disk on the wall of the apparatus. Time and again, we have applauded their success, moved on to see if other students needed help, and returned to find the bird no longer pecking. After helping one student reshape pecking three times, we were finally able to verbalize the problem. During shaping, the student has probably reinforced as many as 30 different movements the pigeon has made: cocking its head and attending to the disk, a slight movement of the beak in the direction of the disk, pecking the wall near the disk, pecking the edge of the disk, pecking the disk, and so forth. All of these movements have been reinforced. How the hell is the pigeon supposed to know which is the one the student wants? When shaping behavior, help the learner achieve the goal as rapidly as possible, and then let him know he's reached it by reinforcing frequently and consistently.

Once behavior is well established, however, there are several reasons for transferring from continuous to some form of intermittent reinforcement. Intermittent reinforcement is more economical, more likely to apply in the natural environment where parents and teachers have competing demands on their attention, and it produces behavior that is more resistent to extinction.

e. Schedules of reinforcement

Once behavior is well established, reinforcement need not occur on a continuous basis; but the contingency relation should be maintained. That is, the desired behavior does not always have to be followed by a reinforcer, but a reinforcer should always be preceded by (some form of) desired behavior. As we saw in the study of Martha (Figure 4.5), when reinforcement is independent of behavior, the strength of that behavior declines.

Behavior can be reinforced intermittently according to a number of different *schedules*. A schedule of reinforcement is a statement of the contingencies on which reinforcement depends. Some schedules specify a certain amount or frequency or rate of behavior; other schedules are based on the passage of time. Some schedules have both temporal and ratio requirements; and of these complex schedules, some have correlated stimuli of various kinds and some do not. Just about any requirement or restriction you can think of can be (and probably has been) studied as a schedule of reinforcement.

Ferster and Skinner (1957) condensed their early work on schedules into a book of 739 pages, with 921 graphs that describe the characteristics of various schedules of reinforcement. The data comprise a quarter of a *billion* responses: 70,000 hours of recorded behavior. There are certain characteristics of performance on each basic schedule common to humans and other species, whether the schedule is in effect alone or in combination with others. Furthermore, these characteristics are sufficiently stable so that performance on a given schedule can be used as a baseline to measure the effects of other variables, such as motivation, lack of sleep, or various drugs. (Lindsley's study of the

effects of benactyzine on hallucinatory vocalizations is shown in Figures 2.5 and 2.6.) Obviously, this is a complex subject. Less obviously, perhaps, it is an important one. To take just one example, there has been extensive research on drug effects. The effects on behavior of various dosages of various drugs have been well-established. Yet in nearly every case, both *the effects and the side effects of the drug depend on the schedule of reinforcement in effect.*[3]

Each of the many possible schedules produces a characteristic rate and pattern of responding, both while the schedule is in effect and in extinction when reinforcement is discontinued. The characteristics of performance maintained by the four basic intermittent schedules are shown in Figure 4.7. The components of complex schedules, which are combinations of these simple schedules, also reveal these basic characteristics.

i. Continuous reinforcement (CRF). When a reinforcer is delivered after each occurrence of the behavior, a stable performance results—until other variables intervene. In the laboratory, especially when the reinforcer is food or water, CRF produces a high, stable performance, broken only by any pauses to eat or drink. (Rats don't pause to eat the small food pellets commonly used as reinforcers: they seem to "inhale" them.) But performance is not usually sustained for long because of satiation. For this reason, CRF provides a way of looking at some animals' patterns of eating.[4] For example, when the Japanese quail (*Coturnix coturnix*) pecks a key that permits brief access to food, pecking and eating occur in bouts throughout the day,

3. Thompson, Pickens, and Neish, 1970, is an excellent source. See also *Federation Proceedings* (August, 1975),a special issue on the behavioral assessment of drug effects.

4. The method is probably appropriate for many rodents and seed-eating birds who normally get their food in small pieces. It would probably *not* be appropriate for predators who catch and consume large meals at infrequent intervals.

Stylized Records of Basic Schedules

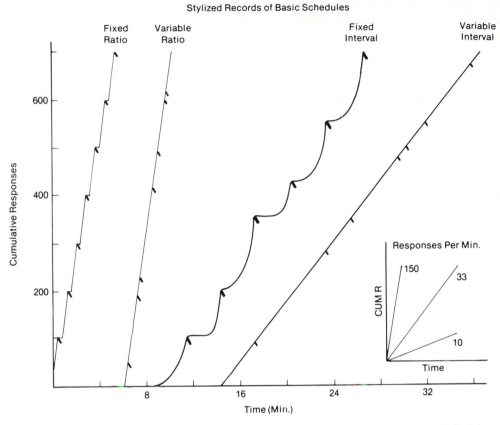

Figure 4.7. Stylized records showing characteristics of responding under basic schedules of reinforcement. Diagonal marks indicate reinforcement; the slope of various rates indicated at lower right. Fixed Ratio (FR 100): high rate, with brief pause following reinforcement and abrupt change to terminal rate. Variable Ratio (VR 100): high sustained rate; no pausing after reinforcement. Fixed Interval (FI 3 min.): low overall rate due to pause following reinforcement; length of pause increases with length of interval; gradual increase to high terminal rate as interval ends. Variable Interval (VI 3.3 min.): low sustained rate; no pausing after reinforcement. (From Reese, 1966, p. 18.)

separated by pauses of approximately 15 minutes. Other animals do most of their eating at night; others at dawn and dusk. Outside of the laboratory, many of the ordinary things we do are reinforced on a schedule that approximates CRF: braking the car (it usually slows), raising food to the mouth with a fork (we usually make it); flicking the electric light switch (and there usually *is* light). But many social, intellectual, and athletic activities fail to meet with uniform success. When we are trying to *establish* these

skills, we can do so most rapidly by using continuous reinforcement; but to *maintain* them in the natural environment, we should gradually transfer to the schedules of intermittent reinforcement that will operate in the home and classroom.

ii. Ratio schedules (FR; VR). Ratio schedules deliver reinforcement according to the number of times the behavior is emitted. On a *Fixed Ratio* (FR) schedule, the ratio of performance to reinforcement is fixed or constant. For a laboratory rat, a schedule of FR 20 would mean that every twentieth lever press would be reinforced. In a factory that paid according to the number of items produced (piecework), a schedule of FR 20 would mean that every 20 items produced added a certain increment to the pay check. A student might take a break after completing every tenth problem (FR 10) or after reading every third article (FR 3) or after doing fifteen pushups (FR 15).

On a *Variable Ratio* (VR) schedule, the ratio of performance to reinforcement varies about a given mean. On VR 20, the behavior might have to occur the following numbers of times for successive reinforcements: 15, 30, 20, 5, 25, 35, 10. Slot machines pay off according to a variable ratio schedule.

The first record in Figure 4.7 is typical of performance on a fixed ratio schedule in which every 100th response is reinforced (FR100). There is a brief pause after reinforcement (diagonal mark on record) followed by an abrupt return to a high rate of responding. In this case, approximately 700 responses are emitted over a period of 5 minutes, giving an average rate of 140 responses per minute. The second record shows the sustained high rate typical of performance on a variable ratio schedule such as VR100. On the average, every 100th response is reinforced; and in this example, the rate is 175 responses per minute (700 responses in four min.).

Ratio schedules differentially reinforce rapid responding because the more rapidly the behavior is emitted, the sooner the reinforcer is delivered. Ratio schedules are therefore characterized by high rates. If the ratio is fixed, there is a pause after reinforcement, but if the ratio is variable, the high rate is sustained (Figure 4.7). The reason for the difference is that reinforcement can come at any time on variable ratio schedules; but on fixed ratio schedules, one reinforcement will never follow another until the behavior has been emitted the specified

number of times. Since the occurrence of behavior immediately following reinforcement is never reinforced, the events connected with reinforcement become discriminative stimuli for nonreinforcement. Fixed ratio performances, then, are characterized by high rates with a pause following reinforcement. This pause and *abrupt* change to a high, stable rate is the hallmark of fixed ratio performance. The postreinforcement pause, which is very brief for low ratios such as FR 20, generally increases with the size of the ratio. The hallmark of variable ratio performance is the high, stable rate without pausing.

The behavioral requirement for reinforcement can be quite high if the increase is gradual or if progress along the way is indicated. But an abrupt increase in ratio size can lead to "ratio strain"—extended pausing after reinforcement and often a breakdown of the performance. Findley and Brady (1965) established stable performances in chimpanzees working on extremely high fixed ratios by gradually increasing the size of the ratio and by periodically presenting a green light as a conditioned reinforcer. One chimpanzee worked on a schedule of FR 120,000, with the conditioned reinforcer presented after each 4,000 lever presses and an almost unlimited supply of food at the completion of the ratio. The chimp paused for approximately 15 minutes when the conditioned reinforcer was presented and then emitted the next 4,000 responses in rapid succession.

iii. Interval schedules (FI; VI). Schedules based primarily on the passage of time are called *interval* schedules. The interval is fixed (FI) when a constant period of time must elapse between reinforced responses, e.g., FI 5, when an interval of five minutes elapses before the next occurrence of the behavior will be reinforced. On a variable interval schedule (VI), the length of the interval varies about some given mean time.

The fixed interval record in Figure 4.7 represents performance on a schedule of FI 3 min. The overall rate is approximately 40 responses a minute, and the scalloping is due to extended pausing after reinforcement followed by a *gradual* increase to a high rate at the end of the interval. Performance on a comparable variable interval schedule (VI 3.3 min.) is characterized by a uniform low rate (here 32 responses per minute) without pausing.

Compared to ratio schedules, the overall rate of performance maintained on interval schedules is low (Figure 4.7). Because reinforcement depends on the occurrence of behavior after a specified period of time has elapsed since the preceding reinforcement, rapid responding is not differentially reinforced. *Fixed interval* performance is characterized by a pause after reinforcement and then a gradual increase to a very high rate at the end of the interval. The characteristic scallop reflects the fact that the probability of one reinforcement following another is zero and increases with the passage of time. The delivery of mail occurs on a fixed interval of approximately 24 hours, and the behavior of looking for the carrier or going to the mailbox is negligible until the interval is nearly over. Then, if motivation is high, these activities occur in strength.

Variable Interval reinforcement produces sustained responding at a low rate. The stability of the performance, plus the fact that relatively little effort is required, make this schedule useful for basic research. As was mentioned earlier, many of Lindsley's patients worked on a schedule of VI 1 minute for sessions lasting five or six hours (Figure 2.6).

The longer the interval, the lower the rate. On fixed interval schedules, the decrease in overall rate with longer intervals is due to an increase in the pause after reinforcement. The terminal rate, as reinforcement is due, remains high. If the interval is FI 5, the subject may pause two or three minutes; if it is FI 30, the pause will be much longer, perhaps 20 minutes. On variable interval schedules, the overall rate is fairly constant, and longer intervals produce lower rates.

The effects of the various schedules apply to escape and avoidance behavior as well as to behavior maintained by reinforcement. Assuming that at least some of your studying is maintained by avoidance of low grades or failure, (and not entirely by good grades and the positive reinforcers inherent in the work), when do you study for various courses? If one course has only a mid-term and a final exam, the chances are good that most of your studying occurs within a few days preceding these events. If another course has weekly exams, a plot of your studying for that course would probably show a more stable rate of studying over the course of the semester.

Born and Davis (1974) compared the study patterns of college students enrolled in two sections of the same course. One section was a traditional lecture course; the other used the PSI (Personalized System of Instruction) format developed by Fred Keller (Keller, 1968; Keller & Koen, in press; Sherman, 1974). The PSI format divides the work into small units which the students master at their own pace. Each unit contains study questions and is followed by a short test. The students must demonstrate mastery of the material in one unit by passing the test with a score of at least 90 percent before they may start working on the next unit. (Alternate versions of the unit tests are available, and proctors provide remedial help if it is needed.) Born and Davis could compare the students' patterns of studying because the work assignments were the same for both sections of the course, and the study materials were available only in a study center open 12 hours a day during the week as well as Saturday morning. The same mid-term and final exam were given to both sections. Figure 4.8 shows how students from the two sections of the course distributed their studying. These particular graphs are selected because they are those of students closest to the median for each section. Both the mid-term and the final were scheduled

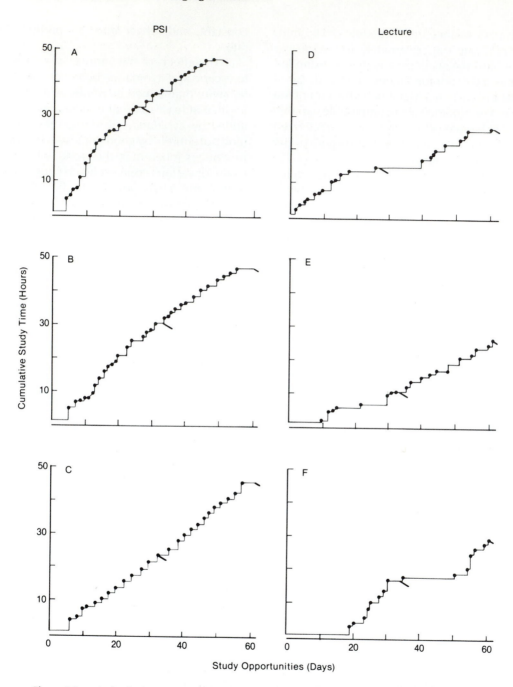

Figure 4.8.   Individual study profiles for students from PSI and lecture classes who were closest to the median number of study hours in each of these sections. The day each student took the midterm and final exam is indicated with a "hash mark." (Redrawn from Born & Davis, 1974, p. 372.)

twice, one week apart, and the date the students took these exams is shown by a "hash mark" on the record. Students in the PSI course (left) showed a stable pattern of studying throughout the semester; the records for those in the lecture section show fixed interval scalloping. Student (F) waited 20 days before starting to study for the mid-term, and then studied at a fairly high rate. The pattern is repeated before the final. The other students from the lecture section show scalloping before the mid-term (E) or before the final (D). Students in the PSI course spent 50 percent more time working in the study center, but the total exposure to course content was about the same (the other students spent approximately 20 hours in lectures.) As a group, PSI students scored significantly higher on both exams, and generally took the exams on the earlier date.

iv. Differential reinforcement of rate (DRL, DRH, and Pacing). Some schedules were developed specifically to control the rate of behavior. Most of the work has been done with laboratory animals, but variations of these schedules have provided a useful alternative to punishment and extinction. DRL refers to the differential reinforcement of low rate; DRH to the differential reinforcement of high rate; and Pacing—as the name implies—refers to a schedule that specifies both upper and lower limits on rate. The restrictions on rate may be added to the restrictions imposed by other schedules. For example, the schedule FR 20 DRH 3 sec. would signify that reinforcement would arrive only when the behavior occurred 20 times *and* the last two occurrences were within three seconds. The effect is to raise the rate over the whole ratio.

A variation of DRL schedules has been used by Dietz and Repp (1973) to reduce inappropriate classroom behavior. In one study, the students were high school seniors, and the problem was changing the subject when the teacher was trying to conduct discussions of academic matters. During baseline, the students changed the subject (usually to social topics) nearly seven times per class period. The teacher didn't want to punish this diversionary tactic, nor did she particularly want to eliminate it entirely, even though the academic discussions were suffering. It was therefore decided to reinforce a low rate of this kind of misbehavior. The first week, the students earned free time on Friday if they didn't change the subject of class discussions more than six times during the 50-minute class periods on Monday through Thursday. During succeeding weeks, the DRL limit was progressively reduced. Each week, the low rate was met and the class earned free time on Friday. Interestingly, the students did not take the DRL contingencies as license to change the subject the specified number of times. On all of the DRL schedules, they stayed well below criterion. When the DRL contingencies were terminated, the rate recovered somewhat, but remained well below baseline for the remaining two weeks of the study.

v. Extinction following various schedules of reinforcement. The duration, rate, and pattern of behavior during extinction depends on the schedule of reinforcement previously in effect. Given the same total number of reinforcements, behavior that has been reinforced continuously (CRF) is least resistant to extinction: the number of responses and the time over which they are emitted are less than when extinction follows intermittent reinforcement. Extinction following CRF is characterized by bursts of responding interspersed with plateaus of nonresponding, and by emotional behavior that often includes aggression. Extinction following conditioning on ratio schedules is characterized by a large number of responses emitted at a high rate over a relatively short period of time (compared to interval schedules). Extinction following interval schedules is characterized by a low, sustained rate that gradually tapers off. These schedules produce the longest extinction curves—so this is the way to maintain behavior if you want it to persist long after reinforcement is discontinued. Interval reinforcement is *not* the way to maintain behavior that you will wish to extinguish quickly: behavior such as a child's asking for a drink of water after being put to bed. If the parents decide the child is really seeking attention, not water, and if they decide that this attention is unwarranted, they should discontinue reinforcement abruptly. Extinction following intermittent reinforcement, particularly on a variable interval schedule, will produce a great deal of frustration for all parties concerned.

vi. Summary.   Continuous reinforcement is the most efficient way to establish new behavior or to increase behavior that seldom occurs. This schedule requires continuous attention, but it establishes behavior more rapidly than do other schedules. "Real life," however, seldom provides continuous reinforcement for social and academic skills, so intermittent reinforcement should be introduced gradually if the behavior is to be sustained in the normal home or school environment. Generally, variable interval reinforcement is appropriate unless it is important to sustain a high rate of behavior. In that case, a ratio schedule would be appropriate. Students who are increasing their studying efficiency often reward themselves when they have read or written a given number of pages. In the case of writing, an interval schedule favors sitting at the desk with pen in hand, but a ratio schedule favors output.

Continuous reinforcement, then, is used to establish new behavior or to increase its frequency or duration; and intermittent reinforcement is used to maintain it. To extend behavior to new situations, such as completing homework assignments in math as well as in English, one should be prepared to go back to continuous reinforcement for a time.

The other message in this section concerns extinction following intermittent reinforcement. The persistence of behavior is a major advantage when we want to sustain it in the normal environment; but it is extraordinarily difficult to carry out extinction procedures when the behavior is either dangerous or aversive. If you have ever tried to extinguish temper tantrums, you know what we mean. "Giving in" to a tantrum "just once" amounts to putting the behavior on an intermittent schedule of reinforcement; and when it is reinforced only occasionally, it becomes very resistant to extinction. As we become more aware of the powerful effects of social reinforcement, we can examine our own behavior more closely to see if we are inadvertently reinforcing problem behavior. If we find that we are and decide to stop, we have to stick with it or run the risk of making the problem even worse. A dreadful example of this problem can be seen in Figure 5.12, which shows the extinction of self-injurious behavior in an autistic child. Fortunately, other procedures can be combined with extinction to eliminate problem behavior more rapidly, and with far less strain on all concerned.

2. Escape Conditioning (Negative Reinforcement)

Behavior is strengthened when its consequence is the removal of a punisher. The monkey in Figure 2.2 learned to press a lever when that behavior terminated electric shock. The strengthening of behavior by the removal of a punisher is called *negative reinforcement*. But since that term is often confused with punishment, we call the removal of a punisher *escape conditioning*. This procedure is more pervasive than we sometimes realize. When parents "give in" to annoying behavior such as whining or temper tantrums, they escape these aversive events. The parents' behavior of giving in can thus be strengthened by escape conditioning; and, since the child's tantrum behavior is reinforced by the parents' compliance, further tantrums can be expected. Even though many parents recognize this vicious circle, they find it a particularly difficult one to break.

Flanagan, Goldiamond, and Azrin (1958, 1959) used escape from a punisher to show that stuttering can be controlled by operant procedures. In the first study, done with chronic stutterers, the punisher was a one-second blast of a 105-decibel (db), 6 kHz tone in the subject's earphones. Subjects were run under two conditions: a punishment condition, during which stuttering produced the blast of noise; and an

escape condition, during which the noise was continually present and stuttering removed it for five seconds. Under the punishment condition, when the noise was contingent on stuttering, stuttering decreased markedly. Under the escape condition, when the removal of noise was contingent on stuttering, the behavior increased appreciably.

The same authors (1959) then used an escape procedure to condition stuttering in normally fluent subjects. The punisher used was shock, which was removed for ten seconds each time the subject stuttered. Actually, the subjects could avoid shock by stuttering at intervals of 10 seconds or less. The records of one subject are shown in Figure 4.9. The escape procedure produced a high rate of stuttering in this normally fluent subject. Goldiamond, now at the Univer-

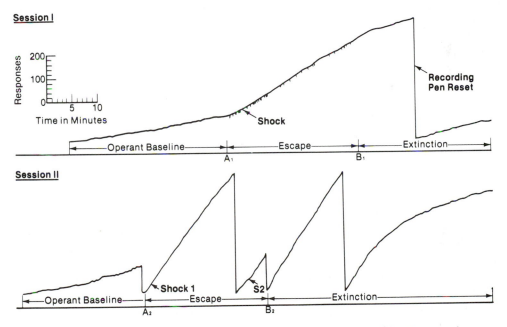

Figure 4.9. Conditioning and extinction of stuttering in a normally fluent subject by escape from shock. Stuttering eliminated shock during escape period, and stuttering at intervals of 10 seconds or less avoided shock. Stuttering occurred at such a high rate during session II that only two shocks were given. Extinction of stuttering during session II shows appropriately 1,000 stutters over 40 minutes. (From Flanagan, Goldiamond, & Azrin, 1959, p. 980.)

sity of Chicago, and Azrin, at Southern Illinois University, wanted to discover the conditions that control stuttering so that they could devise ways to eliminate the problem. Since their early basic research with Flanagan, they have developed successful programs for stutterers at their respective universities.[5]

Escape conditioning has been used to correct a common problem in outpatient treatment: the failure of many outpatients to take their prescribed medication. Azrin and Powell (1969) designed a special apparatus, small enough to fit in a purse or a pocket, to increase the amount of medication taken on time. When 30 minutes had elapsed since the last pill was taken a 50 db, 100 Hz tone was sounded. The tone could be terminated only by turning a small knob on the side of the apparatus. This ejected a pill into the individual's hand and also reset the timing device. The combination of escape conditioning and response priming (pill ejection) resulted in only 3 percent of the pills being missed.

Escape conditioning is possible even when the subject cannot discriminate the behavior being conditioned. Using human subjects, Hefferline, Keenan, and Harford (1959) decided to condition a tiny muscle twitch in the subject's hand. The muscle activity was too small for the subject to observe. For the experimenters to observe it, however, the physiological action potential was amplified one million times and displayed on a meter. During the study the subjects listened to music over which a disagreeably loud 60 Hz hum was superimposed. When the muscle twitch occurred, the hum was turned off or postponed for 15 seconds. One group of subjects was not told about the contingencies in effect: that the muscle twitch would terminate or postpone the loud hum. Although this activity was readily conditioned in all subjects, none was able to identify the behavior. In fact, they did not realize that they had anything to do with terminating or postponing the aversive noise. The message applies not only to escape conditioning, but to all other operant procedures as

well: it is not necessary for an individual to be aware of the contingencies for them to affect behavior.

3. Avoidance

The conditioning of behavior by the *removal* or termination of a punisher is escape conditioning. Conditioning by the *postponement* of an aversive event is avoidance conditioning. In a typical animal laboratory example, a tone precedes the delivery of shock. Behavior, such as lever pressing, which is emitted during the pre-shock tone postpones the shock for a period of time, perhaps 10 seconds. Unless the lever is pressed, the shock is delivered on schedule; but by pressing whenever the tone is presented, the animal can avoid all of the shocks.

Avoidance behavior can be conditioned when it postpones either the delivery of a punisher or the removal of a reinforcer. Much of our behavior seems to be maintained by avoidance contingencies. Paying taxes and obeying traffic signals are probably maintained by the avoidance of aversive consequences such as fines rather than by reinforcers.

Escape and avoidance conditioning have been used to induce two psychiatric patients to feed themselves (Ayllon & Michael, 1959). Both patients had "eating problems" in that they generally refused to eat unless they were spoonfed by nurses. In addition, both were

5. Another fluency-shaping program, which is now on film (Reese & Huberth, 1975), has been developed by Dr. Ronald Webster at Hollins College in Virginia. This program, like Goldiamond's, requires only two or three weeks and teaches the client how to initiate sounds properly and maintain continuous speech. Webster has now developed a small computer that monitors the clients' speech and tells them when they are making the sounds correctly. Several hundred clients have now gone through this program. A two-year follow-up, conducted by people unknown to the former stutterers, showed that 70 percent maintained normal fluency. The remaining 30 percent had lost some ground, but still showed considerable gains over their pretherapy fluency rates.

reported to be relatively indifferent to social reinforcers but to care a great deal about the neatness of their appearance. The procedure involves escape and avoidance conditioning, with spilled food as the punisher, combined with praise and attention for self-feeding. The nurses were given the following instructions:

Continue spoonfeeding the patient; but from now on, do it in such a careless way that the patient will have a few drops of food fall on her dress. Be sure not to overdo the food dropping, since what we want to convey to the patient is that it is difficult to spoonfeed a grown-up person, and not that we are mean to her. What we expect is that the patient will find it difficult to depend on your skill to feed her. You will still be feeding her, but you will simply be less efficient in doing a good job of it. As the patient likes having her clothes clean, she will have to choose between feeding herself and keeping her clothes clean, or being fed by others and risking getting her clothes soiled. Whenever she eats on her own, be sure to stay with her for a while (3 minutes is enough), talking to her, or simply being seated with her. We do this to reinforce her eating on her own. In the experience of the patient, people become nicer when she eats on her own. (Ayllon & Michael, 1959, p. 330-331.)

During the eight-day period when a baseline was established, one patient ate only five meals on her own and weighed 99 pounds. Treatment lasted eight weeks and the patient ate all but four of the last twenty-four meals. When she was discharged from the hospital she weighed 120 pounds.

Another example of behavior maintained by the avoidance of an aversive event is shown in Figure 4.10. This study was conducted by a recent bride whose husband left his clothing, particularly his jacket and shoes, scattered about the living room. Baseline records were taken of the number of items of clothing left in the living room for more than 15 minutes, with the average being two a day. The couple then agreed that whoever left more clothing in the living room would have to do the dishes. During the two weeks in which this avoidance contingency was in effect, no clothing was left in the living room. The wife then removed the

avoidance contingency because "there was no longer a problem," whereupon the problem promptly returned. After a week of this return to baseline, the dishes contingency was reinstated; and once again it proved effective. This time the problem really was solved because when the avoidance contingency was removed for the second time, clothing was left in the living room only twice over the post check period of 20 days. The wife said that she thought her husband had "caught on to the fact that she preferred him not to leave them out" (Hall, 1971a).

Completion of a thesis or dissertation is a familiar problem for many graduate students. Zimmerman has used a "productive avoidance" procedure in a self-control program with a 31-year-old assistant professor at a liberal arts college (Nurnberger & Zimmerman, 1970; Zimmerman, 1972). The professor had completed all the course and research requirements for his Ph.D. and had written ten pages of the introduction to his dissertation; but for the past two years, he had been unable to write another page. The program consisted of a self-control chart that specified the number of pages to be written over a 30-week period (sufficient time for a first draft). Two-week vacations during the summer and Christmas were also scheduled. An avoidance procedure was arranged to "back up" the chart. The client made out five pre-dated checks for $100 each to his favorite charities. If Zimmerman received carbons of the required number of pages by a specified deadline, a check would be torn up; if not, the check would be mailed off to the charity. All went well for the first eight weeks, during which three deadlines were scheduled at relatively short intervals. The fourth deadline was five weeks later, and the client did no writing for half that period. Realizing that he'd never be able to complete the required number of pages in the time remaining, he put in an emergency call to Zimmerman, and the program was revised. Daily, and then weekly, writing requirements were assigned, and a new avoidance contin-

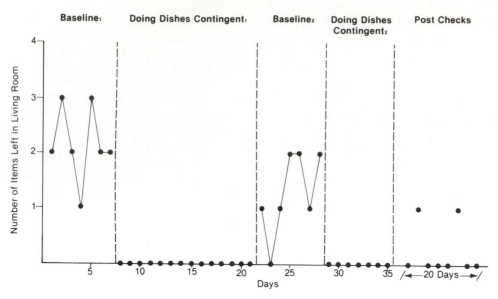

Figure 4.10. The number of items of clothing left in the living room by a newlywed husband. (From Hall, 1971a, p. 42.)

gency was added. This time, the client wrote out checks for $25, and failure to meet a deadline would result in Zimmerman's sending a $25 check to an organization the client *strongly opposed:* the Ku Klux Klan, the American Nazi Party, or the John Birch Society. Thereafter, the client missed no deadlines, and the thesis was completed on schedule.

In addition to being an example of maintaining behavior by an avoidance procedure, this case study illustrates a central tenet of applied behavior analysis. That is, when Zimmerman realized that the first procedure was not working, he "blamed" the procedure, not the professor. ("The subject knows best.") When the procedure was changed, so was the professor's behavior.

4. Recovery

If behavior is being suppressed or weakened by punishment, response cost, or by some other reductive procedure, and if we can identify and remove the contingencies responsible for the suppression, then the behavior may recover. We sometimes find that a student who has actively participated in classroom discussions throughout high school contributes very little to discussions after a few months in college. These students can usually name several aversive consequences that have attended their own—or others—attempts to speak up during class. The instructor or another student disparages their questions and comments; other students complain that they are taking up too much time; they answer a question incorrectly and "feel stupid," and so forth. Even in classes where the instructor and the students agree that discussions are valuable, it may require a deliberate effort to avoid the conditions that have suppressed discussion in another class or with another instructor. It may also be necessary to prompt and reinforce even minimal contributions from some students before their verbal behavior starts to recover. Later on, when verbal output is maintained by intermittent reinforcement, these students will be better able to handle the give and take of a good argument and to defend their ideas in the face of criticism.

5

Operant Procedures for Changing Behavior — II

A. Procedures which Restrict, Reduce, or Eliminate Behavior
1. Extinction
   a. Behavior maintained by reinforcement
   b. Side effects
   c. Behavior maintained by avoidance
2. Satiation
3. Response cost
4. Time out
5. Restraint and confinement
6. Reinforcement of omission (OT, DRO)
7. Reinforcement of alternative behavior (Alt R)
8. Differential reinforcement of low rate (DRL)
9. Punishment
   a. Punishment using painful stimulation
   b. Aversive consequences other than shock
   c. Conditioned punishers
   d. Variables that determine the effectiveness of punishment
      i. Intensity
      ii. Duration
      iii. Immediacy
      iv. Introduction of punishing events
      v. Frequency and consistency: the schedule of punishment
      vi. Motivation to emit the punished behavior: schedules of reinforcement
      vii. Reinforcement of alternative behavior
   e. Generalization of suppression
   f. Collateral effects of punishment
      i. Beneficial side effects
      ii. Escape and avoidance
      iii. Aggression
      iv. Conditioned suppression and anxiety

B. Comparisons and Generalizations
1. Extinction
2. Satiation
3. Response cost
4. Time out
5. Prolonged restraint or confinement
6. Removing the opportunity
7. Omission training (OT or DRO)
8. Reinforcement of alternative behavior (Alt R)
9. Differential reinforcement of low rate (DLR)
10. Punishment

C. Guidelines for Using Reductive Procedures

A. Procedures Which Restrict, Reduce, or Eliminate Behavior

The nine reductive procedures listed in Table 4.1 can be used to eliminate a particular class of behavior, to reduce its frequency or duration, or to restrict its occurrence to specified situations. The effectiveness of a given procedure is evaluated in terms of the *speed*, the *extent*, and the *duration* of its effects. However, these procedures sometimes have "side effects" which must also be considered. Potentially undesirable side effects of reductive procedures include "emotional" behavior, aggression, the suppression of other classes of behavior, and the tendency of the individual to escape or avoid the situation in which the procedure is being applied. Sometimes, however, the side effects are beneficial, as when the suppression of self-injurious behavior allows social behavior to emerge and be reinforced. Undesirable side effects seem most likely to occur in conjunction with punishment and extinction, but they may be minimal if these procedures are used in conjunction with others. In any case, it is wise to consider all of the alternatives before deciding which is most appropriate for a given situation.

1. Extinction

Extinction procedures involve the termination of contingencies which strengthen behavior, either by the presentation of a reinforcer or by the removal or postponement of a punisher. Depending upon which procedure has been used to strengthen behavior, the characteristics of operant extinction may be quite different.

a. Behavior maintained by reinforcement

The time required to extinguish behavior that has been maintained by reinforcement depends upon a great many variables such as the past history of reinforcement, the motivation or deprivation level at the time of extinction, and the availability of reinforcement for incompatible behavior. Extinction following the basic schedules of reinforcement was described in Chapter 4. To review: Behavior that has been maintained by continuous reinforcement is least resistant to extinction in terms of both time and number of responses. Extinction is characterized by bursts of responding, and at first the behavior may occur at an even higher rate than when it was reinforced. Extinction following reinforcement on ratio schedules is also quite rapid; but the behavior occurs at a high, sustained rate. In terms of total number of responses, it is far more resistant to extinction than is behavior that has been maintained by continuous reinforcement. Extinction following behavior maintained by interval schedules is characterized by a low, sustained rate of responding. The total number of responses is often less than following ratio reinforcement, but responding is maintained for a longer period of time and only gradually tapers off.

Those with the experience of being around parents of small children might recognize the following situation. A 20-month-old child was making life miserable for his parents and aunt by screaming and crying when he was put to bed—unless, of course, someone stayed with him until he fell asleep. Temper tantrums were reinforced by having someone keep him company (sometimes for as long as two hours). (The behavior of staying with him was being maintained by escape and/or avoidance contingencies.) Finally, the parents were advised to implement an extinction procedure that required them to leave the room and close the door after putting the child to bed (Williams, 1959).

The first time the child was put to bed under this extinction procedure he cried and screamed for 45 minutes (see Figure 5.1). The second time he didn't cry, and the third he cried for only 10 minutes. As the solid line in Figure 5.1 shows, the duration of crying continued to decrease with the number of times the child was put to bed. By the 10th time he smiled at his parents when they left. Unfortunately, at this time the aunt reinforced a temper tantrum by coming back and staying with him until he went to sleep. This single reinforcement necessitated a second extinction (Figure 5.1, dotted line). Notice that during the second extinction the duration of crying was generally longer than during the first extinction: The temper tantrums had been reinforced on an intermittent schedule, and behavior maintained by intermittent reinforcement is generally more resistant to extinction. Finally, by the ninth time the child was put to bed the curve reached zero and no further temper tantrums were reported during the next two years. Before one can carry out extinction, one has to locate the relevant reinforcers. If staying with the child until he fell asleep had not been the reinforcer maintaining temper tantrums there would not have been a decrease in behavior when the parents no longer stayed with the child.

Another example of the use of an extinction procedure is Ayllon and Haughton's control of

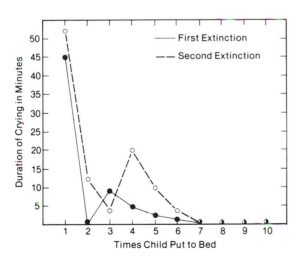

Figure 5.1. Extinction of bedtime temper tantrums: Length of crying on successive occasions of being put to bed. A single reinforcement required second extinction (dotted lines). (From Williams, 1959, p. 269.)

the psychotic verbal behavior of a chronic schizophrenic hospitalized for 16 years. Her psychotic verbal behavior consisted of references to the "royal family"; and the hospital staff stated that references to herself as "Queen" had been virtually her only topic of conversation for eight years. A bilateral prefrontal lobotomy had produced no observed effect on her verbal behavior.

Two classes of verbal behavior were recorded: "psychotic" verbalizations including references to royalty, and "neutral" verbalizations including "What time is it?" and "I'd like some soap." Each class was both reinforced and extinguished during different stages of the experiment, to control for the possibility that any change in behavior might be due to some systematic bias or to the passage of time. Both reinforcement and extinction were controlled by psychiatric nurses. Reinforcement consisted of giving the patient one cigarette and talking with her for three minutes. Extinction was the withholding of cigarettes and social attention: the nurse looked away from the patient and acted interested in something else.

Figure 5.2 shows the control of psychotic verbal behavior by these procedures. For the first 15 days, during which verbal behavior was recorded but not differentially reinforced, the two classes of verbal behavior occurred equally often. During the next 75 days, when psychotic verbalizations were reinforced and neutral ones extinguished, there was a marked change in the patient's verbal behavior. Psychotic verbalizations occurred at twice the baseline frequency, and neutral ones nearly disappeared. When the reinforcement contingencies were reversed, so was verbal content. The success of this and similar experiments in modifying the verbal behavior of psychotics has important implications for psychiatry. If the bizarre verbal behavior that characterizes some forms of schizophrenia can be controlled by social reinforcement, it need not be a symptom of the malfunction of some hypothesized inner process (Ayllon & Haughton, 1964).

This study, unlike Williams (1959), combined the extinction of one class of behavior with the reinforcement of another. The reinforcement of alternative behavior, which is a particularly good way to reduce inappropriate behavior, is described below.

b. Side effects

As noted previously, there may be an initial increase in the occurrence of behavior at the start of extinction, and this alone makes extinction a difficult procedure to carry out. Further difficulties arise from the fact that extinction is often accompanied by aggression and other "emotional" behavior. Artist-psychologist David Thorne tells it from one species' point of view (Figure 5.3). There is documentation for

the side effects portrayed in these cartoons. Among animal studies, one pigeon will attack another during periods of extinction (Azrin, Hutchinson and Hake, 1966), and emit emotional behavior such as wing-flapping, freezing, and pacing back and forth along the walls of the experimental apparatus (Girton and Reese, 1973). Given the opportunity, teenage boys will punch a padded cushion during periods of extinction (Kelly & Hake, 1970); and college women will report high levels of annoyance on an "annoyance meter" (Fuller & Reese, 1974).

In addition to aggression, annoyance, and other "emotional" behavior, the side effects of extinction may include the weakening or strengthening of other classes of behavior. As Sajwaj, Twardosz, and Burke (1972) point out, four possible categories of side effects may accompany extinction—or any other procedure

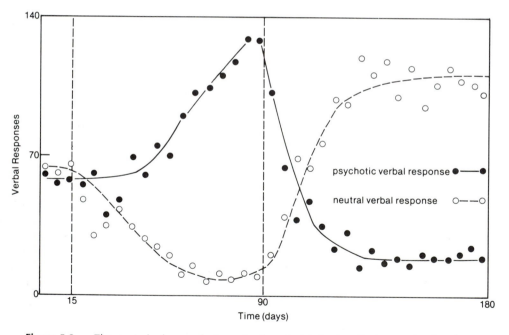

Figure 5.2. The control of a psychotic patient's verbal behavior. During 15-day baseline, psychotic and neutral speech occurred equally often. From the 15th to the 90th day, psychotic verbal behavior was reinforced and increased while unreinforced neutral speech nearly disappeared. During the final 90 days, neutral verbal behavior was reinforced and psychotic verbal behavior was extinguished. (From Ayllon & Haughton, 1964, p. 91.)

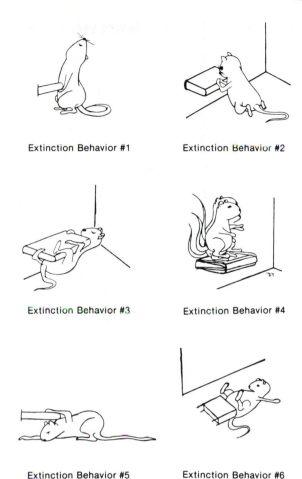

Extinction Behavior #1   Extinction Behavior #2

Extinction Behavior #3   Extinction Behavior #4

Extinction Behavior #5   Extinction Behavior #6

Figure 5.3. Extinction from the subject's perspective. (Illustrations by David Thorne.) (From Whaley & Malott, 1971, p. 58.)

for that matter: desirable behavior may increase or decrease and inappropriate behavior may increase or decrease. In the following example, Wayne, a 7-year old boy in a remedial program for disturbed and retarded children, was engaging in excessive conversation with his teacher instead of speaking or playing with the other children. When the teacher ignored his attempts to engage him in conversation during free play, this behavior decreased (extinguished). But extinction also had effects on four

other classes of behavior: (1) social behavior with other children increased, (2) his use of girls' toys decreased, (3) appropriate academic behavior decreased, and (4) disruptive behavior increased. These last two side effects were dealt with by implementing additional contingencies.

In summary: extinction does *not* produce a rapid decline in the strength of behavior. In fact, the rate of behavior may be higher immediately after the introduction of extinction than before. Extinction can eliminate behavior completely, and its effects are durable unless the behavior recurs and is reinforced. Accompanying side effects, in terms of changes in the strength of other classes of behavior, may be desirable or undesirable. Beneficial side effects are likely when the extinguished behavior is incompatible with appropriate behavior. For example, it would be difficult for Wayne to develop social skills with his peers if he were constantly attending to the teacher. But if this behavior were reduced to a reasonable level, he would be more likely to talk and play with the other children.

Extinction procedures require identification and termination of the contingencies that have maintained the behavior. The initial increase in the strength of behavior accompanied by aggression and "emotional" outbursts may make it difficult to systematically maintain this procedure. (This is especially true if attention is the reinforcer.) Fortunately, the decrease in behavior can be accelerated, and the whole process can be made easier when extinction is used in conjunction with the other procedures described later in this chapter.

c. Behavior maintained by avoidance

Extinction of avoidance behavior can be accomplished by two different methods. Remember that avoidance behavior is maintained by the postponement of a punisher. Thus to extinguish avoidance behavior we could: (1)

eliminate the punisher entirely from the situation, that is, the punisher would not be delivered even if the avoidance behavior did not occur; or (2) deliver the punisher whether or not the behavior occurred.

Whichever type of extinction procedure is used, avoidance behavior is quite resistant to extinction. The behavior may occur many, many times over a long period of time with no substantial decrease in rate. It's rather like carrying around a rabbit's foot to prevent bad luck. You can carry around the rabbit's foot and have nothing bad happen to you for quite a long time. And even if something unfortunate *does* happen, you might think how much worse it would have been had you left the rabbit's foot at home.

A monkey who has learned to press a lever that postpones electric shock for 10 seconds will avoid all potential shocks as long as he presses at least once every 10 seconds. Lever pressing is being reinforced and maintained by the avoidance of shock. He presses and he does not get shocked. If we now disconnect the shock apparatus so that no further shocks are possible, he still presses and he still does not get shocked! There is no change in the experimental operations affecting the monkey until he presses less often than once every 10 seconds; but even at this lowered rate, he is still pressing and still not getting shocked. There is, of course, no relation between pressing and the absence of shock.

If the aversive stimulus is reintroduced, the avoidance behavior increases, even when it is no longer successful. In other words, the introduction of *unavoidable* noncontingent shock will strengthen behavior that previously has been successful in avoiding shock, thus prolonging extinction. If shock is made contingent on lever pressing, lever pressing may decrease; but the operations are those of punishment, not extinction. In some cases, however, even the operations of punishment do not suppress behavior that has previously been maintained by avoidance contingencies. The electric shock that would function as a punisher were there no past history of avoidance can actually function as a reinforcer. Kelleher and Morse have explored these parameters in an extraordinary series of studies; and they have found that, following avoidance training, monkeys will press a lever for months when the only consequence of pressing is painful electric shock (Kelleher & Morse, 1969). Similar findings have been reported for cats by Byrd (1969).

There is relatively little work with human subjects on the extinction of behavior that has avoided a punisher. (The extinction of anxiety is discussed at some length in the next chapter.) However, one extinction record was shown in Figure 4.9: the extinction of stuttering following its conditioning by the avoidance of shock (Flanagan et al., 1959). In this study, the behavior was conditioned without the subjects' awareness of the relation between stuttering and shock avoidance; and when the shock apparatus was discontinued during extinction, nearly 1,000 instances of stuttering occurred within 45 minutes, and the curve is still rising. The persistence of behavior during extinction following avoidance contingencies is probably related to the problem of discriminating the contingencies. If the Flanagan et al. subjects had recognized that their initial increase in stuttering was correlated with shock avoidance, and if they had been told at the start of extinction that shock would no longer be forthcoming, it is possible that extinction would have occurred more rapidly.

2. Satiation

Satiation refers to a decrease in behavior resulting from the loss of effectiveness of the reinforcer that is maintaining that behavior. The most frequently cited example is behavior maintained by food, behavior that decreases and eventually ceases as more food is consumed. The loss of effectiveness of food as a reinforcer is a function of its continued presentation. The decrease in behavior reinforced with food is gradual and temporary, and it will recover after a period of no eating. For this reason, satiation is rarely used in an applied setting. However, procedures analogous to satiation have been successful, especially when combined with other procedures.

Many parents who have caught their children smoking cigarettes have used a modified "satiation" technique. Instead of punishing, they have sat down with a couple of packs of cigarettes and insisted that the child smoke all of them, one after another. A similar procedure has been used with adults who responded to a public service radio announcement and met in a motel conference room on two consecutive weekends (Marrone, Merksamer, & Salzberg, 1970). Of those who smoked continuously for a total of 20 hours, 60 percent were no longer smoking at a four-month follow up. Of those who went through the treatment for only 10 hours, only 18 percent were abstinent at the end of four months.

Many young children are fascinated by lighted matches, and some become juvenile firebugs. Welsh (1968) has treated two such cases by an "oversatiation" procedure. The children, both 7-year-olds, had extensive histories of deliberate fire-setting, and the mother of one had discovered his bed in flames "just in the nick of time." Therapy took place in a well-equipped playroom. When the client was brought in, he was taught how to light matches: one at a time, closing the cover before striking, holding the lighted match over the ash tray, and blowing out the match when it burned down. For one child, an additional requirement was made to insure fatigue: the lighted match had to be held at arm's length, and he could not rest his arm on a table or support it with his other arm. Both clients seem to enjoy their

"lessons"—at least for a while. One went through one and a half boxes of small wooden matches in 40 minutes, but showed "some discomfort" toward the end of the session. Fewer matches were lit during the second session, and during the third he had to be forced to light 10 matches before he was allowed to play with the toys in the room. After only three sessions, his parents allowed him to help burn the trash because "he no longer has that look in his eyes when the trash burns." The problem had not returned four months later. The other child required seven sessions before he refused to light any more matches, and a six-month follow up showed no return of the problem.

Ayllon (1963) has used a variation of satiation to control hoarding behavior in psychiatric patients. One patient collected towels and stored them in her room. The room count ranged from 19 to 29, even though the nurses repeatedly retrieved the towels. When "satiation" treatment started, the towels were no longer removed from her room. Instead, the nurses began giving the patient towels, handing them to her without comment. She was presented seven towels a day during the first week and 60 a day by the third week. When 625 towels had accumulated in her room, the patient began taking them out; and the nurse stopped bringing her towels.

Figure 5.4 shows a baseline of approximately 20 towels established over a period of seven weeks. During the four weeks of treatment the curve rises sharply to 625, at which point the patient started removing towels. The accumulated hoard disappeared over the next eleven weeks, and for the next year only one to five towels were found in her room. The patient never returned to hoarding towels, nor was hoarding replaced by any other problem behavior.

Actually, Ayllon's procedure resembles an old trick of hunters. Hunting dogs can be cured of running unwanted game by giving them an

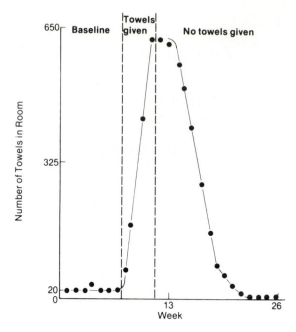

Figure 5.4.   Elimination of a psychiatric patient's towel hoarding by satiation procedures. After establishing baseline, nurses gave the patient towels. When 625 towels had accumulated in her room, the patient started removing them. (From Ayllon, 1963, p. 51.)

overdose of the animal's scent. Concentrated "breaking scent" is applied to the dog's head or to an absorbent felt pad attached to his collar. To quote from an advertisement for one product, Super Stop Deer: "The idea is to really dose him up good, get him so thoroughly dosed with the odor that it gags him to even think of it."

Technically, overwhelming a patient with a supply of towels or a dog with breaking scent is not satiation. The scent and the towels are not contingent on specific activities initiated by the individual. The point is that providing excessive amounts of a reinforcer (that is, more than the individual would normally work to obtain) appears to be aversive, or at least to reduce the effectiveness of that reinforcer.

3. Response Cost

Response cost is the removal of a reinforcer contingent on the occurrence of some behavior.

As mentioned earlier, having to pay a speeding ticket is an example of response cost as is paying a fine for an overdue book at the library. Most research with response cost has been concerned with the loss of generalized conditioned reinforcers such as money, points, or tokens; although it may also include loss of such privileges as television or recess.

It is important to differentiate between response cost, time out, and extinction. A review of the literature on response cost has been conducted by Kazdin (1972a), and let us start as he does by saying what response cost is *not*. Response cost is not extinction, because an extinction procedure contains no programmed consequence for behavior. In extinction, reinforcement is not delivered, but neither are reinforcers lost. Response cost can be distinguished from time out in that time out, as defined by Leitenberg (1965, p. 428), includes a brief period of time when reinforcers are not available. Response cost has no such time limit. Nor does time out specify the loss of reinforcers; but, rather, their unavailability. Response cost does not refer to the effort required to emit the behavior, nor does it refer to the *exchange* of points or tokens for backup reinforcers. The "cost" involved in token exchange, unlike response cost, does not involve a net loss of reinforcers.

In the laboratory, Harold Weiner has been studying response cost with normal human subjects since at least 1962. His subjects push a response button and can earn or lose points according to various schedules of reinforcement. Point loss can be conducted in either of two ways: the subjects can earn points for appropriate responding and lose them for inappropriate responding (Weiner, 1962); or they can be given a set number of points at the start of the session and lose some for inappropriate responding (Weiner, 1963). Both procedures are effective in lowering inappropriately high rates of responding, as, for example, under a fixed interval schedule of reinforcement.

The procedure in which points can be both earned and lost has been used to suppress violent behavior in a token economy program for psychiatric patients (Winkler, 1970); to suppress swearing, personal assault, and property damage in a token economy for mildly retarded delinquents (Burchard & Barrera, 1972); and to decrease crying in a psychiatric patient being treated for "anxiety-depression" (Reisinger, 1972).

Point loss without the opportunity to gain points has been used as a procedure to decrease the disruptive behavior of adolescents in a psychiatric hospital classroom (Kaufman & O'Leary, 1972); to suppress speech disfluencies in normally-speaking college students (Siegel, Lenske, & Broen 1969); and to decrease out-of-seat behavior in an elementary-school child (Wolf, Hanley, King, Lachowicz, & Giles, 1970). In this last study, extra points that could be lost were added to a classroom program in which the students earned points for academic work and exchanged them for backup reinforcers. Sue, whose out-of-seat behavior had not been affected by a procedure in which points were given for in-seat behavior, was given 50 extra points at the start of each class period. She was told that she would lose 10 of these points every time she was out of seat. In this condition, she could retain all 50 points by staying in her seat. In another response-cost condition, the extra points that Sue retained were divided among herself and four peers; meaning that she could retain a maximum of 10 points. The results of these various response cost conditions are shown in Figure 5.5. Before the response-cost contingency, Sue was out of seat during approximately 30 intervals. (Sessions lasted one and a half hours a day, and Sue's out-of-seat behavior was recorded in 30-second intervals.) The response-cost condition during which Sue kept all of the points she didn't lose was successful in reducing out-of-seat behavior below 10 percent; but when she shared the points with

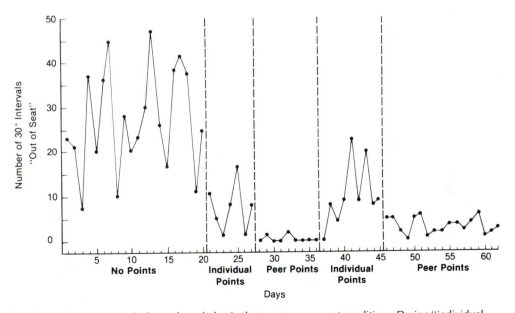

Figure 5.5.   Control of out-of-seat behavior by two response cost conditions. During "individual points" all points were exchanged at end of session for back-up reinforcers. During "peer points" condition, points were divided equally among subject and four peers before being exchanged. (From Wolf, Hanley, King, Lachowicz, & Giles, 1970, p. 116.)

her peers, her out-of-seat behavior was essentially eliminated. As it happened, Sue was receiving a little help from her friends. The authors' note: "... if she stood up, she was immediately reminded to sit down. If she broke her pencil, which she often did, one of the four peers would volunteer to sharpen it for her. If she went to the lavatory, she was reminded to hurry." (Wolf et al., 1970, p. 116.)

Avoidance of response cost has been used as a procedure to decrease smoking (Elliott & Tighe, 1968) and facilitate weight loss (Mann, 1972; Aragona, Cassady, & Drabman, 1975). In these studies, valuables (usually money) were deposited at the start of treatment; and the subjects could gradually "earn" them back if they met a specified criterion or lose them if they did not.

The subjects in the Aragona et al. (1975) study were overweight children ranging in age from five to eleven years. The subjects were randomly assigned to one of three groups: response-cost-plus-reinforcement, response-cost-only, or a no-treatment (control) group. In the response-cost-plus-reinforcement group, the parents of the overweight children would lose some of the money that they deposited at the beginning of treatment if any of the following occurred: (1) they failed to attend a weekly meeting, (2) failed to fill out charts and graphs pertaining to their child's program, or (3) the child failed to meet her specified weekly weight-loss goal. In addition, the parents in this group contracted to deliver a reinforcer to their child for each week the weight-loss goal was met. In the response-cost-only group, the parents did not contract to deliver any such reinforcer to their child for meeting the weekly weight-loss goal, but they were subject to the same response-cost contingencies described above. Children in the control or no-treatment group were told that the program was full at this time, but measurements of their weight were taken periodically during the course of the study.

The mean weight loss/gain for the three groups is shown in Figure 5.6. There was no difference in terms of effectiveness between the response-cost-only group and the response-cost-plus-reinforcement group. The procedures were equally effective in producing weight loss as compared to the no-treatment group. However, 31 weeks after the termination of the program follow-up data indicated that all subjects were gaining weight, but the children whose parents had been in the response-cost plus reinforcement group were gaining weight much more slowly.

These data illustrate the importance of long-term follow-up measures (discussed in Chapter 3), and point up the need for procedures to insure the maintenance of gains made during treatment.

A few years ago, I heard that the Hyatt Hotel people would be paying a substantial bonus to the builder of the Hyatt Regency in San Francisco for completing the hotel ahead of schedule. This sounded like a splendid application of reinforcement principles, so I wrote for further information. It seems the arrangement also includes a form of response cost, not unique to the construction business. After deciding the maximum number of working days required to complete a building, the contractor agrees to pay a penalty for any days he runs beyond this building time. On the other hand, he receives a bonus if he finishes ahead of schedule, the penalty usually being twice the bonus. My informant[1] wrote "I must say it creates incentive," and noted that the San Francisco job was well ahead of schedule.

One point must be remembered when using a response cost procedure. Although it seems obvious, it bears mentioning: response cost means that some reinforcer must be taken away. Think a minute about Sue, the ele-

---

1. Edward G. Sullivan, Vice President and General Manager, Hyatt on Union Square, San Francisco. Personal communication, August 4, 1972.

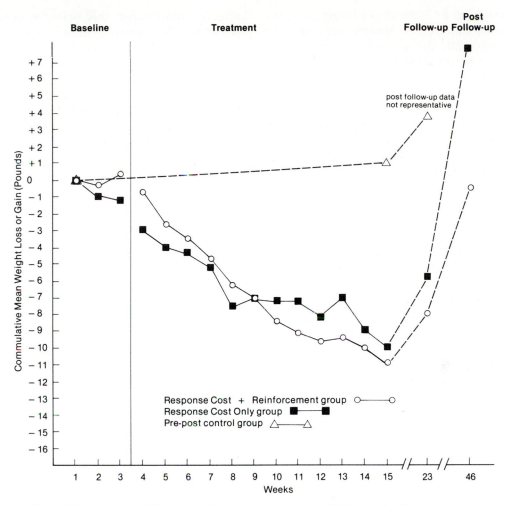

Figure 5.6. Mean weight loss or gain during treatment and follow-up for three groups; no treatment (control), response cost only, and response cost plus reinforcement. (From Aragona, Cassady, & Drabman, 1975, p. 274.)

mentary-school student. Suppose that in the first 15 minutes of class she left her chair five times. Since each time would cost her 10 tokens, she would be "pointless" for the rest of the class. And having lost all her points, there would be no incentive for staying in her chair.

Kazdin (1972a) has reviewed the literature comparing response cost with other reductive procedures. He found that response cost is generally as effective as other procedures with respect to degree of suppression, that its effects are durable, and that adverse side effects are seldom reported.

4. Time Out

Time out is a procedure that weakens behavior by imposing a period of time during which reinforcers are not available. Sending a hockey player to the penalty box as a consequence of a personal foul is an example. Originally, time out meant time away from the opportunity to gain reinforcement. An individual earning monetary reinforcers by doing shopwork might be sent from the room for a brief period of time whenever he engaged in disruptive behavior (e.g., Burchard, 1967). Or, the opportunity to receive social reinforcers might be withdrawn as when an individual is temporarily removed from a group to an empty room, contingent on some behavior. Time out has now been extended to include the brief withdrawal of a reinforcing event. The difference is that in one instance the *individual is being removed* from the reinforcing situation and in the other a *reinforcing event is temporarily withdrawn* from the individual.

Examples of this latter form of time out are shown in the following studies. McReynolds (1969) both removed reinforcers and turned her back on the subject in a very successful program to reduce inappropriate verbal behavior while teaching imitative speech. Baer (1962) suppressed thumbsucking in preschool children by turning off a cartoon whenever the child had his thumb in his mouth; and multiple tics in a neurological patient were suppressed by the interruption of music contingent on the occurrence of tics (Barrett, 1962).

It may have occurred to you, while reading about these three studies, that time out seems very close to response cost. It is—except that a period of time is involved. In his review of the literature, Leitenberg (1965, p. 428) concludes: "There is no single set of operations which adequately defines time-out (TO) from positive reinforcement. The essential feature is a period of time in which positive reinforcement is no longer available."

Both kinds of time out were utilized in a study to decrease the inappropriate meal time behavior of institutionalized retardates. If they stole food, all subjects were removed from the dining area to a time-out room for the duration of a meal. But for another class of behavior, eating with fingers, one of two procedures was used. Eleven of the subjects were removed to the

time-out room when this behavior occurred; while for the other five subjects, eating with fingers resulted in their tray being removed for 15 seconds. The time out procedures appeared to be equally effective in suppressing this unwanted behavior. At the end of six months, after time out had also been introduced for other, related activities, essentially all inappropriate mealtime behavior had been suppressed (Barton, Guess, Garcia, & Baer, 1970).

Ayllon (1963) has also used the withdrawal of food reinforcement to eliminate the behavior of stealing food in a chronic schizophrenic. The patient weighed more than 250 pounds, which the medical staff considered detrimental to her health, and she had not weighed less than 230 pounds during her nine years of hospitalization. Earlier attempts to control her stealing from the food counter and from other patients included coaxing, persuasion, and forcing her to return the stolen food.

Treatment consisted of removing the patient from the dining room whenever she stole food. Figure 5.7 shows that during the three weeks the baseline was established, she stole at more than two-thirds of all meals. When stealing resulted in missing her meal, it was rapidly eliminated. As an additional benefit, the patient

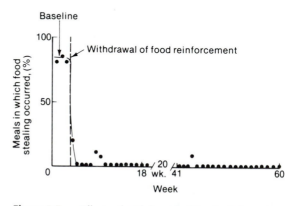

Figure 5.7.   Effects of withdrawal of food reinforcement on the behavior of stealing food by a psychiatric patient. Stealing food was eliminated in one week, and recurred but rarely during the following year. (See also Figure 5.8.) (From Ayllon, 1963, p. 55.)

lost weight when she ate only her prescribed food. At the end of treatment, her weight had stabilized at 180 pounds, and she was pronounced in excellent physical condition (Figure 5.8).

Time out, like most other procedures that decrease the strength of behavior, is probably most effective when combined with reinforcement of appropriate behavior. Vukelich and Hake (1971) were able to suppress the dangerously aggressive behavior of an institutionalized patient by employing both time out for aggressive behavior and social reinforcement for appropriate behavior; time out alone was ineffective. Before treatment the patient "was restrained to a mattress by four sheets and was stuporous due to a heavy drug dose" (p. 217). When the drug dosage was reduced and she was unrestrained for brief periods, she choked another resident within minutes of her release. Even with time out, choking occurred at a rate of eight per hour. Choking was suppressed when continued extra attention—contingent on *not* choking—was added to the time-out contingency; but, when the extra attention was removed, the patient began grabbing other patients by the clothes and hair, even though choking and grabbing resulted in time out. In the final phase, when extra social attention (about seven minutes per hour) was again made contingent on her not being in time out, she could be left unrestrained for 12 hours a day.

Parents have used time out successfully in at least two very difficult cases: a four-year-old with frequent tantrums and periods of aggression (Hawkins, Peterson, Schweid, & Bijou, 1966); and a four-year-old who was extremely aggressive, bossy, and disobedient (Zeilberger, Sampen, & Sloane, 1968). In both studies, the mother was the therapist. As many parents and teachers have learned, time out is a difficult procedure to implement. There are, however, a number of guidelines for its effective use, the following being particularly important. First, the time-out room must not be reinforcing or it will

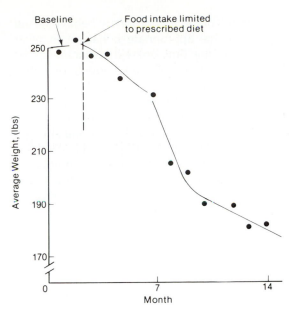

Figure 5.8   Control of food stealing (Figure 5.7) was accompanied by a loss of body weight when the patient's eating was limited to her prescribed diet. (From Ayllon, 1963, p. 55.)

increase, rather than decrease, the problem behavior. Hawkins et al. modified a family bedroom, removing all the toys and other items of interest. Second, getting someone to time out must be done with as little fuss as possible so that attention does not maintain the problem behavior. In fact, all identifiable reinforcers of the problem behavior must be withheld, and that includes elaborate explanations or expressions of sympathy concerning either the behavior or the time out procedure itself. Third, leave the individual in time out until he has been quiet for a couple of minutes. If he has been put there because of a temper tantrum, removing him from time out while the tantrum is still going on will only make matters worse. Fourth, be consistent.[2] Time out should follow *each*

2. Clark, Rowbury, Baer, and Baer (1973) suggest that time out delivered on some intermittent schedule may be as effective as time out on a continuous schedule, at least in the case of behavior that has already been reduced to a low rate.

occurrence of the inappropriate behavior. And fifth, reinforce appropriate behavior. In other words, combine time out with extinction of the problem behavior and reinforcement of appropriate behavior.

A variation of time out called *contingent observation* has been used to reduce disruptive and aggressive behavior in very young children in a day-care setting (Porterfield, Herbert-Jackson, & Risley, 1976). When inappropriate behavior occurred, the child was instructed in appropriate alternative behavior and then required to sit at the periphery of the group for a short time and watch the appropriate social behavior of the other children. This "sit and watch" procedure was more effective than instructions combined with redirecting the child to an alternative toy or activity. Contingent observation appealed to the parents and teachers as an appropriate way to reduce problem behavior, and it has a potential educational value that many other reductive procedures lack.

In most applied settings, the duration of time out is a brief two to five minutes. White, Nielsen, and Johnson (1972) compared three time out durations in suppressing such behavior as aggression, tantrums, and self-destruction. When it was used *first*, a one-minute time out suppressed behavior to a greater extent than did 15- or 30-minute time outs (which did not differ from one another). However, when the short time out came after an extended experience with the longer durations, it generally resulted in an increase in the problem behavior. The one-minute time out may have lost its effectiveness by being contrasted with the longer durations.

Response cost and time out were compared in a study by Burchard and Barrera (1972). Two durations of time out (five and thirty minutes) and two levels of response cost (five and thirty tokens) were used in this study of mildly retarded delinquents in a token economy. For five of the six subjects, the greater cost or the longer time out suppressed swearing, assault, property damage, and certain other classes of problem behavior to a greater extent than did the lower values of cost or time out. There was little difference between the two suppression procedures. However, there was evidence that both time out and response cost were more effective when combined than when either was used alone. The authors make two important points about the use of these procedures. Cost has the advantage of not removing individuals from a situation in which they might engage in desirable behavior. On the other hand, they may continue to engage in the problem behavior, which will result in further costs. Time out may mean time away from the opportunity for learning, but it allows the individual (and the staff) a chance to "cool off."

A final caution when considering the use of time out: What is intended as time out from reinforcement may actually constitute escape from some unspecified punishing event (negative reinforcement). If so, the problem behavior will increase rather than decrease. This was the case when time out was used to suppress disruptive behavior and inappropriate eating, respectively, in an autistic and a retarded preschool child (Plummer, Baer, & LeBlanc, in press), and when junior high school students were sent to a detention room, contingent upon disruptive classroom behavior (Silverman & Silverman, 1973). In a practice that resembles time out, suspension from school is the consequence of unexcused absences in some school systems. But if the student finds school and classroom activities aversive, suspension is unlikely to provide a remedy unless other contingencies are also in effect. (If the environment outside of school were not more attractive than the school environment, the unexcused absences might not occur in the first place.)

5. Restraint and Confinement

Destructive or self-injurious behavior is sometimes prevented by strapping people to their beds or by putting them into straitjackets to protect them and those around them. If some-one is restrained in this way for long periods of time, the contingencies are likely to become obscured. We know of few studies in which restraint has been made contingent upon spe-cific instances of problem behavior. However, when it is applied in a consistent and a con-tingent manner, the procedure appears to be effective. Physical restraint was used in a *time out* procedure with a 16-year-old girl who was restrained to her bed during most of the day because of a high rate of breaking windows with her head (Hamilton, Stephens, & Allen, 1967). When she was released even briefly, for eating, toileting, and exercise, she managed to break an average of one window a day. Instead of *keeping* her restrained, the authors made re-straint contingent upon the problem behavior. When she broke a window with her head, she was restrained to her bed for two hours. The first week, she broke six windows; then two a week for the next six weeks; then none for the remain-ing 11 months of the study.

Rehabilitation is a major argument for con-fining people to hospitals and prisons. Presum-ably, the confinement provides an opportunity to strengthen behavior that is incompatible with criminal behavior, drug abuse, and so forth, and thus provide the individual with an alternative means of surviving when returned to society. Confinement *per se* would contribute little toward this goal.

This assumption is supported by the work of Vaillant (1965) on drug addicts. Vaillant ex-amined the 12-year history of 100 drug addicts who were first admitted to the U.S. Public Health Service Hospital at Lexington in 1952. Not one of these men became abstinent simply because he was unable to get drugs, nor were voluntary hospitalization or prison terms with-out parole effective. The combination of vari-ables that produced abstinence for at least a year, in more than 60 percent of the addicts concerned, was more than eight months in the prison hospital and more than a year of parole.

Lexington did not merely withdraw drugs. It provided supervised work programs, and regu-lar work is incompatible with the behavior in-volved in maintaining an expensive drug habit. Parole after release also required stable em-ployment, a requirement that would help to maintain incompatible behavior in the situa-tion where drug-seeking behavior formerly oc-curred. Men on parole also had to avoid certain of their former associates, which probably helped to remove some of the discriminative stimuli for drug seeking.

6. Reinforcement of Omission (OT, DRO)

When reinforcement is made contingent upon the absence or omission of behavior, the fre-quency or duration of that behavior usually de-clines. This procedure, which is beginning to receive a good deal of attention in the labora-tory, is called *omission training* (OT).[3] In OT,

3. Grant (1964) called this procedure omission training. In applied settings, however, it is usually called by its earlier name, DRO (Reynolds, 1961), which stands for Differential Reinforcement of Other Behavior. Since the "other" behavior presumably reinforced by DRO is usually inferred, the term is a bit misleading: what the procedure amounts to is the "Differential reinforcement of *unspecified* Other Behavior." This being the case, the term omission training seems more descriptive of the experimental operations than does DRO and is therefore the term used here.

The name of this procedure raises another problem in terminology. The words, reinforcer and reinforcement, are defined in terms of their effects upon behavior. In operant conditioning, an event is not a reinforcer unless it increases the strength of the behavior it follows. What behavior is reinforced or strengthened when a potential reinforcer is made contingent upon the absence of some other behavior? The implication of the term, DRO, is that some unspecified behavior is reinforced; the implication of the term, OT, is that nonresponding is a class of behavior that can be reinforced. More precisely, the implication of OT is that the absence of a particular class of behavior is another class of behavior.

Going back to the experimental operations, a potential reinforcer is delivered whenever a particular class of behavior does not occur for a certain period of time. If we judged the effectiveness of the procedure by measuring the change in other classes of behavior, the term DRO would be appropriate. Instead, we judge its effectiveness by measuring the change in the particular class of behavior that has not occurred when reinforcers are delivered. So both the

reinforcement is made contingent on the failure to emit a given class of behavior for a specified period of time. That is, the essential requirement for reinforcement is that a period of time must pass during which the behavior is omitted or does not occur.

Studies with animals have found that reinforcement of nonresponding is as effective as extinction or mild punishment in suppressing behavior. Omission training sometimes requires more time, but its effects have been found to be more durable (Nevin, 1968; Topping, Larmi & Johnson, 1972; Uhl & Sherman, 1971; Zeiler, 1971). Though much remains to be learned about the reinforcement of nonresponding, it seems to be an effective procedure for reducing unwanted behavior in applied settings.

Perhaps the earliest report of omission training in an applied setting is the case study of a child, Fay, whose face and other parts of her body were covered with open sores and scabs from almost a year of excessive scratching. Fay was treated by her mother with the help of Eileen Allen and Florence Harris (1966). Allen and Harris first suggested that Fay's mother ignore the scratching, but she said that this procedure had been tried for a whole month and had not worked. During this period Fay often came to her parents to show them that she had not scratched herself for a whole morning or afternoon; but instead of reinforcing non-scratching, the mother had responded by saying "I told you, we're not going to talk about it. We do not care whether you scratch or not. You are a big girl and it is up to you." (p. 81.)

Fay's mother was advised to do three things: (1) ignore scratching or any evidence of recent scratching; (2) give approval and attention for appropriate behavior such as reading, playing, or helping around the house; and (3) give token reinforcement, as well as approval, every 20 or 30 minutes if Fay had not scratched during that time. The token reinforcement was instituted because it seemed difficult for the

mother to use social reinforcement. (The authors report that Fay's mother "verbally punished and criticized her continuously" for minor misdemeanors "perpetuating between herself and the child a constant state of friction," p. 81.) The tokens were gold stars to be pasted in a booklet, and they were redeemable for food and trinkets. The program was tried for a week and was successful during the day. However, Fay continued to scratch herself during the night. Then a more powerful reinforcer was found—Barbie doll clothes. If Fay did not scratch during the day, she went shopping with her mother for a Barbie doll item that was placed in her bedroom at night. If there was no evidence of scratching by morning, Fay was given the item. By the sixth session, Fay's skin was practically healed, and they began to reduce the extrinsic reinforcers. The daytime trinkets were gradually eliminated, and the number of stars for a Barbie doll item was gradually increased until items were given only occasionally at intervals of more than a week. However, the perceptive Allen and Harris advised the mother to continue giving gold stars, and for a very good reason: The stars served to remind Fay's mother of the many examples of desirable behavior she should look for and reinforce. *One of the great advantages of tokens is that they help the person dispensing them become attentive to appropriate behavior.* After only six weeks of reinforcement procedures, all of Fay's sores had completely healed. A four-month follow-up showed that "the scars had faded to a pale pink barely discernible without close scrutiny" (Allen & Harris, 1966, p. 84).

Omission training has been used in an innovative approach to seizure control by Zlutnick, Mayville, and Moffat (1975). One of their

---

procedure itself and the evaluation of its effectiveness seem to favor the use of the term, OT, and the conceptualization of the omission of one class of behavior as another class of behavior.

five subjects was a 17-year-old girl diagnosed as mentally retarded with major motor epilepsy. She had a long history of seizures that—despite the use of Dilantin and phenobarbitol—were a daily occurrence. The authors analyzed her seizures into the following chain of behavior: (1) her body became tense and rigid; (2) she clenched her fists and raised her arms to a 90 degree angle from her body; (3) her head snapped back and she grimaced; then (4) a motor seizure ensued. Figure 5.9 shows that during baseline she was having approximately 16 seizures a day. Treatment consisted of having a staff member lower the girl's arms as soon as the second phase in the behavioral chain occurred. If she then kept her hands down for five seconds, lavish praise was given and an M & M was offered. This procedure was effective immediately, and seizures occurred only when the staff were unable to reach the girl in time to lower her arms before her head snapped back. To confirm that omission training was responsible for the great reduction in seizures, a reversal phase was implemented and the OT procedure removed. (The staff continued to lower her arms, but discontinued reinforcement.) The subsequent increase in the number of seizures, and the fact that seizures

were virtually eliminated when OT was reintroduced, indicate that OT was a major variable responsible for controlling the seizures.

The authors report that six months after the OT procedure was discontinued, there was a short period of renewed seizure activity; but seizures were again eliminated by a brief return to omission training. Nine months after treatment ended, the frequency of seizures was close to zero.

Omission training has also been used to suppress disruptive behavior (Sewell, McCoy & Sewell, 1973) and aggressive behavior (Bostow & Bailey, 1969; Repp & Deitz [sic], 1974) in retarded children. In the latter two studies OT was used in combination with other suppression procedures. Repp and Dietz found that OT could be easily and effectively combined with either mild punishment (a firm "no" when the unwanted behavior occurred), response cost, or time out to reduce such inappropriate behavior as dangerous aggression or self-injury. As Repp and Dietz point out, OT is a useful procedure to suppress behavior in situations where more aversive techniques may be prohibited or restricted. In another positive note, they report that one of the children, whose aggressive behavior was successfully eliminated by OT and

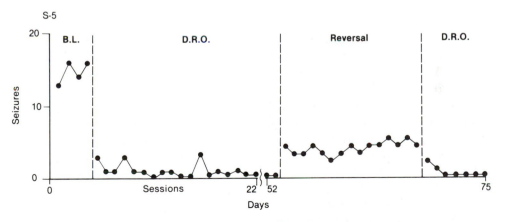

Figure 5.9.   The daily number of motor seizures during phases of study employing omission training (DRO). (From Zlutnik, Mayville, & Moffat, 1975, p. 10.)

time out, developed a high but appropriate rate of saying "I've been good" (p. 323). We don't usually count on reductive procedures to enhance self-esteem—except, perhaps, the procedure described next.

7. Reinforcement of Alternative Behavior (Alt R)

One way to decrease the frequency or duration of problem behavior is to increase the strength of some *other* behavior. The procedure that weakens behavior by the reinforcement of alternative behavior is called *Alt R*. If two activities are incompatible in that they cannot occur at the same time, and if they occur at a very high rate, then the strengthening of one would almost have to be accompanied by a weakening of the other. But it is not necessary that the activities be incompatible, nor must the rate be so high that engaging in one activity leaves little time to engage in the other.

When Fay's mother gave her gold stars for playing and helping with chores, as well as for failure to scratch at other times, she combined the reinforcement of alternative behavior with omission training. Fay could have continued to scratch herself while playing with toys, but she did not. Ayllon and Haughton (1964) also used Alt R when they reinforced neutral verbalizations while extinguishing psychotic verbalizations. (See Figure 5.2.) Neutral and psychotic verbalizations were mutually exclusive, but it is conceivable that they might have varied together, that both classes of verbal behavior might have increased when one was reinforced. Instead, and in both stages of the study, the procedure was highly selective. In this study, we have no way of knowing whether or not extinction alone would have decreased the incidence of psychotic verbalizations; but the rapid decline in one class of verbal behavior when the other was reinforced testifies to the effectiveness of the Alt R procedure.

Reinforcement of alternative behavior has also been used to suppress unwanted behavior in the classroom. Ayllon and Roberts (1974) were able to virtually eliminate the disruptive behavior of five fifth-grade boys by reinforcing academic performance. Disruptive behavior, which was occurring 50 percent of the time during baseline conditions, declined to approximately five percent during the final reinforcement phase, and academic performance increased from 50 to 85 percent.

Ayllon has also used reinforcement of academic behavior to maintain low levels of hyperactivity in children who had previously been taking medication to suppress this behavior (Ayllon, Layman, & Kandel, 1975). The authors provide a description of some of the hyperactive behavior observed during the course of this study:

> The most frequently recorded category for these hyperactive children was gross motor behaviors, which included running around the room, rocking in chairs, and jumping on one or both feet. Disruptive noise with objects included the constant turning of notebook pages and the excessive flipping of book paper. Disturbing others and blurting out included the constant movement of arms, resulting in the destruction of objects and hitting others, screaming, and high-pitched and rapid speech.
>
> (Ayllon, Layman, & Kandel, 1975, p. 140.)

Hyperactivity in children is often controlled by drugs, one of the most common being methylphenidate (Ritalin).[4] Given the conflicting evidence on the effectiveness of such medication and concern for the general practice of administering medication to children, Ayllon decided to try another approach.

One of the three subjects in this study was an eight-year-old girl named Crystal who was enrolled in a learning disabilities class. Clinically diagnosed as chronically hyperactive,

---

4. Ayllon notes that it is estimated that 200,000 children in the United States are currently taking medication to control their hyperactivity.

Crystal had been on medication since she was five years old.

Data collected on academic and hyperactive behavior during reading and math, while Crystal was taking such medication, are shown in Figure 5.10. Ritalin seems to be controlling her hyperactivity (solid circles); but, it is also clear that Crystal was not making much progress academically (open circles). Beginning with the seventh three-day block, Crystal was taken off medication. Hyperactivity rose to 87 percent in math and 91 percent in reading; while academic performance increased slightly but was still much too low. (The children were taken off medication at the start of a holiday weekend. This allowed three days for the effects of the drug to dissipate before their classroom performance was assessed.) In a multiple-baseline design, reinforcement was then introduced for correct academic responses *in math*. Checks were given for each correct item and could be traded in for a variety of backup reinforcers. Hyperactivity during math class dropped to nine percent and academic performance rose to 65 percent. These data strongly suggest that reinforcement for academic performance in math was responsible for the low level of hyperactivity and the improvement in academic performance during that class. If some factor other than reinforcement caused the very desirable effects in math class, we would expect to see similar effects in reading—but this did not happen. When reinforcement procedures were then introduced during reading (while still being maintained in math) Crystal's hyperactivity decreased immediately, and her performance in this subject area improved dramatically. Data from the other two children in the study showed the same reduction of hyperactivity, even without medication, when academic performance was reinforced.

The group data on academic work and hyperactivity, during medication and during reinforcement of academic work, show that

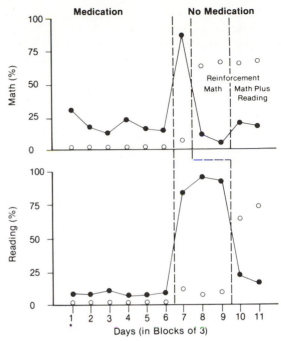

●-● Hyperactivity
○ ○ Academic

Figure 5.10.   Hyperactivity and academic performance of one student (Crystal) during medication and during reinforcement of academic performance. Medication was withdrawn before the seventh 3-day block, and hyperactivity increased sharply. The introduction of reinforcement programs for math (third panel, upper graph) and reading (last panel, lower graph) were accompanied by a marked reduction in hyperactivity as academic performance increased. (After Ayllon, Layman, & Kandel, 1975, p. 142.)

Alt R was as effective as Ritalin in controlling hyperactivity, but with additional benefits (Figure 5.11). Presumably, one of the reasons that children are put on medication is that their hyperactive behavior interferes with learning. Although medication may effectively reduce hyperactivity, academic gains are likely to be greater when reinforcement is contingent upon those gains. The work of Ayllon et al. provides an approach to the treatment of hyperactivity that also strengthens academic performance—a more direct and a more effective approach than medication.

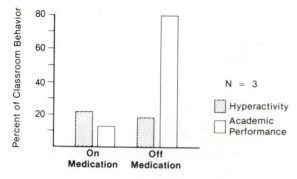

Figure 5.11. Average percentage of hyperactivity and academic performance in math and reading for three children. The first two bars summarize findings from the 17-day baseline under drug therapy. The last two bars show results for the final six-day period without drug therapy but with a reinforcement program for both math and reading performance. (From Ayllon, Layman, & Kandel, 1975, p. 143.)

In basic research with animals, Alt R has been more effective than OT in reducing intraspecific aggression in rats (Baisinger & Roberts, 1972); and it has been more effective than either OT or extinction in reducing lever pressing by squirrel monkeys (Mulick, Leitenberg, & Rawson, 1976). But as the hyperactive children demonstrated, there is another advantage to Alt R that is especially important in applied settings. Many reductive procedures are "negative" in the sense that they suppress one class of behavior while adding nothing to the behavioral repertoire. In such a "vacuum," other problems may develop. The main advantage of the Alt R procedure is that it can decrease unwanted behavior while strengthening behavior that is beneficial to the individual. However, considerable care should be taken in selecting alternative behavior that will be maintained in the normal environment. Otherwise, if the alternative behavior is allowed to extinguish, the problem behavior may return (Girton & Reese, 1973; Leitenberg, Rawson, & Bath, 1970). An important criterion for selecting alternative behavior is that it contribute to the welfare of the individual and be welcomed and sustained by others in the environment.

8. Differential Reinforcement of Low Rate (DRL)

The differential reinforcement of *low rates* of problem behavior has been described above under schedules of reinforcement. In their earlier studies, conducted in special-education classrooms, Dietz and Repp (1973) reduced disruptive verbalizations by reinforcing low rates of this behavior. The procedure was effective whether applied to individuals or to groups of students. Dietz and Repp (1974) have now used the DRL procedure in other programs, designed to reduce misbehavior in a normal elementary classroom. By making gold stars contingent on low rates of children's talking out of turn or leaving their chairs without permission, teachers have greatly reduced these activities. Many classes of behavior, including these examples, become a problem only when their frequency or duration interferes with other classroom activities. The DRL procedure is particularly appropriate when one wishes to reduce "misbehavior" rather than eliminate it entirely.

9. Punishment

The *systematic* application of punishment is usually a procedure of last resort, occasionally employed in institutional settings or in the office of a licensed therapist. The *un*systematic use of punishment is a procedure commonly seen in institutions, and between parent and child, husband and wife, supervisor and worker, teacher and student. Strangely enough, there is considerable moral outrage about the systematic use of punishment but very little concern about its use in everyday life. Furthermore, there seems to be a reluctance to learn about the variables that determine its effectiveness. Among the major issues are questions concerning what sort of punishment will be used, what sort of behavior will be punished, who is to decide whether or not punishment will be used, and who is to apply a punishing event.

In a broad sense, punishment refers to any consequence of behavior that suppresses the behavior by reducing its subsequent frequency or duration. Used in this way, punishment would subsume the operations of response cost and time out. The definition of punishment used here, however, has a more restricted meaning. Punishment is the *presentation* of any stimulus event that suppresses the behavior on which it is contingent (Table 2.1). When an event is used in this way and has this suppressive effect on behavior, it is a punisher. Punishment is thus the presentation of a punisher and therefore does not include the removal of a reinforcer (response cost) or of the opportunity to earn reinforcement (time out).[5] Most people think of a punisher as a painful or aversive event, such as a spanking. Unpleasant social consequences, such as ridicule, could also be punishing events; but the withdrawal of ongoing social consequences such as attention or approval would be the operations of response cost or time out, depending on the period of time involved.

Although the natural environment provides many potential punishing events, most of the basic research on punishment has been conducted with electric shock. If the effectiveness of a punisher is to be evaluated, it is important to be able to specify its parameters and to control its presentation. Electric shock applied to the skin meets these criteria reasonably well, and —at the intensities used—it apparently does the individual no physical harm. This fairly consistent use of shock has provided a good deal of information about the variables that determine its effectiveness in suppressing behavior. On the other hand, one wonders if findings from studies using shock punishment (which, besides being aversive, can involve physical pain) can be extrapolated to other forms of aversive stimulation. The following discussion of punishment is based almost entirely on the use of electric shock and should be read in that context.

Whether the decision to use punishment is made by the individual or by someone with the authority to represent his interests, systematic punishment is seldom used unless the behavior is extremely dangerous to the individual or to others. Neither is it used until other procedures have been tried and found wanting.

a. Punishment using painful stimulation.

The work of Lovaas and his colleagues at UCLA with autistic children is a good example of the exploration of other procedures before the application of punishment. Lovaas learned from his first autistic child, Beth, that self-injurious behavior could be increased and maintained by sympathetic attention. Beth's self-injurious behavior took the forms of beating her head against the wall or the sharp corners of furniture and tearing open her skin with her teeth and nails. They tried strengthening alternative behavior with programs designed to teach her to talk, dress, and play, "But it seemed pointless, since we would take her home to her parents in the afternoon with her head and face still bleeding" (Lovaas, 1973, p. 4). Lovaas and Beth's parents were given professional advice to reassure Beth when she was self-injurious and to express their love and concern. They did this and found she was *worse* on days when she received affectionate attention in conjunction with her self-injurious activities (Lovaas, 1973). Somewhat later, Lovaas found that the frequency of self-injurious behavior increased when it was followed by sympathetic comments and decreased when it was ignored. He also found that the frequency of self-injury was affected when singing, hand clapping, and rocking to music were conditioned. When appropriate musical activities were followed by praise from the experimenter, they were strengthened while self-injurious activities decreased (Lovaas, Freitag, Gold, & Kassorla, 1965).

If self-injurious behavior is maintained by social reinforcement, then it should be possible

5. Unlike time out or restraint, punishment does not remove the individual from the situation or otherwise *prevent* the occurrence of the behavior.

to extinguish it by withholding social reinforcement. This procedure was carried out with John, a seven-year-old boy who had been self-injurious since the age of two. John had only minimal social behavior, no speech or play behavior, was unable to dress himself, and was not toilet trained. In short, John was greatly in need of professional help. He had been in continuous restraints during the six months before Lovaas began to work with him, and he needed complete care in feeding and hygiene. Tranquilizers had no apparent effect on his self-injurious behavior, and when he arrived at UCLA his head was covered with scar tissue and his ears were swollen and bleeding (Bucher & Lovaas, 1968, p. 86; Lovaas & Simmons, 1969, p. 144–145).

During extinction sessions, John was left on a bed without restraints for one and a half hours a day. Self-injurious behavior was recorded from an adjoining observation booth. Data from these sessions are shown in Figure 5.12, where self-injurious acts are plotted cumulatively for each of the successive extinction sessions. On the first day, he hit himself nearly 3,000 times in 90 minutes but the rate declined toward the end of the session. The number of self-injurious acts decreased over the remaining sessions (a long, slow, agonizing process); and John hit himself approximately 10,000 times during the 12 hours he spent in these sessions (Bucher & Lovaas, 1968; Lovaas, 1973).

At this point, Lovaas and his colleagues had found that self-injury could be eliminated by withholding social attention contingent on its occurrence. However, considering the amount of self-injury that took place during extinction, this procedure could hardly be considered humane. In addition, the extinction of John's self-injury in bed had no effect on this behavior in other situations; in other words, generalization did not occur. If children such as John were not to be restrained or drugged, some other

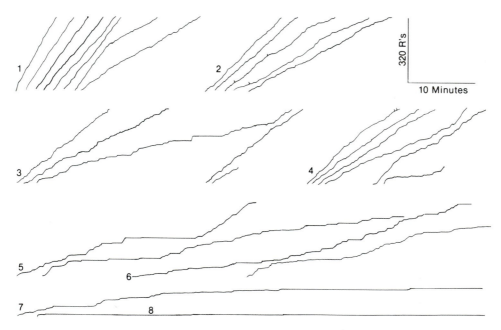

Figure 5.12.   Cumulative record of self-injurious behavior in bed during successive extinction sessions (labeled 1-8). John hit himself approximately 10,000 times during the 12 hours spent in these sessions before this behavior was eliminated. (From Bucher & Lovaas, 1969, p. 87.)

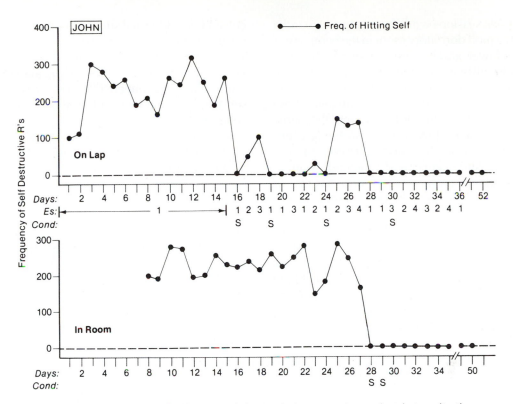

Figure 5.13.   Frequency of self-injurious behavior during successive sessions in two situations: daily 5-min. sessions "on the lap" (upper graph) and daily 10-min. sessions "in the room" (lower graph). The particular experimenter present is shown beneath the upper graph. Sessions when shock (S) was administered are also indicated. Shock was given by Experimenter 1 on days 16, 19, and 24, and by Experimenter 3 on day 30 while John was in the experimenter's lap. Shock was given on days 28 and 29 in the room. (Adapted from Lovaas & Simmons, 1969, p. 148.)

procedure had to be found. Lovaas (1973) says he discovered another procedure by accident. He was working with Beth, his first autistic child, who spent so much time with him that she became like a member of the family.

. . . one day while I was talking to Beth's teacher about her language program, Beth hit her head against the wall right behind me. This made me turn around and, without thinking, slap her quite hard on her rear. She turned around, visibly surprised, but delayed hitting herself for about 30 seconds. She then went back to the wall and hit herself once more, but by that time we had the upper hand. The second time she hit her head she was smacked even harder on the rear. She did not hit herself on the head the rest of the day. Later we 'sharpened' up this treatment (using

painful but harmless electric shock), replicated its effects on other kids, and published on it . . . The point, of course, is that we would never have spanked Beth if we had viewed her as a patient; no one hits a 'sick child'.

(Lovaas, 1973, p. 6.)

This accidental discovery of the beneficial effects of spanking Beth led Lovaas to use shock as punishment with John (Lovaas and Simmons, 1969). This was done after self-injury in bed had been extinguished (Figure 5.12). John's data are presented in Figure 5.13, which shows self-injurious behavior in two situations: during five-minute sessions while sitting on the atten-dant nurse's lap (upper graph) and during

10-minute sessions while he was free to wander about a small dormitory room in the company of adults (lower graph). Sessions in which shock was administered are indicated by the letter S, and the experimenter present during the session is indicated by the numbers 1 through 4. These data were being recorded during the same period that self-injury in bed was being extinguished. By the tenth session in Figure 5.13, self-injury was still occurring at a high rate, both in the attendant's lap and when John was free in the room, even though the behavior had essentially extinguished in bed (Figure 5.12).

On the sixteenth day, while sitting in the attendant's lap, John was shocked on the leg by Experimenter 1 as soon as he hit himself. The effect was immediate (upper graph), but did not generalize to the room (lower graph). Furthermore, self-injury occurred again on the following two days when different experimenters were present. On the 19th day, contingent shock again suppressed self-injury, but again there was no transfer to the other situation, and the behavior reappeared on day 23 with Experimenter 2. On days 25–27, the frequency of self-injury with non-punishing adults increased to more than 100 in these five-minute sessions, but disappeared on days 28 and 29 with the return of the experimenter who had previously administered shock. After a second person, Experimenter 3, administered shock on day 30, there was no further recurrence of self-injury even in the presence of experimenters who had never delivered shock.

By day 27, self-injury was still occurring at a high rate in the dormitory room (lower graph). Suppression of self-injury by shock did not transfer from the attendant's lap to this setting, just as it had not transferred from the bed where it was extinguished. However, two one-second shocks on days 28 and 29 eliminated self-injury in this situation and it did not reappear for the remaining 18 days of the study, even with different experimenters. After these sessions, John received five additional shocks in other situations on the ward and in the street. A total of 19 shocks (12 while sitting on an experimenter's lap, two while in the room, and five in other situations) effectively suppressed John's self-injurious behavior in a wide variety of situations.

John's self-injurious behavior was effectively suppressed by shock; he was no longer a danger to himself, and he could be released from his restraints. *Now* the experimenters could begin to help him develop physical and social skills, something that was impossible before. It also meant that he could run around and explore and discover reinforcing activities on his own. Lovaas and Simmons note that on the first day of shock

he allowed himself a full hour of scratching himself, a luxury he had not been allowed while his hands were tied behind his back. He had been so self-destructive that it had been impossible to give him a bath in a tub. *Freed of self-destructive behavior*, he behaved much like a seal when he was placed in a tub, screaming in happiness and scooting underneath the water with his face up and eyes open.

(Lovaas and Simmons, 1969, p. 149, italics ours.)

Lovaas used shock to suppress self-injury so that he could then apply reinforcement procedures to build adaptive behavior, including speech (e.g., Lovaas, Berberich, Perloff, & Schaeffer, 1966). Sometimes a child was slapped when he was inattentive or engaging in inappropriate behavior; but shock was no longer necessary when self-injury decreased to the point where the children could be released from restraints and other activities could emerge and be reinforced.

Social behavior has also been shaped by shock-avoidance at the same time that self-stimulation and tantrums were suppressed (Lovaas, Schaeffer, & Simmons, 1965). The children in this study were two five-year-old twins who had no verbal behavior, and apparently could not recognize adults or even each other. They spent 70–80 percent of the day in self-stimulating behavior: rocking, fondling themselves, and moving their arms and hands in a stereotyped fashion. They also had frequent temper tantrums during which they screamed, threw things, and hit themselves.

The subjects were placed barefoot in a 12 x 12-foot experimental room, the floor of which could deliver a "painful and frightening" electric shock. During preshock sessions, the baseline performance of the following activities was determined: physical contact with the experimenter, self-stimulatory and tantrum behaviors, and responses to the experimenter's command of "come here." As can be seen in Figures 5.14 and 5.15, during the preshock sessions, the children neither responded to the command nor did they have any physical contact with the experimenters. They did, however,

engage in self-stimulatory behavior and aggression (Figure 5.15).

During the shock sessions, the shock was turned on when the child engaged in self-stimulatory or tantrum behavior, and it was turned off when the child responded to the experimenter's invitation to approach. (Approach behavior was shaped by this shock-avoidance procedure.) The data show that this combination of punishment and avoidance training produced a marked increase in responding to the experimenter's commands (Figure 5.14) together with a moderate increase in physical contact with the experimenter and a complete suppression of the self-stimulation and tantrum behavior (Figure 5.15). The pathological behavior was suppressed, and the children learned to approach the experimenters. These salutary effects were maintained

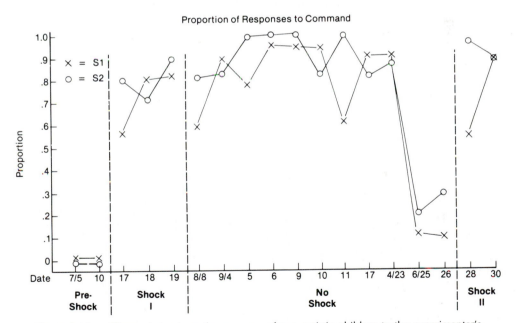

Figure 5.14.   Effects of shock on the response of two autistic children to the experimenter's command, "Come here." Shock, which was contingent upon inappropriate behavior (Figure 5.15), was terminated when the child approached. Prior to shock, the children did not respond; after three sessions with shock, they usually did, for a period of nine months. A single shock at eleven months reinstated the behavior. (From Lovaas, Schaeffer, & Simmons, 1965, p. 102.)

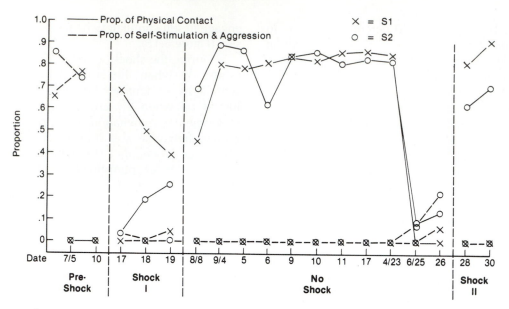

Figure 5.15.   Effect of a punishment-escape procedure on pathological behavior (tantrums and self-stimulation, dotted lines) and social behavior (physical contact with experimenters, solid lines) of two autistic children. Three shock sessions eliminated the pathological behavior and instated social behavior for nine months. A single shock at 11 months reinstated the social behavior. (See also Figure 5.14.) (From Lovaas, Schaeffer, & Simmons, 1965, p. 102.)

without shock for approximately 10 months, at which time they were reinstated with a single non-contingent shock.

A shock punishment-escape procedure, combined with continuous reinforcement of any other behavior, has also been used to suppress self-injury (Tate, 1972). Suzie was 18 years old and blind. She had been restrained in bed for seven and one-half years prior to this treatment, and most of her teeth had been removed to prevent her from biting her lips and shoulders. Brief contingent shock combined with reinforcement for not biting did not suppress self-injury for long; but shock delivered during self-injury and *continued until this behavior ceased* did prove effective. In this procedure, self-injury was punished by shock and the cessation of self-injury was reinforced by escape from shock.

Changing the behavior of autistic children is one of the most difficult tasks therapists face. Self-injury eventually extinguished with John

when attention or sympathy were withheld, but most therapists and attendants would find it difficult to recommend or carry out a procedure that takes this long and is potentially so dangerous for the individual. Since contingent electric shock appears to suppress self-injurious behavior so rapidly, it would seem preferable to the potentially damaging effects of either extinction or continued restraint when reinforcement procedures have failed. Furthermore, the side effects that have been reported are generally beneficial and include increased awareness and appropriate interaction with the environment, *including* the people who administered the shock (Bucher & Lovaas, 1968; Kushner, 1970; Lovaas & Simmons, 1969; Tate and Baroff, 1966).

b. Aversive consequences other than shock
The behavior selected for punishment and the punisher itself depend on who makes the decisions. In one study, high-school seniors volun-

teered to work with Ann Dell Duncan (1971) on a variety of self-management projects. Dave wanted to stop swearing and decided to put a surgical mask over his face and wear it for three minutes every time he swore, no matter where he was. Ben also decided to wear a mask, but as a consequence of making sarcastic remarks. Emma wore a flaming red mitten for five minutes whenever she bit her nails, and Patty wore her brother's boxing glove whenever she cracked her knuckles. Debbie bought herself a "joke" cigarette pack and shocked herself for 10 seconds whenever she ate a snack between meals. The behavior problems went down and stayed down—except for Dave. His follow-up showed that he did start to swear again, but only in the fraternity house! Other punishing events selected by other students in self-management projects are listed in Table 3.9.

A loud noise can constitute aversive stimulation and has been studied as a punishing consequence (Azrin, 1958; Flanagan et al., 1958). The staff in a state institution blew a police whistle whenever a resident stuffed string and other objects up his nose, and succeeded in suppressing this dangerous behavior.[6] Noise has also been used to suppress poor posture, detected by a special apparatus worn by the client (Azrin, Rubin, O'Brien, Ayllon, and Roll, 1968).

In other studies, unpleasant tastes and odors have proved to be effective punishers. Tabasco sauce (Bright & Whaley, 1968) and lemon juice (Sajwaj, Libit & Agras, 1974) have been used to suppress chronic regurgitation and rumination in children. The self-injurious behavior of an autistic woman was eliminated by the contingent presentation of aromatic ammonia (Tanner & Zeiler, 1975). Aversion therapy for smoking sometimes employs a blast of stale cigarette smoke as a punisher and requires the client to smoke one cigarette after another in rapid succession. (Aversion therapies are discussed in Chapter 6.)

The following study illustrates the punishment of severe problem behavior with an aver-sive event other than electric shock. Sajwaj et al. (1974) used lemon juice to suppress rumination in a six-month-old infant, Sandra, who was in danger of starving. After the failure of a number of other treatment procedures, it seemed clear that immediate and dramatic suppression of rumination was needed. The authors were reluctant to use electric shock, because whatever procedure proved effective in the hospital might occasionally be needed at home; and there was evidence of instability and child neglect in Sandra's family. They therefore decided to try lemon juice, injected into Sandra's mouth at the first sign of rumination: vigorous tongue movements. This punishment procedure effectively suppressed rumination, and Sandra was able to go home with her foster parents eight weeks after the start of therapy. Two ruminating episodes were later reported by Sandra's foster mother who immediately injected lemon juice. As at the hospital, the procedure was effective; and Sandra continued to gain weight. There were additional salutory changes in other classes of behavior. The authors note that Sandra became more attentive of adults, and that she began to smile, babble, and grab at nearby objects. Follow-up visits one year later showed that motor, social, and speech skills continued to develop, while rumination was effectively eliminated.

c. Conditioned punishers

Most of us learn at an early age to attend to such conditioned punishers as "No" and "Don't." When these words have semantic value, a great deal of learning and generalization takes place without the use of unconditioned punishers. In several studies using shock or other aversive stimuli, the word "No" has been paired with shock, so that if the behavior recurred or if it appeared in another setting it could be suppressed with only the word. "No" has often

6. Marilyn Gordon, Monson State Hospital, Palmer, Massachusetts. Personal communication, May, 1973.

acquired some conditioned aversive properties prior to its use in a particular setting, but it may require a few additional pairings with an unconditioned punisher when used in a new setting (e.g., Birnbrauer, 1968; Risley, 1968).

Lovaas, Schaeffer and Simmons (1965) used shock to suppress tantrum and self-stimulatory behavior in autistic twins and escape from shock to condition appropriate responses to the experimenter's requests (Figures 5.14 and 5.15). At the same time, they used shock to establish the word "No" as a conditioned punisher. During the few shock sessions "No" was paired with shock at the onset of self-stimulatory or tantrum behavior. The suppressing effect of "No" was then tested with a different class of behavior, pressing a bar, that was maintained with candy. Figure 5.16 shows that before the word "No" was paired with shock, it had little effect on bar pressing. After being paired with shock, however, the verbal command had become a conditioned punisher and suppressed bar pressing. The establishing of responsiveness to social stimuli was a major goal in Lovaas's program, and the use of shock was instrumental in achieving this goal as well as in eliminating the nearly-continuous self-stimulation (Figure 5.15). The authors also report that after adults had been associated with the *avoidance* of shock in the experimental situation, there was an increase in social behavior toward adults in other situations. For example, when the children were hurt in the play yard, they would go to the nurses.

d. Variables that determine the effectiveness of punishment as a procedure to suppress behavior

The effectiveness of punishment—as measured by the immediacy, the extent, and the duration of suppression—depends on a great many variables. Some, such as the intensity of the punisher, are *stimulus variables*; others, such as the manner in which the punisher is introduced,

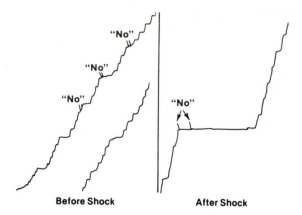

Figure 5.16   Effect of "No" as a conditioned punisher before and after it was paired with shock. Cumulative record of lever pressing for candy by an autistic child. (See also Figures 5.14 and 5.15.) (From Lovaas, Schaeffer, & Simmons, 1965, p. 103.)

are *procedural variables*. And, in addition to the complications that arise from the interactions of these variables, one must consider the events that instigate or maintain the behavior in the first place.

Stimulus variables governing the effectiveness of a punisher include its intensity and duration, and the type of aversive stimulus used. The laboratory studies of Azrin and his colleagues, conducted primarily with lower animals and with shock as the punisher, have produced quantities of systematic data and defined the major parameters that need to be examined in applied settings. (See Azrin & Holz, 1966, and Campbell & Church, 1969, for reviews of the basic research on punishment.) Even though some of their findings have been replicated outside of the laboratory, we must still exercise caution when extrapolating from animals to human subjects, from shock to other punishers, and from the laboratory to applied settings.

i. Intensity. Many laboratory studies with animals show that the greater the intensity of shock, the greater the degree of response suppression. Shock of sufficient intensity suppresses behavior rapidly, completely, and permanently (Azrin, 1960; Holz & Azrin, 1963). Powell and Azrin (1968) report a similar effect of shock intensity on cigarette smoking. They provided smokers with a special cigarette case that delivered shock when it was opened, and found a decrease in the number of cigarettes smoked with an increase in shock intensity. However, when the shock reached a certain intensity, two of the three clients stopped using the apparatus. (The third had essentially stopped smoking by that time.) The intensity of noise also determines the extent to which it suppresses behavior. However, unlike shock, noise does not appear to suppress behavior permanently (Azrin & Holz, 1966).

The intensity, or severity, of the punisher thus is one variable that determines its effectiveness. But as Azrin and Powell's cigarette smokers attest, punishers of high intensity also generate escape and avoidance behavior. In most counseling situations, punishment will "work" only when the client is sufficiently motivated to continue treatment.

ii. Duration.   As in the case of intensity, laboratory studies with shock report an increase in suppression with an increase in the duration of a punisher. Together, these variables determine the severity of punishment (Campbell & Church, 1969). However, Azrin (1958) has found that brief, response-contingent noise is more effective than continuous noise in suppressing human behavior; and in applied settings, the usual duration of shock or noise is one second or less.

It is important to remember that the use of punishment to suppress one class of behavior sets up the possibility of conditioning some other behavior by escape. Rather than use a constant duration of punishment and thus lose some measure of control over the behavior that might be conditioned by escape, one can use the punishment-escape paradigm and suppress one class of behavior while shaping another that is more useful. We have already described how Lovaas used shock to suppress self-stimulation and tantrums, and escape from shock to increase social behavior in two autistic children (Figure 5.15). Lang and Melamed (1969) employed a similar procedure with an infant whose chronic vomiting had brought him close to death. Alternative measures had been tried without success, so Lang and Melamed used a punishment-escape paradigm to suppress vomiting and strengthen normal peristalsis. The result is shown in Figure 6.6.

iii. Immediacy.   The immediacy of punishment has a great deal to do with its effectiveness in suppressing behavior. As in the case of reinforcers, punishers must be contingent upon the behavior to be suppressed. A punisher should thus coincide with or follow the behavior immediately, lest some other behavior intervene. This is one reason for establishing the word "No" as a conditioned punisher for children and pets. The word can be spoken immediately, so that it is contingent upon the behavior one wants to suppress. If you see your puppy trotting off with your slipper, the word "No" may reduce future recurrences of the behavior. If, instead, you call him over and punish him, then coming-when-called is the behavior most likely to be suppressed. Data from laboratory studies indicate that delayed punishment suppresses behavior only during the initial stages of punishment (Azrin and Holz, 1966).

With most people, of course, one can use verbal behavior to bridge the delay between behavior and its consequences. Whether or not this is as effective as immediate punishment requires further exploration. It is, however, something to be considered when punishment is used in applied settings. There is often a considerable delay between the occurrence of behavior and the delivery of punishment, either because the misbehavior is not detected for some time or because the parent or teacher decides to wait for an "appropriate" moment to deliver a punisher.

iv. Introduction of punishing events. The manner in which punishment is introduced is another important consideration. We might expect that electric shock of a given intensity will always suppress behavior to the same extent, but Azrin, Holz, and Hake (1963) found this is not the case. With quite different species of animals (rats, pigeons, monkeys), and with quite different punishers (shock, noise, and bar-slap), they found that behavior is initially suppressed but then recovers unless the intensity of the punisher is very severe. *If the intensity of the punisher is gradually increased, the behavior may continue under far greater intensities than would have been required to completely suppress responding when punishment was first introduced.* With pigeons, for example, if the initial shock is 80 volts, pecking is completely and irreversibly suppressed. But if punishment is introduced at intensities of 60 volts or less, performance can be maintained while shock intensity is gradually increased to 130 volts.

In these laboratory studies, the behavior that is punished is also maintained by intermittent reinforcement. When using punishment in an applied setting, one hopes to locate and withhold all of the reinforcers that might be maintaining the problem behavior. Since this is often difficult, the laboratory studies may shed some light on the problems one faces when behavior to be suppressed is also reinforced. Consider the use of punishment in the classroom. One "violation" may produce a scowl from the teacher; two of them, a reprimand or warning; three or four may result in an extra homework assignment—all building up to a visit to the principal's office or a conference with the parents. Although the type of punisher is continually changing, the teacher is also attempting to increase its severity. If Azrin's data apply, we might expect that the problem behavior would

continue to occur for a longer period of time when the "intensity" of punishment is gradually increased than when some intermediate value is applied first.

v. Frequency and consistency: the schedule of punishment. If behavior is punished intermittently, the degree of suppression is directly related to the frequency of punishment. The laboratory data (e.g., Azrin, Holz, & Hake, 1963) are clear and convincing; and the available data from applied studies also indicate that intermittent punishment is less effective than punishment of every occurrence of the behavior (Birnbrauer, 1968; Kircher, Pear, & Martin, 1971).

Further evidence comes from two clinical studies that ran into apparatus failures. In both of these studies, electric shock was used to suppress behavior that was extremely dangerous for the individual. Scotty was a self-injurious six-year-old who spent his entire day and night in a modified straitjacket and a modified football helmet to protect his head. His baseline rate of pounding his head was 80 times a *minute*. Whaley and Tough (1968) first shocked self-injury and then used shock avoidance to establish the incompatible behavior of holding a toy. In the first few sessions, the apparatus was not working properly. As a result, Scotty was receiving shock on an intermittent schedule, and there was little suppression of self-injury. When the apparatus was repaired, consistent shock rapidly suppressed his self-injurious behavior, and Scotty quickly learned to touch and hold a toy when these activities avoided shock. He was soon freed from his restraints and able to participate in the ward activities and training programs.[7]

---

7. The description of the period of intermittent shock does not appear in the abbreviated published report of this study. The data appear in a mimeographed report available from Dr. Whaley, Center for Behavioral Studies, Box 13592, North Texas State University, Denton, Texas 76203.

The other apparatus failure is reported by Kushner (1970) who was treating a case of uncontrollable sneezing. The patient was a 17-year-old girl who had been

vigorously and rapidly sneezing for 6 months with no relief. She had been thoroughly examined from neurological, endocrinological, allergic, urologic, and psychiatric viewpoints; she had been exposed to a wide variety of medication; had undergone hypnosis and sleep therapy, and was in psychotherapy—all to no avail.

(Kushner, 1970, p. 39.)

Kushner put a microphone around her neck, and sneezing activated a sound relay which in turn activated a brief 3.5 ma. shock to her fingers. Initially, the shock had little effect. Then it was discovered that the fingertip electrodes were not making good contact. When the apparatus was repaired, sneezing decreased from a baseline rate of once every 40 seconds to approximately once in three minutes. When the electrodes were moved from her fingers to her arm, sneezing was completely suppressed within two blocks of trials. At the time of Kushner's report, 13 months had passed with no relapse. Thus chronic sneezing, which had not responded to a variety of other treatments, was eliminated by contingent shock. However, these two studies lend support to laboratory findings that if shock is to have immediate and enduring effects, it should be applied consistently rather than intermittently.

vi. Motivation to emit the punished behavior: schedules of reinforcement. Locating and withholding the reinforcers maintaining unwanted behavior is always the first step in trying to eliminate that behavior. The combination of extinction and punishment is more effective than is either alone (Azrin & Holz, 1966). However, if unable to discontinue reinforcement, remember that behavior maintained by intermittent reinforcement is particularly resistant to both extinction and punishment. Probably the major importance of reinforcement

schedules to the use of punishment in applied settings is their direct effect on the behavior they are maintaining. When behavior is maintained by a ratio schedule, reinforcement rate depends on response rate. As a result, when the addition of punishment suppresses response rate, it also reduces the reinforcement rate. This decrease in reinforcement density will also tend to weaken behavior. When behavior is maintained by interval schedules, however, punishment can reduce response rate without reducing reinforcement density. The persistence of behavior generated by interval schedules of reinforcement makes them particularly useful when we want to *maintain* behavior in the natural environment. But a past history of interval reinforcement becomes a problem when we want to *reduce* or *eliminate* behavior. Often, the solution can be found in the reinforcement of alternative behavior.

vii. Reinforcement of alternative behavior. Even relatively mild or infrequent punishment can eliminate behavior if an alternative means of obtaining reinforcers is available. The psychologists who have used punishment to suppress self-injury have usually tried reinforcing incompatible behavior first. If that procedure alone failed, then punishment was combined with the reinforcement of other behavior. The combination of punishment with the reinforcement of other behavior is desirable for two reasons. Not only does reinforcement of other behavior facilitate the suppressive effects of punishment, it also provides an opportunity to develop desirable behavior.

Alternative behavior can be strengthened by an avoidance paradigm—the way in which Whaley and Tough established playing with toys in place of head banging, for instance—or the alternative behavior can be reinforced directly. If your puppy is chewing your Aubusson carpets and Chippendale chairs, you can hit him and momentarily interrupt these activities. Eventually, you will probably make a conditioned aversive stimulus out of anyone who approaches with an outstretched hand. Alternatively, you can disengage his teeth from the furniture (murmuring a weary "No, puppy" as you do so) and give him a marrow bone, a rubber toy, and a rag tied in knots. Of course, your living room may resemble a charnel house; but by channeling teething in other directions, you will save your furniture and be further rewarded with a happy and entertaining puppy. The avoidance paradigm may be necessary if the problem behavior, such as self-injury, is dangerous and occurs at such a high rate that alternative behavior has little chance to emerge.

e. Generalization of suppression

In applied settings, there has been little recovery following the termination of punishment when the punisher has been (1) electric shock of (2) high intensity and (3) delivered after each occurrence of the problem behavior. In addition, as with any procedure to suppress behavior, the reinforcers maintaining the problem behavior should be located and withheld, and alternative behavior should be reinforced. However, the effects of punishment appear to be very specific: problem behavior may be suppressed in one setting but continue to occur in other settings and in the presence of other people. It thus becomes necessary to take specific steps to promote generalization.

A number of studies have shown that even when punishment has suppressed self-injury or destructive behavior in one setting, there is little reduction of behavior in other settings. Two of the most carefully documented examples are those of Corte, Wolf, and Locke (1971), and Lovaas and Simmons (1969). We have already discussed the Lovaas and Simmons study and seen that suppression of John's self-injury in the attendant's lap did not transfer to another room or to the presence of other experimenters (Figure 5.13). Generalization did not occur until the behavior had been punished by two different experimenters and in more than two settings. Corte et al. (1971) report very similar findings with four institutionalized retarded adolescents with long histories of self-injury. In these and other studies, at least two individuals were needed to punish severe self-injury in at least three different settings before the effects of punishment generalized to different settings. Similar findings apply to destructive behavior. Both Birnbrauer (1968), and Bucher and King (1971) found it necessary to punish the destruction of different kinds of objects in different locations. Fortunately, generalization increases with an increase in the range and variety of situations in which the behavior is punished. Other ways to promote generalization are described in Chapter 3.

f. Collateral effects of punishment

Several collateral or side effects have been reported in studies using punishment. Some are beneficial to the welfare of the individual; others may create new problems.

i. Beneficial side effects. The most obvious advantage of eliminating persistent and severe problem behavior is in the resulting opportunity to develop social, motor, and intellectual behavior. It is extremely difficult to reinforce these classes of behavior if a child engages in self-stimulation 80 percent of the time or begins banging his head and biting his flesh the moment he is released from restraints. Bucher and Lovaas (1968) say that shock is so effective it essentially eliminates these classes of behavior within the first minute. This, of course, would allow the therapist to begin reinforcing appropriate behavior almost immediately.

A very different, and perhaps surprising, side effect of electric-shock punishment has often been reported. On days when punishment was used, whining and fussing decreased and alertness and responsiveness to the environment increased, including eye contacts with the experimenter (Risley, 1968), smiling (Tate & Baroff, 1966), and affection (Lovaas, Schaeffer, & Simmons, 1965). The net effect of such changes was improved relations among the children and those who care for them—an important factor in their future development.

ii. Escape and avoidance. When punishment is employed to suppress a given class of problem behavior, any activities that avoid or escape the punishment will be strengthened. These activities may be even less desirable than the punished behavior: lying to escape the punishing consequences of being late to dinner, or cheating to avoid a low grade on an examination. The hit-and-run driver is probably the most tragic example.

Of the twenty subjects Powell and Azrin (1968) asked to participate in a program using shock to suppress cigarette smoking, only six started the program; only three stayed more than a day after shock was introduced; and two of these stopped carrying the cigarette case when the shock intensity reached high levels. However, escape can be turned toward beneficial ends, as when the Lovaas group established social behavior by terminating shock at the children's approach to the attendant. The point to remember is that punishment will tend to generate escape and avoidance behavior. Those involved in the administration of punishment should bear this in mind, either to preclude escape and avoidance or to use these procedures to the client's advantage.

iii. Aggression. Two kinds of aggressive behavior may occur when punishment is used. One is an attempt to hurt or destroy the person or the instrument delivering the punisher. This kind of aggression does not seem to have occurred with the use of shock following self-injury or aggressive behavior in children. However, Whaley, Rosenkranz, and Knowles (1967) report aggressive behavior in conjunc-

tion with the use of a shock-delivering electronic cigarette pack. They tried the apparatus with a psychiatric patient who "returned the unit damaged as a result of the beating he had given it. The unit had shocked him and he retaliated" (p. 13).

Aggressive behavior can be conditioned, so aggression that occurs in conjunction with punishment could be maintained by its consequences. If aggressive behavior damaged the punishing apparatus or dissuaded the experimenter, we could expect an increase in aggression.

Another type of aggressive behavior that can occur in conjunction with punishment is *pain-elicited aggression*. This type of aggression, rather than being maintained by its consequences, occurs immediately following painful stimulation and dissipates very quickly. Pain-elicited aggression has been studied in many species, including hamsters, cats, squirrel monkeys, raccoons, foxes, turtles, alligators, crayfish, and several species of snakes. Aggressive attacks have been elicited against the individuals themselves (self-injury), members of the same species, members of different species, and against inanimate objects. In short, the stimulus characteristics of the victim do not appear critical. (For research in the area of pain-elicited aggression, see Azrin, 1967; Ulrich, 1966; Ulrich, Hutchinson, & Azrin, 1965.)

There is another, sobering dimension of pain-elicited aggression. It has been shown that the *opportunity for aggression during aversive stimulation is a reinforcer* (Azrin, Hutchinson, & McLaughlin, 1965). In a study using squirrel monkeys, pulling a chain made a canvas-covered ball available for two seconds. The ball was a suitable target for attack, and if the monkey learned to pull the chain the ball would be, by definition, a reinforcer. A painful tail shock was used to induce aggression. In the absence of shock, the monkey virtually never pulled the chain or attacked the ball; but when shock was presented, the ball was attacked consistently and immediately. Attack was elicited by shock, and pulling the chain was reinforced by the opportunity to attack the ball. Pulling the chain was conditioned, extinguished, reconditioned, and again extinguished by presenting or withholding the ball as a reinforcer. (In related work on extinction-produced aggression, Azrin, 1967, found that a pigeon will peck a key when this behavior produces a target pigeon, or victim, which is then attacked.)

To our knowledge, pain-elicited aggression has not been documented in conjunction with punishment in applied settings. Nonetheless, we have probably all seen someone stumble into a chair and kick the object that "hurt" him. The incidence of pain-elicited attack is reduced when there is an opportunity to avoid the painful stimulation (Azrin, 1967), and when the amount of floor space is increased (Ulrich & Azrin, 1962).

It is also worth noting that the major variables governing the frequency of pain-elicited aggression are the intensity, frequency, duration, and consistency of the shock—the same variables that govern the effectiveness of shock as a punisher.

iv. Conditioned suppression and anxiety. The stimuli that precede or accompany punishment may acquire several different properties. They may become discriminative stimuli that signal contingencies of punishment or avoidance. They may become conditioned punishers, suppressing the behavior on which they are contingent or increasing the behavior that removes them. They may more generally suppress behavior in the absence of specific contingencies involving behavior: the phenomenon known as *conditioned suppression*. Finally, as a result of respondent conditioning, they may elicit behavior such as attack or the physiological components of anxiety. To fur-

ther complicate the analysis, any particular event that accompanies punishment may acquire all of these properties—or none of them.

We have already mentioned conditioned punishers, particularly the generalized punisher "No." Like the word, "No," the word "Wrong" and the symbol "X" beside the answer to a homework problem play a prominent role in our education, and often obviate the necessity for unconditioned punishers. So, too, do discriminative stimuli such as ONE WAY—DO NOT ENTER and WARNING: HIGH VOLTAGE, designed to prevent rather than punish behavior.

Conditioned suppression and conditioned anxiety can be viewed as emotional reactions resulting from respondent conditioning. When intense or painful stimulation is contingent on behavior and suppresses that behavior, we are dealing with the operant procedure, punishment. But respondent procedures may also be involved. Intense or painful stimulation may elicit attack (as we have seen), and it may also elicit startle, "freezing," flight, and many physiological activities. Intense stimulation arouses the sympathetic branch of the autonomic nervous system, which in turn "mobilizes" the organism to act in an emergency. (The accompanying physiological changes include increases in heart rate, blood pressure, respiration, and other activities that favor emergency action, and decreases in gastrointestinal activities that do not.) Physiological arousal and other components of anxiety are discussed at some length in the next chapter. They are mentioned here because, whether by design or by accident, they are likely to accompany the use of punishment, particularly in the early stages. Physiological arousal by design is the major emphasis of the aversion therapies described in Chapter 6. But physiological arousal may also occur as a collateral effect of punishment. It is the possibility of respondent *conditioning* that concerns us here, not the properties of punishing events as *unconditional* stimuli. Physiological arousal in response to real danger is adaptive and probably necessary for survival. Conditioned arousal is sometimes adaptive and sometimes not.

Conditioned suppression and conditioned anxiety have been studied extensively in the animal laboratory. An experiment reported by Nathan and Smith (1968) illustrates both phenomena. Monkeys were trained to press a lever in the presence of two signal lights. One light always preceded shock; the other never preceded shock. Neither of the lights nor the shock was contingent on lever pressing or any other class of behavior. Nonetheless, while the light that consistently preceded shock was turned on there was a decrease in lever pressing (conditioned suppression), and an increase in heart rate and blood-flow velocity (conditioned emotional responses, often used as measures of anxiety). Neither of these changes occurred in the presence of the other light.

Although we can offer no data, something comparable to conditioned anxiety and conditioned suppression seems to occur when children are in the presence of a person associated with indiscriminate aversive stimulation—the class bully perhaps, or sometimes a relative. When such a person enters the situation, there may be a general suppression of on-going behavior and an apparent atmosphere of anxiety and tension, *even though* the children have not been doing anything that has been punished in the past. These reactions seem to be different from the more specific anxiety, called guilt, which may arise when we engage in a particular class of behavior that has been punished, or threatened with punishment. The anxiety generated by lying, cheating, plagiarism, and other forms of social misconduct is deliberately cultivated by parents and teachers as well as by formal codes (such as the Ten Commandments). In these cases, the goal is not conditioned suppression, but conditioned anxiety in connection with restricted events, including restricted classes of our own behavior.

B. Comparisons and Generalizations

From the experimental and clinical data obtained thus far, we can draw the following generalizations about procedures to decrease the frequency or duration of behavior or to limit the situations in which it occurs. (We must always keep in mind, however, the levels of such relevant parameters as motivation, intensity of stimulation, schedule of reinforcement or punishment—and the particular talents and weaknesses of all of the people involved.)

1. Extinction

Extinction reduces behavior completely and permanently, but not immediately. If reinforcement has been intermittent, which is nearly always the case with social reinforcers, the behavior will be particularly resistant to extinction. Another problem is the fact that it may be difficult to identify the reinforcers maintaining a particular class of behavior; and, once identified, it may be difficult to withhold them. Drugs and alcohol, and the social reinforcers that accompany their use, are examples. Finally, there is often an increase in the rate and intensity of behavior at the start of extinction, and these temporary increases are likely to be accompanied by aggressive behavior.

All in all, it requires a great deal of patience and fortitude to stick to a program of extinction. It also takes constant reminding that, once extinction is under way, even a single reinforcement will greatly prolong the process. However, when parents, teachers, spouses, and friends have discovered that they, themselves, were inadvertently reinforcing problem behavior, and especially when they have found other, competing behavior to reinforce instead, then extinction has been very effective. Most problems that arise when extinction is used alone fail to appear when extinction is combined with other procedures. In fact, no other procedure to reduce problem behavior will stand much chance of success unless we also stop reinforcing the behavior we are trying to eliminate.

2. Satiation

Satiation also reduces behavior completely— but with renewed deprivation, the behavior usually recovers. The cases cited that resulted in permanent suppression of problem behavior —lighting matches and hoarding towels—are difficult to analyze. It is possible that the behavior was intrinsically reinforcing, but lost its reinforcing properties with forced repetition (the treatment for lighting matches) or when excessive amounts of the reinforcer were provided (625 towels left little room for anything else in the patient's room). It is also possible that the behavior had been maintained by other reinforcers, perhaps social reinforcement in the form of attention, and that this was withdrawn or altered when the satiation treatment was applied.

3. Response Cost

Response cost appears to be a rapid and effective procedure, with few adverse side effects. However, one has to be careful that the procedure does not force the subject into debt by removing more reinforcers than can reasonably be earned. This procedure, like many others, is probably most effective when all concerned parties have agreed to the economy: to the quantity and quality of the reinforcers to be earned and to be withdrawn, and to which specific classes of behavior the rules will apply. Cost has an advantage over time out and con-

finement because it does not remove the individual from a situation where appropriate behavior might be developed and reinforced.

4. Time Out

Like extinction, time out can be a difficult procedure to implement. It takes a good deal of skill (and sometimes strength) to remove a rambunctious or violent person to a "quiet room" in a matter-of-fact manner that is neither reinforcing nor punishing. Once the contingencies or rules are established, however, the procedure can work smoothly and well; and it gives everyone involved a chance to "calm down." Relatively brief time out, on the order of three to five minutes without disruptive behavior, is usually effective. A short time out also minimizes the time the individual is away from the situation where the transgression occurred. Time out is similar to the familiar tactic of sending a child to his room —except, of course, that it won't work if the room provides entertaining diversions. The Silvermans (1973) report a classic misuse of time out in a junior high-school program. Disruptive classroom behavior was penalized by sending the offenders to a detention room. The procedure was a glorious failure because the "detention room" was really a learning center that provided a variety of activities. It probably could have been used as a reinforcer for appropriate, rather than inappropriate, schoolwork.

5. Prolonged Restraint or Confinement

By itself, prolonged restraint or confinement does not permanently eliminate problem behavior, but it can effectively prevent or restrict its occurrence while other measures are taken. However, a *brief* period of restraint, as in the study by Hamilton et al. (1967) can eliminate even severe problem behavior so long as it is made contingent upon the behavior.

6. Removing the Opportunity

Removing the chance to emit the behavior is often a practical measure. Fragile objects can be put out of the reach of two-year-olds and shoes kept away from puppies. Children outgrow this kind of exploratory behavior, and puppies eventually stop teething.

7. Omission Training (OT or DRO)

Omission training is one way that reinforcement can be employed to reduce problem behavior. It therefore avoids the possible negative side effects of aversive procedures. Omission training is not advisable for behavior that is dangerous to the client or to others because extensive damage may be done while one is waiting for a period of time when the behavior does not occur. For this reason, punishment is sometimes used initially to suppress behavior; then, when the rate declines, omission training can be introduced during the periods of time when the behavior does not occur. At first, the omission requirement would be very brief; progressively longer periods of omission would then be required. With ordinary problem behavior, omission training can be very effective and easy to carry out. Sometimes parents and teachers can simply thank their charges for refraining from annoying behavior for specified periods of time.

8. Reinforcement of Alternative Behavior (Alt R)

Eliminating problem behavior by reinforcing alternative behavior is usually the procedure of choice, whether used alone or in combination with other procedures. Its effects can be rapid and durable. It avoids the potential deleterious side effects of punishment, the temporary nature of satiation, and the delayed effectiveness of extinction. It is the one procedure that explicitly reinforces beneficial behavior in place of detrimental behavior. While any harmless behavior could probably serve as an alternative to the behavior one wants to reduce, the Alt R procedure can be used to facilitate growth and development. When used in therapy or in an educational "crash" program, it is particularly important to select behavior that will continue to be reinforced in the natural environment. Otherwise, the gains will be lost, and the problem behavior may recover.

This procedure, like omission training, is difficult to implement if one is dealing with dangerous behavior that occurs at a very high rate. If self-injury, for example, occurs nearly all of the time the individual is not restrained, then it will be very difficult to find alternative behavior to reinforce. In these cases, the restraints may be only partially removed, or punishment may be employed in the initial stages.

9. Differential Reinforcement of Low Rate (DRL)

DRL is especially appropriate when we want to reduce, but not eliminate, a particular class of behavior. In the laboratory, where the term originated, the procedure involves reinforcing the occurrence of behavior if a specified period of time has elapsed since the last occurrence of the behavior. In applied settings, where one does not particularly want to *maintain* the behavior, the contingencies have been changed. Instead of reinforcing a particular occurrence of the behavior, a reinforcer is delivered at the end of a period of time during which the behavior has not occurred more than a specified number of times. The procedure can reduce high rates of disruptive behavior to manageable levels. Omission training is one end of the DRL continuum; DRH is the other. Baseline generally falls somewhere in between.

10. Punishment

Punishment of sufficient severity suppresses behavior rapidly, completely, and permanently. This is why it is sometimes the procedure of choice when one is dealing with excessively dangerous behavior. However, unless the punishment is severe, the behavior recovers when punishment is discontinued. In addition, punishment is often accompanied by aggression, anxiety, and avoidance behavior that does not contribute to the individual's future well-being. In therapy and in self-management projects, many people select punishment over other procedures because it is likely to produce the most immediate results. But for punishment to be maximally effective, *and ultimately productive*, it should be combined with the reinforcement of beneficial alternative behavior.

Covert procedures, including covert extinction and covert punishment, are often effective in self-management programs. They are described in Chapter 7.

C. Guidelines for Using Reductive Procedures

All of us sometimes wish to restrict or eliminate behavior, either our own or that of someone else whom we want to (or must) get along with. The behavior may be a problem in itself or, like much of classroom disruptive behavior, it may simply occur at high rates and thus compete with other, more productive behavior. There are a great many procedures to choose from; and, in any given situation, some will be more appropriate than others. But whatever procedures are selected, they should be used effectively. Otherwise, the attempt may only exacerbate the problem. Assuming that genuine problem behavior has been identified, and that a responsible individual is to reduce this behavior in a responsible and accountable manner, here are some further guidelines for using the procedures described in this section.

a. Locate and withhold the reinforcers maintaining the unwanted behavior

Whatever else we may do about problem behavior, we should try to stop reinforcing it. Unfortunately, extinction is easier to prescribe than to carry out. But we can at least *look for* the reinforcers maintaining the behavior and *try to* withhold them or to make them contingent on other, more desirable behavior.

b. Remove the discriminative stimuli for unwanted behavior

"Lead us not into temptation." Alcoholics first practicing abstinence do well to avoid bars and cocktail parties, and gamblers to avoid casinos. People giving up smoking sometimes give up coffee as well, if drinking coffee has normally been the occasion for a cigarette. Since beer commercials on television often prompt the viewer to open a bottle of beer, you might switch to another channel if you are trying to limit your consumption of beer.

c. Select a COMBINATION of procedures

For both ethical and practical reasons, we should always try to incorporate extinction and the reinforcement of alternative behavior, no matter what other procedures may be employed. Extinction prevents the maintenance of the behavior we want to eliminate, and Alt R provides a way to replace it with behavior that will prove more beneficial in the long run.

d. Select appropriate consequences that are easy to manage

Educational programs that use contrived reinforcers must eventually transfer control to intrinsic or to naturally occurring extrinsic reinforcers or the behavior will not be maintained in the natural environment. But whatever reinforcers are used in applied settings, the individual is learning something that the parents, teachers, or therapist consider beneficial. In the sense that it functions only to suppress behavior, rather than to shape or develop it, punishment by itself does not have any comparable educational value. There are, however, two ways in which punishment can be used constructively. One is indirect: punishment can be used in conjunction with a conditioning procedure, either reinforcement (Alt R) or avoidance, so that some form of adaptive behavior is strengthened while the problem behavior is suppressed. A more direct method is to use natural punishing consequences so that the individual learns something about the environment. Children can learn something valuable about red burners on electric stoves by the natural punishing consequences of touching one. They can learn some of the motor skills involved in riding a bicycle by developing those postures and movements that avoid the punishing consequences of falling off. Of course, there are many times when natural punishing consequences are inappropriate. They may be too dangerous: being run over by a car; being poisoned or blinded after swallowing household ammonia or lye; being bitten after teasing a tethered dog. Or natural punishing consequences may be too difficult to arrange. Errors in arithmetic can have unpleasant consequences if they occur when we are balancing our checkbooks or filing income tax returns, but comparable, logical outcomes might be difficult to arrange in the first-grade classroom. Nevertheless, in any given situation, certain punishers may be more "appropriate" than others. A spanking might be an appropriate consequence of physical aggression against others. Docking a child's allowance might be appropriate for stealing money. As a young child, I once demolished a lemon meringue pie, neatly lifting off each lovely peak with my finger, savoring them one by one. It was an especially fine pie because company was coming to Sunday dinner. Nothing much was said when the deed was discovered, but when it came time for dessert, I was given the "honor" of bringing the remains of my mother's creation to the table and explaining its unusual appearance. It was 20 years before I ate another piece of lemon meringue pie.

e. Most people have verbal behavior. Use it

Our language is rich in discriminative stimuli that tell us what behavior is appropriate or inappropriate in a given situation and what consequence will follow. Instructions and warnings spare us a lot of floundering around, trying to identify the contingencies that govern our behavior.

There are at least four ways we can take advantage of verbal behavior in implementing a program to change behavior. First, we can state the contingencies clearly. Second, we can issue a warning or reminder that the behavior is unacceptable and if initiated or continued will be followed by a specified consequence. (Repeated warnings violate the rules of immediacy and consistency, but a single warning may serve as a welcome reminder and avoid the need for punishment.) Third, we can explain the rationale of a program. Granted, young children who have not even arrived at a conceptual understanding of area and volume are certainly not going to understand a philosophical analysis of the mutual responsibilities that govern harmony in the home. Elaborate explanations may serve only to confuse the child or the issue. Besides, parents and teachers need not justify to their charges everything they do. But we are more likely to abide by rules when we understand (and agree with) the reasons behind them than if we perceive them as utterly arbitrary. And even if nothing else is gained, stating the rationale for a program helps us to weed out our minor or trivial goals from our major ones. Fourth, verbal behavior allows us to negotiate. Contingencies that are fair and acceptable to all parties can be formalized in a contract that specifies each party's responsibilities and the consequences for meeting or not meeting them. Contracts can be as flexible as the people and the occasion warrant. Sometimes a variety of rewards or aversive consequences are listed for different classes of behavior, and the person can exercise options.

f. Contingency
g. Immediacy
h. Consistency

These three rules have been discussed at length in conjunction with both reinforcement and punishment. They apply to all procedures for changing behavior by changing its consequences.

i. Don't build up tolerance by gradually increasing the severity of aversive consequences

Just as we can adapt to aversive stimulation if the intensity is gradually increased, so a 30-token response cost, following an ascending series of lesser fines, may be less effective than a 10-token fine would have been initially. Likewise, a 15-minute time out following a series of ineffective shorter intervals may be less effective than a five-minute time out would have been in the first place.

j. Either prevent escape and avoidance or use them productively

Whining, wheedling, arguing, and telling lies are activities that will be strengthened if they escape or avoid the planned aversive consequences of some other behavior. Once rules are established and agreed on, the specified consequences should follow any infractions. The exception, of course, is when avoidance contingencies are deliberately used to establish or maintain behavior. Some professors use avoidance of the final examination as an incentive for studying and getting good grades on weekly quizzes.

k. Be alert to the possibilities of conditioned anxiety and elicited aggression

When a young child runs in front of a moving car, the situation should be made aversive so that the behavior does not recur. Some people advocate holding the child near a car while someone else "guns" the motor. Like a near miss, the frightening noise is a good approximation of the natural aversive consequences of getting too close to a moving vehicle. But the long-term result might be a child who was afraid to approach a car or cross a street, even under appropriate circumstances. If such procedures are used, one should also establish discriminative stimuli (*moving* cars) and the appropriate behavior of looking and listening.

Elicited aggression is another possible side effect when one is trying to suppress unwanted behavior. Aggression may be elicited by either extinction or painful stimulation; and this aggression could be directed at any convenient target, including a child or a pet.

l. Evaluate

If you don't monitor the results, you won't know how well the procedures are working. Continuous records can alert you to problems before they get out of hand. Alternatively, continuous records can demonstrate steady progress, even though daily improvements may be scarcely noticeable.

m. Maintain a successful program and transfer when able

When remedial or emergency measures meet with success, gradually move over to the conditions of the natural environment. Transfer to social, intrinsic, and naturally occurring reinforcers and punishers. Gradually reduce the density of reinforcement for desired behavior or punishment for problem behavior until it approximates that of the natural environment. Build up self-control by helping the individual assume increasing responsibility for record keeping and for decisions involving procedures, consequences, and scheduling. Meanwhile, keep on monitoring the behavior and prepare to back up if you are moving too fast.

6

Respondent Procedures

A. Anxiety
B. Respondent Conditioning
    1. Classical conditioning
    2. Anxiety-relief conditioning
C. Extinction Procedures
    1. Graduated extinction
    2. Flooding
        a. *In vivo* flooding
        b. Imaginal flooding
    3. Implosion
D. Desensitization (Counterconditioning)
    1. Systematic desensitization (Imaginal)
        a. Relaxation
        b. Construction of hierarchy
        c. Desensitization
        d. Transfer
    2. Variations of systematic desensitization
        a. Emotive imagery
        b. Other alternatives to relaxation
    3. *In vivo* desensitization
    4. Modeling: contact and vicarious desensitization
    5. Automated and group desensitization
E. Anxiety Reduction: Procedures and "Process"
F. Aversion Therapies
    1. Aversive consequences (punishment)
    2. Escape and avoidance
    3. Aversive conditioning
        a. Classical aversive conditioning
        b. Aversion-relief
        c. Covert sensitization

For the most part, the procedures described in this section have been designed and developed for the treatment of severe emotional disturbances. The procedures are generally employed by psychiatrists and psychologists, seldom by paraprofessionals, after careful medical evaluation to ascertain that the problem behavior has no identifiable organic cause. Grouping them under the heading of respondent procedures means only that the *basic experimental operations* are—or are presumed to be—those of respondent conditioning and extinction. Operant procedures are frequently incorporated into treatment, and the general procedure described in Chapter 3 is followed. Perhaps more emphasis is placed on knowing the subject, particularly the past history, and less on experimental designs and techniques of measurement; but the major difference is the investigation and manipulation of the stimulus events that elicit anxiety.[1]

A. Anxiety

Most of the procedures described in this section were developed by therapists who view conditioned anxiety as both the primary cause of neurotic behavior and as the focus of its cure. Some procedures are designed to eliminate the debilitating anxiety that prevents or interferes with normal functioning. Others are designed to create anxiety as a means of suppressing such unwanted behavior as excessive drinking or other drug addiction.

We can all think of examples of anxiety: being totally unprepared for an important exam; feeling the brakes give way as you're driving downhill in the middle lane of an interstate highway during rush hour; working late in the lab at night when someone (was it really the janitor?) turns off all the lights, and you hear sounds of creaking floorboards and suppressed breathing. Defining anxiety, however, is more of a problem.

Nearly all definitions of anxiety, especially when the term is used in conjunction with respondent procedures, include physiological activities mediated by the sympathetic branch of the autonomic nervous system. Generally, these physiological activities enable us to function effectively in an emergency: sympathetic arousal releases epinephrine from the adrenal glands, sugar from the liver, and red blood cells from the spleen, while suppressing gastrointestinal activities. Arousal includes rises in heart rate, blood pressure, respiration rate, sweat gland activity, muscle tension and tremors, pupillary dilation, and dilation of the bronchi—activities that favor rapid and effective response to danger. The sympathetic nervous system also inhibits gastrointestinal activities, which are less adaptive in an emergency, as reflected by the decrease in saliva flow and visceral blood supply and by contraction of the sphincters of the bladder and anus. (Under extreme stress, sphincter "control" may be lost.)

These physiological components of anxiety can be elicited by a loud noise, a flash of light, or by almost any other stimulus that is sufficiently intense. A clap of thunder or unexpected loss of support are familiar examples. They can also be elicited by thoughts and images, as when we recall a frightening experience or watch an exciting event on television. But physiological arousal is not restricted to fearful or emotional situations. Many of the physiological activities we have described can be induced by exercise, drugs, temperature, and other variables; and a degree of physiological arousal accompanies joyful experiences and even such activities as reading, writing, and problem solving. The "alertness" accompanying sympathetic arousal

---

1. If a patient experiences periodic attacks of anxiety unrelated to particular stimulus conditions, then the problem may have an organic basis. Wolpe (1969, p. 29) notes that hyperthyroidism and hypoglycemia are common organic causes of anxiety. These problems, of course, require medical attention, not behavior therapy.

contributes to our ability to handle physical and intellectual problems other than those that arise in emergencies. In their excellent monograph on anxiety and clinical problems, Paul and Bernstein (1973) relate behavioral efficiency to physiological arousal and propose that the optimal level of arousal is lower for complex tasks than for easy ones.

Since a behavioral definition requires a statement of how the behavior will be measured, and since many physiological changes are measureable, a definition of anxiety based solely on physiological arousal would solve a lot of problems. Unfortunately, it doesn't seem to solve enough of them. For one thing, a definition should be useful as well as precise, and physiological arousal may accompany activities (such as physical exercise) that most people consider unrelated to anxiety. For another, physiological activities are expensive and difficult to monitor in an applied setting; and, due to various artifacts, the measures are not always highly correlated. For still another, in most instances of therapy neither the client nor the therapist takes quantitative measures of arousal. In some cases a psychogalvanometer is used to measure electrical resistance of the skin (the psychogalvanic response is a decrease in skin resistance that accompanies activities of the sweat glands) or an electromyograph is used to measure muscle tension; but much of the research on anxiety-reducing procedures must be evaluated without physiological data. For these reasons, anxiety is often defined as the subjective feelings of tension and apprehension *that accompany* physiological arousal of the sympathetic nervous system.

To the extent that subjective feelings and physiological arousal are responses to the threat of real danger, and to the extent that the arousal level is appropriate to the particular setting, anxiety is adaptive and probably necessary for survival. Not only does physiological arousal prepare us to take rapid action in an emergency, many people appear to find the sensations enjoyable. Presumably, physiological arousal is one of the reinforcers maintaining such behavior as riding on a roller coaster and shooting rapids on a river. An ex-vandal announced on television that he used to throw rocks at school windows for the fun and excitement of being chased by a police officer. Anxiety becomes a clinical problem requiring medical or psychological treatment only when it occurs in response to inappropriate or unidentified stimulus events *and* when it is sufficiently intense or pervasive to interfere with normal functioning.

The following attempt to define clinical, or "inappropriate," anxiety in terms of behavior, context, criteria, and measurement is broad enough to cover most of the material under discussion. It is not, however, a very satisfactory attempt, partly because it lacks precision and partly because measures of the various classes of behavior are not always highly correlated nor are they always valid or reliable. It is important to remember these reservations when interpreting data and evaluating therapeutic procedures. With these apologies and warnings, we define clinical anxiety as follows:

1) *Behavior:* Internal responses of the sympathetic branch of the autonomic nervous system such as hormonal or vascular changes; external responses such as sweating, blanching, muscle tension or tremors; subjective reports of fear, tension, and apprehension.

2) *Context:* The internal and external responses are *not* elicited by an *un*conditioned stimulus such as intense sound, pain, or sudden movement, but rather the behavior occurs in the absence of any actual identifiable danger or threat.

3) *Criteria:* The behavior occurs so frequently, or with such intensity or duration, that normal functioning is impaired.

4) *Measurement:* Physiological activities may be measured by a variety of instruments, some of which monitor electrical and chemical changes inside the body while others measure skin resistance, skin temperature, muscle tension, and other peripheral changes. Observational measures may be taken of sweating, muscle tension or tremors, blanching, or rapid breathing. Subjective reports of fear, apprehension, and tension may be quantified with the help of rating scales.

These measures of anxiety may be unreliable for a number of reasons: autonomic activities may be elicited by extraneous events, and many are subject to voluntary control; verbal reports are subject to bias, expectancy, and to consequences that may reinforce lying; observational recording, which requires training, is also subject to bias and expectancy and should be confirmed by an independent observer.

Fortunately, other measures may be taken which, if they are not direct assessments of anxiety, may be of even greater concern to the client. Relatively few clients seek medical or psychological help specifically because they are "anxious." Often the problem is a persistent inability to work or to enjoy sexual relations; to speak in public or to ride in an airplane; it may be a physical problem such as asthma or migraine headaches; or it may be persistent hallucinations or a compulsion to clean the house 16 hours a day. In many such cases, the therapist views conditioned anxiety as the "cause" of the problem behavior, which in turn serves an "anxiety-reducing function." Whether or not one accepts this view, there is every reason to measure the problem behavior directly. If, after therapy, the client works 40 hours a week, has satisfactory sexual relations on 90 percent of the occasions either partner wishes them, speaks in public or rides on an airplane each time the

occasion demands; or if asthma, headaches, delusions, or compulsions are eliminated, then therapy has been successful. Whether the problem was maintained by its anxiety-reducing function or by other variables is of secondary importance to the client. (It is, of course, of major importance to scientists, whose job it is to analyze all of the relations, and to future clients who will benefit from their research.)

Clinical or "inappropriate" anxiety is the primary concern of this chapter, because it so often seems to be the result of respondent conditioning, because it has so often been eliminated by respondent procedures, and because it is viewed as the primary problem in many of the studies to be described. We have noted a few problems, particularly those concerned with measurement. Inconsistencies in measurement plague anyone trying to review an area of reasearch. Since a behavioral definition includes a statement of how the behavior will be measured, and since different measures have been employed in different studies, anxiety has been *defined* differently in different studies. This makes it especially difficult to evaluate the data. Even when a specified change in behavior is reliably demonstrated and can reasonably be attributed to a specified procedure, a change in one measure does not allow us to assume concomitant changes in other measures. Only behavior that is measured and *shown* to have changed is *known* to have changed. Despite these problems, therapists have met with a good deal of success in dealing with anxiety, and many of the procedures they have developed are proving useful with other classes of behavior as well.

The respondent procedures to be described are listed in Table 6.1.

B. Respondent Conditioning

One of the first things you are told when learning to ride a horse is that if you fall off you must immediately climb back on. If the beginning rider is reluctant, that is all the more reason to obey this maxim—at least if one hopes to do much riding in the future. Otherwise, one may develop a persistent fear of riding, not just of falling. The situation can be analyzed in terms of both respondent and operant conditioning, but it is the possibility of respondent conditioning that accounts for the maxim. When the rider falls, the sympathetic branch of the autonomic nervous system is aroused and the rider is likely to experience fear and anxiety. The fear may generalize to riding or even to horses; but if the rider is made to get back on the horse—and if the instructor makes sure the rider doesn't fall again—the conditioned fear elicited by riding can extinguish when it does not accompany the unconditioned fear elicited by falling. Falling may also, of course, constitute punishment; and the behavior preceding the fall may be controlled by this operant consequence. Carriage and control are essential, and the rider may learn that keeping heels down and thighs clamped avoids the punishment of falling.

Either adaptive or maladaptive behavior

Table 6.1   Major respondent procedures.

RESPONDENT PROCEDURES
Respondent Conditioning
   1. Classical Conditioning
   2. Anxiety-Relief Conditioning

Respondent Extinction
   1. Graduated Extinction
   2. Flooding
      a. *In vivo* flooding
      b. Imaginal flooding
   3. Implosion

Desensitization (Counterconditioning)
   1. Systematic Desensitization
   2. *In Vivo* Desensitization
   3. Modeling: Contact and Vicarious Desensitization

Aversion Therapies
   1. Aversive Consequences (Punishment)
   2. Escape and Avoidance
   3. Aversive Conditioning
      a. Classical aversive conditioning
      b. Aversion-relief
      c. Covert sensitization

may be conditioned as a result of events that occur in the natural environment. A driver who has survived an automobile accident may later experience a moderate degree of anxiety at the sight of a car pulling out of line, and be more "sensitive" to other road hazards and thus drive more safely.

The problems that come to the attention of a professional are generally those in which conditioned anxiety prevents or interferes with other activities. But, as we shall see, respondent conditioning procedures are also used when we teach children and pets to be afraid of traffic, electrical appliances, or other hazards.

1. Classical Conditioning

In his work on digestive secretions with dogs, Pavlov showed how reflexes that are not part of our biological inheritance can be acquired. By repeatedly pairing a stimulus (such as a tone) that did *not* elicit salivation with a stimulus (food) that *did*, he established a new reflex in which the tone alone, without the food, elicited salivation. He also found that salivation could be elicited by tones other than the one that was paired with food, a phenomenon called *stimulus generalization*. A number of people have wondered if this sort of respondent conditioning might account for biologically inappropriate behavior in people.

To determine whether or not an emotion such as fear could be conditioned, Watson and Rayner (1920) worked with a fearless child named Albert. The unconditional stimulus they used was a loud noise produced by striking a steel bar with a hammer. The conditional stimulus was a white rat to which Albert had previously shown no signs of fear. The following excerpts from their laboratory notes show how Watson and Rayner made the rat a conditional stimulus for fear by pairing the rat with a loud noise. As in all instances of respondent conditioning, the stimulus events preceded the response.

1. White rat suddenly taken from the basket and presented to Albert. He began to reach for rat with left hand. Just as his hand touched the animal the bar was struck immediately behind his head. The infant jumped violently and fell forward, burying his face in the mattress. He did not cry, however.

2. Just as the right hand touched the rat the bar was again struck. Again the infant jumped violently, fell forward and began to whimper.

(Watson & Rayner, 1920, p. 4.)

A week later, the rat was presented without the sound, and Albert made "tentative reaching movements" with his right hand. However, when the rat nosed his left hand, the hand was immediately withdrawn. There was thus some effect of the two paired presentations of the previous session. After five more paired presentations of the rat with the noise, the rat was presented alone, and Albert's behavior was as follows:

The instant the rat was shown the baby began to cry. Almost instantly he turned sharply to the left, fell over on left side, raised himself on all fours and began to crawl away so rapidly that he was caught with difficulty before reaching the edge of the table. (Watson & Rayner, 1920, p. 5.)

By classical (or Pavlovian or respondent) conditioning, the rat had become a conditional stimulus eliciting startle and crying. The laboratory notes indicate that there probably were operant, as well as respondent, components to the procedure: Not only was the noise an unconditional stimulus that elicited fear, it could also have been a punishing stimulus presented as Albert reached out to touch the rat. Reaching for the rat would thus have been punished (suppressed) by the noise; and if the rat acquired conditioned punishing properties, crawling away from it would function as avoidance behavior.

Figure 6.1A shows the traditional respondent paradigm in which the rat becomes a conditional stimulus eliciting fear. (Presumably, the startle and crying accompanied arousal of the sympathetic branch of the autonomic nervous system.) Figure 6.1B suggests operant components of the procedure. Initially, the rat was probably a reinforcer: reaching for and touching the rat were probably maintained by tactual and perhaps other reinforcers including the rat's behavior. The noise was probably a punisher (S^P) of reaching for the rat as well as an unconditional stimulus (US) for fear; and, after being paired with the noise, the rat probably became a conditioned punisher (S^P). By operant escape-avoidance conditioning, we would then expect an increase in behavior which terminates or avoids a punisher ($R \rightarrow S^P$)—behavior such as crawling away.

A. Respondent Conditioning

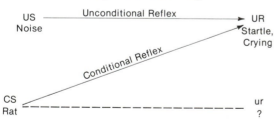

B. Operant Punishment and Avoidance

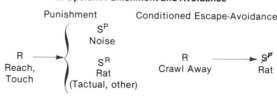

Figure 6.1.   Paradigms illustrating probable respondent and operant components of Watson and Rayner's demonstration of conditioned fear. A. Respondent conditioning: after being paired with a loud noise (an unconditional stimulus which elicited fear), a rat becomes a conditional stimulus capable of eliciting fear. B. Operant punishment and escape-avoidance: initially, contact with rat was probably a reinforcer (S^R), but reaching for the rat was punished by the noise (S^P). After being paired with the noise, the rat becomes a conditioned punisher (S^P), and crawling away from the rat constitutes a conditioned escape-avoidance response.

If this analysis is correct, two classes of behavior were conditioned. Following the respondent pairing procedure,[2] the rat elicited a conditional emotional response—fear; while the operant contingencies favored the acquisition of a conditioned avoidance response —crawling away. Anticipating a problem that will be discussed much later in this chapter, avoidance behavior is critical in therapy because as long as one can successfully avoid an anxiety-evoking situation, there is no opportunity for extinction of conditioned anxiety to occur. Someone who has acquired a fear of riding in elevators usually will not enter one. While this prevents arousal of the fear, it also prevents its extinction.

In one final session, Watson and Rayner found that the fear reaction had generalized to a rabbit, a dog, a fur coat, cotton wool, a Santa Claus mask, and (most appropriately) to Watson's hair. There was no generalization to the room, the table, or Albert's wooden blocks.

The importance of this study—if not to Albert, then to other children—is twofold. It showed that fear can be acquired, and it showed that acquired fear can generalize to events that have never been paired with the unconditional stimulus. These two findings, together with similar findings from animal studies, suggest the possibility that some of our fears are learned rather than the result of genetic endowment or physiological malfunction. And the possibility of learning always provides hope for the possibility of "unlearning."

Watson and Rayner had intended to remove Albert's conditioned emotional reactions, but unfortunately he was taken from the hospital the day the generalization tests were run. The kinds of procedures they had hoped to use were tested by one of Watson's students, Mary Cover Jones (1924), in her efforts to help children who showed marked fears in situations that normally evoke pleasure or only mild anxiety. Some of these children, like Albert, but for unknown

reasons, were afraid of small animals; others feared being alone or being in a darkened room. The procedures described by Jones (who should qualify as the first behavior therapist) are now widely recognized. They include extinction, modeling, and counterconditioning.

Respondent conditioning is not restricted to children or to unpleasant events. Suspecting that sexual "perversions" may also be acquired through respondent conditioning, Rachman has established a boot fetish in adult male volunteers (Rachman, 1966a; Rachman & Hodgson, 1968). The unconditional stimulus was a set of colored slides featuring attractive nude women. These slides elicited sexual arousal prior to any (known) conditioning, and arousal was recorded by changes in penis volume.[3] The conditional stimulus was a color slide of black, knee-high women's boots, which initially elicited no arousal in the men. However, when paired with the slides of nude women, a conditional reflex was established, and the slide of the boots was sufficient to elicit sexual arousal (Figure 6.2). After the reflex was well established, it was ex-

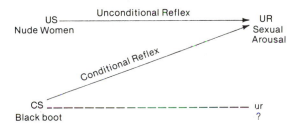

Figure 6.2. Paradigm illustrating respondent conditioning of a boot fetish, based on a study reported by Rachman (1966a).

2: As noted in Chapter 2, the pairing of a neutral stimulus with an unconditional stimulus does not result in conditioning unless the US is preceded by the CS a good deal more often than it occurs in the absence of the CS.

3. Our definition of anxiety included physiological arousal of the *sympathetic* nervous system. In contrast, sexual arousal before orgasm involves the *parasympathetic* branch of the autonomic nervous system. According to Masters and Johnson (1966), the sympathetic branch is involved only during later stages of sexual activity.

tinguished by means of repeated presentations of the boot slide without the accompanying presentation of the erotic ones. In a similar study with both heterosexual and homosexual men, McConaghy (1970) conditioned sexual arousal to geometric forms by pairing these forms with erotic films of nude women or men.

All of these studies were designed as experimental analogues of clinical situations. If we can learn how various classes of behavior are acquired, we are in a better position to remediate problems should the occasion arise. Many phobias appear to have developed as a result of classical conditioning. A person with *cynophobia*, for example, may have been bitten by a ferocious dog at some time and, as a result, exhibit conditioned physiological arousal even in the presence of gentle dogs.

When a child learns a "healthy respect" for dogs or fire or for moving traffic, both operant and respondent procedures may play a part. If the child has actually been burned, then touching a flame or a hot stove has been punished if these objects are not touched on future occasions. Respondent conditioning has also occurred if the child subsequently becomes anxious at the sight of flame or of cigarette lighters, matchbooks, and other objects that may elicit fear by generalization.

Parents often condition anxiety and guilt as a means of deterring their children from lying, stealing, swearing, or from engaging in sexual activities, sometimes invoking aversive events of both earthly and heavenly origin. Although this kind of training may play an important part in the learning of ethical standards, there may be undesirable effects. Therapists of many theoretical persuasions attribute such sexual problems as impotence and frigidity to high-level anxiety conditioned in childhood.

2. Anxiety-Relief Conditioning

This procedure involves the application of continuous faradic (electric) shock to the forearm,

terminated when the patient says a predetermined word such as "calm," or "relax." The theory underlying the anxiety-relief method is illustrated in Figure 6.3. Termination of shock is an unconditional stimulus for relaxation; by the respondent pairing procedure, a neutral word such as "calm" can become a conditional stimulus that elicits relief or relaxation. If relaxation or a feeling of relief can be elicited by the word "calm," then a patient can subsequently control his anxiety and fear by saying the word "calm" to himself. Kushner (1970) reports mixed success with this procedure, and Wolpe (1969) notes that anxiety-relief conditioning will be effective only with people who feel emotional disturbance (as well as pain) in response to shock.

Of course, painful shock must be initiated before it can be terminated. If specific events are paired with the onset of shock, then these events will subsequently elicit anxiety just as the word "calm" subsequently elicits relaxation. This combination of conditioning procedures is called *aversion-relief* therapy. For example, anxiety might be conditioned at the onset of shock in conjunction with problem behavior such as drinking alcohol, while relief was conditioned at the termination of shock in conjunction with rejection of alcohol. This procedure is discussed below under "aversion therapies."

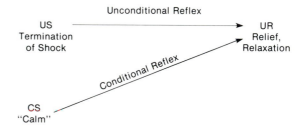

ANXIETY-RELIEF CONDITIONING

Figure 6.3. Theoretical basis of anxiety-relief conditioning. Termination of shock is the unconditional stimulus (US) for relief or relaxation. After respondent conditioning, saying the word "Calm" becomes a conditional stimulus (CS) that can elicit relaxation.

Anxiety-relief conditioning does not seem to be a very popular procedure. The paucity of data may be an indication that such conditioning is difficult, or it may reflect the fact that there are many other, less painful ways of learning to relax.

C. Extinction Procedures

In laboratory studies of respondent conditioning, the conditional reflex can usually be eliminated by repeated presentations of the conditional stimulus without the stimulus that originally elicited the response. But outside the laboratory it is often difficult to eliminate problem behavior that has presumably been acquired through respondent conditioning. If one has a conditioned fear of rats, for example, the logical way to eliminate this fear is to be with a nice, friendly rat that is not in a position to bite or to make sudden movements in one's direction. Eventually, the fear should extinguish. What usually happens is that—for obvious reasons —one avoids the possibility of any contact with a rat, and thus the possibility of extinction. The procedures described in this section are designed to prevent the avoidance of anxiety-producing situations so that the conditional stimuli for anxiety may be presented without the unconditional stimuli, and extinction may take place. There are many variations of this basic procedure. In the following arrangement, the procedures are described in order of increasing intensity of stimulation.

1. Graduated Extinction

A student of ours named Marti was working in the sculpture studio when the alcohol burner she was using exploded in her face. She was badly burned, but thanks to good medical attention her scars healed and her hair grew back. One might never have known of her terrifying experience. A few months later, Marti was one of four students helping me prepare boeuf bourguignon for a mob of psych majors. She was slicing mushrooms some six feet away when I poured brandy on the first batch of beef and set it on fire. As the rest of us admired the flames, Marti gasped, startled, turned pale, and beat a hasty retreat from the kitchen. Since I had known about the explosion, I felt like a fool; and after making apologies, I asked if she'd like to try respondent extinction. Since she had been concerned about her "overreaction" to open flames in other situations in which there was no real danger, Marti said she would like to try.[4] When it was time to flame the next batch of meat, Marti was forewarned, and she watched from outside the kitchen from a distance of approximately 10 feet. With successive batches, she gradually came closer, and she fired the last batch herself. We were all tremendously impressed because the explosion that occurs when brandy is lighted is probably an *unconditional* stimulus for anxiety, even though for most of us the anxiety quickly dissipates. Our admiration may well have contributed to Marti's rapid progress, as might the fact that a trusted individual implied that the procedure would be effective (Wolpin and Raines, 1966).

Marti has since graduated, and when I wrote to ask her if I might publish this account, I also asked if she ever cooks with brandy. Since she is now a graduate student, I should have anticipated her answer: "No—not due to anxiety, but for financial reasons!" It is now three years since the accident, and Marti says that the effects still linger on: she can light a match and put a log on the fire, but she is still afraid of things that might explode. I also asked her if,

---

4. She might have also acquiesced because she thought I wanted her to. Aside from being friends, I was directing her honors research. This class of variables, which might come under the heading "inadvertent social pressure," is seldom analyzed, but is likely to be an important consideration when evaluating therapeutic procedures.

after cooking at our house, she had tried extinguishing anxiety in other situations:

Not "scientifically." At first, I would leave the room when someone would light a cigarette. With time, I would then only go to the door, and not outside the room. Then I would distance myself, and now I don't even budge (although I watch). I guess what was reinforcing was the "nonoccurrence" of an explosion. It didn't take me too long to adjust to cigarettes (maybe a month or so), but it took a couple of years with things that could possibly explode. I now live in a house that is heated by a kerosene stove, which I light with caution and a touch of anxiety. But I do light it. However, at neighbors' houses, I'll casually walk toward the door until the fire is going steadily and then return to where I was sitting.

Feedback concerning the progress of extinction seems to be an important variable. In one study, a claustrophobic patient and a knife-phobic patient were given increasingly longer exposure to the feared situations (Leitenberg, Agras, Thompson, & Wright, 1968). The dependent variable was the length of time the claustrophobic patient stayed in a small, dark room or the length of time the knife-phobic patient kept a knife in view. The patients could terminate a trial whenever they wished. When told how long they remained in the feared situation, they were able to tolerate the situation for increasingly longer periods of time. When this feedback was withdrawn, they made no further progress, but when feedback was reinstated, they continued to improve.

In graduated extinction, the anxiety-producing stimulus is attenuated to a level the individual can tolerate without undue anxiety. As extinction occurs in the presence of attenuated stimulation, the intensity can be gradually increased to a level that formerly elicited marked anxiety.

2. Flooding

Flooding, a term first used by Polin (1959) in an animal study, is now used for a variety of "forced extinction" procedures. What these procedures have in common is prolonged exposure to a conditional anxiety-producing stimulus presented at *full intensity* but in the absence of the unconditional stimulus. Although Polin's rats were free to emit an avoidance response, flooding now usually refers to a procedure in which avoidance is prevented. The client is thus forced to face the object of the (conditioned) anxiety when it is presented at full intensity. This can be accomplished *in vivo* (with the real phobic objects), or the client can be helped to visualize the phobic situation in imagination.

a. In vivo flooding

A case study by Yule, Sacks, and Hersov (1974) illustrates the successful use of flooding after a variation of graduated extinction produced limited success. The client, Bill, was an eleven-year-old boy with a debilitating noise phobia. The authors first extinguished the boy's fear of a cap gun, but had trouble with the sound of bursting balloons. When flooding was initiated, they brought Bill into a small room which contained 50 inflated balloons. Even with no sound, the balloons elicited anxiety: Bill "cowered into his chair, started to sweat and shake, and put his fingers into his ears." When he was asked to burst a balloon, Bill refused, whereupon the therapist promptly burst six. "Bill started to cry, but the therapist continued bursting balloons until he (Bill) no longer flinched . . . After much persuasion, Bill used his feet to push balloons against a nail held by the therapist. In rapid succession, 20 were burst in this fashion" (Yule et al., 1974). The authors note that in a second session, Bill dispatched 320 balloons at a total cost of £4.50.

A number of psychiatrists and psychologists view neurotic behavior as learned behavior which is maintained by its anxiety-reducing function. This position is illustrated by the story of a young girl who has a compulsion to snap her fingers, an activity she engages in for hours at a time. She explains to her therapist that snapping her fingers keeps away the purple elephants; and when the therapist tries to assure her that there *are* no purple elephants, she replies: "See, it works! That's why I keep snapping my fingers!" According to this view, "elephants" come in many forms and colors. A wife who drinks too much or who develops a migraine headache every evening may be said to be avoiding the fear of sexual relations with her husband. Whether such problems are maintained by anxiety-reduction, whether they are maintained simply by the avoidance of unwelcome activities (the husband might be an inept lover)—or neither—is pretty much a matter of speculation and of theoretical persuasion. At any rate, avoidance of a situation effectively prevents the extinction of any anxiety that may occur in conjunction with that situation.

In at least one study (Rainey, 1972), subjective anxiety was recorded before and after the patient engaged in compulsive behavior. There was a marked reduction in anxiety when he completed the compulsive act, which lends some support to the anxiety-reduction hypothesis. The patient had a long history of chronic compulsive and ritualistic behavior associated with a fear of contamination which dated from an incident, 12 years earlier, when he heard a rumor that a female classmate had fleas. He was in the sixth grade, and the year was 1957. At the time of therapy, he had resigned from his job because his company had purchased a piece of equipment manufactured in 1957. Virtually all of his waking hours were then spent in ritualistic decontamination of himself and his belongings. He was unable to open mail from his father who still lived in the city where the original incident had occurred in 1957, and "When such a letter arrived, the patient would pick it up with a piece of kleenex, burn it, and wash out the mail box" (Rainey, 1972, p. 118). *In vivo* flooding, in which the patient carried

with him a 1957 gold sovereign and a 1957 issue of a magazine, eliminated his obsessive thoughts and ritualistic behavior in 48 hours. Rainey reports that 18 months later, the patient was free of symptoms and fully employed.

Flooding is by no means universally successful, and very few studies report the elimination of severe and chronic problems in anything like 48 hours. Wolpe (1969) is among those who urge caution in exposing a patient to high anxiety stimulation. He describes an attempt at *in vivo* flooding with a physician who developed a phobia for psychiatric patients. Treatment consisted of lengthy exposure to schizophrenic patients inside a mental hospital; but instead of decreasing, his anxiety level soared, and flooding had to be discontinued.

b. Imaginal flooding
One way of avoiding the possibility that exposure to high-anxiety stimulation may increase, rather than decrease, the patient's fear is to have him *imagine* the fearful situation rather than face it directly. A person fearful of snakes would be instructed to imagine picking up and holding a snake, watching it writhe and feeling its texture. A person afraid of riding in elevators would imagine entering an elevator, hearing and watching the doors close, feeling the rapid descent as he catches his breath, and so forth. When fear has been reduced in these imaginal flooding sessions, the patient is presented with the frightening situation *in vivo*. As in the case of *in vivo* flooding, this procedure has been used with mixed success. A relevant variable seems to be the duration of exposure: with too brief an exposure to the feared object, seen in imagination, anxiety may actually increase (Morganstern, 1973; Rachman, 1966b).

3. Implosion

Implosion is like flooding, except that instead of having patients imagine realistic scenes of high-intensity anxiety, they imagine unrealistic scenes in which the feared situation is exaggerated to a horrifying degree. The "common sense" rationale of implosion therapy is that if you imagine the very worst and nothing happens, then your anxiety will decrease. Stampfl, who coined the term "implosion therapy," views the process as a special form of extinction. The client is kept at a high level of anxiety until there is a "spontaneous reduction" (hence the term implosion) in the anxiety-inducing properties of the imagined scenes. (See Stampfl & Levis, 1967, for a statement of the rationale and procedures.) Someone with a fear of airplanes might be made to visualize being in a crash, with all the attendant sights, sounds, and odors. When the anxiety level subsided, further scenes involving the warmth and texture of blood might be presented. Someone with claustrophobia might imagine being locked in a stalled elevator during a power failure, and then hearing the cable break as the elevator plunged 38 stories to a subbasement. The therapist who uses this technique, and a similar one called *covert sensitization*, must have a strong stomach and vivid imagery in all sensory modalities.

Stampfl claims that implosion is not cruel because he is dealing only with words and imagery, and because he does not ask the patient to accept or believe in the scenes. Nonetheless, it would seem unwise to employ flooding or implosion with patients having any cardiac or respiratory problems that increased anxiety might exacerbate. Stampfl and his colleagues report good results with a wide variety of neurotic and psychotic disturbances, and with success achieved in a relatively short period of time. Others, however, have reported little success or even a worsening in the patient's condition (see Ayer, 1972; Marks, 1972; and Morganstern, 1973 for reviews). In addition, ethical considerations dictate caution, especially when alternative procedures such as systematic de-

sensitization are less traumatic and generally more effective.

D. Desensitization (Counterconditioning)

Several respondent procedures are designed to reduce or "inhibit" one class of behavior by conditioning another, incompatible class of behavior. In desensitization, the goal is to reduce anxiety by conditioning, for example, such incompatible behavior as relaxation. (Many of the aversion procedures also manipulate anxiety; but in these procedures the goal is to *increase* anxiety in conjunction with drinking, drug taking, fetishism, and so on, as a way of suppressing the problem behavior.)

Counterconditioning is often said to be a process by which a conditioned response is replaced by an incompatible response and, as a result, is no longer elicited by the conditioned stimulus. A person with a fear of snakes, for example, might be taught to relax in the presence of snakes. As relaxation gradually becomes prepotent over anxiety, anxiety is gradually reduced until it is no longer elicited by the presence of a snake.

The term "counterconditioning" suggests that therapy is merely a matter of substituting one conditioned response for another. As we shall see, it's not that simple. In all the many cases where counterconditioned relaxation has eliminated phobias, we know of none in which the formerly phobic object comes to elicit relaxation. The effectiveness of the procedures can be tested more easily than the rationale behind them; it is easier to determine *if* they work than *how* they work. At this point, we can only speculate about the underlying processes, but we can at least describe the procedures.

In what is probably the earliest behavioral description of counterconditioning, Pavlov tells us of an otherwise "very tractable" dog which, over the course of Pavlov's studies, became increasingly excited and disturbed when placed in the restraining stand. The dog struggled to get out of the stand, scratched the floor, gnawed the supports—behavior that Pavlov speculated might be "the expression of a special freedom reflex." When they began giving the dog all of its food in the restraining stand, it gradually became quieter; and Pavlov reports that "the freedom reflex was being inhibited" (Pavlov, 1927, p. 11–12). Pavlov did not exactly say that the restraining stand, which had previously elicited the "freedom reflex," had become a conditioned stimulus for eating; but it seems clear that he thought that eating inhibited the "freedom reflex"—or at least the dog's struggle to escape from the stand. In other terminology, one might say that during the early stages of experimentation, the dog gradually became "sensitized" to the restraining stand; and during the subsequent stages, when it was given all its food in the stand, it gradually became desensitized.

Joseph Wolpe developed desensitization as a therapeutic procedure (e.g., 1952b, 1958, 1962a, 1969). In his early work with cats, Wolpe first conditioned a "neurotic" fear of the apparatus in which the animals received painful shock and then eliminated the fear by feeding them in increasingly closer proximity to the cage. He concluded that feeding inhibited the conditioned fear reaction, and he used the term "reciprocal inhibition" to describe what he presumed to be the underlying physiological process (Wolpe, 1952a,b).

Wolpe's treatment of fear in cats resembles Mary Cover Jones's earlier (1924) methods of eliminating inappropriate fears in children. The procedure she called the "Method of Direct Conditioning" consisted of associating the feared object with a situation "capable of arousing a positive (pleasant) reaction." To eliminate an extreme fear of rabbits in a child named

Peter, for example, she placed a caged rabbit a few feet from Peter while he was sitting in his highchair eating candy. When Peter promptly cried and insisted the rabbit be taken away, the cage was moved to a distance (20 feet) at which fear of the rabbit no longer interfered with eating. Gradually, over a number of sessions, the rabbit was brought closer; and in the final session, Peter patted and played with it for several minutes (Jones, 1924, pp. 388-389).

Wolpe's major extension of Jones's work with children and his own work with cats was to substitute *imagined* exposure to the feared object for the real thing. He also substituted relaxation and assertive behavior for feeding as activities incompatible with fear.

1. Systematic Desensitization (Imaginal)

Wolpe's basic assumption is that neurotic anxiety is learned behavior which can be "unlearned" or inhibited by incompatible behavior. Anxiety is reduced by conditioning incompatible behavior while the client imagines anxiety-evoking scenes. When the incompatible behavior is deep muscle relaxation, and when the imagined scenes are ranked in order of the anxiety they arouse, the procedure is called *systematic desensitization*.

Desensitization involves three sets of operations. The patient is trained in the techniques of progressive muscle relaxation, which may take parts of six sessions. During these sessions, the patient and the therapist also identify the stimuli that arouse anxiety and construct an "anxiety hierarchy" for each stimulus class or theme. The items in each hierarchy are arranged in order, according to the intensity of the anxiety aroused. Then the patient (who is sometimes hypnotized) is asked to imagine the least disturbing item on the list until it no longer evokes any anxiety. By progressive steps, the patient gradually works through the whole hierarchy.

Relaxation can counteract only relatively weak anxiety, so it is important to move slowly, sometimes repeating a single item more than 100 times. Treatment usually takes between 5 and 30 sessions. As desensitization progresses, the patient gradually faces real anxiety-evoking situations in natural settings.

a. Relaxation

With training in deep muscle relaxation, clients learn how to alternately tense and relax the various groups of muscles in the body. (Bernstein & Borkovec, 1973; Paul, 1966; Wolpe, 1969; Wolpe & Lazarus, 1966.) They learn to control the muscles of the hands, arms, shoulders, neck, mouth, tongue, forehead, back, stomach, thighs, legs, and feet. Eventually, they can relax on cue. People who have difficulty learning to relax may be assisted by hypnosis (Wolpe, 1952b), by tranquilizers such as Brevital (Brady, 1971; Friedman, 1966; Shorkey & Himle, 1974), or by a mixture of carbon dioxide and oxygen (Wolpe, 1969). Alternatively, Pecknold, Raeburn, and Poser (1972) have used intravenous diazepam to facilitate relaxation in the desensitization of phobias in patients with barbiturate addictions. Budzynski and Stoyva (1973) used biofeedback to shape and maintain relaxation. One can also learn to relax with the help of taped recordings. (Several are now on the market, e.g., Lazarus, 1970; Turner, no date.)

b. Construction of hierarchy

Anxiety hierarchies are sometimes built around a theme, such as the fear of public speaking: clients would imagine scenes covering a variety of situations in which they might be called on to speak. Other hierarchies are built along a spatial-temporal continuum, in which case the client would imagine scenes of varying proximity to the feared object. Some "mixed" hierarchies contain both thematic and spatial-temporal items. In all of these hierarchies, the scenes are ordered along a continuum from least to most fearful. Many therapists use a "fear thermometer" or "sud (subjective unit of disturbance) scale" to arrange the hierarchy. The client rates each scene according to its sud value, with zero corresponding to totally relaxed and 100 corresponding to maximum possible tension and anxiety. Scenes are created to cover the whole range of subjective disturbance and then arranged according to their sud value.

Anxiety hierarchies are usually designed for the individual client. Even so, the subjective ratings may change over time. Table 6.2 is a desensitization hierarchy for test anxiety, with the client's ratings on two different occasions shown at the left (Kanfer & Phillips, 1970, p. 151). The scenes evoked somewhat different ratings on the two occasions, and for scenes with anxiety ratings between 80–95, even the order is slightly different. For this particular client, maximum tension was reported for thinking about being inadequately prepared for an exam, and for studying the night before a big exam. Other clients with test anxiety might work from different scenes arranged in a different order; and, for some, maximum anxiety might not be induced until they imagined themselves entering the examination room and picking up the exam, or seeing a question they could not answer. (Suinn's 1969 *Test Anxiety Scale* describes many study and test-taking situations helpful in constructing individual hierarchies.)

c. Desensitization

At the start of desensitization, the client relaxes, perhaps visualizing a "relaxing scene" such as lying on the beach, basking in the sun. The lowest scene from the hierarchy is then presented by the therapist who elaborates the details to help the client's imagery. If the slightest anxiety is experienced while visualizing the scene, the client signals, usually by raising a finger. The therapist immediately tells the client to "turn off" the scene and return to a relaxed state. If the scene evokes no anxiety, it is terminated after 5–30 seconds, and then the client

Table 6.2   A mixed desensitization hierarchy for test anxiety. (From Kanfer & Phillips, 1970, p. 151.)

ANXIETY HIERARCHY

Fear Ratings[a]

First Ratings	Second Ratings	Hierarchy Items
0	0	Beginning a new course
15	10	Hearing an instructor announce a small quiz two weeks hence
20	25	Having a professor urge you personally to do well on an exam
35	40	Trying to decide how to study for an exam
40	45	Reviewing the material I know should be studied—listing study to do
60	50	Hearing an instructor remind the class of a quiz one week hence
60	65	Hearing an instructor announce a major exam in three weeks and its importance
75	75	Hearing an instructor announce a major exam in one week
80	70	Standing alone in the hall before an exam
80	80	Getting an exam back in class
80	80	Anticipating getting back a graded exam later that day
80	85	Talking to several students about an exam right before taking it
85	80	Thinking about being scared and anxious regarding a specific exam
90	85	Studying with fellow students several days before an exam
90	90	Hearing some "pearls" from another student which you doubt you'll remember, while studying in a group
90	90	Cramming while alone in the library right before an exam
90	95	Thinking about not keeping up in other subjects while preparing for an exam
95	90	Thinking about being anxious over schoolwork in general
95	95	Talking with several students about an exam immediately after
100	100	Thinking about being generally inadequately prepared
100	100	Thinking about not being adequately prepared for a particular exam
100	100	Studying the night before a big exam

[a]Ratings: 0 = Totally relaxed;
100 = As tense as you ever are

relaxes for a half minute or so. Each item from the hierarchy is presented several times with the client relaxing between presentations. However, whenever anxiety is signaled, the therapist terminates the scene, helps the client relax, and selects an item lower on the hierarchy for the next presentation. The procedure demands that the client work through the hierarchy with minimal anxiety at any stage, and some therapists monitor the psychogalvanic skin response (PGR) in case the client does not accurately discriminate—or report—the level of anxiety.

The number of times that an item on an anxiety hierarchy must be imagined before anxiety is eliminated is not uniform throughout the hierarchy. Wolpe (1963) found that for some kinds of phobias the number of visualizations, or "presentations," increases throughout the hierarchy, while for other phobias it decreases. For claustrophobias and others in which anxiety increases with proximity to the phobic object, few visualizations are necessary for the low-anxiety items; but increasingly more visualizations are required as the client works up the hierarchy. On the other hand, agoraphobias and those in which the *number* of objects is frightening require many more visualizations at the early stages and relatively few as the distance or the number of objects increases.

This is illustrated in Figure 6.4, which shows the course of desensitization for one patient who had three phobias. The ordinate is the number of visualizations (presentations) required to eliminate anxiety on a given item. (The number of visualizations is shown as a percentage of the total number required for the whole hierarchy.) The abscissa gives the stimulus for the least anxiety, increasing to the top of the anxiety hierarchy. For example, curve A describes the desensitization of a phobia for a dead dog. Approximately 10 percent of the total number of presentations in the hierarchy were required to eliminate the anxiety aroused by imagining a dead dog at a distance of 200 yards. Another 10 percent of the total number of visualizations was required when the dog was imagined at 150 yards. The curve gradually accelerates, and it took a relatively large number of imagined scenes to close the last twenty yards.

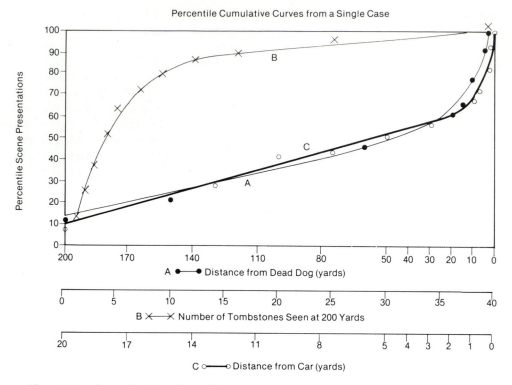

Figure 6.4.   Desensitization of three phobias in a single patient. The proportion of times that items on an anxiety hierarchy were visualized before anxiety for that item was eliminated and the next (more disturbing) item was presented. The ordinate is the number of visualizations required for successive items in the hierarchy (plotted as a cumulative percentage of the number of visualizations for the whole hierarchy). The abscissa is the scene visualized, increasing from the least to the greatest anxiety. Some phobias (A,C) require relatively few visualizations to attenuate the anxiety aroused by items low on the hierarchy, and relatively many visualizations at the top of the hierarchy. Other kinds of phobias (B) require many visualizations of items low on the scale, but once the patient can accept these, progress through the rest of the hierarchy is relatively rapid. (From Wolpe, 1963, p. 1066.)

In contrast, curve B shows that 80 percent of the visualizations for the tombstone hierarchy were required before the patient could accept 10 tombstones at a distance of 200 yards, and that with relatively few additional visualizations he could imagine 40 tombstones without anxiety.

d. Transfer
In at least some cases, generalization from imagined scenes in the therapist's office to real situations in the natural environment occurs very rapidly (Rachman, 1966c). Judging by Sherman's (1972) study with aquaphobic college students, gradual exposure to the real frightening situation should occur during, not at the end of desensitization. Many therapists encourage their clients to "test themselves" in natural situations before completing the hierarchy in imagination, but they caution against exposure to situations further along the hierarchy than those already treated in therapy. Subjects undergoing systematic desensitization for sexual disorders, for example, experienced little anxiety during actual sexual per-

formance when participation was restricted to activities that had already been desensitized (Obler, 1973).

Systematic desensitization has been effective in treating a variety of phobias and irrational fears, including the fear of: heights, open spaces, closed spaces, cars, airplanes, water, rats, dogs, snakes, spiders, lice, blood, hypodermic needles, hospitals, sexual impotence, frigidity, public speaking, and test anxiety. It has also been used in the treatment of nightmares (Geer & Silverman, 1967; Ross, Meichenbaum, & Humphrey, 1971), as well as in the treatment of physical problems such as asthma (Sirota & Mahoney, 1974; Wolpe, 1952b), anorexia (Hallsten, 1965; Lang, 1965), and migraine headache (Lutker, 1971), and to eliminate convulsive seizures occurring an average of 58 times a day prior to treatment (Parrino, 1971). In one study, systematic desensitization in preparation for childbirth significantly reduced both the duration of labor and the intensity of pain as compared to a control group that received more usual "psychoprophylactic" preparation (Kondaš & Śćetniká, 1972).

In an early evaluation of the effectiveness of systematic desensitization, Wolpe (1961) reported less than two percent relapse on a survey of follow-up studies on 249 patients. More recently, Paul (1969b,c) reviewed 75 studies covering nearly 1,000 clients treated by more than 90 therapists. Even though most of the studies lacked appropriate controls, Paul was able to conclude:

The findings were overwhelmingly positive, and for the first time in the history of psychological treatments, a specific therapeutic package reliably produced measurable benefits for clients across a broad range of distressing problems in which anxiety was of fundamental importance. "Relapse" and "symptom substitution" were notably lacking, although the majority of authors were attuned to these problems.

(Paul, 1969c, p. 159.)

2. Variations of Systematic Desensitization

Some adults cannot achieve a state of deep muscle relaxation, and it is a difficult and complex series of exercises to ask of children. As a result, therapists have looked for other classes of behavior incompatible with anxiety.

a. Emotive imagery

Lazarus and Abramovitz (1962) adapted Wolpe's procedure for children by substituting "emotive imagery" for relaxation. Anxiety is reduced by having the child imagine scenes in which he is assertive, amused, or proud of himself. As in systematic desensitization, areas of fear are explored and relevant hierarchies are developed; but instead of muscular relaxation, the child imagines scenes that incorporate his own heroes and daydreams. One 14-year-old boy with an intense fear of dogs had a burning ambition to own an Alfa Romeo and race it at the Indianapolis "500." During the course of therapy, he imagined owning the car as the therapist vividly described its beauty and action. Gradually, the anxiety-producing stimulus was introduced: ". . . the speedometer is climbing into the 90s; you have a wonderful feeling of being in perfect control; you look at the trees whizzing by and you see a little dog standing next to one of them—if you feel any anxiety, just raise your finger." Eventually the child imagines that he is showing off his car to a crowd of envious people in a strange town when a large dog comes up and sniffs at his heels. Therapy was terminated after only five sessions, and reports a year later indicated that there was no return of his phobia.

b. Other alternatives to relaxation

In an early report on systematic desensitization, Wolpe (1952b) states that the autonomic effects of both deep muscle relaxation and assertive behavior are antagonistic to the autonomic components of anxiety. He recommends relaxation to inhibit anxiety evoked by inanimate objects and words, and assertive training to inhibit anxiety evoked by another person. The recommendation for assertive behavior seems to be based on two assumptions: (1) that anxiety evoked by a person is "almost invariably accompanied by some measure of resentment" and (2) that by behaving assertively in the face of anxiety, the client expresses his suppressed resentment and thus "reciprocally inhibits the anxiety" (Wolpe, 1952b, p. 826). (We return to Wolpe's theory of reciprocal inhibition in Section E.)

Whether or not either relaxation or assertive behavior permanently inhibits anxiety in a neurological sense, both classes of behavior can be highly adaptive in anxiety-evoking situations. Relaxed or assertive behavior can be a means of *changing the situation* as well as one's physiological reactions. Furthermore, if one "feels" (or perceives one's behavior as) calm and competent or indignant, one is less likely to "feel" (or perceive one's behavior as) anxious and inadequate.

Lazarus (1965) substituted "directed muscular activity" for relaxation with patients unable to achieve deep muscle relaxation. The anxiety hierarchy is constructed as usual, and the client starts by imagining himself in the least disturbing situation. But instead of relaxing during the scene presentation, he engages in some physical activity such as hitting a pillow or a punching bag. A 32-year-old male patient with a debilitating fear of dentists pounded a leather-padded footstool during visualizations of scenes ranging from the word "dentist" to "the dentist pushes the needle into your gums." The patient was seen for 16 sessions, following which he visited a dentist for the first time in six years. He reported sitting through two extractions and five fillings with only "normal trepidation" (Lazarus, 1965, p. 302). Gershman and Stedman (1971) also report good results with

intense muscular activity: they used the oriental defense exercises, karate and kung fu.

3. In Vivo Desensitization

In vivo, or "real-life," desensitization replaces imagined exposure to a stressful situation with gradual exposure to the real thing. The procedure resembles graduated extinction in that the anxiety-evoking situation is attenuated, and it resembles systematic desensitization in that behavior incompatible with fear is specified and encouraged. *In vivo* desensitization is particularly helpful with clients who have difficulty imagining scenes in vivid detail; and, of course, it obviates the necessity for transfer from imagined to real situations.

Mary Cover Jones (1924) was using *in vivo* desensitization when she eliminated Peter's fear of rabbits by gradually bringing a caged rabbit closer to him as he was eating. When another child who was afraid of frogs wished to play with crayons, she employed her "Method of Distraction" by placing the crayons next to a frog. Bentler (1962) used a similar strategy with one-year-old Margaret who suddenly developed an intense fear of water after slipping in the bathtub. Attractive toys were placed in the *empty* bathtub, then near the kitchen sink, which contained additional toys floating on water. Gradually, over a period of a month, playing with toys involved increasing proximity to water. At the end of that time, Margaret's fear of faucets, bathtubs, and standing water was eliminated; and she played "joyously" in the tub, with the lawn sprinkler, and in her backyard wading pool. Masters and Johnson's (1970) programs for helping men and women overcome sexual problems such as impotence and frigidity are excellent examples of *in vivo* desensitization.

If the feared object is something portable, like a knife or a small animal, *in vivo* desensitization can be carried out in the therapist's office. Turnage and Logan (1974) used this set-ting to conduct *in vivo* desensitization of a young teacher's fear of hypodermic needles. *In vivo* desensitization can also be carried out under simulated conditions. A dog-phobic blind student lost her fear of dogs when desensi-tization was conducted with a tape recording of a barking dog (Monroe & Ahr, 1972). Sim-ilarly, a dog that went berserk during thunder-storms was desensitized when the sound of a taped storm was played at gradually increasing volume (Tuber, Hothersall, & Voith, 1974).

4. Modeling: Contact and Vicarious Desensitization

Contact desensitization (Ritter, 1968) is a form of *in vivo* desensitization that involves physical contact not only with the feared object but also with the therapist who guides or assists the client's participation. In the treatment of a snake phobia, for example, the client might first watch from a distance as the therapist handles a harm-less snake. Gradually the client would approach and then place a (gloved) hand on the therapist's hand as the latter was stroking the snake. Again gradually, the client's hand would be eased onto the snake, and if a glove were worn it would later be removed. Since the procedure involves modeling—by the therapist or by others—it is also called *participant modeling* (Rimm & Mahoney, 1969). As Rimm and Mas-ters (1974) point out, the essentials of the proce-dure are demonstration and gradual participa-tion. Whether or not it should be considered a desensitization procedure is open to question since incompatible behavior such as deep mus-cle relaxation is not specifically required.

Modeling, even without participation, has been effective in the treatment of children's fears, especially when the approach is gradual. Bandura, Grusec, and Menlove (1967), for ex-ample, arranged brief sessions in which chil-dren who were extremely frightened of dogs

could watch a peer model interact with a dog. During the first four sessions, the dog was con-fined in a pen, and the model petted and fed her. In the next two sessions, the model walked the dog around the room on leash; and in the final two sessions, the model climbed into the pen and played with the dog. The success of this graduated modeling procedure was measured by a test in which the children were asked to approach and feed the dog and, finally, to spend time alone with her in the room. There was also a generalization test with another dog of very different appearance. Performance on these tests, both at the end of treatment and at a 30-day follow-up, was far superior to that of control groups, including one control in which the dog was in the room but there was no modeling.

"Symbolic" modeling—filmed modeling, for example—can also be helpful. The pos-sibilities of covert, or imaginary, modeling have been explored in a number of studies by Kazdin. Subjects who are fearful of snakes, for example, imagine both a snake and another person in-teracting with the snake in a hierarchy of 14 scenes. Judging by a variety of subjective and objective measures, covert modeling is effec-tive; and Kazdin has been exploring some of the parameters. For example, he has found that covert modeling is even more effective when the model is initially frightened and gradually overcomes his fears, than when the model is fearless throughout the hierarchy of scenes (Kazdin, 1973, 1974). Meichenbaum (1971) re-ports a similar finding in a study employing filmed models. These studies would seem to have implications for live as well as symbolic modeling: perhaps the model should not be too competent. An initially fearful model who gradually overcomes anxiety would be likely to demonstrate more relevant classes of behavior than would a fearless model.

Several studies indicate that graduated modeling with graduated participation is superior to either modeling or desensitization alone (e.g., Bandura, Blanchard, & Ritter, 1969; Blanchard, 1970; Ritter, 1968, 1969). Mary Cover Jones (as usual) was probably the first behavioral psychologist to examine peer modeling as a procedure to reduce children's fears. She called it the "Method of Social Imitation," and pointed out one of the potential risks: depending on the behavior of the other child, fear might be acquired or exacerbated instead of eliminated (Jones, 1924). Obviously, care must be taken in the selection of models.

5. Automated and Group Desensitization

The therapist's presentation of anxiety-evoking situations can be recorded on audio- or video-tape or film, and this allows for "automated" desensitization with minimal participation by the therapist. Even the relaxation training can be given by tape. The client can control the exposure to each scene in the hierarchy by advancing the tape; and in some cases (e.g., Cotler, 1970; Lang, Melamed, & Hart, 1970) if anxiety increases, the client pushes a switch that returns the tape to a section with instructions for relaxation. Lang's group at the University of Wisconsin has a highly automated system for desensitization which, in one study with snake-phobic college students,[5] was even more effective than "live" desensitization with a therapist present. Others who have employed automated desensitization with snake phobias include Krapfl and Nawas (1969) and Morris and Suckerman (1974).

The development of automated desensitization procedures has at least two practical advantages: (1) the savings in therapist time allows the treatment of more clients, often at a lower fee; and (2) clients may work through the anxiety hierarchy at their own pace. Automation makes it possible for people to conduct their own desensitization. A patient of Migler and Wolpe (1967) experienced great distress in con-

junction with public speaking because he feared derision and disapproval. The authors supervised as the patient recorded instructions for relaxation and the items of an anxiety hierarchy, and then allowed him to carry out desensitization at home. This required only seven sessions. The following week, the patient was asked to speak at a staff meeting, whereupon he confidently gave a long speech expressing disagreement with previous speakers. Two years later he was continuing to speak in public with no anxiety (Wolpe, 1969).

To help the many stutterers who have an agonizing time talking on the telephone, Lee, McGeough, and Peins (1976) have developed an automated desensitization program for telephone use.

Automation also contributes to the *evaluation* of the desensitization procedure because it eliminates many features of therapist participation that might, in themselves, be responsible for the client's improvement. Automation may not eliminate the client's "expectation of success," but it does eliminate the therapist's differential reinforcement of the client's behavior during desensitization sessions. The therapist's general manner of understanding and support is probably an important component of any sort of therapy, including automated desensitization.

Another procedure that saves therapist time and reduces therapist interaction with the client is group desensitization. Wolpe (1969) required only five sessions for group desensitization of fear of public speaking—an average of only 18 minutes of therapist time per patient. Group desensitization has proved effective with a wide

---

5. The relevance of data from snake-phobic college students to clinical populations has been questioned by Bernstein and Paul (1971) and by Cooper, Furst, and Bridger (1969). Most of us don't run into too many snakes during the normal course of events, whereas a pronounced fear of heights, of open or closed spaces, or of cars can be truly debilitating. But basic research can identify many important variables, and the generality of laboratory findings is an empirical question that will be answered in time.

variety of problems: acrophobia and claustrophobia (Lazarus, 1961), interpersonal anxiety (Paul & Shannon, 1966), test anxiety (Donner & Guerney, 1969; Taylor, 1971), and fear of public speaking (Wolpe, 1969). Group and automated desensitization have been combined to reduce test anxiety in college students (Donner and Guerney, 1969); and Nawas (1971) has developed an entire desensitization "package" for the reduction of snake phobias.

E. Anxiety Reduction: Procedures and "Process"

The clinical success of systematic desensitization and related procedures has stimulated a great deal of research and a great deal of heated discussion.[6] The procedures are clearly described (Wolpe, 1958, 1969), and can be analyzed and evaluated. The theory, however, presents more of a problem. At the present time, little is known about how systematic desensitization produces its effects, but some progress has been made toward analyzing the relative contributions of various components of the desensitization procedure. The major components include: (1) locating the conditions in which maladaptive anxiety occurs and constructing the relevant hierarchies; (2) training in deep muscle relaxation or some other behavior that is physically incompatible with arousal of the sympathetic branch of the autonomic nervous system; (3) imagining anxiety-evoking situations while engaging in this incompatible behavior, starting with those situations that evoke the least anxiety and working up the hierarchy; (4) transfer from imagined to real situations; and (5) evaluation of the success of treatment.

Most research on systematic desensitization has been designed to evaluate the three components of desensitization proper: *imagining* the anxiety-evoking situations instead of facing them directly; *attenuating* the level of anxiety by starting at the bottom of the hierarchy and advancing to a higher item only when lower items no longer evoke anxiety; and simultaneously engaging in some *other behavior* that presumably inhibits the physiological components of anxiety.

It is obviously not *mandatory* to imagine the anxiety-evoking situation because the success of *in vivo* desensitization is well documented. The *in vivo* treatment may even be superior (Cooke, 1966, found consistent, but not significant, differences in this direction), and, of course, it programs the transfer to real-life situations right from the start. On the other hand, imaginal desensitization is sometimes easier to carry out—as when the patient is fearful of heights or flying in airplanes. Wolpe's assumption that imagining a fearful situation is accompanied by physiological arousal has received considerable support. In his review of the literature concerning physiological measures of desensitization phenomena, Mathews (1971) concludes that physiological arousal, particularly when measured by heart rate and skin resistance, is greater when the patient imagines fearful than neutral situations, and that arousal to imagined phobic situations decreases during the course of desensitization. This reduction in physiological arousal is generally accompanied by, or followed by, a decrease in the level of anxiety reported by the patient. As Mathews notes, these changes may then allow the patient to make closer contact with the real phobic situation, which, in turn, would allow the *in vivo* reduction in autonomic responses and in subjective reports of anxiety.

6. The following articles include reviews of research from a variety of theoretical positions: Davison, 1968b, Davison & Wilson, 1973; Evans, 1973; Locke, 1971; Mathews, 1971; Morganstern, 1973; Paul, 1969b,c; Seligman, 1971; Van Egeren, 1971; Van Egeren, Feather, & Hein, 1971; Vodde & Gilner, 1971; Weiner, 1973; Wilkins, 1971; Wilson & Davison, 1971.

Another critical feature of Wolpe's desensitization program, given the utility of confronting phobic situations in imagination, is the gradual progression along a hierarchy, advancing to higher items only when lower items no longer evoke anxiety. There is good evidence supporting a positive correlation between the patient's rating of scenes along the hierarchy and the degree of physiological arousal when the patient actually imagines the scene (Lang, et al., 1970; Van Egeren et al., 1971). But it does not necessarily follow that anxiety evoked by items low in the hierarchy will be reduced more rapidly than anxiety evoked by items at the top of the hierarchy. (See Van Egeren et al., 1971; Wolpe, 1963; and Figure 6.4 of this text.)

Just as the success of *in vivo* desensitization refutes the *necessity* for prior imaginal desensitization, so the success of flooding refutes the necessity for progression along an anxiety hierarchy. Table 6.3 compares several anxiety-reducing procedures with respect to these conditions. When the anxiety-evoking situation is imagined, its intensity or duration can be attenuated and then progressively increased, as in systematic desensitization; it can be presented at full strength, starting at the top of the hierarchy, as in flooding; or it can be exaggerated, as in implosion. When the anxiety-evoking situation is confronted directly, the intensity or duration of exposure can also be attenuated and gradually increased, as with *in vivo* desensitization; or it can be presented at full strength, as with *in vivo* flooding or forced extinction. To our knowledge, there is no behavioral therapy based on *in vivo* implosion, although some of the encounter therapies might qualify. Hypothetical *in vivo* implosion "treatments" would include: taking a claustrophobic on a prolonged cruise in a submarine; taking someone with a fear of heights up in an airplane and forcing him to jump with a parachute that would not open for 1,000 feet; making someone with a dog phobia the target while a large number of dogs are given attack training (the patient, of course, would be wearing appropriate padding so that no physical damage would occur). Good results have been reported with all of the procedures shown in Table 6.3, which suggests that neither the imaginal nor the hierarchical components of systematic desensitization is *essential*. Nonetheless, desensitization, either systematic or *in vivo*, has two advantages: the hierarchy provides a flexible program that can be tailored to the individual's responses, and the therapist does not run the risk of exacerbating the clients' fears through the extreme emotional stress of implosion.

The third feature of desensitization proper is the inhibition of the physiological components of anxiety by the action of the parasympathetic branch of the autonomic nervous system. In one statement of his theory, Wolpe says:

In the systematic desensitization technique the effects of muscle relaxation are used to produce reciprocal inhibition of small evocations of anxiety and thereby build up conditioned inhibition of anxiety-responding to the particular stimulus combination. When (and only when) the evocations of anxiety are weakened by the counterposed relaxation does the anxiety response *habit* diminish. (Wolpe, 1962b, p. 325–326.)

Wolpe thus attributes the success of desensitization procedures to an underlying process

Table 6.3   Presentation of anxiety-evoking situation in various respondent procedures designed to eliminate anxiety.

Intensity or Duration of Stimulus

	Attenuated	Full Strength	Exaggerated
Imagined	Systematic desensitization	Flooding	Implosion
Real Life	*In vivo* desensitization	*In vivo* flooding	—
	Graduated extinction	Forced extinction	—

he calls "reciprocal inhibition," a term borrowed from the great English physiologist, Sir Charles Sherrington. Sherrington (1906) used the term to describe the reciprocal action of certain reflexes such as the relaxation of extensor muscles when the corresponding flexor muscles contract. Wolpe has extended the term to the mutually incompatible arousal of the sympathetic and parasympathetic branches of the autonomic nervous system; and he proposes that anxiety—mediated by the sympathetic branch—can be inhibited by assertive behavior, relaxation, or sexual arousal—mediated by the parasympathetic branch. (Conversely, assertive behavior, relaxation, and sexual arousal can be inhibited by anxiety.)

Studies designed to evaluate the role of relaxation in desensitization have produced conflicting results. At present, there is insufficient evidence to conclude that relaxation prevents or inhibits the physiological components of anxiety. Nevertheless, relaxation may facilitate desensitization if, as Mathews suggests, it enhances both the "vividness and the autonomic effects of imagery, while at the same time maximizing the response decrement with repeated presentations" (Mathews, 1971, p. 88).

More troublesome is Wolpe's statement that the inhibition of anxiety by relaxation will build up *conditioned inhibition* of anxiety (see quotation above). As Sherrington used the term, reciprocal inhibition was a temporary and a reversible phenomenon. Wolpe seems to be talking about a more enduring process. One hesitates to endorse the proposition that relaxation leads to permanent *inhibition* of anxiety, when extinction would also account for systematic desensitization's enduring effects. There is now a good deal of evidence that anxiety can be reduced by prolonged exposure to a conditioned anxiety-evoking situation, whether or not the anxiety-evoking stimulus is attenuated, whether or not it is imagined, and

whether or not competing behavior is specifically encouraged. (See Wilson & Davison, 1971, for a review.) What all these procedures have in common is a conditioned fear stimulus presented in the absence of real danger. These are the operations of respondent extinction, which would seem to be the most parsimonious interpretation of the data. The practical problem, of course, is how to get the patient to remain in the presence of an anxiety-evoking situation so that extinction *can* occur. The usual reaction is to avoid the anxiety-evoking situation at any cost.

The problem is further complicated by the fact that both operant and respondent conditioning may play an important role in clinical anxiety. By the operant procedures of escape and avoidance, behavior is conditioned when it removes or postpones an aversive event. And so long as a patient avoids a phobic situation, neither the classically conditioned emotional responses, nor the avoidance behavior conditioned by operant procedures, can extinguish.

One way or another, the various therapies prevent the avoidance of phobic situations so that extinction may take place. All of the procedures we have discussed employ sustained exposure to an anxiety-evoking situation, even though in systematic desensitization and imaginal flooding, it is exposure to visualizations of aversive situations rather than the real thing. Forced exposure to a conditioned aversive stimulus in the absence of the unconditioned aversive stimulus allows conditioned emotional responses to extinguish. Forced exposure also promotes extinction of avoidance behavior (Baum, 1970; Baum & Poser, 1971). Desensitization, graduated extinction, and most modeling procedures also attenuate the intensity or proximity of the anxiety-evoking situation, and this, too, may facilitate extinction of emotional responses. Finally, desensitization (and some flooding procedures) incorporate deep muscle relaxation or another activity presumed to be incompatible with anxiety. While it is quite possible that relaxation (and other activities associated with parasympathetic arousal) inhibit anxiety during desensitization visualizations, the reciprocal inhibition model does not seem adequate to describe the enduring effects of therapy. We are inclined to agree with Wilson and Davison (1971) that relaxation may facilitate exposure to anxiety-evoking situations, thus allowing extinction to take place. Later, when emotional responses to imagined situations have extinguished to some appreciable degree, the patient is more likely to permit exposure to a graduated series of real situations where extinction of both emotional and avoidance responses can occur.

F. Aversion Therapies

As the name implies, the aversion therapies are those that employ aversive stimulation toward some therapeutic end. They are generally used to eliminate problem behavior that is in itself reinforcing and thus not amenable to extinction: behavior such as excessive drinking or smoking. Therapy consists of arranging for an aversive event to occur in conjunction with the unwanted behavior, either to suppress the behavior or to reduce its reinforcing properties.

The three basic ways to manipulate aversive stimulation are operant punishment, operant escape-avoidance conditioning, and respondent (classical) conditioning. In one sense, only the operations of punishment suppress the problem behavior. The two conditioning procedures reduce problem behavior indirectly by strengthening some other behavior that is either prepotent over, or incompatible with, the problem behavior.[7] Although the three procedures are readily distinguished "on paper," the contingencies are such that they are usually combined or confounded in practice. Pun-

ishers—both painful aversive consequences and consequences such as censure or ridicule—are very likely to elicit the physiological components of anxiety; and any behavior that accompanies the termination of aversive consequences is likely to be strengthened by avoidance conditioning (Dunham, 1971).

Aversion therapy for alcoholism, for example, might consist of delivering painful electric shock when the client swallows a sip of an alcoholic drink. The contingencies and the temporal relations of this simple procedure are likely to include the operations of punishment, conditioned escape and avoidance, and conditioned anxiety. Suppose that therapy takes place in a simulated bar or cocktail lounge. The client, who has given informed consent to the treatment, approaches the bar, orders a shot of bourbon, watches the bartender pour the drink, picks up the glass and savors the aroma, tosses it off in one gulp—and gets shocked. First of all, shock is contingent on swallowing the bourbon, so if swallowing bourbon occurs less frequently in the future, then shock is a punisher and the procedure constitutes punishment. The procedure is also one that can generate a conditioned emotional response. Because of their temporal relation to shock, the events (including the client's own behavior) that precede shock can come to elicit the physiological components of anxiety. Following aversion therapy, the client might become anxious when approaching a bar or accepting a drink, and this anxiety might reduce the likelihood of drinking. Finally, the procedure can generate avoidance behavior. The patient can avoid shock by staying away from the bar, by ordering a nonalcoholic drink,

7. There is no respondent procedure comparable to punishment. The respondent pairing procedure can only increase the strength of a reflex. The only ways to weaken a reflex are by fatigue and habituation (which are temporary measures), by extinction, and by the conditioning of incompatible behavior.

or even by ordering bourbon but not drinking it. The paradigms would resemble those in Figure 6.1 if Little Albert had been reaching for a drink instead of a white rat: (1) respondent conditioning whereby bars, bartenders, and bourbon (CSs) are paired with shock (US) and subsequently elicit the autonomic components of anxiety; (2) punishment of drinking bourbon; and (3) escape-avoidance conditioning of behavior that postpones or prevents shock, behavior such as staying away from bars or ordering nonalcoholic drinks.

Much of the literature on aversion therapy is concerned with the relative contributions of punishment, conditioned avoidance, and conditioned autonomic responses; and various procedures have been devised to emphasize one or another of these components. (See Rachman & Teasdale, 1969, for a discussion of these issues.) In our view, they are all important. If one is to use aversion therapy at all, one should try to maximize its effectiveness so that the least amount of aversive stimulation will have the greatest and most enduring effect. We would guess that the most effective aversion therapy will prove to be that which utilizes all three components, incorporates procedures to strengthen adaptive behavior, and trains the client in self-management skills. Mark and Linda Sobell developed just such a program for alcoholics, described at the end of Chapter 3.

The advantage of combining several procedures is that the combination often favors the successful outcome of therapy. The disadvantage is the difficulty of assessing the relative contributions of the component procedures. Most therapy cannot afford this costly and time-consuming analysis, which is a problem for continuing research (Risley, 1971). There are, however, several programs which employ a limited number of procedures, and we will describe a few which emphasize particular components of aversion therapy.

1. Aversive Consequences (Punishment)

The procedures described here are slightly different from those described under "punishment" in Chapter 5. The explicit goal is to change covert behavior, such as desires, cravings, or obsessive thoughts, as well as to suppress a particular class of overt behavior. A "classic" study employing aversion therapy is the work of Marks and Gelder (1967) on the treatment of sexual deviations. Their patients, all of whom had voluntarily sought treatment, were three transvestites (males who dressed in female clothing) and two fetishists. One of the latter had two arrests for stealing panties from clotheslines; the other was attracted by high-heeled shoes and boots, and had once suffered a broken coccyx after imploring his wife to kick him. (He also had fantasies of being stamped on and beaten to death.) Therapy was similar in all cases, so we shall describe the patient whose data are given in most detail.

This 21-year-old patient had been sexually aroused since the age of 13 by dressing as a woman. "He sought treatment because he felt himself abnormal and wanted to have normal sexual relationships" (p. 713). Previous treatment with apomorphine aversion therapy[8] had been unsuccessful. Therapy consisted of two one-hour sessions a day for a period of two weeks during which the patients were hospitalized. "Booster" sessions continued at weekly or monthly intervals for "several

8. Apomorphine aversion is described under "aversive conditioning" procedures. Apomorphine aversion is a classical conditioning procedure in which the US is nausea induced by a drug such as apomorphine. The CS is something related to the behavior that is to be suppressed: alcohol, for example, or in this case women's clothes. The client is given the drug, and the presentation of the potential CS is timed so that it just precedes nausea. The client would take a drink or don women's clothes just before becoming nauseated. Successful therapy depends on the problem behavior (or stimuli associated with it) becoming conditioned stimuli for nausea.

months" after the patient left the hospital. Unpleasant—but not painful—electric shock was administered at irregular intervals to the patient's arm or leg, both when he carried out his deviant behavior and when he *imagined* he was carrying it out. This patient, then, was shocked when he wore or handled women's panties, slips, and other clothing, and when he imagined scenes in which he was wearing women's clothes. The purpose was to shock the whole sequence of covert and overt behavior. The authors note an additional advantage of working with covert behavior: a wide range of activities can be treated. Fortunately for all concerned, the masochistic patients could *imagine* being kicked or whipped.

Several classes of behavior were measured. Sexual arousal was monitored by a penis transducer,[9] which allowed measurement of the latency and the extent of erection to the various real or imagined situations. The semantic differential[10] was used to measure the patient's attitudes about several concepts: his particular sexual deviation (corsets and brassieres; being kicked with boots), more normal sex (women; sexual intercourse), members of the family (my mother; my father; my girlfriend), and two concepts that might be considered controls (my general practitioner; electric shock). Finally, although follow-up data are not presented, outcome of treatment was evaluated by the patients and by members of the family or (in one case) another psychiatrist.

Sexual arousal of the 21-year-old transvestite during the course of treatment is shown in Figure 6.5. The lower graphs represent the extent of erections: a 10-unit deflection on the transducer was just perceptible to the patient; a 60-unit deflection represented a full erection. The upper graphs represent the latency of an erection at the end of each session. If an erection did not occur within three minutes, it did not occur with further exposure, so a 180-second latency is the equivalent of no erection. Before

aversion therapy, the patient had a full erection when he saw a photograph of a nude woman and when he saw or felt women's clothes that he used in cross-dressing (lower graphs, extreme left). The first treatment sessions employed electric shock while the patient was wearing or holding panties. Initially, erection occurred within 30 seconds; but the latency increased over the course of treatment and there was no erection at the end of the sixth session. The specificity of the shock treatment is shown in the lower curves. Shock treatment with panties resulted in no further erections to panties, but responses to the other garments were unaffected. In subsequent sessions, treatment was successively applied to pajamas, skirt and blouse, and slip. The same selective effect can be seen: sexual arousal to a given garment continued until the patient received shock while holding, wearing, or imagining that he was wearing that particular garment. Full arousal to the nude photo was, of course, never shocked and was maintained.

As these physiological changes occurred, the patient reported increasing difficulty in visualizing himself wearing women's clothing; he got the image of a girl instead.

Changes in sexual arousal were accompanied by changes in attitudes, as measured by the semantic differential. For example, the transvestite's ratings of corsets and brassieres were highly positive before treatment; after two weeks of aversion therapy they were highly negative. Ratings of sexual intercourse started just above neutral and ended highly positive; ratings of electric shock were consistently nega-

9. The penis transducer is a strain gauge transducer with a small, mercury-filled plastic loop. The patient slips the loop over the shaft of his penis, and a lead extends from his waist to the recording apparatus, which can be located several feet away. Clothes can be worn as usual. Patients report no discomfort and no embarrassment after wearing the transducer a few times.

10. The semantic differential was developed by Charles Osgood (1953). Concepts are scaled along a series of bipolar adjectives such as good-bad, friendly-unfriendly.

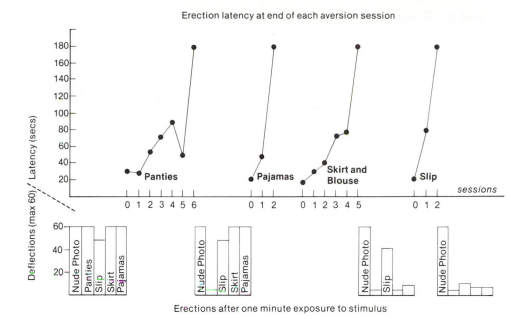

Figure 6.5. Changes in sexual arousal during course of aversion therapy for transvestism. Bar graphs show extent of erection; a 60-unit deflection represents a full erection. Upper graphs show latency; a 180-second latency is the equivalent of no erection. Note specificity of treatment effects. (From Marks & Gelder, 1967, p. 714.)

tive; and ratings on the other items (my girl friend, mother, father, general practitioner) increased from the moderately positive to the highly positive end of the scale.

Following aversion therapy, all patients reported an improvement in sexual relations (the wives of the two married men confirmed more frequent intercourse and better performance); and the patients said that they "felt more self respect." The patient whose data are presented in Figure 6.5 established a close relationship with a girl for the first time in his life.

As already noted, this study emphasizes the punishment components of aversion therapy. As might be expected, the shocks also elicited some anxiety and anger during treatment, but these emotional responses apparently subsided fairly quickly. There is no indication that the fetish objects or women's garments became

conditioned stimuli capable of eliciting anxiety following treatment. Although the study included no control groups, control sessions without shock were employed with three subjects and produced only minor changes. The specificity of the autonomic changes (Figure 6.5) and of the correlated attitudinal changes also support the authors' conclusion that contingent aversive shock was the major variable responsible for the patients' improvement.

An important aspect of the Marks and Gelder program is their attention to the imaginal components of their patients' behavior. Imagining scenes of deviant behavior was shocked not only because certain activities would be difficult to carry out in the clinic, but also because fantasy is an important element in the whole chain of behavior. In fact, fantasy may occur a good deal more often than overt behavior.

2. Escape and Avoidance

A dramatic example of aversion therapy with a punishment-escape paradigm is Lang and Melamed's (1969) treatment of an infant whose chronic vomiting had brought him close to death. The child was nine months old and weighed only 12 pounds. He had gained weight at a normal rate from birth to six months, when he had weighed 17 pounds; but persistent vomiting following each meal had left him in the pathetic condition shown in Figure 6.6A. The behavioral therapists were brought in as a last resort: extensive tests and various treatments during three previous hospitalizations had failed to eliminate the vomiting, and the attending physician attested that the life of the child was threatened.

Lang and Melamed observed the child for two days and took EMG (electromyograph) recordings, which allowed them to monitor his sucking, throat, and chest movements. Sucking movements were clearly distinguishable from the rhythmic movements of reverse peristalsis (vomiting), and vomiting did not occur while the child was feeding. The authors were thus able to initiate shock at the onset of reverse peristalsis without interrupting feeding. A nurse, who assisted in therapy, signaled when she thought the child was starting to vomit; and if the EMG confirmed her judgment, shock was administered to the child's leg. A punishment-escape paradigm was used: a brief shock was contingent upon the onset of reverse peristalsis and continued at one-second intervals until these movements ceased. Thus reverse peristalsis was punished, and normal peristalsis was strengthened by escape from shock. Normal peristalsis was also strengthened by avoidance of shock on those occasions when reverse peristalsis did not occur. To facilitate transfer, sessions were scheduled at different times of day while the child was engaged in different activities such as playing on the floor after feeding.

Vomiting was almost eliminated in two sessions that lasted less than an hour, but occasional vomiting occurred (and was shocked) for three days.

After three sessions with no vomiting, the punishment procedure was discontinued. Two days later, a little rumination and vomiting occurred but were eliminated when a few shocks were given. The child gained nearly a pound on the first day of treatment, and his weight increased from 12 to 16 pounds over the nine days of treatment. He also became more active and playful, and he smiled and reached out to the nurse and to visitors. He was discharged from the hospital five days later, when the photograph in Figure 6.6B was taken. One month later he weighed 21 pounds; and five months later, 26 pounds 1 ounce (Figure 6.6C). His general health and happiness were again confirmed one year after treatment.

The avoidance component of aversion therapy is emphasized in the work of Feldman, MacCulloch, and their colleagues.[11] Their procedure is quite complex, and includes two series of slides, one related to the behavior the client wishes to eliminate, the other to the behavior the client wishes to acquire. For example, a male homosexual who wished to change his orientation would rank according to their attractiveness a series of slides of men and another series of women. Initially, the slide of the *least* attractive man would be projected, and the patient would be shocked *unless* he turned off the slide. Turning off the slide would not only avoid shock, it would also present the slide ranked *most* attractive woman. According to the respondent conditioning paradigm, the sight of a man would thus become a conditioned stimulus for anxiety, while the sight of a woman would become a conditioned stimulus for relief.

11. See, for examples: Feldman and MacCulloch, 1965; MacCulloch and Feldman, 1967; MacCulloch, Birtles, and Feldman, 1971; MacCulloch, Williams, and Birtles, 1971.

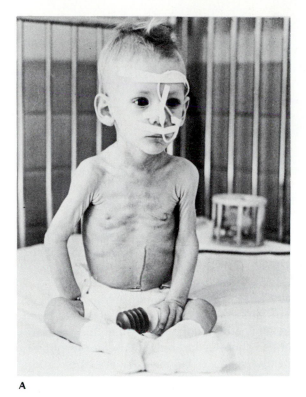

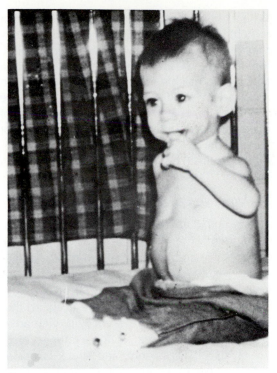

A

B

Figure 6.6. A: Patient just prior to treatment. Tape around face holds tubing for the nasogastric pump. B: Thirteen days later (day of discharge) body weight having increased by 26 percent. C: Five months after treatment. (From Lang & Melamed, 1969, p. 3, 7.)

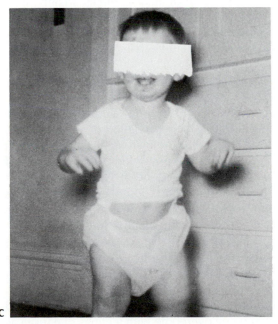

C

When the avoidance response (pressing a switch) is well established, it is placed on intermittent reinforcement. When the client reliably tries to terminate the slide of the male, and when he reports that his former attraction has been replaced by indifference or dislike, then the slides are changed. Gradually, the slides of males increase in attractiveness, and slides of females decrease in attractiveness. The procedure appears to be quite successful.

3. Aversive Conditioning

a. *Classical aversive conditioning* has been applied with varying degrees of success in the treatment of alcoholism and other drug addictions, sexual deviations, and overeating. A counterconditioning procedure, it pairs a noxious stimulus with a pleasurable event so that the formerly pleasurable event will elicit anxiety, disgust, or nausea. If, for example, electric shock elicits anxiety, and shock is paired with the taste of alcohol, then a new reflex, in which the taste of alcohol elicits anxiety, may be conditioned. As noted above, the respondent conditioning of anxiety could accompany and augment the effects of an operant punishment procedure.

If the procedure contained an "escape clause," further respondent conditioning might take place. If rejecting alcohol terminated shock, and if the termination of shock elicited feelings of "relief," then rejecting alcohol might come to elicit the physiological components of relief. This seems to be the basis of the *aversion-relief* procedure described below, and its effects would accompany and augment those of operant escape-avoidance training.

The third aversive conditioning procedure to be described substitutes *imagined* aversive events for real ones. With the help of a skillful therapist, an alcoholic might imagine himself approaching a bar, ordering a drink, and then being overcome with feelings of nausea as he lifts the glass to his lips. This procedure,

called *covert sensitization*, usually includes aversion relief. So after imagining himself vomiting all over his drink, the bar, and his clothes, the alcoholic would imagine a glorious feeling of relief as he put down his drink, left the bar, and entered the clear, fresh air outside. With sufficient training, the taste and smell, and even the thought, of drinking alcohol would elicit feelings of nausea; and rejection of alcohol would elicit feelings of relief. Covert sensitization is the aversive counterpart of Wolpe's systematic desensitization procedure. It is proving successful with a variety of problems, especially when employed by a therapist with the vivid imagination of Cautela (e.g., 1966, 1967, 1970c).

a. Classical aversive conditioning

This procedure has generally been used in the treatment of alcoholism where the unconditioned stimulus has been nausea or respiratory paralysis (e.g., Lemere & Voegtlin, 1950; Madill, Campbell, Laverty, Sanderson, & Vandewater, 1966); or cigarette smoking, where the US has been a puff of stale cigarette smoke (e.g., Lublin, 1968); or sexual problems, where the US has been shock or nausea (e.g., Lavin, Thorpe, Barker, Blakemore, & Conway, 1961). But the following example concerns weight loss.

Foreyt and Kennedy (1971) used aversion therapy with three undergraduates and three members of TOPS (Take Off Pounds Sensibly) who were at least 10 percent overweight. Control subjects were all members of TOPS. The experimental treatment consisted of pairing the subject's favorite high-calorie food (CS) with a noxious odor (US) to make the favorite food less desirable. (The noxious odors included butyric acid and pure skunk oil.)

A subject would be given her favorite food, perhaps a doughnut, and told to take it, feel it, think about tasting and eating it—and when she signaled that she was smelling and thinking about it, she was told to put her nose to an oxygen mask that delivered a puff of the noxious odor. The results were impressive and are shown in Figure 6.7. The graph shows the *total* weight lost or gained by the six experimental and six control subjects both during treatment and throughout the 36-week follow-up period. Note that the curve *rises* with weight loss and drops with weight gain. All experimental subjects lost weight (mean: 13.3 pounds), but only one-half of the control subjects did (mean: 1.0 pounds). At the end of the follow-up, one experimental subject had gained weight, but there was a mean loss of 9.2 pounds. Of the control subjects, only two weighed less than when the program started, and there was a group mean gain of 1.3 pounds. Five of the six experimental subjects reported that they were "conditioned." That is, they felt discomfort or uneasiness in the presence of the foods used during treatment.

b. Aversion relief

A paradigm for the treatment of alcoholism by aversion relief is suggested in Figure 6.8A. The diagonal lines represent the reflexes that are presumably conditioned during this procedure.

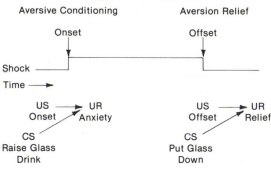

Figure 6.8. Theoretical basis of aversion-relief therapy. A. Respondent components: (left) *aversive conditioning* in which the onset of faradic shock is paired with drinking so that drinking will subsequently elicit anxiety; (right) *aversion relief* in which termination of shock is paired with rejection of drinking so that this behavior subsequently elicits relief. B. Operant components: (left) *punishment*, in which shock is contingent on drinking; (right) *escape*, in which shock offset is contingent on rejection of drinking.

Physiological measures and subjective reports would be necessary to demonstrate that raising a glass and drinking (without shock) actually elicit anxiety and that lowering the glass (without shock termination) elicits the physiological correlates of relief. In Figure 6.8B we have suggested the operant procedures inherent in aversion-relief conditioning. If behavior such as reaching for, touching, and raising a glass to the mouth is suppressed, then the shock is a punisher, and the operations constitute operant punishment as well as respondent conditioning of anxiety. Similarly, if the frequency of putting down the glass increases when this behavior terminates shock, then the operations constitute operant escape (or negative reinforcement) as well as respondent conditioning of relief.

This procedure was introduced by Thorpe, Schmidt, Brown, and Castell (1964). They reported success in treating six clients with sexual

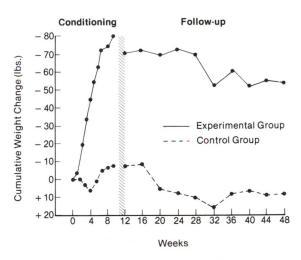

Figure 6.7. Total weight change in pounds during aversive conditioning and 36-week follow-up period for experimental and control subjects. Note: rising curve indicates weight loss and falling curve indicates weight gain. (From Foreyt & Kennedy, 1971, p. 32.)

problems and failure in treating two clients, one diagnosed as obsessive-compulsive neurosis, the other as recurrent depressive. There are relatively little data to evaluate aversion-relief therapy; caution is in order.

c. Covert sensitization

In covert sensitization, as in systematic desensitization, a skillful therapist can help the client visualize completely and specifically all of the events surrounding the behavior to be eliminated. Antecedent stimuli from all sensory modalities are marshalled to help the client imagine in vivid detail the scenes being presented. Cautela (e.g., 1966) is a past master of this art, and so are his students. The following scene is one that Pat Wisocki (1973) created for the benefit of a heroin addict of three years standing:

Imagine that you're in the car, on your way to Boston to get some junk. You see a road sign indicating the distance to that city. You're thinking about how easy it will be to get drugs there. As you have that thought a wasp flies into the car. You can hear it buzzing. You can see it flying in front of your eyes. It's all brown and ugly. A fear starts to rise in you, but you shake it off and think about how you'll feel when you have the fix. Then suddenly that wasp is joined by a horde of other wasps—all buzzing and flying around your eyes. You keep driving to Boston, thinking about your pusher and making the contact. And then you see him—the guy who will sell you the heroin. Suddenly the wasps attack—swarms of them come crashing down on your head. They land on your hands; the steering wheel is covered with them. You can't see in front of you. The sounds are terrible. You can feel a hundred stings all over your body. They're in your clothes, on your face, all over everything. You decide it's not worth it. You decide to turn back. You think how nice it would be to be home and away from this whole scene of copping heroin and everything connected with it. And, as you turn your car away, the wasps begin to leave. The farther away you get, the fewer the wasps around you. Everything is quiet, peaceful, and calm. The radio is playing your favorite song. You begin to feel happy that you resisted the urge.
(Wisocki, 1973, p. 57-58.)

The scenes are devised to elicit maximum anxiety in conjunction with the behavior the client wishes to reduce. Between scenes, the therapist may instruct the client to use covert reinforcement to strengthen thoughts of activities incompatible with the problem behavior: Wisocki's client gets to hear his favorite song when he turns away from the drug scene.

Covert sensitization has been a component of successful treatment of a variety of problems, including alcoholism (Ashem & Donner, 1968), nail-biting (Daniels, 1974), pedophilia (Barlow, Leitenberg, & Agras, 1969), sadistic phantasy (Davison, 1968a), glue-sniffing (Kolvin, 1967), and obsessive-compulsive behavior (Wisocki, 1970). The procedure is also useful in self-management projects: have you ever tried to visualize the black insides of your lungs while you reach for a cigarette? Or pictured your stomach hanging down over your belt while you reach for an extra helping of chocolate cake? Maletzky (1973) attempted covert sensitization with a woman who had trouble losing weight because she could not resist anything made of chocolate. Covert sensitization alone was unsuccessful; but the addition of an overt unconditional stimulus worked well. The client imagined scenes of chocolate goodies infested with lice and maggots, and then she took a whiff of valeric acid, which elicits nausea and gagging. Ten sessions of this treatment curbed her passion for chocolate, and she continued to lose weight throughout the seven-month follow-up period.

7

Self-Control

A. The Control of Behavior

All of us control the behavior of others in the sense that what we do (or fail to do) determines what they do (or fail to do). Some people are professionals, trained and paid to change behavior: counselors and consultants, legislators and law-enforcement officers, teachers and therapists, to name a few. Others assume the responsibility in their roles as parents or friends. The effect is the same, whether or not we ''intend'' to affect the behavior of others. A crying or smiling infant exerts considerable control over the behavior of parents or other caretakers; a responsive audience exerts considerable control over the performance of actors and musicians.

One reason for analyzing the control of behavior is so that we may teach, legislate, and raise children more effectively. Another reason is so that we may recognize and protect ourselves against inhumane or ineffective procedures, by legislation or by other forms of countercontrol. A very important third reason is so that we may control our own behavior.

When we can identify the variables that control a particular class of behavior, we can change that behavior if we can change the level of one or more of the relevant variables. When we can identify and manage the variables that control our own behavior, we are in a position to exercise self-control. It is not really ourselves that we control or manage, of course; it is our behavior.

There are several ''degrees'' of self-management. Given the option, children can select among several reinforcing activities and thus determine or control what they will be doing for a given period of time. They might also select among several kinds of work the one that will earn the reinforcer of their choice and thus control the behavior and the reinforcer. We would probably agree that a greater degree of self-management is involved if the child sets the contingencies by determining the amount or quality of the behavior that will qualify for reinforcement. But what most people mean by self-control or self-management is that given a choice between two conflicting alternatives, we select the one that has long-term benefits for ourselves or others rather than the one that provides more immediate gratification. Studying instead of going to a movie; counting to 10 instead of venting anger on a hapless bystander; buying beverages in returnable bottles or recycling cans and bottles instead of throwing them away would fall into this last category. Under certain conditions, pigeons will ''control their impulses'' and choose a delayed reward over an immediate one, and so will people. With pigeons, the experimenter can control the choice by manipulating the duration of the delay and the magnitude of the reward (Ainslie, 1974; Rachlin & Green, 1972). People can often manipulate these and other variables with respect to their own behavior.

For several years, all students in our advanced course in behavior analysis have conducted a self-control project. They are advised that *they are not to try changing any one else's behavior until they have succeeded in changing their own*. Many select problems related to academic work: increasing class participation or the time and efficiency of studying; decreasing daydreaming in class or falling asleep while reading. Others have been concerned about weight or smoking. Some concentrate on rather specific personal habits such as biting their nails or chewing their lips, while others tackle more pervasive personal problems such as low self-esteem. Still others have been concerned about such matters as getting up in the morning, procrastinating, forgetting things, terminating conversations gracefully, and reducing the time and money spent on long-distance telephone calls.

Our students look for and analyze the conditions that control the behavior they wish to change, and then they look for every feasible way to modify those conditions. They follow the general procedure described in Chapter 3, adapting it to their own particular problem and situation. This general procedure is essentially the same model proposed by other behavioral psychologists (notably Watson and Tharp, 1972, and Williams and Long, 1975) who have helped students and clients to manage their own behavior.[1] Actually, most of the principles were enumerated by Skinner (1953) more than 20 years ago, but they have only recently received the widespread attention they deserve.

B. Analyzing the Situation

1. Preliminary and Continuing:

a. Know thyself

As with any other program to change behavior, one has to start by getting to know the person for whom the program will be designed. Just because the person is oneself doesn't necessarily make this step any easier. We still have to identify skills to build on and deficits to work around. Above all, we have to develop an awareness of particular classes of our own behavior and the context in which they occur or fail to occur. Goldiamond (1965, p. 853) translates the Greek maxim *know thyself* into the behavioral language: "Know thy behaviors, know thy environment, and know the functional relation between the two."

A self-management project requires us to examine our problem behavior closely. Initially, we may examine several classes of behavior, uncertain which is the more troublesome or pervasive or amenable to change. This can be a strange experience (we may be accustomed to closing our eyes and hoping the problem will go away if we don't peek), and it can be a discouraging one, especially when it comes to keeping records. For these reasons, we recommend that people start off by making a list of things they are *good* at. Things that are no problem at all. If they can't think of anything —as may be the case if the problem is low self-esteem—they should get suggestions from friends, and perhaps tape a long list of virtues to their mirror.

b. Consult

When designing a program to change the behavior of someone else, it is important to have frequent consultations with all of the people who will be affected, especially those who will help to carry out the program. Even when designing a program for oneself, there are several reasons for consulting with other people. If you are undertaking a weight-control program, you don't want family and friends plying you with forbidden foods. You *do* want their cooperation and possibly their admiration. If you decide to make letters and phone calls reinforcing events that must be earned, you can prevent a great many misunderstandings by telling your friends about your program. Most people find it helpful to conduct a self-management program along with someone else. It is often easier to forego a second helping of dessert or to go jogging at 6 A.M. if someone else is being noble too. Even when two people are working on different projects, they can discuss problems and share successes. They can also provide that extra incentive to keep accurate records. Our students usually work in pairs and meet once a day to plot the points on their graphs, plan the next day's activities, and "spend" or discuss the reinforcers they have earned. Weight Watchers, Alcoholics Anonymous, Smoke Enders, and Synanon are all organizations that take good advantage of this kind of mutual support and control.

c. Evaluate

As in any other program, the only way to evaluate the success of a self-management program is to collect data. We can start by collecting

---

1. Other books include: Goldfried and Merbaum, 1973, Mahoney and Thoresen, 1974, Thoresen and Mahoney, 1974. The first two contain several excellent readings.

baseline data on some classes of behavior even before choosing specific goals and procedures. In fact, preliminary baseline data on several classes of behavior can help us decide which to select for change. Whatever else we might decide to record in a weight-control program, we would certainly want to keep track of weight. Later on, we might add other measures: perhaps clothes size and body measurements, the number of between-meal snacks, the number of between-meal snacks *refused*, the total number of calories consumed in food and expended in exercise, the number of calories consumed in certain kinds of food only (e.g., "junk" food), admiring or critical comments from significant other people, self-esteem, or anything else that seems important when an analysis of the situation reveals the antecedents and consequences of eating.

We have already noted (Chapter 4) that self-recording is often accompanied by a change in the behavior being recorded. Because the change is often in the desired direction, self-recording in itself can be a procedure to change behavior. The effect is usually temporary, however, and additional procedures are likely to be necessary. There are probably several reasons why self-recording can change behavior in the desired direction, particularly when we record behavior that we ourselves want to change. For one thing, the records reveal the extent of the problem, and this may increase the motivation to do something about it. Before recording, many people do not realize the number of cigarettes, drinks, or calories they consume each day; or the number of times they criticize friends and relations; or the amount of energy and money they waste by keeping their houses at 70° F. in the winter and 68° F. in the summer. (Why otherwise rational people insist on being cooler in summer than in winter is something I've never understood.) Another reason is that recording often makes us more aware of the occasions when the behavior oc-

curs. We may then begin to avoid those occasions that favor problem behavior and to seek out those that favor desired behavior, even before we incorporate stimulus control into a formal program.

Self-recording may also have reinforcing or aversive consequences. If the records show a change in the desired direction, they will probably reinforce further recording. On the other hand, records that show a high rate of problem behavior may be aversive. In this case, one could avoid the aversive consequences of recording in either of two ways: (1) by continuing to keep accurate records but emitting the behavior less often, or (2) by failing to keep accurate records. The first solution would result in a reduction of the problem behavior and records that might serve as reinforcers. The second solution, of course, would be no solution at all.

Finally, the records might provide the means of attaining reinforcers. Glynn and Thomas (1974) instructed elementary-school children to record whether or not they were working at the moment an auditory signal was given. They used a time-sampling procedure, and auditory signals were presented several times, at random intervals, throughout a 50-minute class. If the children were working when they heard the signal, they placed a checkmark on a card provided for that purpose. Each check was worth one minute of free time at the end of class. Independent measures, taken by observers, showed that the procedure worked well: the percentage of intervals during which the children were working increased from a baseline level of 50 percent to 91 percent during the final phase of the study. In this study, self-recording was reinforced by the teacher-imposed contingencies of free time for on-task behavior. But it was the children who determined whether or not they were working when the signal sounded. This is surely a first step in the self-management of behavior.

Of course, if self-recording *per se* is accompanied by a change in behavior, then self-recording cannot provide a valid baseline measure. This is a serious problem in the case of research, and independent records should also be taken. The problem of validity is less important when we are carrying out a personal project. It is usually not essential to know the frequency or duration of our behavior before we start to record it; and if we find that self-recording is producing a desirable change, then we learn something useful. Assuming that baseline recording is continued until the behavior reaches a fairly stable level, we can still evaluate the effectiveness of a program to produce *further* changes. We simply have to remember that the basis of comparison is the end, not the beginning, of baseline.

2. Sequence Analysis

The period of baseline collection is a good time to acquire the information needed to design an effective program. It is a time for observation and for reading. It is a time to learn about ourselves and about the specific events that control our behavior: the situations that prompt or inhibit the behavior we want to change, and the consequences that maintain or suppress it. It is also a time to discover what others have learned about the behavior: about its physiological and environmental determinants, and about alternative means to control it. (See "education," below.)

Since we are keeping track of the frequency or duration of the behavior anyway, it is not much more work to look at the context in which the behavior occurs. Before designing a weight-control project, for example, it may be important to know when and what we eat, with whom, and what else we are doing while eating. Some people are surprised to find that they eat only 800 calories a day at meals, but consume a couple of thousand calories in alcohol and "junk" food. Others eat sensibly except for periodic "binges." One student we know could take in 4,000 calories in potato chips, doughnuts, and frosted cereal in a single evening. If the problem is binges, you want to know what precipitates them. Some people overeat only when they are alone, others only when they are with someone else, still others only when they are watching television or studying for an exam.

If the problem is "tuning out" in class, does this happen equally often in all classes? What is the teaching format: lecture, seminar, lab, films? Is tuning out related to the subject matter, the professor, where you sit or the people you sit next to, the amount of sleep you had the night before? If you are depressed a lot of the time, who are you with and what are you doing or thinking about when you feel depressed *and when you don't* feel depressed? Do you tell certain people when you feel depressed; and, if so, are they generally sympathetic or disinterested? Have you had a physical examination recently? Have you made a list of the things you are good at?

The information that provides an analysis of the current situation can be accumulated in a diary, on scraps of paper, or in the margins of class notes. But it will probably be easier to organize the information if you start with some sort of data sheet that provides columns for the context and antecedents of the behavior, the behavior itself, and the consequences. Table 7.1 is a general form that might be adapted for several classes of behavior. Tables 7.2 and 7.3 are daily record sheets used by several of our students in weight-control and studying programs, respectively. Goldiamond (1974) provides additional forms that he uses with his clients in conjunction with his highly successful *constructional* approach to therapy for stuttering, smoking, drug abuse, time management, and other personal problems. For the forms shown in Tables 7.1–7.3, the students attempted to record all relevant incidents throughout the day. One could also employ a time-sampling proce-

Table 7.1 General form for sequence analysis of problem behavior prior to designing a self-management program. Tentative goals in this example: increase class participation and assertiveness.

| Time | ANTECEDENTS or CONTEXT | | | BEHAVIOR | CONSEQUENCES | COMMENTS |
	Place	Company	Incident	(include number, duration)	(what happened next)	
11 am	Psych. lab	Beth, Amy, Terry	Terry asked for my notes _again_	agreed (1)	Terry said thanks & tore off. Beth said I should have refused or gotten her to type my next paper. Amy said I shouldn't take such good notes!	Felt stupid
2-4	Psych. Seminar	class	questions discussion	Didn't answer 1 question (knew answer); didn't contribute 3 times when could have	nothing	this won't help my grade
9:30	Room (studying)	no one	El's radio blaring again	Tried to ignore for 10 min., then asked her to turn it down	She did!	She was very nice about it.
10:30	Room	Terry	Asked me to decipher my notes – what a nerve	_Furious_ – but I did (1)	She wanted to ask questions on the reading but I said I had to study.	at least I didn't give her those notes.
11:15	"	—	Just thinking	Resolved: 1) Say something terribly clever and erudite in History tomorrow 2) Tell Terry to borrow some one else's notes	?	? (we'll see)

Table 7.2   Example of daily record form used in self-management of weight.

Day *Th* Date *10/11* WEIGHT *138* GOAL *118*					CALORIES, eaten *3828*			
Baseline *X* Program ___ Maintenance ___					Calories, exercise *100*			
Amt. sleep last night *6 h.* Weather *cold*					Total meals *7*			

Time	Place	Activity	People	Mood	Amount	FOOD	Calories	Sum
7:30	Dorm	Breakfast	People?	bitchy	1 1 2	o.j. H.B. egg revolting coffee & crs toast, butter	120 78 40 210	448
10:30	College Inn	break	Debbie, Neal Dinny, Barb	BORED	1 1	Danish coffee	125 40	—165
Noon	Dorm	lunch	Jill, Pearl, Eva, Stephanie	OK	1 1 2	milk spaghetti cake @	160 couldn't eat 500	660
4:30	Snack bar	after lab	Ed, David Jerrilynn	Ravenous	1 1	cheeseburger Fr. fries (make up for lunch)	470 250	720
6:30	Dorm	dinner	Jerri, Betsy, Denise, Chip, Cathy	good	2 1 2 1	meat (lamb??) peas sm potatoes choc. ice cream	470 115 120 100	805
10:30	Snack bar	a well- deserved break	Tim & Marci Cindy, Richard Skye & Talley TOM	tired	2 1	beer sm potato chips	300 230	530
11-12	Room	studying	Rhea for a while; Esther & Madeline came by	zonked	½ box (maybe 10?) choc chip cookies		500?	500

448
165
1380
1835
3828

Total meals *7*   Total Cal. *3828*

EXERCISE

Moderate (200/hr; 33/10 min)		Vigorous (300/hr; 50/10 min)		Strenuous (400/hr; 70/10 min)	
Walking (slow)	*15*	Walking (3 mph)	*10*	Stren. sports	___
Bicycling	___	Horseback riding	___	Dancing (fast)	___
House work	___	Bowling	___	Jogging	___
___	___	Swimming	___	___	___
			___	___	___

Total time *15* Cal. *50*   Time *10* Cal. *50*   Time ___ Cal. ___

COMMENTS: *This was not a good day*

Table 7.3   Example of daily record form used in project to manage studying.

Day **Wed.**   Date **10/3**   Baseline **X** Program _____ Maint._____

AM 7	8	9	10	11	12
up 7:30	breakfast	Ψ313	coffee - Jane, Leslie, Wendy	Bio. 333	lunch; weighed pigeon

PM 1	2	3	4	5	6
Bio. Lab			?	Talked w/ Laurie + EPR-may change project!	T☺ Amherst

7	8	9	10	11	12
dinner - Kent, Leanna	studied with Kent (about one hour)			back around 11:30	bed 12:30ish

	Time	Accomplished
Reading	1 hr. ?	pages 10?
Writing	_____	pages _____
Other	_____	_____
Subtotal	1	10
Classes	2 hr.	
Labs	3 hr.	
Conference (etc.)	1 hr.	
Subtotal	6 hr.	
TOTAL	7	

Total Time **7** = _____ pts.

Accomplished **10p.** = _____ pts.

COMMENTS

Forgot dorm meeting at 8

dure and collect baseline data along with the sequence analysis. Alternatively, one could simply describe events that seemed particularly important. Although this last procedure would not provide baseline data, an analysis of even a few occasions would be helpful in designing a program of treatment.

The entries in Table 7.1 were made by a student who was considering two self-management programs. She wanted to contribute more to class discussions, and she wanted to behave more assertively when people asked what she considered to be unreasonable favors. For classroom discussions, she eventually recorded her total number of contributions and her failures to contribute per opportunity. She decided not to carry out a formal assertiveness program, but to practice "saying 'no' gracefully" with another student who was working in this area.

An analysis of eating behavior should include a daily "weigh in." Many people do not realize how much their weight fluctuates or the variables that control that fluctuation. Some women, for example, don't realize that they usually gain one or two pounds just before their monthly period. Without this information, one could draw the wrong conclusions about the success or failure of the program once it starts.

Students who will be increasing the time or efficiency of studying usually enter their records on data sheets that show how they have spent every hour of the day and what they have accomplished (Table 7.3). The same form is used to schedule activities for the following day. If the student is working on a point system, spaces for points earned and points spent are added to the mimeographed form.

The preliminary analysis should continue throughout baseline and cover as many situations as possible: weekends and possibly vacations as well as "routine" days. The more situations in which you observe your behavior, the better the chances of discovering the variables that control it and thus the better the chances of designing a successful program. Usually, baseline and the preliminary analysis continue for a couple of weeks and until the behavior stabilizes. One has to resist the temptation to jump into a program too soon, and the opposite temptation to prolong baseline and thus avoid starting the program. In her write-up of a weight-control project, one student wrote: "The experience of discovery and virtually guilt-free consumption of naughties during baseline was so enjoyable that the baseline period may have been extended longer than necessary."

3. Education

There are, of course, a great many determinants of behavior that won't be revealed by a sequence analysis. We are not likely to discover the caloric content of different foods simply by weighing ourselves and noting what we eat. But we have to know something about the caloric content of various foods if we are to design a successful weight-control program. This information is widely available, if seldom used. An otherwise bright and informed college student "knew" that fruits and vegetables were low in calories, so she lunched on *two whole avocados*. For fewer calories, she *could* have had: lean roast beef, a baked potato and butter, green beans, and a slice of angel food cake; or she could have skipped the butter and started her meal with a shrimp cocktail.

Many problems have a physiological basis. Chronic anxiety, fatigue, or depression could be related to a hormone imbalance, blood-sugar level, or a low-grade infection. If a sequence analysis does not reveal the major determinants of behavior, a medical examination may.

The problems that beset most of us—whether they be obesity, drug abuse, or inefficient study habits—have been the subject of numerous doctoral dissertations, medical research projects, government publications, and popular articles. There is a wealth of information available in the nearest bookstore or library. In addition to the general information available on most subjects, there is a rapidly growing literature on the use of behavioral procedures to manage problem behavior. Most of the *research* is designed to evaluate one or two procedures, but some authors describe entire programs. The Stuart and Davis *Slim Chance in a Fat World* (1972) has proved both readable and useful for those concerned about weight control; Fox (1962) and Jones (1969) offer several helpful suggestions for increasing the efficiency of studying; Hall (1976) can help you manage your time more efficiently; Goldiamond (1965) is excellent on personal problems. We have already mentioned several books on behavioral self-management. Of these, Williams and Long (1975) devote separate chapters to health problems (eating, smoking, drinking), athletic skills, studying, career planning, thoughts and feelings, and social skills and assertiveness. Craighead, Kazdin, and Mahoney (1976), and Leitenberg (1976) also include chapters on weight-control, smoking, drinking, various social skills (including those that arise in marriage counseling), and physical problems.

4. Motivation

A characteristic problem in self-management is that where the long-term consequences are aversive, the immediate consequences are reinforcing, and vice versa. Consummatory behavior is a good example of the first case. With problems like overeating, drinking too much alcohol, or other drug abuse, the behavior itself and its immediate consequences are usually reinforcing while the unfortunate long-term consequences are usually too distant to exert much control. The opposite is usually true when the goal is to increase the frequency or duration of behavior such as studying or exercising or speaking more effectively: the long-term benefits are usually clear, but the behavior itself

may be aversive or simply less appealing than competing activities.

When we want to weaken behavior, but its immediate consequences are reinforcing, we can follow the procedure suggested by Ferster, Nurnberger, and Levitt (1962) and identify the *ultimate aversive consequences* of the behavior. Their clients, who were overweight, were trained to verbalize an aversive consequence of obesity whenever they broke their program by eating the wrong food or in the wrong place or at the wrong time. The idea is to bridge the delay between the problem behavior and its aversive consequences and thus override the immediate reinforcing consequences. When using this tactic, the aversive consequences should be specific, graphic, and personal, not just general statistics on heart disease and life expectancy. If the goal is to increase, rather than decrease, the frequency or duration of behavior, then one identifies the aversive consequences of *failing* to emit the behavior. The events that made one decide to start a self-management program offer good possibilities: a cutting remark, the inability to fit into one's favorite clothes, the reason one was passed over for a promotion. A few examples, courtesy of our students:

Weight:
"I'm panting and struggling to carry around all that weight. I look much older than I am and have to wear old-looking clothes; why are all the nice clothes made for thin people?"

"I'm dying too soon from heart (respiratory, kidney) problems and I won't be able to attend my son (daughter's) wedding."

"I'm having a baby and labor is much longer and more difficult because I'm so fat."

"No one will ever believe I was a Marine."

"The money I'm spending on "junk" food is at least a dollar a day—$365 a year; $3,650 in ten years. I could feed 10 people on what I don't need."

"I'm on the beach in my ugly, loose-fitting bathing suit, but my 'tire' still shows and I can feel my thighs rubbing and sticking together."

"They have to get an extra cab because I can't fit with four other people and no one wants me to sit on their lap."

Studying:

"I'm flunking out of college and trying to get a job at the dime store."

"I won't get into graduate school, and I'll never be able to do my own research."

"I'm being turned down for a teaching assistantship."

"I won't have anything interesting to talk about at parties."

"Mr. _____ (professor) thinks I'm stupid."

"_____ (boy friend, girl friend) thinks I'm stupid."

"I've lost my scholarship and can't come back next year."

"Now I'll have to pull two all-nighters to get this paper in."

"Everyone else is at _____ and here I am, stewing in my room because I goofed off this morning."

Personal Habits:

"_____ noticed my nails and turned away, revolted."

"My hands (face, head) are infected and repulsive."

"My hair is falling out."

"Mother is nagging again."

"I'm applying for a job and the interviewer obviously thinks I have no self-control."

Smoking:

"I'm too young to be dying of cancer (emphysema, heart problems)."

"The surgeon is removing one lung and is so disgusted that he can't finish the operation."

"I'm polluting the air and forcing other people to inhale it."

"My fingers are completely yellow and I have to wear gloves all the time."

"My teeth are yellow and I can't smile without having people give me a disgusted look."

"My clothes smell so much that other people avoid me."

"_____ says she has to wash her hair after she's been in my room, it stinks so much."

"_____ thinks I'm neurotic."

"I'm spending more than a dollar a day to kill myself??"

Along with identifying aversive consequences, we find it useful to identify the reinforcing consequences of carrying out a successful program. Usually, these are the inverse of the aversive consequences: wearing nice clothes, being admired for self-control, feeling happy, healthy, and proud. Again, these consequences

should be specific: wearing a particular outfit, being admired by a particular person, having time to go on a particular weekend without feeling guilty. Companion lists of aversive and reinforcing consequences can be taped to the mirror or carried around in a notebook for frequent reference. When it comes to designing the program, items from these personalized lists of aversive and reinforcing consequences can be used as covert, or imaginary, reinforcers or punishers. One female student conducting a weight-control program made the distressing discovery that although she could no longer fit into her favorite blue jeans, her boy friend could. When she felt an urge to eat, she conjured up the image of her friend smugly wearing her jeans; when she then resisted the urge to eat, she rewarded herself by visualizing a scene in which she was wearing an attractive dress and thinking "gorgeous me!" One good thing about these kinds of covert reinforcers and punishers is that they represent natural consequences of behavior. Another is that they are free.

5. Taking Stock

Having gotten this far, one should have learned something about oneself and the problem. One should also have identified a good many reasons for undertaking a self-management program. It is a time to decide whether or not one really wants to change the behavior or just fool around with self-control procedures. If the former, it is important to get all the help one can. Simply "making up one's mind" and summoning "will power" may work for a while, but the chances are pretty good that that route has already been tried and found wanting. Witness the cigarette smoker who says, "It's *easy* to give up smoking. I've done it a hundred times." It is not very difficult to lose 10 pounds for a special occasion or to stop smoking for a week; but permanent changes usually require careful planning, frequent revisions, and often a major rearrangement of one's life style.

6. Selecting and Defining Goals

The preliminary analysis may have involved monitoring several classes of behavior prior to selecting one or two to manage. Some may turn out to be less of a problem than originally anticipated. Others may turn out to be related to some other problem that might better become the target of a self-management program. Some may seem too difficult to tackle in a first attempt at self-management. The goals must be realistic, and the program must be something one can live with. The goals should also be personally important so that one doesn't abandon the project when the going gets tough. Given a choice among several potential projects, one might be selected over another because there is someone else to work with.

As always, the major difficulty in defining goals lies in specifying how they will be measured. We can measure products of behavior: number of pages written, number of cigarettes smoked, number of creative ideas written in a notebook, number of pounds gained or lost. We can measure the frequency or duration of ongoing behavior: time spent reading or writing, number of compliments received or given, time spent exercising. And we can measure covert behavior: number of urges to eat or have a drink; time spent feeling good or bad about ourselves; number of times our feelings are hurt; number of times we feel proud or angry or vindictive. It is usually helpful to measure more than one class of behavior and to include products, on-going behavior, and—for many problems—covert behavior. Recording covert behavior and the context in which it occurs often makes us more aware of the environmental variables that control our emotions. But it will be some form of overt behavior that will affect our relations with others and, ultimately, our self-esteem.

It also helps to have at least one dependent variable that is sensitive to small changes. Suppose you are a student who carries a lot of extracurricular activities and you are spending only one hour a day studying. If you measure study time in units of one hour, you would have to double your baseline performance before you could notice any improvement. If you measured studying in 10-minute intervals, you would be in a better position to monitor the success or failure of the procedures you selected. Similarly, when biting nails and cuticles is a problem, it takes several days for the skin to heal and the nails to grow back. One solution is to examine the top, bottom, and sides of each finger once a day, and either press these areas for soreness or look for redness and new wounds. This provides a 40-point scale that is sensitive enough to measure small changes.

Even when a goal is easily defined and measured—stopping smoking, losing 20 pounds, winning an election—there may be different ways to reach the goal and thus different classes of behavior to define and record. If someone decided to lose 20 pounds by restricting between-meal snacks and exercising more, it would be a good idea to record the number and content of the snacks and the time or amount of exercise. If someone decided to eliminate smoking gradually, starting with the situations easiest to control, it would be a good idea to count the number of cigarettes smoked in those situations as well as the daily total. For most problems, there are several possible measures; the choice will depend on the results of the sequence analysis and the procedures selected to change the behavior. A few examples will suggest the range of possibilities:

Weight control:

Weight
Number of calories consumed at meals and
    between meals
Number of calories in "junk" food or
    alcohol

Caloric breakdown into protein, carbohy-drates, and fat (important for diabetics)

Number of second helpings accepted and refused

Time spent eating

Number of between-meal snacks

Urges to eat and whether or not succumbed to the urge

Number of times *did something else* when felt an urge to eat

Time spent in extra exercise

Calories expended in extra exercise

Money saved by not buying "forbidden" foods

Physical measurements: waist, hips, etc.

If a sequence analysis resembled Table 7.2, the individual would realize that more than half of the daily caloric intake (1,980 of 3,828 calories) was due to french fries, potato chips, and cookies consumed as "snacks." If eaten in this quantity every day, these items alone would account for four pounds a week. (Allow 3,400 calories per pound of weight.) If the general goal were to lose a pound a week for 10 weeks, a reasonable program might specify no more than two between-meal snacks a day with a total caloric value not to exceed 400 calories on weekdays or 700 calories on weekends. (This would amount to one pound a week in snacks, which is considerably less than the situation indicated in Table 7.2, and the snacks could be nutritious rather than "junk" food.) Someone else who was just as concerned about flabby muscles as overweight might select a combina-tion of diet and exercise. A program for this person to lose a pound a week might specify reducing caloric intake by 2,200 calories a week and increasing exercise by 1,200 calories.

Studying or Other Work:

Time spent reading, writing, doing other assignments

Time spent in class, lab, conferences

Number of pages written, read

Number of articles summarized in reading notebook

Number of problems solved or projects completed

Proportion of time *available* for study (work) that was spent studying (working)

Proportion of work planned that was accomplished

Time not spent working when should have

Time spent doing something else while intending to study

Grades; comments on papers

Where one person might concentrate on in-creasing the time spent studying, another might concentrate on reducing the time spent in com-peting activities. In either case, it might be wise to record both. It might also be wise to specify a product of behavior such as the number of pages to be read or problems to be solved.

Social Skills:

Time spent listening (attentively) to others

Proportion of listening time to talking time

Number of times changed the conversation to something of personal interest

Number of times noticed something com-mendable in someone else

Number of times expressed approval or appreciation when noticed

Number of compliments received

Number of invitations received, given

Times felt "on defensive"; acted defen-sively or rudely

Times put someone else on the defensive (intentionally or not)

Times precipitated an unpleasant situation

Times calmed or corrected an unpleasant situation

Times apologized gracefully

After analyzing a particular problem in the area of social skills, it should be possible to select some specific goals and ways to measure them. One student who wanted to speak more often, and also more loudly, counted the number of times another person said "What?" or "Huh?"

C. Managing the Situation

We now come to the main reason for carrying out a sequence analysis and laboriously collecting records like those shown in Tables 7.1–7.3. Behavior occurs, or fails to occur, in the context of other events including the physical and social setting, the behavior of others, and the activities that comprise sequences of our own behavior. Drinking alcohol may be especially likely to occur at a party, where other people are drinking and urging drinks, and when one has already had a couple and is warming up to recite a long and hilarious story. Studying may fail to occur at a desk covered with letters and magazines, when other people are present and carrying on an animated discussion of sports, and when one is expecting an important long-distance telephone call. One way to change behavior is to change the context in which it normally occurs or fails to occur. Thus one way to reduce alcohol consumption would be to stay away from parties; one way to increase studying would be to clear off the desk and clear out the people. These and other procedures to change the antecedents of behavior are described under *Stimulus Control*.

Behavior is also followed by consequences, some of which function to maintain it while others function to weaken it. A polite and soft-spoken request may be ignored while nagging or shouting may be reinforced with compliance. If we are interested in maintaining good manners and developing social skills, we would probably have to do something to change these inappropriate consequences. There are several ways to arrange a situation so that reinforcing events will follow the behavior we want to increase and will not follow the behavior that we want to decrease. These procedures are described under *Managing the Consequences*. We can thus gain some control over our behavior by changing its antecedents or its consequences. Usually it makes sense to try both.

(If you are reading this chapter with the hope of finding suggestions for managing some aspect of your own behavior, take a moment to think about any previous attempts at self-control. Recall what was helpful and what was not; where it was relatively easy to stick to your resolutions and where it was difficult. If the program succeeded for a while but then ran into snags, try to account for the change.)

1. Managing the Antecedents of Behavior: Stimulus Control

When a particular class of behavior is likely to occur in a particular context, we say that the context exerts stimulus control. To the extent that we can control the context, we can gain some control over the behavior. In some cases we want to establish stimulus control; in others we want to reduce or remove it. When the problem is a behavioral excess—such as eating, drinking, or swearing too much or too often—we want to break up stimulus control over these classes of behavior; and, where possible, we want to establish stimulus control over other, more desirable behavior. When the problem is a behavioral deficit—such as infrequent studying, forgetting to do things, or speaking less effectively than we would like—then we want to establish stimulus control over these classes of behavior and break up the association between the context and any other activities that compete with those we are trying to strengthen.

a. Disrupting stimulus control

The most obvious way to reduce or eliminate behavior that occurs in a particular situation is to *avoid* that situation. While this will usually not provide a permanent solution, it is often a very good place to start. If a budding alcoholic passes a bar on the way home each night and stops in for a drink, and another, and another, one solution is to take a different route home. At first, of course, the route should not be one that passes a different bar. But later on, when other measures have been taken, it might be a good idea to walk past bars that have few of the discriminative stimuli of the original. When I am in the lab, I often spend more time talking with students than working. It is easier to avoid the sight of students by closing my door than it is to see them and resist the temptation to talk. We all learn to avoid certain topics of conversation with certain friends or relatives because those topics provoke arguments that, in turn, provoke behavior we'd rather not see ourselves emit. An alternative to avoiding an entire situation is to remove the discriminative stimuli for problem behavior. If we eat or drink or smoke too much, we can keep food and liquor and cigarettes out of sight.

In *Walden Two* (p. 87-88) Skinner describes how three- and four-year-old children learn self-control. In the morning they are given a lollipop dipped in powered sugar, and they can have it later in the day if it hasn't been licked. The children quickly learn to put their lollipops out of sight. Obviously there are other, probably social, contingencies in effect. Otherwise the children might as well eat the lollipop in the morning as wait until later in the day. Now, if they were to get *two* lollipops for waiting . . . But Skinner probably preferred to rely on social consequences as they are more likely to characterize the natural environment. Putting money in the bank is one of the few situations where hiding your reinforcer can double its value.

Of course we have to be aware of the stimuli that control our behavior in order to avoid or remove them. This was the reason for the preliminary analysis of the situation. One student on a weight-control program discovered that the first thing she did on arriving home via the back door was to go to the kitchen where the other (thin) boarders were usually eating and socializing. She joined them and only later went to her room and started studying. She decided to enter the house by the *front* door and to go straight to her room and study. Only then would she go to the kitchen; and by this time, most of the fattening food would have disappeared. She might also have followed Williams and Long's (1975) suggestion for increasing awareness and posted pictures of fat and thin people on the refrigerator door.

When we cannot (or don't wish to) avoid the situations that currently control problem behavior, we can try to establish their control over competing behavior. If dinner is the occasion for a hassle about family finances or child-rearing problems, perhaps these subjects can be relegated to another time and place so that dinner can become the occasion for amusing stories that have been saved up during the day, or for making plans for weekends and vacations. If 10 P.M. or "feeling bored" or a certain television commercial is the occasion for having a little snack, perhaps it can instead become the occasion for making a phone call, reading the paper, or letting out the dog.

b. Establishing stimulus control

If behavior occurs less often than we would like, or if it occurs in far too many situations, we will want to bring it under stimulus control. Goldiamond (1965) provides examples. One of his clients was a girl who had difficulty studying, and Goldiamond decided to help her bring studying under the control of her desk:

The program with the young lady started with human engineering of her desk. Since she felt sleepy when she studied, she was told to replace a 40-w lamp with a good one and to turn her desk away from her bed. It was also decided that her desk was to control study behavior. If she wished to write a letter, she should do so but in the dining room; if she wished to read comic books, she should do so but in the kitchen; if she wished to daydream, she should do so but was to go to another room; at her desk she was to engage in her school work and her school work only.

This girl had previously had a course in behavioral analysis and said, "I know what you're up to. You want that desk to assume stimulus control over me. I'm not going to let any piece of wood run my life for me."

"On the contrary," I said, "you *want* that desk to run you. It is you who decides when to put yourself under the control of your desk."
(Goldiamond, 1965, p. 854)

After a week, the girl gleefully reported to Goldiamond that she had spent only 10 minutes at her desk. Unfazed (and unfazable), Goldiamond quietly asked if she had studied while she was at her desk. When she said "Yes," he congratulated her and suggested that she try to double the time the following week. By the end of the semester, she had spent three hours a day at her desk for four weeks in a row; and while she sat at her desk she had studied.

The clothes we wear on certain occasions may serve as discriminative stimuli for behavior that the culture deems appropriate for those occasions. Our carriage is apt to be more erect and our language more elegant when we are groomed and dressed for a formal occasion than when we are slouching around in informal attire. My college roommate used to take advantage of this kind of stimulus control when she prepared herself for an important examination. While the rest of us barely succeeded in dragging ourselves out of bed and into our scruffy blue jeans, my roommate would wash her hair and get all dressed up as though she were off to a job interview or a formal luncheon. Since she was a relatively normal student in most respects, I finally asked for and got an explanation: "If I look neat, I'll think neat." She made Phi Beta Kappa!

When behavior occurs in too many settings, we want to *restrict* the stimulus events that control it. People who eat too much often eat in

a great many situations: while reading, watching television, studying, thinking; at parties, ball games, waiting for a bus, waiting in the checkout line at the supermarket; when they are bored, anxious, tired, happy; at 8 A.M., 10 A.M., noon, mid-afternoon, before, during, and after dinner, before bed—and whenever anyone drops by for a visit. It helps to make some of these situations discriminative stimuli for *other* classes of behavior, but the main thing is to restrict their control over eating. Goldiamond (1965) counseled one of his clients to treat food with the dignity it deserves. The client was instructed to eat to his heart's content, but only under specified conditions. Eating deserved his full attention, so when he ate he was to devote himself exclusively to eating. No more eating while studying or watching television. If he wanted a sandwich, fine. But he was to put it on a plate, take it to the table, sit down, and enjoy it fully. Within a week, the client had disrupted the control that television and studying had formerly exerted over eating, and he had stopped eating between meals. He told Goldiamond: "You've taken all the fun out of it."

Other authorities on weight control (Ferster et al., 1962; Stuart, 1967) also encourage restricting the stimulus occasions for eating, and the procedure is appropriate for other problems as well. In another Goldiamond (1965) case study, his client was a young husband who screamed at his wife for "hours on end" or —ashamed for having done so—spent hours brooding and sulking. Goldiamond advised him to sulk to his heart's content, but to do so in a specified place: a special sulking stool in the garage where he might "sulk and mutter over the indignities of life for as long as he wished." Similarly, Nolan (1968) describes a smoker who allowed herself to smoke only in a "smoking chair," which was uncomfortable and faced away from the television set and other possible sources of reinforcement. When she succeeded in restricting her smoking to the chair, she moved it to the cellar. Ferster et al. (1962) and Penick, Filion, Fox, and Stunkard (1971) recommend establishing similar control over eating: at a table set with a napkin and place mat of a distinctive color.

A student (we'll call her Joan) complained of low self-esteem and said she spent most of her time feeling "depressed." It turned out that when she was feeling depressed she was recounting to herself all of her inadequacies: the "stupid" remarks she had made, her failures to send in any applications to graduate schools, her inability to even start filling out the application forms, and so forth. We decided on three approaches: 1) Every day, she was to make a list of the activities she could reasonably accomplish, even little things. She was to check off those she did accomplish and tell me about them the following day. The first "assignment" was to type the envelopes for the graduate school applications. 2) She was to find a special place to be depressed in, some distinctive place that we hoped would assume stimulus control. A green armchair in her room fit the bill. Whenever she started to feel depressed, she was to go to her room, sit in that chair, and indulge herself. She could make lists of her inadequacies if she wished, but she was not to think or speak negative thoughts about herself anywhere else but in that chair. 3) She was to tell her closest friends about the program and ask their help. They were to reinforce positive statements and actions and to place negative self-statements on extinction. They were also to refrain from modeling these classes of behavior. If Joan made a self-deprecatory remark, they were to ignore it or tell her to go to her green chair if she wanted to be depressed. (Her friends were also advised to watch closely for any indication of serious depression and to alert me and the college psychiatrist at the first sign.) In a very short time, Joan hated the sight of the green chair; but the envelopes got typed on the first day, and the graduate school applications were completed and mailed before the deadlines. She also concentrated on developing verbal behavior that was incompatible with depression, and for a while we had to put up with some pretty flip remarks. But we all survived that stage and welcomed the transition from self-deprecation through caustic comments to the revival of a glorious sense of humor about herself and the world. I am sure that (like most of us) Joan still has frequent periods of discouragement and self-doubt. But she has been capable of sustained and effective work in graduate school, where she is now completing her doctorate; she appears to be happy; and she is a highly entertaining public speaker.

2. Managing the Consequences

Establishing stimulus control may well be the most important step we can take in managing our own behavior. But this control will not be maintained unless the behavior is followed by appropriate consequences. If studying at the desk or eating only in the dining room are not reinforced in some way, these activities will extinguish, and we will probably revert to our former bad habits.

The best reinforcers, of course—and possibly the only kind that will be effective over the long haul—are the natural reinforcing consequences that accompany successful self-management: weight loss in a weight-control program; better grades following efficient studying; better (more reinforcing) social relations following management of social skills, and so forth. Improved self-esteem and sometimes admiration from others are also naturally occurring consequences of successful self-management. But these reinforcers are usually delayed. It may take weeks to lose a noticeable amount of weight or to grow long nails or to research and write a good paper. It may also take weeks for improvements in self-confidence and social skills to affect the behavior of others. Meanwhile, temptations abound, and it is easy to fall by the wayside and undo all the good work.

Friends can help by refraining from tempting us to break the rules we set up and by noticing and reinforcing the behavior we are trying to increase. We can also ask our friends to extinguish behavior that we want to eliminate; but if we want to keep our friends, we probably should not ask them to administer aversive consequences.

To bridge the delay between managing their behavior and the reinforcing consequences of success, many people rely on other reinforcers to maintain the effort and abstinence required during the early stages of the program.

a. Is self-reinforcement possible?

More than a year ago, in a desperate attempt to speed up the writing of this book, I marked a stack of 3 x 5 cards with things I could do when I had written a page of manuscript. One card said GET COFFEE; others said FEED FISH, GET MAIL, SMOKE A CIGARETTE, and so forth: all the things I am apt to do to "help along" my writing or as a break when I can incubate Great Thoughts. Then I shuffled the cards, turned over the top one, and settled down to work for a cup of coffee. Coffee and feeding the fish worked fine (or perhaps it was the novelty of the situation). Some of the others did not. When GET MAIL turned up, I diddled around or looked up an interesting reference (which always leads to looking up another interesting reference) or rewrote the last page a few times. Maybe getting mail was not reinforcing because of the high proportion of book ads and bills. As for cigarettes, I spent more time peeking at the cards to see when the next cigarette was due than I did writing to earn one. I smoked at least four before I had earned even one. In other words,

I cheated; and the ensuing guilt and frustration did nothing to facilitate my writing.

Now, there were a lot of things wrong with this arrangement as you can tell from two dismal facts: I cheated, and I am still working on the manuscript. For one thing, a whole page of writing was far too much to require. I write very slowly, revising as I go, and it often takes hours to come up with a single acceptable page. (Which is why I don't reinforce *time* spent working. That is already excessive.) For another, I should have programmed *options* for a given amount of work: coffee *or* feeding the fish *or* getting the mail. For another—and this may just be a personal preference that doesn't apply to others—the events that were supposed to reinforce writing either had nothing to do with writing or bore the wrong temporal relation to writing. Coffee and cigarettes are discriminative stimuli for my writing, not effective consequences; and the others seemed too contrived. Even though they are "high probability behavior," I picked them "out of the blue," and back to the blue they went. On the other hand, counting and graphing accomplishments are excellent reinforcers for me, and I monitor several classes of behavior. The data seem to me to be logical and natural consequences, and since I enter the records every night, they are relatively immediate. But there are other consequences as well, and data alone would probably not have maintained certain classes of "good" behavior for four years. When I care to stick my neck out, having someone else read and appreciate something I think is well written or innovative or useful is also reinforcing and a natural consequence of writing. Buying new, "slim" clothes would seem to be an appropriate reinforcer for weight loss, and the fact that one can wear them is a natural consequence of weight control. Even splurging the money one saves by not buying cigarettes or "junk" food seems logical.

Maybe my real problem was that writing a whole page was too difficult while having an illicit cigarette was too easy. And that raises an important point about self-management: *Can we, in fact, reinforce or punish our own behavior?* Granted that the terms *self-reinforcement* and *self-punishment* are misleading,[2] I am inclined to answer both yes and no. No, not without supporting external control; yes, *but with supporting external control, which we ourselves can often arrange.*[3] If the only reinforcer for writing is getting a cup of coffee, and if there are no aversive consequences for failure to complete the manuscript, and if I can easily get a cup of coffee without writing, then sooner or later, alas, I probably will. But if the writing-then-coffee contingency is backed up by some external contingency, then maybe I won't. If I have to submit five pages a week to the publisher (instead of 400 pages at the end of two years), or if I have to demonstrate my progress to someone whose respect I want; or if I assign 10 as-yet-unwritten-pages to my class to be read two weeks from now, then there will be a good deal of external control exerted on my behavior, and I will probably write to avoid the aversive consequences of failing to do so. Now, if *I* am the one to institute these avoidance contingencies, rather than my publisher, friend, or students; and if I actually do the writing, then I think it is reasonable to say that I have played an important role in managing the consequences of my own behavior. Similarly, if I tell a colleague or a student that I am trying to learn how to speak in complete sentences when I lecture, and I ask for (and get) differential feedback, then I have been instrumental in bringing about this form of external control.

There is good evidence that other sorts of self-determined consequences can be effective in self-management programs. Even contrived reinforcers can be symbols of progress toward a goal, an extra value they would lack had they not been earned. And if we use points or tokens, we can arrange that they be delivered immediately, thus bridging the delay between our behavior and the natural or externally imposed reinforcing consequences.

b. Establishing effective consequences

Several reinforcers that have been used in successful self-management programs have been listed in Table 3.6. Table 3.8 from Watson and Tharp, is a list of questions to ask oneself when trying to identify effective reinforcers. Our students who are on weight-control programs often select consequences that are directly related to their problem. The major reinforcers, after a 5- or 10-pound loss, are often new clothes, one or two sizes smaller than the ones they can wear at the start of the program. Sometimes the clothes are bought before they fit, which is a nice example of stimulus control and apparently provides a little extra incentive to stick to the program. Smaller reinforcers for keeping records and stay-

2. One sense in which the terms self-reinforcement and self-punishment are misleading has been mentioned in conjunction with the term self-control. If the terms are used correctly, it is not the self that is reinforced or punished; it is some behavior. Goldiamond (1976b) raises another issue. He says that the term *self-reinforcement* is inappropriate because the contingencies of reinforcement require that the evaluation of the response requirement be independent of the subject. In the laboratory, it is usually the apparatus that defines the behavior that qualifies for reinforcement; in applied settings, it is usually another person; in self-management, it is the subject who makes this evaluation. We agree with Goldiamond and with Catania (1975) that self-reinforcement is a misleading term for the evaluation of one's own behavior. If we are to examine the variables that allow us to control our behavior, we should draw a distinction between the evaluation of performance and the management of consequences. The term *self-reinforcement* does not seem appropriate for either.

3. Watson and Tharp (1972) maintain that we *can* reinforce our own behavior; Catania (1975), and Morgan and Bass (1973) maintain that, on the basis of present evidence, external agents are necessary. They agree with Stuart (1972) and Goldiamond (1965) that stimulus control is the more effective strategy.

ing within calorie limits might include going out to dinner or even 200 "free" calories to be "spent" on any food or drink the person wants. (If someone has saved 3,000 calories a week by sticking to a sensible diet and given up a favorite food in the process, 200 calories is but a small step backwards and may prevent excessive deprivation of the food in question.)

Students engaged in other sorts of self-management projects seem more likely to select activities as reinforcers. Unfortunately, we have not kept data on this point. As a punisher, should the need arise, some students on weight-control programs choose to "exercise off" the number of calories by which they have exceeded their limit. (Since it takes a great deal of exercise to burn up a few calories, this procedure is practical only for small excesses in caloric consumption.) Other punishers and response costs are listed in Table 3.9.

Besides earning things or activities for themselves, people sometimes find altruism reinforcing. Some of our students have earned points for someone else; and in one group study, the participants earned points by controlling their eating behavior and then exchanged their points for money which they voted to give to different charities (Penick et al., 1971).

3. Selecting Procedures

Having located potential reinforcers and possibly punishers, one could conceivably use any of the procedures described in Chapters 4 and 5. Combinations of procedures are probably most effective. In any case, one would be advised to make reinforcement contingent upon all constructive behavior that occurs in conjunction with the program. "Constructive" behavior includes keeping records and arranging for stimulus control as well as observable progress towards the goal. ("Constructive" behavior also includes spending the reinforcers earned.

Hoarded tokens or points may reinforce behavior for a while, but sometimes the progress comes to an abrupt halt. On such occasions, we have sometimes urged students to award themselves points for spending points!)

Additional procedures will depend upon the problem. Modeling and role playing, for example, are particularly useful when we want to acquire physical or social skills. Differential reinforcement of low rate is sometimes appropriate for a gradual reduction in smoking or drinking or other bad habits. Omission training and reinforcement of alternative behavior are *always* appropriate when we want to eliminate problem behavior. A 30-year-old woman in the Penick et al., (1971) weight-control program realized for the first time during her preliminary sequence analysis that when she felt angry, she ate. Therefore, at the slightest sign of anger, she left the kitchen and wrote down her feelings, thereby decreasing both her anger and her food consumption.

Response cost is another reductive procedure frequently used in self-control programs, especially in conjunction with a point system. If compliance with the rules of the program earns points, failure to comply may lose points. As in any response cost procedure, the contingencies must be carefully arranged so that more points are earned than lost, and the individual does not go into "debt."

a. Covert procedures

Most of the research on self-management has been concerned with the effectiveness of overt procedures: overt reinforcers or punishers as consequences of overt behavior. But there is now evidence that covert procedures may also be effective. The term "covert" may apply to the behavior, the consequence, or both. An overweight person at a party might feel the urge (covert behavior) for another canapé and immediately visualize an aversive scene of buttons popping from critical places as the other guests snicker or avert their eyes (covert punishment). The person might then eat a piece of celery (overt behavior) and either earn points toward some overt reinforcer or else imagine another scene, this time a pleasant one, which would constitute covert reinforcement. The definitions are a bit tenuous because we are dealing with private events. Only the person who is imagining the reinforcing or punishing events can ascertain whether or not they have occurred and whether or not they have changed his covert behavior. But if we are willing to grant that people can make these judgments, and if we are willing to accept their reports, there is evidence that both overt behavior (such as smoking and drinking) and covert behavior (such as compulsive thoughts or urges) can be changed by covert procedures.

Lloyd Homme (1965) was one of the first to explore the possibilities of covert reinforcement; and Cautela and his colleagues have investigated covert parallels of most of the major overt operant procedures—covert reinforcement, covert escape,[4] covert punishment, covert extinction—as well as the respondent conditioning procedures, covert sensitization and covert aversion relief (e.g., Ascher & Cautela, 1972; Cautela, 1966, 1967, 1970a, b, 1971; Wisocki, 1970, 1973).

For the use of covert reinforcing procedures, Cautela has compiled a Reinforcement Survey Schedule (Cautela & Kastenbaum, 1967) from which the client may select among hundreds of potentially reinforcing events in some 54 categories. When clients want to increase a particular class of behavior, they imagine they are engaging in one of the reinforcing activities they selected. Covert reinforcement can be used in the shaping and reinforcement paradigm, to develop or maintain behavior; and it can be used in the Alt R paradigm to reduce problem behavior by the covert reinforcement of alternative behavior. Wisocki (1970) describes a young wife who spent most of her day engaging in obsessive-compulsive housework, which included folding and refolding clothes to remove invisible wrinkles. Since this compulsive neatness interfered with her other activities, the client was told to imagine herself either refraining from repetitiously sorting and folding clothes or engaging in some incompatible behavior. She was then to follow this covert behavior by imagining herself in a reinforcing scene. If, for example, she imagined herself throwing her son's unmatched sock into the bureau and immediately shutting the drawer, she could then imagine herself eating Italian food, practicing ballet, or completing a difficult task. Within six weeks, there was a decrease in all obsessive-compulsive behavior, not just folding clothes. The daily time occupied in making beds decreased from 30 minutes to 10 minutes, and in rinsing dishes from 60 to 20 minutes. Progress in this and other areas was maintained at a 12-month follow-up when the client also reported being pleased with her ability to exert some control over her environment.[5]

Covert extinction has been used by Cautela (1971) in the treatment of stuttering, and by Gotestam, Melin, and Dockens (1975) in the treatment of intravenous amphetamine addiction. The subjects in the latter study imagined, as vividly as possible, the whole sequence of events involved in injecting amphetamines, but at the end of the sequence they were to feel nothing, no "flash" or any other effect. The authors monitored respiration, pulse rate, pulse volume, and GSR. After 100 extinction trials spread over a week, the clients no longer exhibited physiological reactions during the imagined sequences. At one time or another dur-

---

4. Covert escape would also be called covert negative reinforcement.

5. Some of our students who start with elaborate point systems for tangible reinforcers later switch to covert reinforcement. I seem to notice this happening after they have read some of Wisocki's papers, prior to her annual visit to my class.

ing treatment, all four clients "went AWOL" and injected amphetamines, but they said that they failed to experience the flash. During the nine-month follow-up, three of the four remained off drugs, while one returned to the use of stimulants.

Under the *covert escape* procedure, clients imagine a frightening situation, and then they imagine escaping from this situation by engaging in some activity that is appropriate for their problem. A girl who was unable to leave her house for fear of being sexually attacked imagined escaping from sirens by walking outside her house on a sunny day; an alcoholic imagined escaping from having his teeth drilled in the dentist's chair by resolving not to take another drink (Cautela, 1970a). Just as in systematic desensitization, the best documented of the covert procedures, in this procedure *in vivo* transfer is usually programmed along the way as the client practices the adaptive behavior in the natural environment.

Thought-stopping is a covert procedure used to interrupt urges or compulsive thinking. As used in therapy, the client starts a train of compulsive thinking or visualizes himself about to engage in problem behavior. In the latter case, the therapist would help along the imagery. If the client were an alcoholic whose specialty was dry martinis, the therapist might say something like this:

Shut your eyes and relax. Really relax. Imagine that you are on your way home, hot and tired after an exhausting day at work. You pass the _____ (name of favorite bar) and decide you really deserve a drink. You open the door and immediately feel the coolness. You sigh and feel better already. (Can you visualize the bar? The room, the people, the friendly atmosphere? The welcome coolness after the hot pavement? Good.) You go to the bar and ask _____ (name of bartender) for the special. He nods and smiles and turns to the rows of bottles behind him. You glance around the room, notice two familiar faces, then sit on the stool. You can feel yourself relaxing. _____ takes a bottle of Beefeaters from the shelf and pours some, crystal clear, over the ice in the shaker. He adds just a drop of dry vermouth. He stirs

your drink, and you see it swirling around the glass shaker. He pours it into your glass, right up to the top. Amazing how they always know just how much to make. He cuts a thin peel of lemon, gives it a twist. You see the drops of oil fly off and smell the pungent odor. He drops it into the glass. Beautiful. As he passes over the glass, you can smell the juniper in the gin, and you notice that you're salivating. You sigh and reach slowly for the glass, and you see some of the moisture on the outside condense as you carefully lift it to your lips. It feels so cool. You part your lips to take the first sip . . .

Whereupon the therapist shouts "Stop!" and perhaps bangs the table. This startles the client out of his wits, and certainly out of his lovely scene at the bar.[6] If nothing else, the client learns that compulsive thoughts or urges can be disrupted. Next, the client imagines the scene again and shouts (or imagines shouting) "Stop" to himself. Then he is taught how to practice the exercise at home.

b. Combining overt and covert procedures

Covert procedures have generally been used in combination with other procedures. This, plus the scarcity of controlled studies, makes it difficult to evaluate their effectiveness at this time. There are, however, at least three reasons they merit attention. Most of us think (at least occasionally), and much of our overt behavior occurs in sequences that also incorporate covert activities. Procedures that allow us to manage either class of behavior would seem to be worth investigating. The other reasons are more immediately practical. We can practice covert procedures anywhere, and they are free. These are likely to be important considerations in self-management.

There are thus a wide variety of procedures that may be used to manage one's own behavior. In addition to covert sensitization and desensitization, described in Chapter 6, the co-

---

6. I once watched Joe Cautela demonstrate thought-stopping in a similar scenario and literally jumped out of my seat.

vert counterparts of many overt procedures offer a number of possibilities and probably would not require professional help. (See Table 7.4.)

4. Contingencies and Contracts

Having dwelled at some length on contingencies and contracts in Chapter 3, we will say little more here except that they are just as important in self-management as they are in any other program. Some people work out rather simple arrangements: a certain amount of studying or exercise, for example, will be followed by a shower before bed. No work, no shower. Others may design an elaborate point system whereby they can earn 100 or more points a day and then

use their points to "purchase" several reinforcing items or activities such as those shown in Table 3.6.

One student, who was working on weight loss and assertiveness, carried around a set of blue 3 x 5 cards on which she had written her major goals. Some of the weight-control cards read: "Fought inflation by not buying nonnutritive foods; helped conserve the world food supply; increased musculature by using natural energy." The assertiveness cards included: "Talked to a stranger that she didn't have to; participated in class or in a meeting" (followed by a list of her classes); "Showed GREAT COURAGE by speaking to a PROFESSOR; felt very good about something she did today; was told she talked louder." When she performed

Figure 7.1.   Examples of record cards kept by a student conducting self-management program for weight control and assertiveness.

Table 7.4   Self-management procedures.

OVERT PROCEDURES	COVERT PROCEDURES
Self-instruction	
Writing down the rules in a contingency contract; reading or saying them out loud.	Recalling the rules; telling yourself to relax, count to ten, pay attention.
Modeling and Role Playing	
Watching someone performing skillfully or appropriately (speaking with confidence; overcoming a problem; demonstrating a skill) then practicing the behavior that has been modeled.	Imagining yourself or another person performing skillfully or appropriately.
Reinforcement	
Rewarding performance of the desired behavior by engaging in a preferred activity or by gaining a token or point that you may exchange for a back-up reinforcer.	Imagining yourself in a pleasant situation or telling yourself that you are noble, brave, virtuous, and in command, contingent on imagining or actually performing the desired behavior.
Escape-Avoidance	
Making a deposit of money or goods that will be forfeited if the desired behavior is not emitted. "Storing a bag of ugly fat (representing one's own obesity) in the refrigerator and removing pieces as one loses weight." (From Mahoney & Thoreson, 1974, p. 50)	Imagining yourself escaping from an aversive or anxiety-producing situation when you imagine you are performing the desired behavior, or when you actually perform the behavior.
Extinction	
Asking friends not to reinforce behavior (such as complaining, swearing) that you are trying to eliminate.	Imagining that the behavior (eating, drug-taking) is emitted but is not followed by the usual reinforcing consequences.
Satiation	
?? (If you are spending too much time reading pornographic literature, you might, in one sitting, go through eight or ten of those with the fewest redeeming features. But it might be better to program this as a reinforcer for competing behavior.)	Imagining yourself engaging in the problem behavior until it is no longer enjoyable (eating forbidden food until you feel stuffed, sated.)
Punishment	
Doing something you dislike: cleaning the room; exercising; wearing the button of a hated politician (also from Mahoney & Thoresen), contingent on problem behavior. Arranging to be embarrassed: confessing to someone important; wearing a sign on your back or a glove on one hand that will make people ask why. (Not recommended for self-esteem projects.)	Thinking an unpleasant thought or imagining an aversive consequence, contingent upon emitting the problem behavior or upon the urge to do so. Telling yourself you're stupid, slovenly, gluttonous.
Response Cost	
Subtracting tokens or points from those earned, contingent on the problem behavior.	Imagining the loss of a valuable possession, contingent upon overt or covert problem behavior.
Omission Training and DRL	
Reinforcing the failure to emit the problem behavior for a specified period of time. (Behavior may be omitted altogether or in a specified situation.) Reinforcing a specified low rate of the behavior.	Imagining a reinforcing event, contingent upon real or imagined omission of the behavior for a specified period of time.
Reinforcement of Alternative Behavior (Alt R)	
Reinforcing behavior that prevents or competes with the problem behavior.	Imagining a reinforcing consequence for overt or covert competing behavior, e.g., imagining a pleasant situation following resisting the urge to eat by leaving the table.

one of these activities she placed a brightly colored star (sticker) on the card and noted the date. The number of stars corresponded to various back-up reinforcers, but I imagine that earning them and placing them on the cards were the more effective reinforcing events. This was the student mentioned above who was trying to speak more loudly and counted the number of times someone said "What?" or "Huh?" during the course of a conversation. (It really was very difficult to hear what she was saying, and that was a shame because it was usually something interesting and original.) She did independent work the following semester; and following her oral presentation in a fairly large classroom, I was delighted to be able to tell her that we could hear every word from the back row.

The main reason for writing a contract with oneself for a self-management program is that it clarifies the contingencies. Specifying the rules makes it easier to follow them and also makes it easier to discover the source of problems when they arise. As in any other contract, a self-management contract should specify exactly what is to be done and the consequences for doing it or failing to do it. For the first few weeks at least, we recommend stating consequences for all aspects of the program: keeping records and arranging stimulus control as well as the behavior one is trying to change. A general contract now used by our students is shown in Table 7.5. It has been filled out by a student on a weight-control program, but it can be adapted for other problems.

Contracts can be revised as often as necessary and should be reviewed at weekly intervals. After a week, the student who wrote the contract shown in Table 7.5 wanted to stop giving herself points for stimulus control. She'd do it anyway. I urged her to continue, reminding her that eating alone in her room had accounted for several hundred calories a day during baseline. She also thought it was silly to give herself points for keeping records because she had to do that

anyway in conjunction with the course. Again, I urged her to continue—mostly, I guess, because I wanted this behavior under reinforcement as well as avoidance contingencies. I also wanted to make sure that she could easily earn enough points to meet her daily needs. She did make some changes. She wasn't doing any exercising, so she changed that point value from 10 points for 15 minutes to two points a minute; and she decided to include any kind of "vigorous" or "strenuous" exercise (Table 7.2), not just calisthenics.

5. Programming

a. Deprivation
Too severe deprivation can be the downfall of any self-management program, whether in conjunction with the behavior (e.g., eating) or with the withholding of important events so that they may be used as reinforcers. Crash diets in a weight-control program can make self-management much more difficult than need be; and if a diet is limited to one or two foods, then the deprivation for other foods is increased. A balanced diet and a program of *gradual* weight-loss are better for long-term management as well as for health. Other ways to handle the deprivation problem in weight-control include eating the least preferred food first and drinking a glass of water just before the meal. It also helps to space out the eating process by chewing the food carefully and by pausing a few seconds between mouthfuls. As for other kinds of self-management programs, deprivation of important reinforcers that will be used to maintain self-management procedures can lead to cheating.

b. Cheating
There are two clarion calls that a self-management program is in trouble. One is that there is no apparent progress toward the goal.

Table 7.5   **Self-management contract** for weight control.

Name: _____   General Goal: _20 lb. weight loss_____

Duration of Contract (dates) _oct 4_ to _oct 11_.   Program _✓_   Maintenance _____

Data
    Keep daily _✓_ or _____ records of:

      _weight_____   _extra exercise (time)_

      _calories_____   _____

      # between meal snacks   _____

    Data will be analysed and plotted: _every night_____

Program
    <u>Behavior</u>   <u>Consequences</u>

      Keep records at 5 pts each; 10 pts graph   _30 pts_
      1600 cal. weekdays; 1800 weekends (2 days)   _50_
      only 2 snacks a day: Total 300 cal. (500 weekend)   _10_
      Eat at least 2 balanced meals a day   _10_
      Exercise 15 min/day (during week)   _10_

    <u>Stimulus control</u>
      No food in room   _10_
      Eat only with someone, in regular place   _10_

    <u>Alternative behavior</u> (if applicable)
      when feel urge to eat, remember Richard can
      wear my jeans and I can't Resist urge –
      think "gorgeous me."
    <u>Covert</u> (behavior, consequences)

                    If points, possible daily total   _130_
  Bonus?
    50 points each pound lost
    200 "free" calories if stay within limit whole week
Exchange
             <u>Reinforcers</u>   (<u>Aversive Consequences?</u>)

    movies, TV, reading etc – 10 pts/hr   _Point cost: 1 pt each 10 cal._
    Shower – 10 pts   _over limit_
    Weekend away – 100 pts   _Also: if 200 cal. over,_
    gas for car – 10 pts   _tell Richard I blew it_
    clothes – 100 pts per $10.00 worth   _if 300 cal. over, all calls_
                               from pay phone for a
                               week

Signature _____   Date _____

The other is cheating. In either case, the solution is to revise the program: the reinforcers, the contingencies, or both.

Two of our students regularly "blew" their weight-control programs on weekends at Dartmouth. Rather than scrap the program (or the weekends) they earned extra calories during the week, which could be spent on the weekend. The result was a considerable savings in the total number of calories consumed and a parallel savings in self-esteem. If we start with the possible, and if we gradually raise the requirements, the problem of cheating can often be averted.

c. Start with the possible

One year, just after Christmas, I got a call from the mother of a student who had taken my course in behavior analysis the preceding semester. The student, whom we shall call Susan, would not be coming back second semester because she couldn't do the independent research project required of all majors. Actually, Susan had been looking forward to *doing* the independent work, but she couldn't face the final oral report. (Students doing independent work report their research in symposia patterned after professional meetings. It is the highlight of the semester for their proud faculty sponsors.) Susan's mother was naturally concerned that her daughter would not graduate. I was dumbfounded, even though I knew perfectly well that Susan had a problem with public speaking because that was her self-management project the previous semester. It was difficult for an outsider to recognize the severity of the problem because she is a delightful person who converses easily in small groups. It was only in larger groups and on formal occasions that she became silent. I thought we had made great progress the previous semester—she spoke a few times in my class and in others, and participated in all of the small-group discussions. As I was about to tell her mother that Susan had already given an oral report at the end of my course, I remembered that she hadn't. She'd

gotten sick and gone home early, reporting on neither her self-management project nor her other applied project for the course. It hadn't occurred to me until I was speaking with her mother that the illness was almost certainly related to Susan's anxiety about these oral reports. Realizing for the 88th time that I would never make a good clinician, I told Susan's mother that I was certain we could work something out. We could probably eliminate this anxiety before the end of the semester; but if we didn't, and if Susan still did not want to give an oral report, I thought I could arrange some alternative with the chairman of the department. I would find out and let her know the next day. Meanwhile, the mother would call Susan (who was out of town) and see if she would reconsider returning to college. She would and did.

Susan did her independent work with another student who also was worried about the final oral presentation; and they did their research under my direction, which made it easier for all of us to get together. In direct preparation for the oral report, they practiced telling me about their independent work. They described the apparatus, the behavior of the animals, their data, and so forth—all of the things they would eventually be telling other students and the assembled department. Then they told other people about these matters: first one person at a time, then two or three. Meanwhile, they worked on speaking up in class. As an early approximation, they wrote down the comments and questions that they *might* raise *if* they weren't afraid to. Later, they told a couple of professors what they were doing and got these instructors to forewarn them of questions that would be raised in class. They got friends to sit next to them and nudge them when it was appropriate to answer a "prepared" question from the instructor or to make one of the bright comments that they continued to write down during class. I also recommended the Lazarus (1970) relaxation tapes to counteract anxiety, but I am not sure how much time they spent with them.

As the time drew near, they decided that they did want to give an oral presentation —partly, I think, because they were excited about their data and wanted to share it. It was an imprinting study, so we took charming slides of chicks with hens and goats and puppies and donkeys; and we made transparencies of everything else to do with their talk so that they would never have to speak without something on the screen. They taped note cards to the transparencies so that they could appear to be looking at the data and not have to shuffle nervously through papers or cards. They practiced placing the pointer firmly *on* the transparency, not holding it above the transparency where the slightest tremble of the hand is magnified on the screen. They programmed interesting anecdotes for every section of the report. They planned and rehearsed every blessed detail of the presentation, with close friends and then with me, first in the familiar lab, and then in the room where the meetings would be held. I played the role of the chairman and introduced their paper. The great day dawned and no one was sick. By evening, no one was sick. They gave their report and it was beautiful. The following fall, Susan entered a paralegal program and she is now a lawyer's assistant, talking frequently—and apparently easily—before small groups and large.

It seems fairly obvious to "start with the possible" when we are building skills or prerequisite skills. It is also a reasonable procedure when we are trying to reduce or eliminate problem behavior. With consummatory behavior such as eating or drinking too much or smoking, we could start with those situations easiest to control. We are not saying that people shouldn't quit certain habits "cold turkey"; but if that solution has been tried a number of times without success, then perhaps something else is called for. A sequence analysis tells us the relative frequency of engaging in problem behavior in different settings. We can also rate the situations according to their importance. Someone

might smoke only one cigarette after breakfast, but that might be the "most important" cigarette of the day and thus the last to eliminate. One friend told me that waiting in the checkout line at the supermarket and thinking about all the money she would be spending was her most important occasion for a cigarette. So we might start with something relatively easy, perhaps not smoking while driving to work. And once successful in that situation, we might be encouraged to try another.

Goldiamond (1974) points out another reason why uniform programs to eliminate smoking have been unsuccessful. People smoke "for different reasons at different times," which is to say that in different situations, smoking is controlled by different stimuli. It might be relatively easy to change the discriminative stimuli for smoking in one room of the house (remove the ash trays and put up signs saying DANGER: EXPLOSIVES); and it might be relatively easy to find an alternative response to smoking while watching television (doing something like knitting that occupies both hands); but different programs may be needed in different settings.

d. Gradually raise the requirements

Any sort of programming involves starting with the possible and then gradually raising the requirements for reinforcement. In self-management, this is especially important because not only are we learning *how* to manage our behavior, we are learning that we *can* manage it. If we don't succeed in the early stages, we are likely to throw in the sponge.

Start with baseline. If you are averaging 3,000 calories a day, but this varies between 2,000 and 4,000 calories, then earning points for staying at or below 3,000 will usually lower the average. When you discover that life is worth living on 3,000 calories a day, then go for 2,700—or whatever seems reasonable in light of the problems encountered thus far. Remember that 3,400 calories corresponds to a pound of body weight. If your daily intake is 500 calories less than baseline, you'll lose a pound a week.

If studying averages only one hour a day, don't start by trying to increase the time *every* day. Some days will be so occupied with other important activities that it would be difficult to find extra time. Pick a day and a time that the sequence analysis shows you generally "do nothing," and raise the requirements for the week as a whole. If you are working on personal relations, start with small—or large—groups, whichever is more comfortable, and with the easiest possible topic of conversation. Increase the time you spend "relating" by seconds or by minutes. Get up a few minutes earlier in the morning; postpone the first cigarette of the day by a few minutes, and so forth. Then gradually increase the demands you place on your behavior as it becomes relatively easy to do so.

The other major principle of programming is to back up a little if you get in trouble. Failure to meet a subgoal or cheating or an almost intolerable temptation to cheat is an indication that you are moving ahead too rapidly.

6. Maintenance

Almost everyone who enters a self-management program to lose weight or stop smoking or drinking has done so before. And most people have succeeded for a while, but then gone off the diet or off the wagon and perhaps ended up worse off than before. Maintaining the gains is as important a goal as achieving them in the first place. The knowledge we acquire about our own behavior and the general information about the problem are probably permanent gains. If we stop a program too soon and lose the ground we've gained, we probably will not have to start again at the beginning with an analysis of the situation. But we will have to go back on some kind of program. Presumably, we have

learned how to manage our behavior and it should be easier a second time, but it is discouraging nonetheless. Better to program maintenance and transfer to the natural environment *before* a program is terminated and to gradually withdraw any "artificial" support.

The general rules for transferring to naturally occurring reinforcers and for broadening stimulus control have been described in Chapter 3. In one sense, they may be easier to follow with a self-management project than with a program designed by someone else (e.g., a parent or professor) because we ourselves have selected the goals. Presumably these are goals that will be useful in our particular environment: useful either because they enable us to accomplish something else that we want or because people will treat us more kindly or with more respect. In other words, there will probably be naturally occurring reinforcers to maintain our gains, but they may not occur as frequently—or on as many critical occasions—as during the program.

One way to handle maintenance is to write a series of contracts that gradually reduce the density of reinforcement and increase the settings in which the behavior will occur (or not occur). As with the earlier contracts, the purpose is to clarify and formalize the contingencies. If we have been monitoring and recording several classes of behavior, we might gradually eliminate some records; but it is essential to keep track of the main product or class of behavior (weight, hours worked, number of drinks) because we need this feedback to know how well the maintenance program is succeeding. Table 7.6 is a "forever contract," the last maintenance contract, written by the student who designed the program contract shown in Table 7.5. She has dropped nearly all of the requirements of her program and is now working under what amounts to avoidance contingencies. She will continue to weigh herself once a week and limit herself to two snacks a day. But she doesn't have

Table 7.6   **Maintenance contract** for weight control.

Name: _____   General Goal: *maintain weight loss* _____

Duration of Contract (dates) *4/20* to *5/20*.   Program ____ Maintenance *✓*

Data

    Keep daily ____ or *weekly* records of:

    _____   _____

    weight _____   _____

    _____   _____

    Data will be analysed and plotted: *weekly* _____

Program

    Behavior   Consequences

        only 2 snacks a day
        Try keep calories to 1800/day, but }   *see below*
            don't have to count

    Stimulus control

        no food in room

    Alternative behavior (if applicable)

    Covert (behavior, consequences)

                                    If points, possible daily total ____

    Bonus?

Exchange

                Reinforcers   (Aversive Consequences?)

        If gain more than 1 lb, go back to counting calories
        If "   "   "   3 ", back on whole program

Signature _____   Date _____

to count calories and keep all the records of Table 7.5 *unless* she starts to gain weight again. If she does gain more than one pound, then she has to go back to counting calories; and if she gains more than three pounds, she has to reinstate the entire program.

Because the maintenance of gains is the acid test of a program, we recommend practicing maintenance procedures before the final goal is reached. This could be especially helpful when achieving the final goal takes a long time. In a program for gradual weight loss, for example, we would recommend adhering to the program for three or four weeks—or until four or five pounds had been lost—and then going on a maintenance program for a week or ten days before resuming the program. Other things being equal, if you had been losing a pound a week you could take in 3,400 more calories a week during maintenance without gaining weight. This might be good for morale, and the experience might well prove valuable in designing the final maintenance program.

8

Ethical and Other Concerns

A. The Scope of Behavior Analysis
   1. Settings
   2. Areas of concern
      a. Education
      b. Programs in residential treatment facilities
      c. Rehabilitation
      d. Therapy, counseling, and social work
      e. Medicine
      f. Athletics
      g. Ecology and environmental concerns
      h. Communities
      i. Measurement of sensory capacities
      j. Self-control
      k. Teaching applied behavior analysis

B. Accountability
   1. Therapist competence
   2. Informed consent
      a. Goals
      b. Procedures
      c. Cost and duration of treatment
      d. Measures to evaluate treatment
   3. Continuing evaluation of treatment
   4. Right to terminate treatment
   5. Right to privacy
   6. Transfer to natural environment and self-management
   7. Follow-up
   8. Fees
   9. Written agreement
C. The Transitory Nature of Models
D. Freedom

A. The Scope of Behavior Analysis

A few decades ago, the naturalist who wanted to observe that rare specimen, a behaviorist, would have traveled to its natural habitat: a small burrow in the basement (or attic) of a university laboratory. If the behaviorist could not be spotted foraging for data among its usual prey, *Rattus rattus*, it could easily be traced to a neighboring burrow where it engaged in the curious behavior of designing and building apparatus. (Like Darwin's finches, it had discovered the use of tools.) Data-gathering behavior has proved adaptive; and behaviorists have increased, multiplied and spread across the land where they now occupy a broad ecological niche. Before addressing some of the questions these developments have raised, let us briefly survey the territory that behaviorists have now "invaded."

The activities of behaviorists are chronicled in a dozen journals founded for this purpose,[1] and a great many articles on applied behavior analysis appear in other journals as well.[2] There are also five annual reviews of behavioral publications. More than 520 books, published between 1900–1972, are listed in Drash and Freeman's (1973) bibliography of behavior modification, behavior therapy, and operant conditioning; and most of the thousands of published articles can be located with the help of Klein's (1973) *bibliography of bibliographies* on behavior modification.[3] There are also professional meetings, both national and regional, at which psychologists gather to present their research and discuss the issues it raises.

Table 8.1 lists *some* of the topics discussed at a recent gathering of behaviorists: The second Annual Convention of the Midwestern Association of Behavior Analysis (May 1–4, 1976). The 441 research papers, workshops, symposia, and major speeches covered a wide range of topics and addressed a number of practical and theoretical issues. Although MABA is not the largest organization of behavioral psychologists,

the convention proceedings fairly represent the concerns and activities of other behaviorists throughout the country, and indeed, the world. Table 8.1 indicates some of the areas where they are directing their efforts.

1. Settings

Behaviorists have joined forces with teachers and other members of the educational profession to develop and implement more effective teaching procedures. They first entered the pre-

1. English-language journals and the date of first publication include: *Journal of the Experimental Analysis of Behavior* (1958), *Behaviour Research and Therapy* (1963), *Journal of Applied Behavior Analysis* (1968), *SALT: School Applications of Learning Theory* (1968), *Behavior Therapy* (1970), *Journal of Behavior Therapy and Experimental Psychiatry* (1970), *Learning and Motivation* (1970), *Behaviorism* (1972), and *Behavior Modification* (1977). Annuals and their publishers include: *Advances in Behavior Therapy* (Academic Press), *Annual Review of Behavior Therapy: Theory and Practice* (Brunner/Mazel), *Behavior Change* (formerly *Psychotherapy and Behavior Change*; Aldine), *Biofeedback and Self-Control* (Aldine), and *Progress in Behavior Modification* (Academic Press). Foreign journals include: the *European Journal of Behavioural Analysis and Modification*, the *Mexican Journal of Behavior Analysis/Revista Mexicana de Análisis de la Conducta*, and the *Scandinavian Journal of Behaviour Therapy*. Societies for behavior analysis have been founded in Brazil, Canada, Greece, Great Britain, Mexico, The Netherlands, and Sweden.

2. In 1974, more than 10 percent of the articles published in the following journals reported research in applied behavior analysis: *American Educational Research Journal* (14.3 percent), *Journal of Child Psychology and Psychiatry* (11.1 percent), *Journal of Speech and Hearing Disorders* (13.6 percent), *Mental Retardation* (10.7 percent), *Psychology in the Schools* (15.9 percent). (Figures from Kazdin, 1975b.)

3. Klein's annotated list describes 32 bibliographies, some of which contain more than 1,000 entries. These bibliographies cover a wide range of topics, including: *alcoholism* (Wisocki & Cautela, 1968, 107 items), *children* (Shack & Barnett, 1973, 462 items), *educational settings* (Berkowitz, 1968, 268 items), *nursing* (Baron, 1969, 21 items), and *token economies* (Kazdin, 1972b, 134 items). Additional specialized bibliographies which have appeared since 1973 include Bornstein's (1974) list of 209 books and articles concerning the *training of parents* as behavior modifiers; Shorkey, Himle, and Collins's (1974) annotated bibliography of behavior modification in *groups* (77 items); and Wenrich and LeTendre's (1975) annotated bibliography on the operant control of *autonomic behavior* (237 items).

Table 8.1 **Summary of addresses, paper sessions, workshops and symposia** presented at a single meeting of the Midwestern Association of Behavior Analysis.[4]

TOPICS TREATED AT A SINGLE MEETING OF MABA

Assessment
Autism
   design and management of programs
   self-injury
   self-stimulation
   student *practica* with

Basic Research
   adjunctive behavior
   alcohol
   animal psychophysics
   apparatus
   autoshaping
   aversive control
   choice and preference
   classical conditioning
   comparative psychology
   conditioned suppression
   comparisons among procedures
   fading
   memory
   past history
   pharmacology (drug effects)
   physiology
   schedules of reinforcement
   stimulus control
Biofeedback
   migraine headaches
   sensory mode and muscle relaxation
   skin temperature
   variables affecting success of
Business and Industry
   absenteeism
   accidents (assembly lines; open-pit mining)
   employee turnover
   employees: grocery clerks, machinists, miners, textile
      workers, unit staff, university faculty
   "in-house" training in behavior analysis
   job accountability
   pay schedules and performance
   projects in large industrial corporations

Community Settings
   community-based education
   experimental communities ("Walden")
   mass-media techniques
   multiple-handicapped center
   rehabilitation programs
   senior citizens
   sheltered workshops
Contracting (Contingency)
   designing and implementing
   in foster homes
   with high-school students
   and PSI
   and self-control
Counseling
   career
   consultation skills

drugs
high school
marriage
parent
Creative Behavior
   defining
   training
   transfer of

Delinquency
   behavioral analysis of criminal responsibility
   community-based treatment
   home-based treatment of probationers
   resocialization of delinquent girls
   shoplifting (prevention of)
   stealing in second graders
   truancy and school failure
Drugs
   basic research
   drug-counselor training
   high-school students
   paraprofessional help
   self-regulation in alcohol treatment
   smoking
   social drinking
   use of with young children, retardates

Ecology
   behavioral analysis of transportation problems
   car pooling
   conservation of electricity, gasoline
   environmental health
   littering

Education
   Special Education
      classroom programming
      programs for mainstreaming
   Preschool
      academic skills (math, reading, handwriting)
      compensatory education
      motor skills
      preschool education at home
      programs and learning environments
   Elementary
      attention from principal as reinforcer
      lunchroom behavior
      multiplication
      syntactical reasoning
      systems approach
   Junior High School
      classroom programs
      teaching behavioral psychology in
   High School
      behavioral counseling programs

4.The 2nd Annual Convention of the Midwestern Association of Behavior Analysis, May 1-4, 1976.

Table 8.1 (Continued)

Table 8.1 (Continued)

low-income paraprofessionals
parents and future parents
practica and internship training
students: elementary, high school, undergraduate,
    graduate
	sentences; approximations to ordinary conversation;
	    social prerequisites of,
	speech anxiety
	spelling and reading
	stuttering
	syntactical reasoning

Verbal Behavior communication skills of therapy supervisors conditioning verbal behavior in control of rage development of stimulus classes family-based speech programs functional analysis of delusional speech language acquisition in children and retarded: complex	**Weight Control** anorexia nervosa excessive eating nutritionists as therapists transfer from therapist control to self-control

school classroom and have now progressed through elementary and high school to university and graduate programs. Other institutional settings include hospitals and clinics of all kinds, nursing homes, summer camps, and the armed services. Educational and other rehabilitation programs have been developed in prisons and in homes or special schools that offer an alternative to prison. Community programs are located in day-care centers, sheltered workshops, and halfway houses. The family home has long been a setting for applied behavior analysis; the business establishment is becoming one. Hamner and Hamner (1976) review applications of behavioral procedures in a variety of industrial settings; and Feeney publishes *Performance Improvement Magazine,* which integrates behavioral procedures with those of industrial management. Another recent setting is the veterinarian's office where behavioral procedures are being used to eliminate neurotic behavior in animals (Tuber et al., 1974).

2. Areas of Concern

a. Education

The early efforts of behaviorists working in classroom settings were often aimed at reducing disruptive behavior (Winett & Winkler, 1972). This was partly on request: Teachers were the ex-

perts on educational matters; psychologists were called in to handle "problem" behavior. (It may also have had something to do with the fact that most early behaviorists were not personally concerned with elementary education until their own children entered the school system.) At any rate, they are now actively involved in both normal and special education and in the development of effective procedures to teach physical, social, and vocational skills as well as academic subject matter. In 1968, Sidney Bijou outlined the possibilities in an address to the School Psychologists of the American Psychological Association. His paper, *What psychology has to offer education–Now,* is still well worth reading. Bijou's offer has found many takers, and the contributions of behavior analysis to elementary and secondary education are now well documented (e.g., O'Leary & O'Leary, 1972; Sulzer & Mayer, 1972, 1977). One highly successful program—Don Bushell's "Follow Through"[5]—has enabled more than 7,000 disadvantaged children to function at or above the level of their more fortunate peers, and their gains have been maintained for years. Behavioral psychologists are also concerned with the conditions and procedures that favor the development of creative behavior (the topic

5. For further information, write Dr. Donald Bushell, Dept. of Human Development, University of Kansas, Lawrence, Kansas 66045.

of four papers and one invited address at MABA).

Behavior analysis is also contributing to higher education. At the college level (and in industry and the armed services) self-paced or personalized instruction (PSI) is enabling large numbers of students to acquire new levels of competence. Mastery, rather than mere exposure to the material, is the goal and the result. Programs have been developed for more than 40 academic disciplines, ranging from architecture to zoology and including poetry, music, and medicine. Keller and Koen (in press) and Sherman (1974) review the history, the potential, and the current status of personalized systems of instruction.

b. Programs in residential treatment facilities for retarded and psychiatric patients

Many programs are concerned with the development of self-help skills. Residents learn (or relearn) to dress and feed themselves and to care for their personal hygiene. Other programs prepare the resident for eventual discharge and cover a broad range of abilities: asking questions, telling time, making change, reading and ordering from menus, using public telephones and transportation, shopping and housekeeping chores, as well as vocational training (See Atthowe, 1976; Ayllon & Azrin, 1968).

c. Rehabilitation

Many residents move from institutions to halfway houses or sheltered workshops, some sponsored by the local community and some by the institution from which the resident has been discharged (See Atthowe, 1973, 1976; Cull & Hardy, 1974; Sanders, 1975). These settings are designed to favor the maintenance and generalization of previously acquired skills as well as the acquisition of new ones. Project Threshold (Southeastern Massachusetts University) draws up contracts with community rehabilitation programs on behalf of retarded adults who fail to meet the acceptance criteria of the particular programs. The missing skills are specified, and the individual is guaranteed admission to the program when the Project Threshold personnel have taught the prerequisite skills (Riley & Holt, 1976).

Physical therapy is another area of rehabilitation, one where shaping procedures are particularly useful. As an adjunct to shaping, biofeedback from muscle activity (EMG) has enabled paralyzed patients to regain muscular control (Blanchard & Young, 1974). Ince (1976) describes the application of a broad range of behavioral procedures to the field of rehabilitation medicine.

The rehabilitation of criminals and juvenile delinquents poses many ethical and practical problems, particularly among prison populations. Although some behavioral programs (Cohen & Filipczak, 1971; Milan & McKee, 1974) appear promising, others do not. (See Kennedy, 1976, for a review and analysis of behavior modification programs in prisons.) Programs for delinquents outside the prison environment have fared better. The "family-style" program, exemplified by Achievement Place, is probably the most successful of all (Fixsen et al., 1976; Phillips, 1968; Phillips et al., 1973). The original program and its encouraging results are briefly described in Chapter 3. There are now several homes across the country, patterned after Achievement Place—and 400 ex-delinquents (Braukman & Kirigan, 1976).

d. Therapy, counseling, and social work

The use of both operant and respondent procedures in therapy has been documented throughout this book. Behavioral procedures are also proving useful in marriage and family counseling; in social skills training; in high school and college centers for career counseling as well as test anxiety, study skills, and other academic problems; and in "hot line" emergency services such as the American University crisis intervention telephone service (Krieger, Wasserman, Berman, McCarthy, & Krieger, 1975). Community programs using behavioral procedures are described by Liberman (1973) and Tharp and Wetzel (1969). Fischer and Gochros (1976) and Jehu, Hardiker, Yelloly, and Shaw (1972) have adapted the basic procedures to the needs of social workers (See also Hersen & Eisler, 1976; Knox, 1971; Krumboltz & Thoresen, 1969, 1976; Miller & Miller, 1970; Schwartz & Goldiamond, 1975).

e. Medicine

Behavioral principles procedures are now being taught in some medical schools and incorporated into the analysis and treatment of many medical problems. In addition to the case studies already described, relaxation training and sometimes biofeedback training have been helpful in treating cardiovascular problems, tension headaches, and asthma; and a variety of gastrointestinal and neurological problems have responded to omission training and the reinforcement of alternative behavior. Fordyce (1976), who has long been a leader in the field, describes the treatment and management of chronic pain. (See also Houts & Hench, 1976; Ince, 1976; Katz & Zlutnick, 1974; Knapp & Peterson, 1976; LeBow, 1973; Williams & Gentry, 1976.)

f. Athletics

Rushall and Siedentop (1972) have written a book on the applications of behavioral procedures to physical education, and Suinn (1976) is counseling Olympic athletes.

g. Ecology and environmental concerns

Behavioral procedures are now being directed toward the solution of such ecological problems as littering, the purchase of nonreturnable bottles, the use of public transportation, and the other topics listed in Table 8.1. This literature is reviewed by Kazdin (1977). Efforts are also being made to identify and manage the relevant variables in family planning and population control (Zifferblatt & Hendricks, 1974). (See also Chapman & Risley, 1974; Clark, Burgess, & Hendee, 1972; Everett, Hayward, & Meyers, 1974; Geller, Farris, & Post, 1973; Geller, Wylie, & Farris, 1971; Hayes, Johnson, & Cone, 1975; Poché & Bailey, 1976; Powers, Osborne & Anderson, 1973.)

h. Communities designed on behavioral principles

In an attempt to manage many aspects of their environment, some people have joined together in communities organized around the principles of applied behavior analysis. Two of the better known behavioral communities are Twin Oaks in Virginia and The University of Kansas Experimental Living Project. Twin Oaks, inspired by Skinner's *Walden Two*, was established in 1967 and has survived many vicissitudes, carefully documented by Kincade (1973). The Kansas project is a small community of 30 university students; and, unlike Twin Oaks, was founded in 1972 by practicing behavioral psychologists who are collecting data on several aspects of the program (Miller, 1976; Miller & Feallock, 1975). This project appears to be quite successful, but since all of the students are unmarried, it has not yet encountered the particular problems that arise in communities of families.

i. The measurement of sensory capacities

In many cases, particularly with retarded or brain-damaged individuals, it is difficult to measure visual and auditory capacities. Yet this diagnostic information is needed to select remedial aids, such as prescription glasses, and to design effective training programs for the particular individual. Behavioral procedures, including fading and special programming of reinforcement, have provided sensitive threshold measures (Bricker & Bricker, 1970; Macht, 1971; Meyerson & Michael, 1964; Reese et al.,

1977; Rosenberger, 1974; Sidman & Stoddard, 1967).

j. Self-control

This major area of concern to behavior analysts has been discussed in Chapter 7.

k. Teaching applied behavior analysis

The burgeoning application of behavioral procedures has created problems in the training of a sufficient number of practitioners. The principles and procedures are gradually being included into the curricula of several graduate and professional schools (particularly in psychology and education; more slowly in medicine, nursing, and social work); and courses are now being offered in some high schools and many colleges. But probably few of the parents, siblings, peers, teachers, students, counselors, nurses, social workers, and institutional staff who are currently using behavioral procedures received any training in behavior analysis as part of their formal education. More likely, their training was provided by individual therapists or counselors working with individual clients and their families, or by consultants who offer workshops and concentrated training programs.[6] A recent book, edited by Yen and McIntire (1976), assesses the effectiveness of several training programs for parents and teachers, and describes a number of programs and practica now being offered at the undergraduate and graduate level in universities and professional schools. The major problem of evaluating the effectiveness of training is addressed by several of the authors and by Wood (1975). See also Ramp & Semb, 1975.

B. Accountability

The widespread application of behavioral procedures has naturally aroused concern among behaviorists as well as many laymen and members of other professions. Some of the concern arises from misinformation; but in some cases, programs have been implemented without proper supervision and evaluation, and without due regard for the ethical considerations that should govern all of the helping professions. As Brown, Wienckowski, and Stolz (1975) point out, "Behavior modification programs have an additional special ethical problem because the procedures are generally simple enough to be used by persons lacking the training to evaluate them properly." These authors suggest that all decision-making responsibilities be assumed by a supervisory committee of three persons with the necessary expertise.

Behavioral psychologists are carefully examining the competencies that should be required of those who have varying degrees of responsibility for implementing programs (Sulzer-Azaroff, Thaw, & Thomas, 1975); and consideration is being given to certification requirements for those who would call themselves behavior therapists or behavior modifiers. Whether or not these additional certification requirements are finally adopted, the client's surest protection will rest upon therapist accountability.

We said earlier, and it bears repeating, that a defining characteristic of behavior modification is the objective evaluation of treatment. This means (1) that educational and therapeutic procedures *derive* from empirical research and (2) that as these procedures are *applied* to individual cases, objective criteria are used to evaluate their effectiveness in each particular

---

6. The dates and places of many workshops are listed in two monthly publications of the American Psychological Association: *American Psychologist* and *The APA Monitor*. Two people who have had extensive experience in conducting workshops and other training programs for parents, teachers, and institutional staff are Vance Hall (H & H Enterprises, Dept. J, Box 3342, Lawrence, Kansas) and Luke Watson (Behavior Modification Technology, Box 597, Libertyville, Illinois). Hall's programs are primarily for school personnel and parents, Watson's for institutional personnel.

case. This allows the client to examine the evidence concerning any procedure that might be used and to judge its effectiveness during therapy.

But accountability goes beyond these generalities. Accountability depends upon data because no objective evaluation is possible without data. Beyond this obvious fact, it seems reasonable to expect that all those who engage in therapy, particularly those who accept compensation for their services, will specify the responsibilities they will assume and the ways in which they will be accountable to their clients. Therapists should also specify the responsibilities they will *not* assume and the ways in which they will *not* be accountable to their client. In other words, the therapeutic ''package'' should be clearly labeled.

Table 8.2 is an attempt to list the major dimensions of therapist accountability. Although the terms are addressed to therapy, we look forward to the day when they will be more widely adopted by educators.

Table 8.2   Dimensions of accountability in therapy.

DIMENSIONS OF ACCOUNTABILITY

1. Therapist Competence

2. Informed Consent
   a. goals
   b. procedures (including negative effects)
   c. cost and duration of treatment
   d. measures to evaluate treatment

3. Continuing Evaluation of Treatment

4. Right to Terminate

5. Right to Privacy

6. Transfer to Natural Environment and Self-Management

7. Follow-up

8. Fees: Contingent on Expenses and Success

9. Written Agreement

Their willingness to accept the remaining measures of accountability listed in Table 8.2 might be considered an indirect measure of competence, particularly if they agree that treatment should be defined in terms of success.

1. Therapist Competence

Competence is determined by licensing and certification programs, and the client can get some notion of the therapist's qualifications from the degrees, licenses, and memberships held. Along with stating their qualifications, therapists are expected to inform their clients of those medical or technical areas in which they are *not* qualified, and to refer them to specialists as the occasion warrants. At present, there is no official program (several are under consideration) for licensing behavior therapists as distinguished from psychologists and psychiatrists of other orientations.[7] Those who are not psychiatrists would be expected to be licensed to practice psychology.

It is difficult to gauge the *continuing* competence of therapists, particularly when they develop or incorporate new procedures.

2. Informed Consent

Informed consent is an accepted precondition of therapy, but it is not always clear who is qualified to give consent and under what conditions of possible duress, nor is it always clear what the consenter should be informed about.

Usually, consent is obtained from the client or from a parent or legal guardian, but there is now a movement to interest other people in serving as *advocates* for those who cannot act on their own behalf. For example, at the Mansfield Training School, Mansfield, Connecticut, several residents are represented by advocates to whom the school is accountable. The advo-

7. Beth Sulzer-Azaroff has proposed a list of competencies for behavior modifiers. Whether or not these competencies are adopted for certification, they constitute a clear ''definition'' of a behavior modifier (Sulzer-Azaroff et al., 1975).

cates may be law students, teachers, members of the clergy, or other interested citizens.[8]

Informed consent should, of course, be free consent, not consent obtained under duress. If a patient or prisoner is promised release contingent upon completing a course of treatment, the consent to undergo treatment can hardly be called free. (See Goldiamond, 1976a, for a discussion of this issue.)

To be considered informed, the client or the client's advocate should have detailed information about the goals of the program, the alternative procedures that might be employed, the probable cost and duration of treatment with various procedures, and the measures that will be used to evaluate the outcome of treatment.

a. Goals

We have already said that the goals in behavior-change programs should be those that enable the individuals to maximize their physical, social, and intellectual potential, taking into consideration the future consequences of their behavior for other individuals and for the environment. In a given instance, there may be alternate routes to this ideal state; or the therapist may be aware of problems—to the client or to others—that might accompany the attainment of a particular goal. In either case, the client must be fully informed of alternative goals and the possible concomitants of achieving them before a reasonable choice can be made.

Many residents in mental institutions are now being taught self-help or self-maintenance skills. Programs have been developed for a number of basic skills including toilet training, feeding, and dressing. Here, a question is sometimes raised as to who is the client: the resident or the attendant? Does the resident really *want* to acquire cleaning, feeding, or dressing skills? Or to serve meals and sort laundry? Do these skills enable residents to realize their physical, social, or intellectual potential, or do they just make life easier for the staff? The answer is probably both. When residents have acquired such

self-maintenance skills then they will probably become eligible for grounds passes and for educational programs and occupational therapy. Ayllon has said that "our goal must be to enable the patient to experience dignity by becoming useful to himself and to others" (Ayllon, 1967, p. 248).

b. Procedures

Accountability means that therapeutic procedures derive from empirical research and that the evidence is made available to the client, who may examine the results of clinical tests. Some nonbehavioral procedures (such as surgery or electroconvulsive shock) are irreversible. Here, it is especially important that the client be informed of the incidence of negative results. In any case, alternative procedures should be explored, and their effects and possible side effects discussed. If drugs, such as amphetamines for "hyperactive" children, are recommended, the client should inquire what *else* is to be done. If the answer amounts to "nothing," consent might be withheld, at least until more data are available on the short- and long-term effects of these drugs.[9]

c. Cost and duration of treatment

Consent can hardly be informed unless the client is apprised of the cost, in time, money, emotion, and stress, of various procedures to

---

8. For further information about the advocacy movement, write Jack Thaw, Mansfield Training School, Mansfield Depot, Connecticut.

9. Sprague is assessing the short- and long-term effects of stimulant medication on hyperactive and minimally brain-damaged children. He reports that a dose of 0.30mg./kg. methylphenidate provides the greatest enhancement of learning performance and that significant increases in heart rate and blood pressure accompany higher dosages of 0.60 mg./kg. even though "these dosages are considerably below the recommended dose of 2.00 mg./kg. From these data, it is quite clear that the clinical titration method is resulting in much higher dosages for children than are needed to control hyperactivity and to produce the optimal learning enhancement" (Sprague, 1974, p. 4). (See also Liberman & Davis, 1975.)

achieve various goals. The cost would include therapist fees, number of visits, duration of treatment, and any other expenses or effort that might be incurred in conjunction with the proposed program: data collection, telephone calls, or even a new wardrobe to enhance the client's self-esteem. Where costs and efforts vary, the range and median can be indicated.

d. Measures to evaluate treatment

Finally, informed consent should be based upon a knowledge of what measures will be taken to evaluate the success of the program and a guarantee that these data will be shared with the client.

In a behavioral program, the client will almost certainly be required to keep data, perhaps on several classes of behavior. If such an agreement is not reached, or if the client agrees but then fails to keep accurate records, it may not be possible to assess the progress of treatment. There are thus practical, as well as ethical, reasons that the client be fully informed of all responsibilities before consenting to a course of treatment.

3. Continuing Evaluation of Treatment

The client aims to get help, the therapist to give it. Both go to considerable trouble to establish goals and to select procedures to achieve them. How will they know if their goals are reached? If the procedures are effective? What *is* treatment anyway? In an article which appeared in the *Harvard Civil Rights-Civil Liberties Law Review*, Schwitzgebel (1973) argues that "Treatment should be defined in terms of results, not just procedures or the intent to produce results" (p. 522) and that "Ineffective treatment is not better than no treatment, it's just more expensive (p. 521).[10]

If Schwitzgebel's position is accepted—as it most emphatically is by behaviorists—then the problem becomes one of selecting valid measures of effective treatment. There are many sorts of data, but we need measures of *improvement*, not just the kind and amount of medication or the number of hours in therapy. These statistics are important in evaluating the relative effectiveness of different procedures with different clients, but they do not measure the effectiveness of therapy with a particular client.

A client who wants to cut down on drinking can decide how much alcohol constitutes "a drink" and then count the number of drinks consumed each day. The client might also count the number of times a drink is desired and note the conditions under which this desire occurs. If the therapist and client conclude that drinking is only part of the problem, they might decide to measure additional classes of behavior such as the amount of time the client engages in productive work or the number of times a family argument takes place. If the goals include drinking less than three ounces of alcohol a day as well as working at least 30 hours and arguing no more than twice a week, then treatment is effective to the extent that these goals are reached.

If the problem is one of increasing the client's self-esteem, the client and therapist must decide what they mean by self-esteem in order to know when they have increased it. One person might count the number of compliments and invitations received. Another might count the number of times he spoke up in class or otherwise behaved in an assertive manner. Yet another might decide on a rating scale, either a standardized test or a scale devised for the individual. Very different measures, true; but *what we mean is what we measure*. If we don't measure anything . . . ?

---

10. Schwitzgebel, whose degrees include a Doctor of Education and a Doctor of Jurisprudence, is a Lecturer in Psychology in the Department of Psychiatry at Harvard Medical School.

Even when therapists recognize the need for data, it may be some time before the clients recognize that they really want data, too: Without objective measures, neither of them will be able to assess the progress of treatment. Therapists who fail to get this point across may also fail to get the data that allow them to be accountable to their clients and to their profession.

4. Right to Terminate Treatment

The client may move out of state, become ill, go broke, fall in or out of love with the therapist, become disenchanted with data collection, or become disenchanted with what the data show. For any of the above, or for any other reason, the client should have the right to terminate participation in the program. Even if the client does not request it, the therapist should suggest termination if there is no measurable progress.

5. Right to Privacy

Even when therapy is not specifically part of a program of research, many therapists incorporate clinical material in their teaching or writing. Many valuable contributions to psychology and medicine first appear in case histories. However, unless the client gives specific written permission, clinical material is confidential and can be used only when the client's identity is disguised beyond possibility of recognition. Even then, written consent is advisable.

Clients should also be protected from unnecessary inconvenience and intrusions into their private affairs. In many cases, data obtained by the client are subjected to reliability checks by either a covert or overt observer. The client should be informed in advance of the fact, if not the timing, of these observations; and the observer should be as unobtrusive as possible.

6. Transfer to Natural Environment and Self-Management

From the very beginning, therapists should plan for the time when their counsel is no longer needed and incorporate procedures that will facilitate transfer from the office, clinic, or special classroom. Whenever possible, the program should be designed in consultation with those who will carry it out: if not the client, then members of the family, or classroom or institutional personnel. These individuals will then be in a better position to assume increasing responsibility as the therapist gradually withdraws support.

Preparation for transfer might include education in self-management or training in the use of special procedures. In the classroom or institutional situation, it is important that several different people consistently employ any special procedures in several different settings. Otherwise the client's improvement may be restricted to one setting or to the presence of one person.

It is essential that evaluation continue during transfer so the therapist will know how well it is going and be able to make any necessary changes. Unless the client is doing the recording, other people may have to be trained to collect and assess data. In either case, reliability checks may be required.

7. Follow-Up

Continued evaluation in the form of follow-up data benefits the therapist and other clients as well as the client whose formal treatment has ended. It benefits the client because the therapist may detect potential problems at an early stage when remediation is relatively easy. Follow-up data benefit the therapist and other clients no matter what they show. If all is well, the data are a general endorsement of the treatment and transfer procedures, and the therapist will be encouraged to adapt them to similar situations. If all is not well, the problem may be traced to some aspect of these procedures that would then be scrapped or revised.

8. Fees

Before agreeing to a course of therapy, the client should be informed of the therapist's fees, what they will cover, and when they will be paid. If a per-session rate is established, then the probable number of sessions should be stated in advance.

There is a growing feeling among behaviorists that professional fees should be based on the success of therapy. For example, Ayllon and Skuban (1973) made an agreement with their clients that if the specified objectives of therapy were not reached in 35 days, the therapist would forfeit one-third of the fee (Table 3.12). Robertshaw and Johnson (1974) charged a minimal fee of two dollars per session, with additional amounts to be paid as the client attained each of the several goals of the program.

Fees are sometimes made contingent upon some aspect of the client's performance that the therapist considers essential to treatment. Knox (1973) uses this procedure in marriage counseling when the clients agree to keep daily records of the behavior they wish to increase. By contractual agreement, if the clients bring the data to their weekly session with the therapist, the fee for the next session is reduced by a certain amount. If the client "forgets," the fee for the next session is increased by that same amount. Similarly, Eyberg and Johnson (1974) gradually returned the client's advance deposit, contingent upon attendance at therapy sessions and collection of data.

9. Written Agreement

When the conditions of therapy—including fees, goals and procedures, and the specific re-

sponsibilities of both parties—have been agreed upon, it is good policy to put these conditions in writing. Even if the signed agreement is not legally binding, it represents a formal commitment from both client and therapist. It may also serve to jog their memories and to prevent misunderstandings. An agreement can cover the expected duration of therapy, or it can be changed from week to week or upon the attainment of a specified goal.

As early as 1962, Edward Sulzer proposed that the therapist is the agent of the client and that a formal contract should be agreed to before therapy begins. Apparently Sulzer did not publish any examples of a therapeutic contract, but other therapists now have. Table 8.3 is a general contract prepared by Richard Stuart. (Other contracts and general rules for writing them have been described in Chapter 3.) Stuart's contract illustrates nearly all of the criteria that have been suggested for accountability: therapist competence (item 1); informed consent with respect to goals (2; A) and procedures (3, 4; B) including references to published research (3a, b) and the possibility of undesirable side effects (5; E); the cost (D) and duration (4) of treatment; specification of the measures that will be taken to evaluate the effectiveness of the program (6; C); the right to privacy (G); and the right to terminate treatment (F). The only issues not specifically mentioned in the form are transfer and follow-up, and these might be included among the procedures entered under (3).

C. The Transitory Nature of Models

Another matter that might be considered an ethical issue is the tendency of some scientists to cling to a model "till death do them part." We are referring to scientific dogmatism and an attitude that says "my model must be right." Throughout this text we have stressed procedures, but taken all together they constitute a

Table 8.3   Client-therapist treatment contract illustrating major dimensions of accountability. (Prepared by Richard B. Stuart; copyright Research Press, Champaign, Ill.)

Name of Client: Name of therapist:

  Address: Title:

  Phone: Organization:

                                                       Highest academic degree:

                                                       License:

1. I, the above named therapist, certify that I am (circle one) duly licensed to offer the services described below or under the supervision of _____
                                   (Name, address)
who is so licensed.

2. I have assessed the client's behavior change objective(s) in the following manner: _____

3. I propose to use the following intervention technique(s) in my effort to assist the client to achieve the above objective(s):

   a. This (these) technique(s) have been fully described in the following standard professional reference: _____

   b. The most recent comprehensive account of the clinical results achieved with this (these) technique(s) may be found in the following source(s):_____

4. It is expected that this (these) intervention technique(s) will have the following beneficial effects for the client by the dates specified: _____

5. It is also noted that this (these) intervention technique(s) may be associated with the following undesirable side effect(s): __

6. Both the progress toward achieving the specified objectives and the potential side effects will be monitored continuously in the following manner(s): _____

_____   _____
   Date   Signature of Therapist

A. I, the above named client, assert that I have discussed the above named objectives for the change of my behavior and that I consent to work toward the achievement of those objectives.
B. I further assert that I have discussed the above named intervention technique(s) with the therapist and that I consent to apply these techniques.
C. I further assert that I shall provide the above named data in order to determine the effectiveness of the use of the intervention technique(s).
D. I further assert that I shall provide the therapist with the following compensation for his or her efforts in my behalf: _____
E. I further assert that I have freely entered into this contract knowing the therapeutic objectives and both the positive and negative potential effects of the intervention technique(s).
F. I further assert that I have been assured of my right to terminate my participation in treatment at any time, for any reason, and without the need to offer an explanation.
G. I further specifically limit the above named therapist's use of any information which can in any way identify me to others unless I have offered my specific, written permission.

_____ _____ _____
   Date   Signature of Client   Signature of Witness

Copyright 1975, Research Press, Champaign, Ill.

model for behavior modification. There are many other models, or if you prefer, procedures for behavior modification. It is probably a truism that everyone who ever engaged in helping people has been successful with someone. It makes no difference whether the therapist be behaviorist, parish priest, rabbi, family physician, psychiatrist, or psychoanalyst. All have been successful in helping people, and all will continue to do so. The fact that the procedures described in this book have been responsible for what may be described as a ''breakthrough'' in handling behavioral problems that have long proved intractable, and in handling less stubborn problems with greater efficiency, should blind no one to the other fact that this is just a beginning. There will always be a better way. The history of science is the history of the rise and fall of models.

We hope that we can avoid the problem of dogmatism by our emphasis on empirical data and objective evaluation, by treasuring the component of behavior modification that sets it apart from other clinical models: *accountability*.

D. Freedom

And now we have come full circle, or if not full circle, back to Chapter 1 where we briefly discussed that bugaboo of uninformed critics of behavior modification and the legitimate concern of its informed critics: the control of behavior. Not so long ago, many critics maintained that while operant procedures might affect certain classes of behavior in certain lower organisms confined to certain sorts of very restricted environments, these same procedures would never adequately describe or affect the behavior of higher organisms (like critics). Now it is generally recognized that our behavior is, indeed, affected by its consequences, and in

fairly predictable ways. So, recent objections to operant procedures are not that the procedures are *in*effective, but that they may be *too* effective, and that they may be employed by a few powerful souls to make robots of us all. This possibility is as abhorrent to behaviorists as to anyone else. And this is one reason they are so adamant about effective guarantees of accountability. It is quite true that behavioral procedures could be used to restrict the diversity of interests and actions that most of us now enjoy. We could, for example, decrease a person's behavioral repertoire by withholding reinforcement for various classes of behavior or by removing the opportunity to engage in these activities. But we can do just the opposite; we can enlarge a person's repertoire by making reinforcement contingent upon a greater variety of activities. Presumably this is one of the objectives of a college education. A person who has a limited behavioral repertoire and whose behavior produces a limited variety of reinforcers may be considered a person with very little freedom. On the other hand, a person who can read and write and speak effectively—who has, perhaps, artistic, or athletic, or mechanical skills—such a person has the freedom to pursue a variety of vocational and avocational endeavors.

Freedom, defined in these terms, is indeed a function of behavioral control, but the relation need not be inverse. We can design an environment that favors an extensive behavioral repertoire and thereby increases our freedom, or we can design an environment that restricts our repertoire and thereby our freedom. The effective control of behavior can do much more. Speaking before the Royal Society, Skinner offers us this alternative:

It could well be that an effective technology of teaching will be unwisely used. It could destroy initiative and creativity, it could make men all alike (and not necessarily in being equally excellent), it could suppress the beneficial effect of accidents upon the development of the individual and upon the evolution of a culture. On the other hand, it could maximize the genetic endowment of each student, it could make him as skillful, competent, and informed as possible, it could build the greatest diversity of interests, it could lead him to make the greatest possible contribution to the survival and development of his culture. (Skinner, B. F. The technology of teaching. *Proceedings of the Royal Society,* B, 1965, *162,* 427–443. [p. 442])

The question is not one of control *per se*. That is what parents, educators, therapists, clergymen, and statesmen have been doing all along, and what they will continue to do unless they forfeit their opportunities and responsibilities and leave the modification of behavior to others or to chance. The essential question is how do we use our increasing knowledge of

behavior to best advantage?—A question that becomes more pressing as the techniques of behavioral control become more effective. This is a matter that concerns all of us, as all of us exercise control over our families and friends, and all of us delegate control to professionals in education, government, and law. We can close our eyes to the techniques of behavior control and risk everything, or we can use these techniques effectively to create the kind of world we want to live in. The latter course requires that we keep informed. Fortunately, the science of behavior is neither esoteric nor obscure. It is a young science, an exciting one, and an important one; for surely a proper study of mankind is his behavior.

References

AABT (Newsletter published by the Association for Advancement of Behavior Therapy), 1974, *1*, (3).

The ABC's of Education. Baltimore, Md.: Hallmark films. (Film)

Addison, R. M., & Homme, L. E. The reinforcing event (RE) menu. *NSPI Journal*, 1966, *1*, 8–9.

Ainslie, G. W. Impulse control in pigeons. *Journal of the Experimental Analysis of Behavior*, 1974, *21*, 485–489.

Alevizos, P. N., Berck, P. L., Campbell, M. D., & Callahan, E. J. Communication. (An instructional aid for staff training in behavioral assessment.) *Journal of Applied Behavior Analysis*, 1974, *7*, 472. (Original flow chart available from Dr. Alevizos, Camarillo–UCLA Neuropsychiatric Research Program, Box A, Camarillo, Calif. 93010.)

Allen, K. E., & Harris, F. R. Elimination of a child's excessive scratching by training the mother in reinforcement procedures. *Behaviour Research and Therapy*, 1966, *4*, 79–84.

Allen, K. E., Turner, K. D., & Everett, P. M. A behavior modification classroom for Head Start children with problem behaviors. *Exceptional Children*, 1970, *37*, 119–127.

American Psychological Association. *Ethical standards of psychologists*. Washington, D.C.: American Psychological Association, 1963.

American Psychological Association. *Standards for educational and psychological tests and manuals*. Washington, D.C.: American Psychological Association, 1966.

American Psychological Association. *Ethical principles in the conduct of research with human participants*. Washington, D.C.: American Psychological Association, 1973.

Aragona, J., Cassady, J., & Drabman, R. S. Treating overweight children through parental training and contingency contracting. *Journal of Applied Behavior Analysis*, 1975, *8*, 269–278.

Ascher, L. M., & Cautela, J. R. Covert negative reinforcement: An experimental test. *Journal of Behavior Therapy and Experimental Psychiatry*, 1972, *3*, 1–5.

Ashem, B., & Donner, L. Covert sensitization with alcoholics: A controlled replication. *Behaviour Research and Therapy*, 1968, *6*, 7–12.

Atthowe, J. M., Jr. Behavior innovation and persistence. *American Psychologist*, 1973, *28*, 34–41.

Atthowe, J. M., Jr. Treating the hospitalized person. In W. E. Craighead, A. E. Kazdin, & M. J. Mahoney (Eds.), *Behavior modification: Principles, issues, and applications*. Boston: Houghton Mifflin, 1976.

Axelrod, S., Hall, R. V., Weis, L., & Rohrer, S. Use of self-imposed contingencies to reduce the frequency of smoking behavior. In M. J. Mahoney & C. E. Thoresen (Eds.), *Self-control: Power to the person*. Monterey, Calif.: Brooks/Cole, 1974.

Ayer, W. A. Implosive therapy: A review. *Psychotherapy: Theory, Research and Practice*, 1972, *9*, 242–250.

Ayllon, T. Intensive treatment of psychotic behaviour by stimulus satiation and food reinforcement. *Behaviour Research and Therapy*, 1963, *1*, 53–61.

Ayllon, T. The practical modification of deviant behavior through operant techniques. *Comparative Psychopathology*, 1967, 240–248.

Ayllon, T., & Azrin, N. H. The measurement and reinforcement of behavior of psychotics. *Journal of the Experimental Analysis of Behavior*, 1965, *8*, 357–383.

Ayllon, T., & Azrin, N. *The token economy: A motivational system for therapy and rehabilitation*. New York: Appleton-Century-Crofts, 1968.

Ayllon, T., & Haughton, E. Modification of symptomatic verbal behaviour of mental patients. *Behaviour Research and Therapy*, 1964, *2*, 87–97.

Ayllon, T., Haughton, E., & Hughes, H. B. Interpretation of symptoms: Fact or fiction. *Behaviour Research and Therapy*, 1965, *3*, 1–7.

Ayllon, T., Layman, D., & Kandel, H. J. A behavioral-educational alternative to drug control of hyperactive children. *Journal of Applied Behavior Analysis*, 1975, *8*, 137–146.

Ayllon, T., & Michael, J. The psychiatric nurse as a behavioral engineer. *Journal of the Experimental Analysis of Behavior*, 1959, *2*, 323–334.

Ayllon, T., & Roberts, M. D. Eliminating discipline

problems by strengthening academic performance. *Journal of Applied Behavior Analysis*, 1974, *7*, 71–76.

Ayllon, T., & Skuban, W. Accountability in psychotherapy: A test case. *Journal of Behavior Therapy and Experimental Psychiatry*, 1973, *4*, 19–29.

Azrin, N. H. Some effects of noise on human behavior. *Journal of the Experimental Analysis of Behavior*, 1958, *1*, 183–200.

Azrin, N. H. Effects of punishment intensity during variable-interval reinforcement. *Journal of the Experimental Analysis of Behavior*, 1960, *3*, 123–142.

Azrin, N. H. Pain and aggression. *Psychology Today*, May 1967, pp. 27–33.

Azrin, N. H., & Foxx, R. M. *Toilet training in less than a day*. New York: Simon and Schuster, 1974.

Azrin, N. H., & Holz, W. C. Punishment. In W. K. Honig (Ed.), *Operant behavior: Areas of research and application*. New York: Appleton-Century-Crofts, 1966.

Azrin, N. H., Holz, W. C., & Hake, D. F. Fixed-ratio punishment. *Journal of the Experimental Analysis of Behavior*, 1963, *6*, 141–148.

Azrin, N. H., Hutchinson, R. R., & Hake, D. F. Extinction-induced aggression. *Journal of the Experimental Analysis of Behavior*, 1966, *9*, 191–204.

Azrin, N. H., Hutchinson, R. R., & McLaughlin, R. The opportunity for aggression as an operant reinforcer during aversive stimulation. *Journal of the Experimental Analysis of Behavior*, 1965, *8*, 171–180.

Azrin, N. H., & Nunn, R. G. A rapid method of eliminating stuttering by a regulated breathing approach. *Behaviour Research and Therapy*, 1974, *12*, 279–286.

Azrin, N. H., & Powell, J. Behavioral engineering: The use of response priming to improve prescribed self-medication. *Journal of Applied Behavior Analysis*, 1969, *2*, 39–42.

Azrin, N., Rubin, H., O'Brien, F., Ayllon, T., & Roll, D. Behavioral engineering: Postural control by a portable operant apparatus. *Journal of Applied Behavior Analysis*, 1968, *1*, 99–108.

Bachrach, A. J., Erwin, W. J., & Mohr, J. P. The control of eating behavior in an anorexic by operant conditioning techniques. In L. P. Ullmann & L. Krasner (Eds.), *Case studies in behavior modification*. New York: Holt, Rinehart and Winston, 1965.

Baer, D. M. Laboratory control of thumbsucking by withdrawal and re-presentation of reinforcement. *Journal of the Experimental Analysis of Behavior*, 1962, *5*, 525–528.

Baer, D. M. In the beginning, there was the response. In E. Ramp & G. Semb (Eds.), *Behavior analysis: Areas of research and application*. Englewood Cliffs, N. J.: Prentice-Hall, 1975.

Baer, D. M., Peterson, R. F., & Sherman, J. A. The development of imitation by reinforcing behavioral similarity to a model. *Journal of the Experimental Analysis of Behavior*, 1967, *10*, 405–416.

Baer, D. M., Wolf, M. M., & Risley, T. R. Some current dimensions of applied behavior analysis. *Journal of Applied Behavior Analysis*, 1968, *1*, 91–97.

Baisinger, J., & Roberts, C. L. Reduction of intraspecies aggression in rats by positive reinforcement of incompatible behaviors. *Journal of the Experimental Analysis of Behavior*, 1972, *18*, 535–540.

Baker, B. L. Symptom treatment and symptom substitution in enuresis. *Journal of Abnormal Psychology*, 1969, *74*, 42–49.

Bandura, A. Behavioral modifications through modeling procedures. In L. Krasner & L. P. Ullmann (Eds.), *Research in behavior modification*. New York: Holt, Rinehart and Winston, 1965.

Bandura, A. Psychotherapy based upon modeling principles. In A. E. Bergin & S. L. Garfield (Eds.), *Handbook of psychotherapy and behavior change: An empirical analysis*. New York: Wiley, 1971. (a)

Bandura, A. *Social learning theory*. New York: General Learning Press, 1971. (b)

Bandura, A., Blanchard, E. B., & Ritter, B. The relative efficacy of desensitization and modeling approaches for inducing behavioral, affective, and attitudinal changes. *Journal of Personality and Social Psychology*, 1969, *13*, 173–199.

Bandura, A., Grusec, J. E., & Menlove, F. L. Vicarious extinction of avoidance behavior. *Journal of Personality and Social Psychology*, 1967, *5*, 16–23.

Barlow, D. H. Increasing heterosexual responsiveness in the treatment of sexual deviation: A review of the clinical and experimental evidence. *Behavior Therapy*, 1973, *4*, 655–671.

Barlow, D. H., & Hersen, M. Single-case experimental designs: Uses in applied clinical research. *Archives of General Psychiatry*, 1973, *29*, 319–325.

Barlow, D. H., Leitenberg, H., & Agras, W. S. Experimental control of sexual deviation through manipulation of the noxious scene in covert sensitization. *Journal of Abnormal Psychology*, 1969, *74*, 597–601.

Baron, M. G. Psychiatric nursing and behavior therapy: An annotated bibliography. Boston, Mass.: Boston State Hospital, 1969. (Available from Mary Grace Baron, Boston State Hospital, 591 Morton Street, Boston, MA 02124.)

Barrett, B. H. Reduction in rate of multiple tics by free operant conditioning methods. *Journal of Nervous and Mental Disease*, 1962, *135*, 187–195.

Barton, E. S., Guess, D., Garcia, E., & Baer, D. M. Improvement of retardates' mealtime behaviors by timeout procedures using multiple baseline techniques. *Journal of Applied Behavior Analysis*, 1970, *3*, 77–84.

Baum, M. Extinction of avoidance responding through response prevention (flooding). *Psychological Bulletin*, 1970, *74*, 276–284.

Baum, M., & Poser, E. G. Comparison of flooding procedures in animals and man. *Behaviour Research and Therapy*, 1971, *9*, 249–254.

Bentler, P. M. An infant's phobia treated with reciprocal inhibition therapy. *Journal of Child Psychology and Psychiatry and Allied Disciplines*, 1962, *3*, 185–189.

Berkowitz, B. P., & Graziano, A. M. Training parents as behavior therapists: A review. *Behaviour Research and Therapy*, 1972, *10*, 297–317.

Berkowitz, L. The case for bottling up rage. *Psychology Today*, July 1973, pp. 24–31.

Berkowitz, S. *Behavior modification in educational settings: A selected bibliography*. Baltimore, Md.: Behavioral Information and Technology, 1968.

Bernstein, D. A., & Borkovec, T. D. *Progressive relaxation training: A manual for the helping professions*. Champaign, Ill.: Research Press, 1973.

Bernstein, D. A., & Paul, G. L. Some comments on therapy analogue research with small animal "phobias." *Journal of Behavior Therapy and Experimental Psychiatry*, 1971, *2*, 225–237.

Bijou, S. W. Behavior modification in the mentally retarded. *Pediatric Clinics of North America*, 1968, *15*, 969–987.

Bijou, S. W. What psychology has to offer education—Now. *Journal of Applied Behavior Analysis*, 1971, *3*, 65–71.

Bijou, S. W., Peterson, R. F., & Ault, M. H. A method to integrate descriptive and experimental studies at the level of data and empirical concepts. *Journal of Applied Behavior Analysis*, 1968, *1*, 175–191.

Birnbrauer, J. S. Generalization of punishment effects—A case study. *Journal of Applied Behavior Analysis*, 1968, *1*, 201–211.

Birnbrauer, J. S., Wolf, M. M., Kidder, J. D., & Tague, C. E. Classroom behavior of retarded pupils with token reinforcement. *Journal of Experimental Child Psychology*, 1965, *2*, 219–235.

Blanchard, E. B. Relative contributions of modeling, informational influences, and physical contact in extinction of phobic behavior. *Journal of Abnormal Psychology*, 1970, *76*, 55–61.

Blanchard, E. B., & Young, L. D. Clinical applications of biofeedback training: A review of evidence. *Archives of General Psychiatry*, 1974, *30*, 573–589.

Bondy, A. S., & Erickson, M. T. Comparison of modelling and reinforcement procedures in increasing question-asking of mildly retarded children. *Journal of Applied Behavior Analysis*, 1976, *9*, 108.

Boren, J. J., & Colman, A. D. Some experiments on reinforcement principles within a psychiatric ward for delinquent soldiers. *Journal of Applied Behavior Analysis*, 1970, *3*, 29–37.

Born, D. G., & Davis, M. L. Amount and distribution of study in a personalized instruction course and in a lecture course. *Journal of Applied Behavior Analysis*, 1974, *7*, 365–375.

Bornstein, P. H. Training parents as behavior modifiers: A bibliography 1959-1973. JSAS *Catalog of Selected Documents in Psychology*, 1974, *4*, 130. (Ms. No. 777.)

Bostow, D. E., & Bailey, J. Modification of severe disruptive and aggressive behavior using brief timeout and reinforcement procedures. *Journal of Applied Behavior Analysis*, 1969, *2*, 31–37.

Boudin, H. M. Contingency contracting as a therapeutic tool in the deceleration of amphetamine use. *Behavior Therapy*, 1972, *3*, 604–608.

Boudin, H. M., & Valentine, V. E., III. Contingency contracting: A major treatment modality for drug abuse. Mimeograph, 1974. (Available from Henry M. Boudin, 728 East University Av., Gainesville, FL 32601.)

Brady, J. P. Brevital-aided systematic desensitization. In R. D. Rubin, H. Fensterheim, A. A. Lazarus, & C. M. Franks (Eds.), *Advances in behavior therapy*. New York: Academic Press, 1971.

Braukman, C., & Kirigan, K. Achievement Place homes for 400 delinquent youth. Invited symposium at the Second Annual Convention of the Midwestern Association of Behavior Analysis, Chicago, May, 1976.

Bricker, W. A., & Bricker, D. D. A program of language training for the severely handicapped child. *Exceptional Children*, 1970, *37*, 101–111.

Bright, G. D., & Whaley, D. L. Suppression of regurgitation and rumination with aversive events. *Michigan Mental Health Research Bulletin*, 1968, *2* (2), 17–20.

Bristol, M. M., & Sloane, H. N., Jr. Effects of contingency contracting on study rate and test performance. *Journal of Applied Behavior Analysis*, 1974, *7*, 271–285.

Broden, M., Hall, R. V., & Mitts, B. The effect of self-recording on the classroom behavior of two eighth-grade students. *Journal of Applied Behavior Analysis*, 1971, *4*, 191–199.

Brown, B. S., Wienckowski, L. A., & Stolz, S. B. *Behavior modification: Perspective on a current issue*. Rockville, Md.: DHEW No. (ADM) 75-202, 1975. (Available from Office of Public Information, NIMH, 5600 Fishers Lane, Rockville, MD 20852.)

Brown, L., Van Deventer, P., Johnson, P., & Sontag, E. Teaching adolescent trainable level retarded students to read a restaurant menu. *School Applications of Learning Theory*, 1974, *6*(3), 1–13.

Bucher, B., & King, L. W. Generalization of punishment effects in the deviant behavior of a psychotic child. *Behavior Therapy*, 1971, *2*, 68–77.

Bucher, B., & Lovaas, O. I. Use of aversive stimulation in behavior modification. In M. R. Jones (Ed.), *Miami symposium on the prediction of behavior, 1967: Aversive stimulation*. Coral Gables, Fl.: University of Miami Press, 1968.

Budzynski, T. H., & Stoyva, J. Biofeedback techniques in behavior therapy. In D. Shapiro, T. X. Barber, L. V. DiCara, J. Kamiya, N. E. Miller, & J. Stoyva (Eds.), *Biofeedback and self-control 1972*. Chicago: Aldine, 1973. (English translation of a chapter from *Die Bewaltigung von Angst. Beitrage der Neuropsychologie zur Angstforschunge. Reihe Fortschritte der Klinischen Psychologie*, Bd. 4, 1973.)

Burchard, J. D. Systematic socialization: A programmed environment for the habilitation of antisocial retardates. *The Psychological Record*, 1967, *17*, 461–476.

Burchard, J. D., & Barrera, F. An analysis of timeout and response cost in a programmed environment. *Journal of Applied Behavior Analysis*, 1972, *5*, 271–282.

Bushell, D., Jr. *Classroom behavior: A little book for teachers*. Englewood Cliffs, N.J.: Prentice-Hall, 1973.

Butler, J. F. The toilet training success of parents after reading *Toilet Training in Less than a Day. Behavior Therapy*, 1976, *7*, 185–191.

Byrd, L. D. Responding in the cat maintained under response-independent electric shock and response-produced electric shock. *Journal of the Experimental Analysis of Behavior*, 1969, *12*, 1–10.

Cahoon, D. D. Symptom substitution and the behavior therapies. *Psychological Bulletin*, 1968, *69*, 149–156.

Cameron, P., & Giuntoli, D. Consciousness sampling in the college classroom or is anybody listening? *Intellect*, October 1972, pp. 63–64.

Campbell, B. A., & Church, R. M. (Eds.). *Punishment and aversive behavior*. New York: Appleton-Century-Crofts, 1969.

Catania, A. C. Introduction. In A. C. Catania (Ed.), *Contemporary research in operant behavior*. Glenview, Ill.: Scott, Foresman, 1968.

Catania, A. C. The myth of self-reinforcement. *Behaviorism*, 1975, *3*, 192–199.

Cautela, J. R. Treatment of compulsive behavior by covert sensitization. *The Psychological Record*, 1966, *16*, 33–41.

Cautela, J. R. Covert sensitization. *Psychological Reports*, 1967, *20*, 459–468.

Cautela, J. R. Covert negative reinforcement. *Journal of Behavior Therapy and Experimental Psychiatry*, 1970, *1*, 273–278. (a)

Cautela, J. R. Covert reinforcement. *Behavior Therapy*, 1970, *1*, 33–50. (b)

Cautela, J. R. Treatment of smoking by covert sensitization. *Psychological Reports*, 1970, *26*, 415–420. (c)

Cautela, J. R. Covert extinction. *Behavior Therapy*, 1971, *2*, 192–200.

Cautela, J. R., & Kastenbaum, R. A reinforcement survey schedule for use in therapy, training, and research. *Psychological Reports*, 1967, *20*, 1115–1130.

Chapman, C., & Risley, T. R. Anti-litter procedures in an urban high-density area. *Journal of Applied Behavior Analysis*, 1974, *7*, 377–383.

Cherek, D. R., Thompson, T., & Heistad, G. T. Effects of Δ'-Tetrahydrocannabinol and food deprivation level on responding maintained by the opportunity to attack. *Physiology and Behavior*, 1972, *9*, 795–800.

Clark, H. B., Rowbury, T., Baer, A. M., & Baer, D. M. Timeout as a punishing stimulus in continuous and intermittent schedules. *Journal of Applied Behavior Analysis*, 1973, *6*, 443–455.

Clark, R. N., Burgess, R. L., & Hendee, J. C. The development of anti-litter behavior in a forest campground. *Journal of Applied Behavior Analysis*, 1972, *5*, 1–5.

Cohen, H. L., & Filipczak, J. *A new learning environment: A case for learning.* San Francisco, Calif.: Jossey–Bass, 1971.

Cohen, S. I., Keyworth, J. M., Kleiner, R. I., & Libert, J. M. The support of school behaviors by home-based reinforcement via parent-child contingency contracts. In E. A. Ramp & B. L. Hopkins (Eds.), *A new direction for education: Behavior analysis, 1971.* Lawrence, Kans.: Department of Human Development, University of Kansas, 1971.

Cooke, G. The efficacy of two desensitization procedures: An analogue study. *Behaviour Research and Therapy*, 1966, *4*, 17–24.

Cooper, A., Furst, J. B., & Bridger, W. H. A brief commentary on the usefulness of studying fears of snakes. *Journal of Abnormal Psychology*, 1969, *74*, 413–414.

Copeland, R. E., Brown, R. E., & Hall, R. V. The effects of principal-implemented techniques on the behavior of pupils. *Journal of Applied Behavior Analysis*, 1974, *7*, 77–86.

Corey, J. R., & Shamow, J. The effects of fading on the acquisition and retention of oral reading. *Journal of Applied Behavior Analysis*, 1972, *5*, 311–315.

Corte, H. E., Wolf, M. M., & Locke, B. J. A comparison of procedures for eliminating self-injurious behavior of retarded adolescents. *Journal of Applied Behavior Analysis*, 1971, *4*, 201–213.

Cotler, S. B. Sex differences and generalization of anxiety reduction with automated desensitization and minimal therapist interaction. *Behaviour Research and Therapy*, 1970, *8*, 273–285.

Cotler, S. B., Applegate, G., King, L. W., & Kristal, S. Establishing a token economy program in a state hospital classroom: A lesson in training student and teacher. *Behavior Therapy*, 1972, *3*, 209–222.

Craighead, W. E., Kazdin, A. E., & Mahoney, M. J. (Eds.). *Behavior modification: Principles, issues, and applications.* Boston: Houghton Mifflin, 1976.

Csapo, M. Peer models reverse the "One bad apple spoils the barrel" theory. *Teaching Exceptional Children*, 1972, *5*, 20–24.

Cull, J. G., & Hardy, R. E. *Behavior modification in rehabilitation settings: Applied principles.* Springfield, Ill.: Charles C Thomas, 1974.

Daley, M. F. The "reinforcement menu": Finding effective reinforcers. In J. D. Krumboltz & C. E. Thoresen (Eds.), *Behavioral counseling: Cases and techniques.* New York: Holt, Rinehart and Winston, 1969.

Daniels, L. K. Rapid extinction of nail biting by covert sensitization: A case study. *Journal of Behavior Therapy and Experimental Psychiatry*, 1974, *5*, 91–92.

Davison, G. C. Elimination of a sadistic fantasy by a client-controlled counterconditioning technique: A case study. *Journal of Abnormal Psychology*, 1968, *73*, 84–90. (a)

Davison, G. C. Systematic desensitization as a counter-conditioning process. *Journal of Abnormal Psychology*, 1968, *73*, 91–99. (b)

Davison, G. C., & Wilson, G. T. Processes of fear-reduction in systematic desensitization: Cognitive and social reinforcement factors in humans. *Behavior Therapy*, 1973, *4*, 1–21.

Dietz, S. M., & Repp, A. C. Decreasing classroom misbehavior through the use of DRL schedules of reinforcement. *Journal of Applied Behavior Analysis*, 1973, *6*, 457–463.

Dietz, S. M., & Repp, A. C. Differentially reinforcing low rates of misbehavior with normal elementary school children. *Journal of Applied Behavior Analysis*, 1974, *7*, 622.

Donner, L., & Guerney, B. G., Jr. Automated group desensitization for test anxiety. *Behaviour Research and Therapy*, 1969, *7*, 1–13.

Drash, P. H., & Freeman, B. J. *Behavior modification, behavior therapy, and operant conditioning: An historical survey and a bibliography of books in print, 1900-1972.* Baltimore, Md., Behavioral Information and Technology, 1973.

Duncan, A. D. Self-application of behavior modification techniques by teenagers. In C. E. Pitts (Ed.), *Operant conditioning in the classroom: Introductory readings in educational psychology.* New York: Thomas Y. Crowell, 1971.

Dunham, P. J. Punishment: Method and theory. *Psychological Review*, 1971, *78*, 58–70.

Elliott, R., & Tighe, T. Breaking the cigarette habit: Effects of a technique involving threatened loss of money. *Psychological Record*, 1968, *18*, 503–513.

Engelmann, S. *Your child can succeed.* New York: Simon and Schuster, 1975.

Essock, S. M., & Reese, E. P. Preference for and effects of variable- as opposed to fixed-reinforcer duration. *Journal of the Experimental Analysis of Behavior*, 1974, *21*, 89–97.

Evans, I. M. The logical requirements for explanations of systematic desensitization. *Behavior Therapy*, 1973, *4*, 506–514.

Everett, P. B., Hayward, S. C., & Meyers, A. W. The effects of a token reinforcement procedure on bus ridership. *Journal of Applied Behavior Analysis*, 1974, *7*, 1–9.

Eyberg, S. M., & Johnson, S. M. Multiple assessment of behavior modification with families: Effects of contingency contracting and order of treated problems. *Journal of Consulting and Clinical Psychology*, 1974, *42*, 594–606.

Fast, B. L. Contingency contracting. *Journal of Health, Physical Education, and Recreation*, September 1971, pp. 31–32.

Fawcett, S. B., & Miller, L. K. Training public-speaking behavior: An experimental analysis and social validation. *Journal of Applied Behavior Analysis*, 1975, *8*, 125–135.

Federation Proceedings, 1975, 34, No. 9. (August) (Published by the Federation of American Societies for Experimental Biology.)

Feldman, M. P., & MacCulloch, M. J. The application of anticipatory avoidance learning to the treatment of homosexuality. I. Theory, technique and preliminary results. *Behaviour Research and Therapy*, 1965, *2*, 165–183.

Felixbrod, J. J., & O'Leary, K. D. Effects of reinforcement on children's academic behavior as a function of self-determined and externally imposed contingencies. *Journal of Applied Behavior Analysis*, 1973, *6*, 241–250.

Ferster, C. B., Nurnberger, J. I., & Levitt, E. B. The control of eating. *Journal of Mathetics*, 1962, *1*, 87–109.

Ferster, C. B., & Skinner, B. F. *Schedules of reinforcement*. New York: Appleton-Century-Crofts, 1957.

Findley, J. D., & Brady, J. V. Facilitation of large ratio performance by use of conditioned reinforcement. *Journal of the Experimental Analysis of Behavior*, 1965, *8*, 125–129.

Fink, W. T., & Carnine, D. W. Control of arithmetic errors using informational feedback and graphing. *Journal of Applied Behavior Analysis*, 1975, *8*, 461.

Fisher, J., & Gochros, H. L. *Planned behavior change: Behavior modification in social work*. Riverside, N. J.: the Free Press, 1976.

Fixsen, D. L., Phillips, E. L., Phillips, E. A., & Wolf, M. M. The teaching-family model of group home treatment. In W. E. Craighead, A. E. Kazdin, & M. J. Mahoney (Eds.), *Behavior modification: Principles, issues, and applications*. Boston: Houghton Mifflin, 1976.

Flanagan, B., Goldiamond, I., & Azrin, N. Operant stuttering: the control of stuttering behavior through response-contingent consequences. *Journal of the Experimental Analysis of Behavior*, 1958, *1*, 173–177.

Flanagan, B., Goldiamond, I., & Azrin, N. H. Instatement of stuttering in normally fluent individuals through operant procedures. *Science*, 1959, *130*, 979–981.

Fordyce, W. E. *Behavioral methods for chronic pain and illness*. St. Louis, Mo.: C. V. Mosby, 1976.

Foreyt, J. P., & Kennedy, W. A. Treatment of over-weight by aversion therapy. *Behaviour Research and Therapy*, 1971, *9*, 29–34.

Fox, L. Effecting the use of efficient study habits. *Journal of Mathetics*, 1962, *1*, 75–86.

Fox, R. G., Copeland, R. E., Harris, J. W., Rieth, H. J., & Hall, R. V. A computerized system for selecting responsive teaching studies, catalogued along twenty-eight important dimensions. In E. Ramp & G. Semb (Eds.), *Behavior analysis: Areas of research and application*. Englewood Cliffs, N.J.: Prentice-Hall, 1975.

Foxx, R. M., & Azrin, N. H. Restitution: A method of eliminating aggressive-disruptive behavior of mentally retarded and brain damaged patients. *Behaviour Research and Therapy*, 1972, *10*, 15–27.

Foxx, R. M., & Azrin, N. H. *Toilet training the retarded: A rapid program for day and nighttime independent toileting*. Champaign, Ill.: Research Press, 1973.

Franks, C. M. Behavior therapy and its Pavlovian origins. In C. M. Franks (Ed.), *Behavior therapy: Appraisal and status*. New York: McGraw-Hill, 1969.

Friedman, D. A new technique for systematic desensitization of phobic symptoms. *Behaviour Research and Therapy*, 1966, *4*, 139–140.

Fuller, E., & Reese, E. P. A comparison of four procedures in suppressing human response rates during a five-component multiple schedule of reinforcement. Paper presented at the Annual Meeting of the American Psychological Association. New Orleans, La., September, 1974.

Geer, J. R., & Silverman, I. Treatment of a recurrent nightmare by behavior-modification procedures: A case study. *Journal of Abnormal Psychology*, 1967, *72*, 188–190.

Geller, E. S., Farris, J. C., & Post, D. S. Prompting a consumer behavior for pollution control. *Journal of Applied Behavior Analysis*, 1973, 6, 367–376.

Geller, E. S., Wylie, R. C., & Farris, J. C. An attempt at applying prompting and reinforcement toward pollution control. *Proceedings of the 79th Annual Convention of the American Psychological Association*, 1971, 6, 701–702. (Summary)

Gersham, L., & Stedman, J. M. Oriental defense exercises as reciprocal inhibitors of anxiety. *Journal of Behavior Therapy and Experimental Psychiatry*, 1971, 2, 117–119.

Girton, M., & Reese, E. P. Response topography as a variable in the reinforcement of incompatible behavior. *Proceedings of the 81st Annual Convention of the American Psychological Association*, 1973, 8, 883–884. (Summary)

Glynn, E. L., & Thomas, J. D. Effect of cueing on self-control of classroom behavior. *Journal of Applied Behavior Analysis*, 1974, 7, 299–306.

Goldfried, M. R., & Merbaum, M. (Eds.). *Behavior change through self-control*. New York: Holt, Rinehart and Winston, 1973.

Goldiamond, I. Self-control procedures in personal behavior problems. *Psychological Reports*, 1965, 17, 851–868.

Goldiamond, I. Toward a constructional approach to social problems: Ethical and constitutional issues raised by applied behavior analysis. *Behaviorism*, 1974, 2, 1–8.

Goldiamond, I. Protection of human subjects and patients: A social contingency analysis of distinctions between research and practice, and its implications. *Behaviorism*, 1976, 4, 1–41. (a)

Goldiamond, I. Self-reinforcement. *Journal of Applied Behavior Analysis*, 1976, 9, 509–514. (b)

Gotestam, K. G., Melin, G. L., & Dockens, W. S., III. A behavioral program for intravenous amphetamine addicts. In T. Thompson & W. S. Dockens III (Eds.), *Applications of behavior modification*. New York: Academic Press, 1975.

Grant, D. A. Classical and operant conditioning. In A. W. Melton (Ed.), *Categories of human learning*, New York: Academic Press, 1964.

Hall, B. L. Behavioral techniques of time management. Workshop presented at the Second Annual Convention of the Midwestern Association of Behavior Analysis, Chicago, May, 1976.

Hall, R. V. *Managing behavior 1: Behavior modification: The measurement of behavior. 3: Applications in school and home*. Lawrence, Kans.: H & H Enterprises, 1971. (a)

Hall, R. V. Training teachers in classroom use of contingency management. *Educational Technology*, April 1971, pp. 33–38. (b)

Hall, R. V., Axelrod, S., Tyler, L., Grief, E., Jones, F. C., & Robertson, R. Modification of behavior problems in the home with a parent as observer and experimenter. *Journal of Applied Behavior Analysis*, 1972, 5, 53–64.

Hall, S. M., & Hall, R. G. Outcome and methodological considerations in behavioral treatment of obesity. *Behavior Therapy*, 1974, 5, 352–364.

Hallsten, E. A., Jr. Adolescent anorexia nervosa treated by desensitization. *Behaviour Research and Therapy*, 1965, 3, 87–91.

Hamilton, J., Stephens, L., & Allen, P. Controlling aggressive and destructive behavior in severely retarded institutionalized residents. *American Journal of Mental Deficiency*, 1967, 71, 852–856.

Hamner, W. C., & Hamner, E. P. Behavior modification on the bottom line, *Organizational Dynamics*, 1976, 4, 2–21.

Hampe, E., Noble, H., Miller, L. C., & Barrett, C. L. Phobic children one and two years posttreatment. *Journal of Abnormal Psychology*, 1973, 82, 446–453.

Hart, B. M., Reynolds, N. J., Baer, D. M., Brawley, E. R., & Harris, F. R. Effect of contingent and non-contingent social reinforcement on the cooperative play of a preschool child. *Journal of Applied Behavior Analysis*, 1968, 1, 73–76.

Hasazi, J. E., & Hasazi, S. E. Effects of teacher attention on digit-reversal behavior in an elementary school child. *Journal of Applied Behavior Analysis*, 1972, 5, 157–162.

Hawkins, R. P. Who decided *that* was the problem? Two stages of responsibility for applied behavior analysis. In W. S. Wood (Ed.), *Issues in evaluating behavior modification: Proceedings of the First Drake Conference on Professional Issues in Applied Behavior Analysis, 1974*. Champaign, Ill.: Research Press, 1975.

Hawkins, R. P., Axelrod, S., & Hall, R. V. Teachers as behavior analysts: Precisely monitoring student performance. In T. A. Brigham, R. P. Hawkins, J. Scott, & T. F. McLaughlin (Eds.), *Behavior analysis in education: Self-control and reading*. Dubuque, Iowa: Kendall-Hunt, 1976.

Hawkins, R. P., & Dobes, R. W. Behavioral definitions in applied behavior analysis: Explicit or implicit. In B. C. Etzel, J. M. LeBlanc, & D. M. Baer (Eds.), *New developments in behavioral research: Theory, methods, and applications. In honor of Sidney W. Bijou*. Hillsdale, N.J.: Lawrence Erlbaum Associates, in press.

Hawkins, R. P., & Dotson, V. A. Reliability scores that delude: An Alice in Wonderland trip through the misleading characteristics of interobserver agreement scores in interval recording. In E. Ramp & G. Semb (Eds.), *Behavior analysis: Areas of research and application*. Englewood Cliffs, N.J.: Prentice-Hall, 1975.

Hawkins, R. P., Peterson, R. F., Schweid, E., & Bijou, S. W. Behavior therapy in the home: Amelioration of problem parent-child relations with the parent in a therapeutic role. *Journal of Experimental Child Psychology*, 1966, *4*, 99–107.

Hawkins, R. P., Sluyter, D. J., & Smith, C. D. Modification of achievement by a simple technique involving parents and teacher. In M. B. Harris (Ed.), *Classroom uses of behavior modification*. Columbus, Ohio: Charles E. Merrill, 1972.

Hayes, S. C., Johnson, V. S., & Cone, J. D. The marked item technique: A practical procedure for litter control. *Journal of Applied Behavior Analysis*, 1975, *8*, 381–386.

Hefferline, R. F., Keenan, B., & Harford, R. A. Escape and avoidance conditioning in human subjects without their observation of the response. *Science*, 1959, *130*, 1338–1339.

Herbert, E. W., & Baer, D. M. Training parents as behavior modifiers: Self-recording of contingent attention. *Journal of Applied Behavior Analysis*, 1972, *5*, 139–149.

Hermann, J. A., de Montes, A. I., Domínquez, B., Montes, F., & Hopkins, B. L. Effects of bonuses for punctuality on the tardiness of industrial workers. *Journal of Applied Behavior Analysis*, 1973, *6*, 563–570.

Hersen, M., & Barlow, D. H. *Single case experimental designs: Strategies for studying behavior change*. Elmsford, N.Y.: Pergamon Press, 1976.

Hersen, M., & Bellack, A. S. (Eds.). *Behavioral assessment: A practical handbook*. Elmsford, N.Y.: Pergamon Press, 1976.

Hersen, M., & Eisler, R. M. Social skills training. In W. E. Craighead, A. E. Kazdin, & M. J. Mahoney (Eds.), *Behavior modification: Principles, issues, and applications*. Boston: Houghton Mifflin, 1976.

Hewett, F. M. Teaching reading to an autistic boy through operant conditioning. *Reading Teacher*, 1964, *17*, 613–618.

Hively, W. Programming stimuli in matching to sample. *Journal of the Experimental Analysis of Behavior*, 1962, *5*, 279–298.

Holland, C. J. An interview guide for behavioural counseling with parents. *Behavior Therapy*, 1970, *1*, 70–79.

Holland, C. J. Directive parental counseling: The parents' manual. *Behavior Therapy*, 1976, *7*, 123–127.

Holz, W. C., & Azrin, N. H. A comparison of several procedures for eliminating behavior. *Journal of the Experimental Analysis of Behavior*, 1963, *6*, 399–406.

Homme, L. E. Perspectives in psychology: XXIV Control of coverants, the operants of the mind. *The Psychological Record*, 1965, *15*, 501–511.

Homme, L., Csanyi, A. P., Gonzales, M. A., & Rechs, J. R. *How to use contingency contracting in the classroom*. Champaign, Ill.: Research Press, 1970.

Homme, L. E., deBaca, P. C., Devine, J. V., Steinhorst, R., & Rickert, E. J. Use of the Premack principle in controlling the behavior of nursery school children. *Journal of the Experimental Analysis of Behavior*, 1963, *6*, 544.

Hops, H. Behavioral treatment of marital problems. In W. E. Craighead, A. E. Kazdin, & M. J. Mahoney (Eds.), *Behavior modification: Principles, issues, and applications*. Boston: Houghton Mifflin, 1976.

Houts, P. S., & Hench, R. W., Jr. Teaching behavior modification in professional schools. In S. Yen & R. W. McIntire (Eds.), *Teaching behavior modification*. Kalamazoo, Mich.: Behaviordelia, 1976.

Hunt, W. A., Barnett, L. W., & Branch, L. G. Relapse rates in addiction programs. *Journal of Clinical Psychology*, 1971, *27*, 455–456.

Ince, L. P. *Behavior modification in rehabilitation medicine*. Springfield, Ill.: Charles C Thomas, 1976.

Jeffrey, D. B. Self-control: Methodological issues and research trends. In M. J. Mahoney & C. E. Thoresen (Eds.), *Self-control: Power to the person*. Monterey, Calif.: Brooks/Cole, 1974.

Jeffrey, W. E. Variables in early discrimination learning: I. Motor responses in the training of a left-right discrimination. *Child Development*, 1958, *29*, 269–275.

Jehu, D., Hardiker, P., Yelloly, M., & Shaw, M. *Behaviour modification in social work*. New York: Wiley-Interscience, 1972.

Johnson, J. *838 ways to amuse a child*. New York: Gramercy, 1960.

Johnson, S. M., & White, G. Self-observation as an agent of behavioral change. *Behavior Therapy*, 1971, *2*, 488–497.

Jones, G. B. Improving study behaviors. In J. D. Krumboltz & C. E. Thoresen (Eds.), *Behavioral counseling: Cases and techniques.* New York: Holt, Rinehart and Winston, 1969.

Jones, M. C. The elimination of children's fears. *Journal of Experimental Psychology*, 1924, *7*, 382–390.

Jones, R. T., & Kazdin, A. E. Programming response maintenance after withdrawing token reinforcement. *Behavior Therapy*, 1975, 6, 153–164.

Kanfer, F. H., & Phillips, J. S. *Learning foundations of behavior therapy.* New York: Wiley, 1970.

Kanfer, F. H., & Saslow, G. Behavioral diagnosis. In C. M. Franks (Ed.), *Behavior therapy: Appraisal and status.* New York: McGraw-Hill, 1969.

Kapfer, M. B. *Behavioral objectives in curriculum development; selected readings and bibliography.* Englewood Cliffs, N.J.: Educational Technology Publications, 1971.

Karen, R. L. *An introduction to behavior theory and its applications.* New York: Harper & Row, 1974.

Katz, R. C., & Zlutnick, S. (Eds.). *Behavioral therapy and health care: Principles and applications.* Elmsford, N.Y.: Pergamon Press, 1974.

Kaufman, K. F., & O'Leary, K. D. Reward, cost, and self-evaluation procedures for disruptive adolescents in a psychiatric hospital school. *Journal of Applied Behavior Analysis*, 1972, *5*, 293–309.

Kazdin, A. E. Response cost: The removal of conditioned reinforcers for therapeutic change. *Behavior Therapy*, 1972, *3*, 533–546. (a)

Kazdin, A. E. The token economy: An annotated bibliography. JSAS *Catalog of Selected Documents in Psychology*, 1972, *2*, 22–23. *(Ms. No. 86) (b)*

Kazdin, A. E. Covert modeling and the reduction of avoidance behavior. *Journal of Abnormal Psychology*, 1973, *81*, 87–95.

Kazdin, A. E. Comparative effects of some variations of covert modeling. *Journal of Behavior Therapy and Experimental Psychiatry*, 1974, *5*, 225–231. (a)

Kazdin, A. E. The effect of model identity and fear-relevant similarity on covert modeling. *Behavior Therapy*, 1974, *5*, 624–635. (b)

Kazdin, A. E. Self-monitoring and behavior change. In M. J. Mahoney & C. E. Thoresen (Eds.), *Self-control: Power to the person.* Monterey, Calif.: Brooks/Cole, 1974. (c)

Kazdin, A. E. *Behavior modification in applied settings.* Homewood, Ill.: Dorsey Press, 1975. (a)

Kazdin, A. E. The impact of applied behavior analysis on diverse areas of research. *Journal of Applied Behavior Analysis*, 1975, *8*, 213–229. (b)

Kazdin, A. E. Recent advances in token economy research. In M. Hersen, R. M. Eisler, & P. M. Miller (Eds.), *Progress in behavior modification.* New York: Academic Press, 1975. (c)

Kazdin, A. E. Methodology of applied behavior analysis. In T. A. Brigham & A. C. Catania (Eds.), *Social and instructional processes: Foundations and applications of a behavioral analysis.* New York: Irvington/Naiburg—Wiley, 1976. (a)

Kazdin, A. E. Statistical analyses for single-case designs. In M. Hersen & A. S. Bellack (Eds.), *Single-case experimental designs: Strategies for studying behavior change.* Elmsford, N.Y.: Pergamon Press, 1976. (b)

Kazdin, A. E. Extensions of reinforcement techniques to socially and environmentally relevant behaviors. In M. Hersen, R. M. Eisler, & P. M. Miller (Eds.), *Progress in behavior modification.* New York: Academic Press, in press.

Kazdin, A. E., & Bootzin, R. R. The token economy: An evaluative review. *Journal of Applied Behavior Analysis*, 1972, *5*, 343–372.

Kazdin, A. E., & Klock, J. The effect of nonverbal teacher approval on student attentive behavior. *Journal of Applied Behavior Analysis*, 1973, *6*, 643–654.

Kazdin, A. E., & Polster, R. Intermittent token reinforcement and response maintenance in extinction. *Behavior Therapy*, 1973, *4*, 386–391.

Kazdin, A. E., & Straw, M. K. Assessment of behaviors of the mentally retarded. In M. Hersen & A. S. Bellack (Eds.), *Behavioral assessment: A practical handbook.* Elmsford, N.Y.: Pergamon Press, 1976.

Keeley, S. M., Shemberg, K. M., & Carbonell, J. Operant clinical intervention: Behavior management or beyond? Where are the data? *Behavior Therapy*, 1976, *7*, 292–305.

Kelleher, R. T., & Morse, W. H. Schedules using noxious stimuli: III. Responding maintained with response-produced electric shocks. *Journal of the Experimental Analysis of Behavior*, 1968, *11*, 819–838.

Keller, F. S. "Good-bye, teacher . . ." *Journal of Applied Behavior Analysis*, 1968, *1*, 79–89.

Keller, F. S., & Koen, B. V. (Eds.). *The state of the art of the Keller Plan, 1976.* San Francisco: Jossey Bass, in press.

Kelly, J. F., & Hake, D. F. An extinction-induced increase in an aggressive response with humans. *Journal of the Experimental Analysis of Behavior*, 1970, *14*, 153–164.

Kennedy, R. E. Behavior modification in prisons. In W. E. Craighead, A. E. Kazdin, & M. J. Mahoney, (Eds.), *Behavior modification: Principles, issues, and applications*. Boston: Houghton Mifflin, 1976.

Kincade, K. *A Walden Two experiment*. New York: Morrow, 1973.

Kircher, A. S., Pear, J. J., & Martin, G. L. Shock as punishment in a picture-naming task with retarded children. *Journal of Applied Behavior Analysis*, 1971, *4*, 227–233.

Klein, Z. E. Bibliographies on behavior modification: An annotated listing. *Behavior Therapy*, 1973, *4*, 592–598.

Knapp, T. J., & Peterson, L. W. Behavior management in medical and nursing practice. In W. E. Craighead, A. E. Kazdin, & M. J. Mahoney (Eds.), *Behavior modification: Principles, issues and applications*. Boston: Houghton Mifflin, 1976.

Knox, D. *Marriage happiness: A behavioral approach to counseling*. Champaign, Ill.: Research Press, 1971.

Knox, D. Behavior contracts in marriage counseling. *Journal of Family Counseling*, 1973, *1*, 22–28.

Koegel, R. L., & Rincover, A. Treatment of psychotic children in a classroom environment: I. Learning in a large group. *Journal of Applied Behavior Analysis*, 1974, *7*, 45–59.

Kolvin, I. "Aversive imagery" treatment in adolescents. *Behaviour Research and Therapy*, 1967, *5*, 245–248.

Kondaš, O., & Šćetnická, B. Systematic desensitization as a method of preparation for childbirth. *Journal of Behavior Therapy and Experimental Psychiatry*, 1972, *3*, 51–54.

Krapfl, J. E., & Nawas, M. M. Client-therapist relationship factor in systematic desensitization. *Journal of Consulting and Clinical Psychology*, 1969, *33*, 435–439.

Krasnogorski, N. I. The conditioned reflexes and children's neuroses. *American Journal of Diseases of Children*, 1925, *30*, 753–768.

Krieger, H., Wasserman, C., Berman, A., McCarthy, B., & Krieger, J. The American University "Hotline": A model crisis intervention telephone service. *JSAS Catalogue of Selected Documents in Psychology*, 1975, *5*, 193. (Ms. No. 862.)

Krumboltz, J. D., & Thoresen, C. E. (Eds.). *Behavioral counseling: Cases and techniques*. New York: Holt, Rinehart and Winston, 1969.

Krumboltz, J. D., & Thoresen, C. E. (Eds.). *Counseling methods*. New York: Holt, Rinehart and Winston, 1976.

Kunzelmann, H. P. (Ed.), with Cohen, M. A., Hulten, W. J., Martin, G. L., & Mingo, A. R. *Precision teaching: An initial training sequence*. Seattle, Wash.: Special Child Publications, 1970.

Kushner, M. Faradic aversive controls in clinical practice. In C. Neuringer & J. L. Michael (Eds.), *Behavior modification in clinical psychology*. New York: Appleton-Century-Crofts, 1970.

Lang, P. J. Behavior therapy with a case of nervous anorexia. In L. P. Ullmann & L. Krasner (Eds.), *Case studies in behavior modification*. New York: Holt, Rinehart and Winston, 1965.

Lang, P. J., & Melamed, B. G. Case report: Avoidance conditioning therapy of an infant with chronic ruminative vomiting. *Journal of Abnormal Psychology*, 1969, *74*, 1–8.

Lang, P. J., Melamed, B. G., & Hart, J. A psychophysiological analysis of fear modification using an automated desensitization procedure. *Journal of Abnormal Psychology*, 1970, *76*, 220–234.

Lavin, N. I., Thorpe, J. G., Barker, J. C., Blakemore, C. B., & Conway, C. G. Behavior therapy in a case of transvestism. *Journal of Nervous and Mental Disease*, 1961, *133*, 346–353.

Lazarus, A. A. Group therapy of phobic disorders by systematic desensitization. *Journal of Abnormal and Social Psychology*, 1961, *63*, 504–510.

Lazarus, A. A. A preliminary report on the use of directed muscular activity in counter-conditioning. *Behaviour Research and Therapy*, 1965, *2*, 301–303.

Lazarus, A. A. In support of technical eclecticism. *Psychological Reports*, 1967, *21*, 415–416.

Lazarus, A. A. *Daily living: Coping with tensions and anxieties*. Chicago, Ill.: Instructional Dynamics, 1970. (Series of tape cassettes)

Lazarus, A. A. *Clinical behavior therapy*. New York: Brunner/Mazel, 1972.

Lazarus, A. A., & Abramovitz, A. The use of "emotive imagery" in the treatment of children's phobias. *Journal of Mental Science*, 1962, *108*, 191–195.

LeBlanc, J. M., & Etzel, B. C. Predetermined confidence levels vs. predetermined criterion behavior: One argument against the use of statistics in operant research. Invited symposium at the Second Annual Convention of the Midwestern Association of Behavior Analysis, Chicago, May, 1976.

LeBow, M. D. *Behavior modification: A significant*

method in nursing practice. Englewood Cliffs, N.J.: Prentice-Hall, 1973.

Lee, B. S., McGough, W. E., & Peins, M. Automated desensitization of stutterers to use of the telephone. *Behavior Therapy*, 1976, *7*, 110–112.

Leitenberg, H. Is time-out from positive reinforcement an aversive event? A review of the experimental evidence. *Psychological Bulletin*, 1965, *64*, 428–441.

Leitenberg, H. (Ed.). *Handbook of behavior modification and behavior therapy.* Englewood Cliffs, N.J.: Prentice-Hall, 1976.

Leitenberg, H., Agras, W. S., Thompson, L. E., & Wright, D. E. Feedback in behavior modification: An experimental analysis in two phobic cases. *Journal of Applied Behavior Analysis*, 1968, *1*, 131–137.

Leitenberg, H., Rawson, R. A., & Bath, K. Reinforcement of competing behavior during extinction. *Science*, 1970, *169*, 301–303.

Lemere, F., & Voegtlin, W. L. An evaluation of the aversion treatment of alcoholism. *Quarterly Journal of Studies on Alcohol*, 1950, *11*, 199–204.

Liberman, R. P. Applying behavioral techniques in a community mental health center. In R. D. Rubin, J. P. Brady, & J. D. Henderson (Eds.), *Advances in behavior therapy, Vol. 4.* New York: Academic Press, 1973.

Liberman, R. P., & Davis, J. Drugs and behavior analysis. In M. Hersen, R. M. Eisler, & P. M. Miller (Eds.), *Progress in behavior modification Vol. 1.* New York: Academic Press, 1975.

Lindsley, O. R. Operant conditioning methods applied to research in chronic schizophrenia. *Psychiatric Research Reports*, 1956, *5*, 118–139.

Lindsley, O. R. Characteristics of the behavior of chronic psychotics as revealed by free-operant conditioning methods. *Diseases of the Nervous System, Monograph Supplement,* 1960, *2*, 66–78.

Lindsley, O. R. Operant conditioning methods in diagnosis. *The first Hahnemann symposium on psychosomatic medicine.* Philadelphia: Lea & Febiger, 1962, pp. 41–52. (a)

Lindsley, O. R. Operant conditioning techniques in the measurement of psychopharmacologic response. *The first Hahnemann symposium on psychosomatic medicine.* Philadelphia: Lea & Febiger, 1962, pp. 373–383. (b)

Lindsley, O. R. A reliable wrist counter for recording behavior rates. *Journal of Applied Behavior Analysis*, 1968, *1*, 77–78.

Lindsley, O. R. Theoretical basis for behavior modification. In C. E. Pitts (Ed.), *Operant conditioning in the classroom: Introductory readings in educational psychology.* New York: Thomas Y. Crowell, 1971.

Locke, E. A. Is "Behavior Therapy" behavioristic? (An analysis of Wolpe's psychotherapeutic methods). *Psychological Bulletin*, 1971, *76*, 318–327.

Lovaas, O. I. *Behavior modification: Teaching language to psychotic children.* New York: Appleton-Century-Crofts, 1971. (Film)

Lovaas, O. I. *Behavioral treatment of autistic children.* Morristown, N.J.: General Learning Press, 1973.

Lovaas, O. I., Berberich, J. P., Perloff, B. F., & Schaeffer, B. Acquisition of imitative speech by schizophrenic children. *Science*, 1966, *151*, 705–707.

Lovaas, O. I., Freitag, G., Gold, V. J., & Kassorla, I. C. Experimental studies in childhood schizophrenia: Analysis of self-destructive behavior. *Journal of Experimental Child Psychology*, 1965, *2*, 67–84.

Lovaas, O. I., Koegel, R., Simmons, J. Q., & Long, J. S. Some generalization and follow-up measures on autistic children in behavior therapy. *Journal of Applied Behavior Analysis*, 1973, *6*, 131–166.

Lovaas, O. I., Schaeffer, B., & Simmons, J. Q. Building social behavior in autistic children by use of electric shock. *Journal of Experimental Research in Personality*, 1965, *1*, 99–109.

Lovaas, O. I., & Simmons, J. Q. Manipulation of self-destruction in three retarded children. *Journal of Applied Behavior Analysis*, 1969, *2*, 143–157.

Lovitt, T. C., & Curtiss, K. A. Academic response rate as a function of teacher- and self-imposed contingencies. *Journal of Applied Behavior Analysis*, 1969, *2*, 49–53.

Lublin, I. Principles governing the choice of unconditioned stimuli in aversive conditioning. In R. D. Rubin & C. M. Franks (Eds.), *Advances in behavior therapy.* New York: Academic Press, 1968.

Lutker, E. R. Treatment of migraine headache by conditioned relaxation: A case study. *Behavior Therapy*, 1971, *2*, 592–593.

Lutzker, S. Z., & Lutzker, J. R. A two-dimensional marital contract: Weight loss and household responsibility performance. Paper presented at the meetings of the Western Psychological Association, San Francisco, Calif., April, 1974.

MacCulloch, M. J., Birtles, C. J., & Feldman, M. P. Anticipatory avoidance learning for the treatment of homosexuality: Recent developments and an automatic aversion therapy system. *Behavior Therapy*, 1971, *2*, 151–169.

MacCulloch, M. J., & Feldman, M. P. Aversion therapy in the management of 43 homosexuals. *British Medical Journal*, 1967, *2*, 594–597.

MacCulloch, M. J., Williams, C., & Birtles, C. J. The successful application of aversion therapy to an adolescent exhibitionist *Journal of Behavior Therapy and Experimental Psychiatry*, 1971, *2*, 61–66.

Macht, J. Operant measurement of subjective visual acuity in non-verbal children. *Journal of Applied Behavior Analysis*, 1971, *4*, 23–36.

Madill, M. F., Campbell, D., Laverty, S. G., Sanderson, R. E., & Vandewater, S. L. Aversion treatment of alcoholics by succinylcholine-induced apneic paralysis. *Quarterly Journal of Studies on Alcohol*, 1966, *27*, 483–509.

Madsen, C. H., Jr., Madsen, C. K., & Thompson, F. Increasing rural Head Start children's consumption of middle-class meals. *Journal of Applied Behavior Analysis*, 1974, *7*, 257–262.

Madsen, C. K., & Madsen, C. H., Jr. You are already using behavior modification. *Instructor,* October 1971, pp. 47–56.

Mager, R. F. *Preparing instructional objectives.* Belmont, Calif.: Fearon, 1962. (Previously published as *Preparing objectives for programmed instruction.*)

Mager, R. F. *Goal analysis.* Belmont, Calif.: Fearon, 1972.

Mahoney, M. J., & Thoresen, C. E. *Self-control: Power to the person.* Monterey, Calif.: Brooks/Cole, 1974.

Maletzky, B. M. "Assisted" covert sensitization: A preliminary report. *Behavior Therapy*, 1973, *4*, 117–119.

Mann, R. A. The behavior-therapeutic use of contingency contracting to control an adult behavior problem: Weight control. *Journal of Applied Behavior Analysis*, 1972, *5*, 99–109.

Marks, I. Perspectives on flooding. *Seminars in Psychiatry*, 1972, *4*, 129–138.

Marks, I. M., & Gelder, M. G. Transvestism and fetishism: Clinical and psychological changes during faradic aversion. *British Journal of Psychiatry*, 1967, *113*, 711–729.

Marrone, R. L., Merksamer, M. A., & Salzberg, P. M. A short duration group treatment of smoking behavior by stimulus saturation. *Behaviour Research and Therapy*, 1970, *8*, 347–352.

Martin, J. A. Generalizing the use of descriptive adjectives through modeling. *Journal of Applied Behavior Analysis*, 1975, *8*, 203–209.

Masters, W. H., & Johnson, V. E. *Human sexual response.* Boston: Little, Brown, 1966.

Masters, W. H., & Johnson, V. E. *Human sexual inadequacy.* Boston: Little, Brown, 1970.

Mathews, A. M. Psychophysiological approaches to the investigation of desensitization and related procedures. *Psychological Bulletin*, 1971, *76*, 73–91.

McConaghy, N. Penile response conditioning and its relationship to aversion therapy in homosexuals. *Behavior Therapy,* 1970, *1*, 213–221.

McCullough, J. P., Cornell, J. E., McDaniel, M. H., & Mueller, R. K. Utilization of the simultaneous treatment design to improve student behavior in a first-grade classroom. *Journal of Consulting and Clinical Psychology*, 1974, *42*, 288–292.

McDowell, E. E. A programmed method of reading instruction for use with kindergarten children. *The Psychological Record*, 1968, *18*, 233–239.

McFall, R. M. Effects of self-monitoring on normal smoking behavior. *Journal of Consulting and Clinical Psychology*, 1970, *35*, 135–142.

McFall, R. M., & Hammen, C. L. Motivation, structure, and self-monitoring: Role of nonspecific factors in smoking reduction. *Journal of Consulting and Clinical Psychology*, 1971, *37*, 80–86.

McKenzie, T. L., & Rushall, B. S. Effects of self-recording on attendance and performance in a competitive swimming training environment. *Journal of Applied Behavior Analysis*, 1974, *7*, 199–206.

McLaughlin, T. F., & Malaby, J. Intrinsic reinforcers in a classroom token economy. *Journal of Applied Behavior Analysis*, 1972, *5*, 263–270.

McReynolds, L. V. Application of timeout from positive reinforcement for increasing the efficiency of speech training. *Journal of Applied Behavior Analysis*, 1969, *2*, 199–205.

Meehl, P. E. Psychotherapy. *Annual Review of Psychology,* 1955, *6*, 357–378.

Meichenbaum, D. H. Examination of model characteristics in reducing avoidance behavior. *Journal of Personality and Social Psychology*, 1971, *17*, 298–307.

Meichenbaum, D., & Cameron, R. Training schizophrenics to talk to themselves: A means of developing attentional controls. *Behavior Therapy*, 1973, *4*, 515–534.

Meichenbaum, D. H., & Cameron, R. The clinical

potential of modifying what clients say to themselves. In M. J. Mahoney & C. E. Thoresen (Eds.), *Self-control: Power to the person*. Monterey, Calif.: Brooks/Cole, 1974.

Meichenbaum, D. H., & Goodman, J. Training impulsive children to talk to themselves: A means of developing self-control. *Journal of Abnormal Psychology*, 1971, *77*, 115–126.

Meyerson, L., & Michael, J. Assessment of hearing by operant conditioning. In *Report of the Proceedings of the International Congress on Education of the Deaf*. Washington, D.C.: U.S. Govt. Printing Office, 1964, 237–242.

Michael, J. Statistical inference for individual organism research: Mixed blessing or curse? *Journal of Applied Behavior Analysis*, 1974, *7*, 647–653.

Michael, J. Positive and negative reinforcement, a distinction that is no longer necessary; or a better way to talk about bad things. In E. Ramp & G. Semb (Eds.), *Behavior analysis: Areas of research and application*. Englewood Cliffs, N.J.: Prentice-Hall, 1975.

Migler, B., & Wolpe, J. Automated self-desensitization: A case report. *Behaviour Research and Therapy*, 1967, *5*, 133–135.

Milan, M. A., & McKee, J. M. Behavior modification: Principles and applications in corrections. In D. Glaser (Ed.), *Handbook of criminology*. Chicago: Rand McNally, 1974.

Miller, L. K. Behavior principles and experimental communities. In W. E. Craighead, A. E. Kazdin, & M. J. Mahoney (Eds.), *Behavior modification: Principles, issues, and applications*. Boston: Houghton Mifflin, 1976.

Miller, L. K., & Feallock, R. A behavioral system for group living. In E. Ramp & G. Semb (Eds.), *Behavior analysis: Areas of research and application*. Englewood Cliffs, N.J.: Prentice-Hall, 1975.

Miller, L. K., & Miller, O. L. Reinforcing self-help group activities of welfare recipients. *Journal of Applied Behavior Analysis*, 1970, 3, 57–64.

Miller, N. E. Learning of visceral and glandular responses. *Science*, 1969, *163*, 434–445.

Miller, P. M. The use of behavioral contracting in the treatment of alcoholism: A case report. *Behavior Therapy*, 1972, *3*, 593–596.

Mills, K. C., Sobell, M. B., & Schaefer, H. H. Training social drinking as an alternative to abstinence for alcoholics. *Behavior Therapy*, 1971, *2*, 18–27.

Monroe, B. D., & Ahr, C. J. Auditory desensitization of a dog phobia in a blind patient. *Journal of Behavior Therapy and Experimental Psychiatry*, 1972, *3*, 315–317.

Moore, R., & Goldiamond, I. Errorless establishment of visual discrimination using fading procedures. *Journal of the Experimental Analysis of Behavior*, 1964, *7*, 269–272.

Morgan, W. G., & Bass, B. A. Self-control through self-mediated rewards. In R. D. Rubin, J. P. Brady, & J. D. Henderson (Eds.), *Advances in Behavior Therapy, Vol. 4*. New York: Academic Press, 1973.

Morganstern, K. P. Implosive therapy and flooding procedures: A critical review. *Psychological Bulletin*, 1973, *79*, 318–334.

Morris, R. J., & Suckerman, K. R. Therapist warmth as a factor in automated systematic desensitization. *Journal of Consulting and Clinical Psychology*, 1974, *42*, 244–250.

Mosher, P. M., & Reese, E. P. Task difficulty as a variable in teaching word-recognition by fading and non-fading procedures. Paper presented at the Annual Meeting of the Eastern Psychological Association, New York, April, 1976.

Mulick, J. A., Leitenberg, H., & Rawson, R. A. Alternative response training, differential reinforcement of other behavior, and extinction in squirrel monkeys (Saimiri sciureus). *Journal of the Experimental Analysis of Behavior*, 1976, *25*, 311–320.

Nathan, M. A., & Smith, O. A., Jr. Differential conditional emotional and cardiovascular responses—a training technique for monkeys. *Journal of the Experimental Analysis of Behavior*, 1968, *11*, 77–82.

Nawas, M. M. Standardized scheduled desensitization: Some unstable results and an improved program. *Behaviour Research and Therapy*, 1971, *9*, 35–38.

Nelson, C. M., Worell, J., & Polsgrove, L. Behaviorally disordered peers as contingency managers. *Behavior Therapy*, 1973, *4*, 270–276.

Nevin, J. A. Differential reinforcement and stimulus control of not responding. *Journal of the Experimental Analysis of Behavior*, 1968, *11*, 715–726.

Nolan, J. D. Self-control procedures in the modification of smoking behavior. *Journal of Consulting and Clinical Psychology*, 1968, *32*, 92–93.

Nurnberger, J. I., & Zimmerman, J. Applied analysis of human behavior: An alternative to conventional motivational inferences and unconscious determination in therapeutic programming. *Behavior Therapy*, 1970, *1*, 59–69.

Obler, M. Systematic desensitization in sexual disorders. *Journal of Behavior Therapy and Experimental Psychiatry*, 1973, *4*, 93–101.

O'Leary, K. D., & Drabman, R. Token reinforcement in the classroom: A review. *Psychological Bulletin*, 1971, *75*, 379–398.

O'Leary, K. D., & O'Leary, S. G. (Eds.). *Classroom management: The successful use of behavior modification.* New York: Pergamon Press, 1972.

O'Leary, K. D., & Wilson, G. T. *Behavior therapy: Application and outcome.* Englewood Cliffs, N.J.: Prentice-Hall, 1975.

Osborne, J. G. Free-time as a reinforcer in the management of classroom behavior. *Journal of Applied Behavior Analysis*, 1969, *2*, 113–118.

Osgood, C. E. *Method and theory in experimental psychology.* New York: Oxford University Press, 1953.

Parrino, J. J. Reduction of seizures by desensitization. *Journal of Behavior Therapy and Experimental Psychiatry*, 1971, *2*, 215–218.

Patterson, B. R., (sic) McNeal, S., Hawkins, N., & Phelps, R. Reprogramming the social environment. *Journal of Child Psychology and Psychiatry and Allied Disciplines*, 1967, *8*, 181–195.

Patterson, G. R., & Brodskey, G. A behaviour modification programme for a child with multiple problem behaviours. *Journal of Child Psychology and Psychiatry and Allied Disciplines*, 1966, *7*, 277–295.

Patterson, G. R., & Reid, J. B. Reciprocity and coercion: Two facets of social systems. In C. Neuringer & J. L. Michael (Eds.), *Behavior modification in clinical psychology.* New York: Appleton-Century-Crofts, 1970.

Patterson, R. L. (Ed.). *Maintaining effective token economies.* Springfield, Ill.: Charles C Thomas, in press.

Paul, G. L. *Insight versus desensitization in psychotherapy: An experiment in anxiety reduction.* Stanford, Calif.: Stanford University Press, 1966.

Paul, G. L. Behavior modification research: Design and tactics. In C. M. Franks (Ed.), *Behavior Therapy: Appraisal and status.* New York: McGraw-Hill, 1969. (a)

Paul, G. L. Outcome of systematic desensitization. I: Background, procedures, and uncontrolled reports of individual treatment. In C. M. Franks

(Ed.), *Behavior therapy: Appraisal and status.* New York: McGraw-Hill, 1969. (b)

Paul, G. L. Outcome of systematic desensitization. II: Controlled investigations of individual treatment, technique variations, and current status. In C. M. Franks (Ed.), *Behavior therapy: Appraisal and status.* New York: McGraw-Hill, 1969. (c)

Paul, G. L., & Bernstein, D. A. *Anxiety and clinical problems: Systematic desensitization and related techniques.* Morristown, N.J.: General Learning Press, 1973.

Paul, G. L., & Shannon, D. T. Treatment of anxiety through systematic desensitization in therapy groups. *Journal of Abnormal Psychology*, 1966, *71*, 124–135.

Pavlov, I. P. *Conditioned reflexes.* (G. V. Anrep, Ed. and trans.). London: Oxford University Press, 1927.

Pavlov, I. P. *Lectures on conditioned reflexes.* (W. H. Gantt, trans.). New York: International Publishers, 1928.

Pecknold, J. C., Raeburn, J., & Poser, E. G. Intravenous diazepam for facilitating relaxation for desensitization. *Journal of Behavior Therapy and Experimental Psychiatry*, 1972, *3*, 39–41.

Penick, S. B., Filion, R., Fox, S., & Stunkard, A. J. Behavior modification in the treatment of obesity. *Psychosomatic Medicine*, 1971, *33*, 49–55.

Performance improvement magazine. Published by Edward J. Feeney, 99 Danbury Rd., Ridgefield, Conn. 06877.

Phillips, E. L. Achievement place: Token reinforcement procedures in a home-style rehabilitation setting for "pre-delinquent" boys. *Journal of Applied Behavior Analysis*, 1968, *1*, 213–223.

Phillips, E. L., Phillips, E. A., Fixsen, D. L., & Wolf, M. M. Behavior shaping works for delinquents. *Psychology Today*, June 1973, pp. 75–79.

Pierrel, R., & Sherman, J. G. Barnabus, the rat with college training. *Brown Alumni Monthly*, Brown University, Providence, R.I., February 1963, pp. 8–12.

Plummer, S., Baer, D. M., & LeBlanc, J. M. Functional considerations in the use of timeout and an effective alternative procedure. *Journal of Applied Behavior Analysis*, in press.

Poché, C. E., & Bailey, J. S. The development and evaluation of an incentive program to encourage car pooling. Paper presented at the Second Annual Convention of the Midwestern Association of Behavior Analysis, Chicago, May, 1976.

Polin, A. T. The effects of flooding and physical suppression as extinction techniques on an anxiety motivated avoidance locomotor response. *The Journal of Psychology*, 1959, *47*, 235–245.

Popham, W. J., & Baker, E. L. *Establishing instructional goals*. Englewood Cliffs, N.J.: Prentice-Hall, 1970.

Porterfield, J. K., Herbert-Jackson, E., & Risley, T. R. Contingent observation: An effective and acceptable procedure for reducing disruptive behavior of young children in a group setting. *Journal of Applied Behavior Analysis*, 1976, *9*, 55–64.

Powell, J., & Azrin, N. The effects of shock as a punisher for cigarette smoking. *Journal of Applied Behavior Analysis*, 1968, *1*, 63–71.

Powell, J., Martindale, A., & Kulp, S. An evaluation of time-sample measures of behavior. *Journal of Applied Behavior Analysis*, 1975, *8*, 463–469.

Powers, R. B., Osborne, J. G., & Anderson, E. G. Positive reinforcement of litter removal in the natural environment. *Journal of Applied Behavior Analysis*, 1973, *6*, 579–586.

Premack, D. Toward empirical behavior laws: I. Positive reinforcement. *Psychological Review*, 1959, *66*, 219–233.

Premack, D. Reinforcement theory. In D. Levine (Ed.), *Nebraska symposium on motivation*. Lincoln, Nebr.: University of Nebraska Press, 1965.

Quilitch, H. R., & Risley, T. R. The effects of play materials on social play. *Journal of Applied Behavior Analysis*, 1973, *6*, 573–578.

Rachlin, H., & Green, L. Commitment, choice and self-control. *Journal of the Experimental Analysis of Behavior*, 1972, *17*, 15–22.

Rachman, S. Sexual fetishism: An experimental analogue. *The Psychological Record*, 1966, *16*, 293–296. (a)

Rachman, S. Studies in desensitization—II: Flooding. *Behaviour Research and Therapy*, 1966, *4*, 1–6. (b)

Rachman, S. Studies in desensitization—III: Speed of generalization. *Behaviour Research and Therapy*, 1966, *4*, 7–15. (c)

Rachman, S., & Hodgson, R. J. Experimentally-induced "sexual fetishism": Replication and development. *The Psychological Record*, 1968, *18*, 25–27.

Rachman, S., & Teasdale, J. *Aversion therapy and behaviour disorders: An analysis*. Coral Gables, Fla.: University of Miami Press, 1969.

Rainey, C. A. An obsessive-compulsive neurosis treated by flooding. *Journal of Behavior Therapy and Experimental Psychiatry*, 1972, *3*, 117–121.

Ramp, E. & Semb, G. (Eds). *Behavior analysis: Areas of research and application*. Englewood Cliffs, N.J.: Prentice-Hall, 1975.

Redd, W. H., & Birnbrauer, J. S. Adults as discriminative stimuli for different reinforcement contingencies with retarded children. *Journal of Experimental Child Psychology*, 1969, *7*, 440–447.

Reese, E. P. *Behavior theory in practice*. New York: Appleton-Century-Crofts, 1965. (Film; distributed by Prentice-Hall).

Reese, E. P. *The analysis of human operant behavior*. Dubuque, Iowa: William C. Brown, 1966.

Reese, E. P. *Born to succeed: Behavioral procedures for education. Part 1: Concept of number; Part 2: Arithmetic*. Box 625, Northampton, Mass.: Hanover Communications, 1971. (a) (Film)

Reese, E. P. *Born to succeed: Behavioral procedures for education*. 1971. (b) (Film outline and summary of program; available from the author, Mount Holyoke College, South Hadley, MA 01075.)

Reese, E. P. *A demonstration of behavioral processes by B. F. Skinner*. New York: Appleton-Century-Crofts, 1971. (c) (Film; distributed by Prentice-Hall.)

Reese, E. P. *Observing, defining, and recording behavior: A first step toward accountability*, 1977. (Training program)

Reese, E. P., Howard, J. S., & Rosenberger, P. B. Behavioral procedures for assessing visual capacities in nonverbal subjects. In B. C. Etzel, J. M. LeBlanc, & D. M. Baer (Eds.), *New developments in behavioral research: Theory, methods, and applications. In honor of Sidney W. Bijou*. Hillsdale, N.J.: Lawrence Erlbaum Associates, 1977.

Reese, E. P., & Huberth, J. C. *Now I can talk: A fluency-shaping program for stutterers*. Box 625, Northampton, Mass.: Hanover Communications, 1975. (Film)

Reese, E. P., & Werden, D. A fading technique for teaching number concepts to severely retarded children. Paper presented at the Annual Meeting of the Eastern Psychological Association. Atlantic City, N.J., April, 1970.

Reisinger, J. J. The treatment of "anxiety-depression" via positive reinforcement and response cost. *Journal of Applied Behavior Analysis*, 1972, *5*, 125–130.

Repp, A. C., & Deitz, (sic) S. M. Reducing aggressive and self-injurious behavior of institutionalized retarded children through reinforcement of other behaviors. *Journal of Applied Behavior Analysis*, 1974, *7*, 313–325.

Rescorla, R. A. Probability of shock in the presence and absence of CS in fear conditioning. *Journal of Comparative and Physiological Psychology*, 1968, 66, 1–5.

Resnick, L. B., Wang, M. C., & Kaplan, J. Task analysis in curriculum design: A hierarchically sequenced introductory mathematics curriculum. *Journal of Applied Behavior Analysis*, 1973, 6, 679–710.

Reynolds, G. S. Behavioral contrast. *Journal of the Experimental Analysis of Behavior*, 1961, 4, 57–71.

Riley, J. B., & Holt, W. R. Project threshold: A multiphase program of individual and group behavioral management for community-based retardates functioning below minimum acceptance or retention criteria for community rehabilitation programs. Paper presented at the Second Annual Convention of the Midwestern Association of Behavior Analysis, Chicago, May, 1976.

Rimm, D. C., & Mahoney, M. J. The application of reinforcement and participant modeling procedures in the treatment of snake-phobic behavior. *Behaviour Research and Therapy*, 1969, 7, 369–376.

Rimm, D. C., & Masters, J. C. *Behavior therapy: Techniques and empirical findings.* New York: Academic Press, 1974.

Risley, T. R. The effects and side effects of punishing the autistic behaviors of a deviant child. *Journal of Applied Behavior Analysis*, 1968, 1, 21–34.

Risley, T. R. Behavior modification: An experimental-therapeutic endeavor. In L. A. Hamerlynck, P. O. Davidson, & L. E. Acker (Eds.), *Behavior modification and ideal mental health services.* Calgary, Alberta, Canada: University of Calgary Press, 1971.

Ritter, B. The group desensitization of children's snake phobias using vicarious and contact desensitization procedures. *Behaviour Research and Therapy*, 1968, 6, 1–6.

Ritter, B. The use of contact desensitization, demonstration-plus-participation, and demonstration-alone in the treatment of acrophobia. *Behaviour Research and Therapy*, 1969, 7, 157–164.

Robertshaw, C. S., & Johnson, C. A. The remedial contract: A facilitator of accountability in education. *School Applications of Learning Theory*, 1974, 6 (3), 25–31.

Rosenberger, P. B. Discriminative aspects of visual hemi-inattention. *Neurology*, January 1974, pp. 17–23.

Rosenkrans, M. A., & Hartup, W. W. Imitative influences of consistent and inconsistent response consequences to a model on aggressive behavior in children. *Journal of Personality and Social Psychology*, 1967, 7, 429–434.

Ross, R. R., Meichenbaum, D. H., & Humphrey, C. Treatment of nocturnal headbanging by behavior modification techniques: A case report. *Behaviour Research and Therapy*, 1971, 9, 151–154.

Rushall, B. S., & Siedentop, D. *The development and control of behavior in sport and physical education.* Philadelphia: Lea & Febiger, 1972.

Sajwaj, T., Libet, J., & Agras, S. Lemon-juice therapy: The control of life-threatening rumination in a six-month-old infant. *Journal of Applied Behavior Analysis*, 1974, 7, 557–563.

Sajwaj, T., Twardosz, S., & Burke, M. Side effects of extinction procedures in a remedial preschool. *Journal of Applied Behavior Analysis*, 1972, 5, 163–175.

Salzinger, K., Feldman, R. S., Cowan, J. E., & Salzinger, S. Operant conditioning of verbal behavior of two young speech-deficient boys. In L. Krasner & L. P. Ullmann (Eds.), *Research in behavior modification.* New York: Holt, Rinehart and Winston, 1965.

Sanders, R. M. *Behavior modification in a rehabilitation facility.* Carbondale, Ill.: Southern Illinois University Press, 1975.

Santogrossi, D. A., O'Leary, K. D., Romanczyk, R. G., & Kaufman, K. F. Self-evaluation by adolescents in a psychiatric hospital school token program. *Journal of Applied Behavior Analysis*, 1973, 6, 277–287.

Schaefer, H. H., Sobell, M. B., & Mills, K. C. Some sobering data on the use of self-confrontation with alcoholics. *Behavior Therapy*, 1971, 2, 28–39.

Schmidt, G. W., & Ulrich, R. E. Effects of group contingent events upon classroom noise. *Journal of Applied Behavior Analysis*, 1969, 2, 171–179.

Schwartz, A., & Goldiamond, I. with Howe, M. W. *Social casework: A behavioral approach.* New York: Columbia University Press, 1975.

Schwitzgebel, R. K. Right to treatment for the mentally disabled: The need for realistic standards and objective criteria. *Harvard Civil Rights-Civil Liberties Law Review*, 1973, 8, (3), 513–535.

Seligman, M. E. P. Phobias and preparedness. *Behavior Therapy*, 1971, 2, 307–320.

Sewell, E., McCoy, J. F., & Sewell, W. R. Modification of an antagonistic social behavior using positive reinforcement for other behavior. *The Psychological Record*, 1973, *23*, 499–504.

Shack, J. R., & Barnett, L. W. *An annotated and indexed bibliography of behavior management with children.* Chicago, Ill.: Loyola University and Loyola University Child Guidance Center, 1973. (Available from John R. Shack, Child Guidance Center, 1043 West Loyola Avenue, Chicago, Ill. 60626.)

Sherman, A. R. Real-life exposure as a primary therapeutic factor in the desensitization treatment of fear. *Journal of Abnormal Psychology*, 1972, *79*, 19–28.

Sherman, J. G. (Ed.). *Personalized system of instruction: 41 germinal papers.* Menlo Park, Calif.: W. A. Benjamin, 1974.

Sherrington, C. S. *The integrative action of the nervous system.* New Haven, Conn.: Yale University Press, 1906.

Shorkey, C., & Himle, D. P. Systematic desensitization treatment of a recurring nightmare and related insomnia. *Journal of Behavior Therapy and Experimental Psychiatry*, 1974, *5*, 97–98.

Shorkey, C. T., Himle, D. P., & Collins, M. A. Behavior modification in groups: An annotated bibliography. JSAS *Catalog of Selected Documents in Psychology*, 1974, *4*, 129. (Ms. No. 776.)

Sidman, M. *Tactics of scientific research.* New York: Basic Books, 1960.

Sidman, M., & Stoddard, L. T. The effectiveness of fading in programming a simultaneous form discrimination for retarded children. *Journal of the Experimental Analysis of Behavior*, 1967, *10*, 3–15.

Siegel, G. M., Lenske, J., & Broen, P. Suppression of normal speech disfluencies through response cost. *Journal of Applied Behavior Analysis*, 1969, *2*, 265–276.

Silverman, H., & Silverman, S. Report of a failure —"The detention room." *School Applications of Learning Theory*, 1973, *6* (1), 41–43.

Sirota, A. D., & Mahoney, M. J. Relaxing on cue: The self regulation of asthma. *Journal of Behavior Therapy and Experimental Psychiatry*, 1974, *5*, 65–66.

Skinner, B. F. Two types of conditioned reflex and a pseudo type. *Journal of General Psychology*, 1935, *12*, 66–77.

Skinner, B. F. *The behavior of organisms.* New York: D. Appleton Century, 1938.

Skinner, B. F. 'Superstition' in the pigeon. *Journal of Experimental Psychology*, 1948, *38*, 168–172. (a)

Skinner, B. F. *Walden Two.* New York: Macmillan, 1948. (b)

Skinner, B. F. *Science and human behavior.* New York: Macmillan, 1953.

Skinner, B. F. Freedom and the control of men. *American Scholar*, 1955, *25*, 47–65.

Skinner, B. F. The technology of teaching. *Proceedings of the Royal Society*, B, 1965, *162*, 427–443.

Skinner, B. F. *The technology of teaching.* New York: Appleton-Century-Crofts, 1968.

Skinner, B. F. *Beyond freedom and dignity.* New York: Knopf, 1971.

Skinner, B. F., & Krakower, S. *Handwriting with write and see.* Chicago: Lyons & Carnahan, 1968.

Smith, D. D., & Lovitt, T. C. The use of modeling techniques to influence the acquisition of computational arithmetic skills in learning-disabled children. In E. Ramp & G. Semb (Eds.), *Behavior analysis: Areas of research and application.* Englewood Cliffs, N.J.: Prentice-Hall, 1975.

Snyder, C., & Noble, M. Operant conditioning of vasoconstriction. *Journal of Experimental Psychology*, 1968, *77*, 263–268.

Sobell, M. B., & Sobell, L. C. *Individualized behavior therapy for alcoholics.* California Mental Health Research Monograph, No. 13. Bureau of Research, California Department of Mental Hygiene, March 1972. (a)

Sobell, M. B., & Sobell, L. C. One year follow-up of alcoholics treated by the method of individualized behavior therapy. Paper presented at the 80th Annual Convention of the American Psychological Association, Honolulu, Hawaii, Sept. 7, 1972. (b)

Sobell, M. B., & Sobell, L. C. Alcoholics treated by individualized behavior therapy: One year treatment outcome. *Behaviour Research and Therapy*, 1973, *11*, 599–618. (a)

Sobell, M. B., & Sobell, L. C. Evidence of controlled drinking by former alcoholics: A second year evaluation of individualized behavior therapy. Paper presented at the 81st Annual Convention of the American Psychological Association, Montreal, Canada, August 31, 1973. (b)

Sobell, M. B., & Sobell, L. C. Individualized behavior therapy for alcoholics. *Behavior Therapy*, 1973, *4*, 49–72. (c)

Sprague, R. L. What's happening at—Children's Research Center, University of Illinois at Urbana/Champaign. *Psychopharmacology* (Division 28 Newsletter) December 15, 1974.

Staats, A. W., Minke, K. A., Finley, J. R., Wolf, M., & Brooks, L. O. A reinforcer system and experimental procedure for the laboratory study of reading acquisition. *Child Development*, 1964, *35*, 209–231.

Stampfl, T. G., & Levis, D. J. Essentials of implosive therapy: A learning-theory-based psychodynamic behavioral therapy. *Journal of Abnormal Psychology*, 1967, *72*, 496–503.

Steeves, J. M., Martin, G. L., & Pear, J. J. Self-imposed time-out by autistic children during an operant training program. *Behavior Therapy*, 1970, *1*, 371–381.

Stoddard, L. T., & Sidman, M. The effects of errors on children's performance on a circle-ellipse discrimination. *Journal of the Experimental Analysis of Behavior*, 1967, *10*, 261–270.

Stokes, T. F., Baer, D. M., & Jackson, R. L. Programming the generalization of a greeting response in four retarded children. *Journal of Applied Behavior Analysis*, 1974, *7*, 599–610.

Stromer, R. Modifying letter and number reversals in elementary school children. *Journal of Applied Behavior Analysis*, 1975, *8*, 211.

Stuart, R. B. Behavioral control of overeating. *Behaviour Research and Therapy*, 1967, *5*, 357–365.

Stuart, R. B. Behavioral contracting within the families of delinquents. *Journal of Behavior Therapy and Experimental Psychiatry*, 1971, *2*, 1–11.

Stuart, R. B. Situational versus self-control. In R. D. Rubin, H. Fensterheim, J. D. Henderson, & L. P. Ullmann (Eds.), *Advances in behavior therapy*. New York: Academic Press, 1972.

Stuart, R. B., & Davis, B. *Slim chance in a fat world*. Champaign, Ill.: Research Press, 1972.

Stumphauzer, J. S. Increased delay of gratification in young prison inmates through imitation of high-delay peer models. *Journal of Personality and Social Psychology*, 1972, *21*, 10–17.

Suinn, R. M. The STABS, a measure of test anxiety for behavior therapy: Normative data. *Behaviour Research and Therapy*, 1969, *7*, 335–339.

Suinn, R. M. Body thinking: Psychology for olympic champs. *Psychology Today*, July 1976, pp. 38–43.

Sulzer, B., & Mayer, G. R. *Behavior modification procedures for school personnel*. Hinsdale, Ill.: Dryden Press, 1972.

Sulzer, B., & Mayer, G.R. *Applying behavior-analysis procedures with children and youth*. New York: Holt, Rinehart and Winston, 1977.

Sulzer, E. S. Research frontier: Reinforcement and the therapeutic contract. *Journal of Counseling Psychology*, 1962, *9*, 271–276.

Sulzer-Azaroff, B., Thaw, J., & Thomas, C. Behavioral competencies for the evaluation of behavior modifiers. In W. S. Wood (Ed.), *Issues in evaluating behavior modification*. Champaign, Ill.: Research Press, 1975.

Suppes, P., & Ginsberg, R. Experimental studies of mathematical concept formation in young children. *Science Education*, 1962, *46*, 230–240.

Tanner, B. A., & Zeiler, M. Punishment of self-injurious behavior using aromatic ammonia as the aversive stimulus. *Journal of Applied Behavior Analysis*, 1975, *8*, 53–57.

Tate, B. G. Case study: Control of chronic self-injurious behavior by conditioning procedures. *Behavior Therapy*, 1972, *3*, 72–83.

Tate, B. G., & Baroff, G. S. Aversive control of self-injurious behavior in a psychotic boy. *Behaviour Research and Therapy*, 1966, *4*, 281–287.

Taylor, D. W. Group systematic desensitization with test-anxious college students. *Dissertation Abstracts International*, 1971, *31*, (7-B), 4347.

Terrace, H. S. Discrimination learning with and without "errors." *Journal of the Experimental Analysis of Behavior*, 1963, *6*, 1–27. (a)

Terrace, H. S. Errorless discrimination learning in the pigeon: Effects of chlorpromazine and imipramine. *Science*, 1963, *140*, 318–319. (b)

Terrace, H. S. Errorless transfer of a discrimination across continua. *Journal of the Experimental Analysis of Behavior*, 1963, *6*, 223–232. (c)

Tharp, R. G., & Wetzel, R. J. *Behavior modification in the natural environment*. New York: Academic Press, 1969.

Thompson, T., Pickens, R., & Meisch, R. A. (Eds.). *Readings in behavioral pharmacology*. New York: Appleton-Century-Crofts, 1970.

Thoresen, C. E., & Mahoney, M. J. *Behavioral self-control*. New York: Holt, Rinehart and Winston, 1974.

Thorndike, E. L. *Animal intelligence: An experimental study of the associative processes in animals*. Psychological Review, Monograph Supplement, 1898, *2*, No. 8.

Thorpe, J. G., Schmidt, E., Brown, P. T., & Castell, D. Aversion-relief therapy: A new method for general application. *Behaviour Research and Therapy*, 1964, *2*, 71–82.

Topping, J. S., Larmi, O. K., & Johnson, D. L. Omission training: Effects of gradual introduction. *Psychonomic Science*, 1972, *28*, 279–280.

Touchette, P. E. The effects of graduated stimulus change on the acquisition of a simple discrimination in severely retarded boys. *Journal of* the *Experimental Analysis of Behavior*, 1968, *11*, 39–48.

Tuber, D. S., Hothersall, D., & Voith, V. L. Animal clinical psychology. *American Psychologist*, 1974, *29*, 762–766.

Turnage, J. R., & Logan, D. L. Treatment of a hypodermic needle phobia by *in vivo* systematic desensitization. *Journal of Behavior Therapy and Experimental Psychiatry*, 1974, *5*, 67–69.

Turner, A. J. *Relaxation*. Huntsville, Ala.: Cybersystems. (no date) (Tape cassette)

Uhl, C. N., & Sherman, W. O. Comparison of combinations of omission, punishment, and extinction methods in response elimination in rats. *Journal of Comparative and Physiological Psychology*, 1971, *74*, 59–65.

Ulman, J. D., & Sulzer-Azaroff, B. Multielement baseline design in educational research. In E. Ramp & G. Semb (Eds.), *Behavior analysis: Areas of research and application*. Englewood Cliffs, N.J.: Prentice-Hall, 1975.

Ulrich, R. Pain as a cause of aggression. *American Zoologist*, 1966, *6*, 643–662.

Ulrich, R. E. *Understanding aggression*. New York: McGraw-Hill Textfilms, 1971. (Film)

Ulrich, R. E., & Azrin, N. H. Reflexive fighting in response to aversive stimulation. *Journal of the Experimental Analysis of Behavior*, 1962, *5*, 511–520.

Ulrich, R. E., Hutchinson, R. R., & Azrin, N. H. Pain-elicited aggression. *The Psychological Record*, 1965, *15*, 111–126.

Vaillant, G. E. Some determining factors in patterns of drug use among urban addicts. Paper presented at the meetings of the New England Psychological Association, Boston, Mass., November, 1965.

van Egeren, L. F. Psychophysiological aspects of systematic desensitization: Some outstanding issues. *Behaviour Research and Therapy*, 1971, *9*, 65–77.

Van Egeren, L. F., Feather, B. W., & Hein, P. L. Desensitization of phobias: Some psychophysiological propositions. *Psychophysiology*, 1971, *8*, 213–228.

Vargas, J. B. F. Skinner: Father, grandfather, behavior modifier. *Human Behavior*, 1972, *1*, 16–23. (a)

Vargas, J. S. *Writing worthwhile behavioral objectives*. New York: Harper & Row, 1972. (b)

Vodde, T. W., & Gilner, F. H. The effects of exposure to fear stimuli on fear reduction. *Behaviour Research and Therapy*, 1971, *9*, 169–175.

Vukelich, R., & Hake, D. F. Reduction of dangerously aggressive behavior in a severely retarded resident through a combination of positive reinforcement procedures. *Journal of Applied Behavior Analysis*, 1971, *4*, 215–225.

Walker, H. M., & Buckley, N. K. Programming generalization and maintenance of treatment effects across time and across settings. *Journal of Applied Behavior Analysis*, 1972, *5*, 209–224.

Walker, H. M., & Hops, H. Use of normative peer data as a standard for evaluating classroom treatment effects. *Journal of Applied Behavior Analysis*, 1976, *9*, 159–168.

Watson, D. L., & Tharp, R. G. *Self-directed behavior: Self-modification for personal adjustment*. Monterey, Calif.: Brooks/Cole, 1972.

Watson, J. B. *Behaviorism*. New York: W. W. Norton, 1924.

Watson, J. B., & Rayner, R. Conditioned emotional reactions. *Journal of Experimental Psychology*, 1920, *3*, 1–14.

Watson, L. S., Jr. *How to use behavior modification with the mentally retarded*. Columbus, Ohio, 1968. (Mimeographed training manual)

Watson, L. S., Jr. *A manual for teaching behavior modification skills to staff*. Libertyville, Ill.: Behavior Modification Technology, 1974.

Weiner, H. Some effects of response cost upon human operant behavior. *Journal of the Experimental Analysis of Behavior*, 1962, *5*, 201–208.

Weiner, H. Response cost and the aversive control of human operant behavior. *Journal of the Experimental Analysis of Behavior*, 1963, *6*, 415–421.

Weiner, H. Some thoughts on behavioral approaches to therapy. *The Psychological Record*, 1973, *23*, 441–450.

Welsh, R. S. The use of stimulus satiation in the elimination of juvenile fire-setting behavior. In A. M. Graziano (Ed.), *Behavior therapy with children*. Chicago: Aldine, 1971.

Wenrich, W. W., & LeTendre, D. *Operant control of autonomic behavior: An annotated bibliography (1959-1974)*. JSAS Catalog of Selected Documents, 1975, *5*, 231. (Ms. No. 924.)

Whaley, D. L., & Malott, R. W. *Elementary principles of behavior*. New York: Appleton-Century-Crofts, 1971.

Whaley, D. L., Rosenkranz, A., & Knowles, P. A. Automatic punishment of cigarette smoking by a portable electronic device. Unpublished report of research conducted at the V.A. Hospital, Coral Gables, Fla. December, 1967.

Whaley, D. L., & Tough, J. Treatment of a self-injuring mongoloid with shock-induced suppression and avoidance. *Michigan Mental Health Research Bulletin*, 1968, *2*, (1), 33–35.

White, G. D., Nielsen, G., & Johnson, S. M. Timeout duration and the suppression of deviant behavior in children. *Journal of Applied Behavior Analysis*, 1972, *5*, 111–120.

Wilkins, W. Desensitization: Social and cognitive factors underlying the effectiveness of Wolpe's procedure. *Psychological Bulletin*, 1971, *76*, 311–317.

Williams, C. D. The elimination of tantrum behavior by extinction procedures. *Journal of Abnormal and Social Psychology*, 1959, *59*, 269.

Williams, R. B., Jr., & Gentry, W. D. *Behavioral approaches to medical treatment*. Cambridge, Mass.: Ballinger, 1976.

Williams, R. L., & Long, J. D. *Toward a self-managed life style*. Boston: Houghton Mifflin, 1975.

Wilson, G. T., & Davison, G. C. Processes of fear reduction in systematic desensitization: Animal studies. *Psychological Bulletin*, 1971, *76*, 1–14.

Winett, R. A., & Winkler, R. C. Current behavior modification in the classroom: Be still, be quiet, be docile. *Journal of Applied Behavior Analysis*, 1972, *5*, 499–504.

Winkler, R. C. Management of chronic psychiatric patients by a token reinforcement system. *Journal of Applied Behavior Analysis*, 1970, *3*, 47–55.

Wisocki, P. A. Treatment of obsessive-compulsive behavior by covert sensitization and covert reinforcement: A case report. *Journal of Behavior Therapy and Experimental Psychiatry*, 1970, *1*, 233–239.

Wisocki, P. A. The successful treatment of a heroin addict by covert conditioning techniques. *Journal of Behavior Therapy and Experimental Psychiatry*, 1973, *4*, 55–61.

Wisocki, P. A., & Cautela, J. R. The application of learning theory principles to the problem of alcoholism—A bibliography. 1968. (Available from Patricia A. Wisocki, Psychology Dept., University of Massachusetts, Amherst, MA 01002.)

Wolf, M. M., Hanley, E. L., King, L. A., Lachowicz, J., & Giles, D. K. The timer-game: A variable interval contingency for the management of out-of-seat behavior. *Exceptional Children*, 1970, *37*, 113–117.

Wolpe, J. Experimental neurosis as learned behaviour. *British Journal of Psychology*, 1952, *43*, 243–268. (a)

Wolpe, J. Objective psychotherapy of the neuroses. *South African Medical Journal*, 1952, *26*, 825–29. (b)

Wolpe, J. *Psychotherapy by reciprocal inhibition*. Stanford, Calif.: Stanford University Press, 1958.

Wolpe, J. The prognosis in unpsychoanalyzed recovery from neurosis. *American Journal of Psychiatry*, 1961, *118*, 35–39.

Wolpe, J. The experimental foundations of some new psychotherapeutic methods. In A. J. Bachrach (Ed.), *Experimental foundations of clinical psychology*. New York: Basic, 1962. (a)

Wolpe, J. Isolation of a conditioning procedure as the crucial psychotherapeutic factor: A case study. *Journal of Nervous and Mental Disease*, 1962, *134*, 316–329. (b)

Wolpe, J. Quantitative relationships in the systematic desensitization of phobias. *American Journal of Psychiatry*, 1963, *119*, 1062–1068.

Wolpe, J. *The practice of behavior therapy*. Elmsford, N.Y.: Pergamon Press, 1969.

Wolpe, J., & Lazarus, A. A. *Behavior therapy techniques: A guide to the treatment of neuroses*. Elmsford, N.Y.: Pergamon Press, 1966.

Wolpin, M., & Raines, J. Visual imagery, expected roles and extinction as possible factors in reducing fear and avoidance behavior. *Behaviour Research and Therapy*, 1966, *4*, 25–37.

Wood, W. S. (Ed.). *Issues in evaluating behavior modification*. Champaign, Ill.: Research Press, 1975.

Yates, A. J. Symptoms and symptom substitution. *Psychological Review*, 1958, *65*, 371–374.

Yen, S., & McIntire, R. W. (Eds.). *Teaching behavior modification*. Kalamazoo, Mich.: Behaviordelia, 1976.

Yule, W., Sacks, B., & Hersov, L. Successful flooding treatment of a noise phobia in an eleven-year-old. *Journal of Behavior Therapy and Experimental Psychiatry*, 1974, *5*, 209–211.

Zeilberger, J., Sampen, S. E., & Sloane, H. N., Jr. Modification of a child's problem behaviors in the home with the mother as therapist. *Journal of Applied Behavior Analysis*, 1968, *1*, 47–53.

Zeiler, M. D. Eliminating behavior with reinforcement. *Journal of the Experimental Analysis of Behavior*, 1971, *16*, 401–405.

Zifferblatt, S. M., & Hendricks, C. G. Applied behavioral analysis of societal problems: Population change, a case in point. *American Psychologist*, 1974, *29*, 750–761.

Zimmerman, E. H., & Zimmerman, J. The alteration of behavior in a special classroom situation. *Journal of the Experimental Analysis of Behavior*, 1962, *5*, 59–60.

Zimmerman, J. Behavior measurement—The essence of behavior modification. *Medical Bulletin of the Marshfield Clinic and Marshfield Clinic Foundation*, 1972, *4*, 24–52.

Zimmerman, J. If it's what's inside that counts, why not count it? Behavior Modification Workshop, Atlanta, Ga., March, 1973.

Zimmerman, J., Zimmerman, E., with Rider, S. L., Smith, A. F., & Dinn, R. Doing your own thing with precision: The essence of behavior management in the classroom. *Educational Technology*, 1971, *11*, 26–32.

Zlutnick, S., Mayville, W. J., & Moffat, S. Modification of seizure disorders: The interruption of behavioral chains. *Journal of Applied Behavior Analysis*, 1975, *8*, 1–12.

Author Index

Subject Index